Brendan
BEHAN
A Life

Brendan Behan

Published by
ROBERTS RINEHART PUBLISHERS
Post Office Box 666
Niwot, Colorado 80544
TEL 303.652.2685
FAX 303.652.2689
www.robertsrinehart.com

Distributed to the trade by Publishers Group West

International Standard Book Number 1-57098-274-0

Library of Congress Catalog Card Number 99-60836

First published in Ireland by
Blackwater Press
Dublin

Dustjacket photograph of Brendan Behan courtesy
of Lensmen, Dublin, Ireland

Illustration of Brendan Behan used on Part openings
by John Short

10 9 8 7 6 5 4 3 2 1

Manufactured in the United States of America

Brendan BEHAN
A Life

MICHAEL O'SULLIVAN

ROBERTS RINEHART PUBLISHERS
Boulder, Colorado

All will be judged. Master of nuance and scruple,
Pray for me and for all writers, living or dead:
Because there are many whose works
Are in better taste than their lives, because there is no end
to the vanity of our calling, make intercession
For the treason of all clerks.

W.H. Auden

Every man has three lives, public, private, and secret.

Gabriel García Márquez

Do Garech de Brún

For Garech Browne

Contents

Acknowledgements

This is not an 'authorised' or 'official' biography of Brendan Behan, and it was undertaken on my own initiative. Nevertheless I have had such support from members of the Behan family, and from so many of Brendan Behan's friends, that it is difficult to make adequate acknowledgement to them. Some have asked not to be acknowledged. Others will be disappointed that aspects of Behan's life which they may have preferred to see quietly glossed over are included in the book. I have gone to considerable lengths to honour my commitment to use the information given to me exactly in the spirit in which it was given. Some interviewees who were hesitant at first, later gave very generous help and I am particularly grateful to them for that trust.

Before acknowledging the many people who made this book possible I wish to express my special thanks to four members of the Behan family who were endlessly patient with my many varied and sometimes quite forward enquiries on personal family matters. In this regard I am especially grateful to Brendan Behan's brothers, Seamus Behan, Brian Behan and Seán Furlong. Paudge Behan also gave generously of his time and knowledge.

I knew the late Beatrice Behan and her sister, the late Celia ffrench-Salkeld, since I was an undergraduate at Trinity College, Dublin. I benefited from many happy hours spent in their company, listening to their recollections of Brendan Behan. Behan's close friend, Cathal Goulding, gave generously of his time during lengthy interviews in County Carlow and in Dublin. Behan's other great friend, Paddy Collins, answered many enquiries with glad grace and gave me an important written record of his memories of their friendship.

The constant encouragement and support needed to complete the book came from my good friend, Garech Browne. He provided that enlivening motivation which contributed to seeing it through to its conclusion.

At a crucial stage I had the great good fortune to have the selfless dedication of Kate Braithwaite to whose editorial judgement and skill I am deeply indebted. Her incisive critical evaluation of all aspects of the book was the largest single contribution made to it. In that regard I am also indebted to

Bernardine Dewar for her invaluable editorial advice and guidance and to Emily Ormond whose editorial skills and advice saved me from many a pitfall. Through the help and guidance of John Wood, many of the complexities of Behan's New York life and my enquiries about it, were solved with expert efficiency, skill and quiet patience.

Three institutions provided an important cache of previously unpublished source material, some of which was not due for release to scholars until the year 2007, and I wish to express my gratitude to individuals in the institutions concerned. At the British Home Office, Mr J.M. Lloyd; at the Military Archives, Dublin, Comdt. Peter Young and Comdt. Victor Lang; at the Department of Justice, Dublin, the former Minister for Justice, Mrs Nora Owen and departmental officials Fergus Bailey, Seamus Hanrahan and John O'Dwyer.

For interviews, recollections, photographs, the loan of material and for many kindnesses I wish to thank the following people whose names are arranged alphabetically: Muriel Allison (Trinity College Library), Peter Arthurs, Carmel Behan, Sean Boyd, Liam Brady, Dr Luke Brady, Rev Fr P.J. Brophy, Rory Carren, Michael Coogan, Paul Conran, Alan Cook, Anthony Cronin, Thérèse Cronin, Ruda Beresford Dauphin (for her kind help in New York), the late Stan Gebler Davies, Gerry Daly (for his help in unravelling the complexity of Behan's travel to and from England during the period of his IRA membership), Mairead Delaney, Johnny Devlin, Brendan Dohry, J.P Donleavy, Dr Aidan Doyle (for his scholarly guidance on Behan's Irish poems), Austin Doyle, Senator Joe Doyle, Ian Dunlop, Daniel Farson, Liam Finnegan, Joan Countess de Freney, Paula Furlong, the late Allen Ginsberg, Viscount Gormanston, James Gorry, Thérèse Gorry, Valentine Gotti (for her kind help in Paris and New York), Charles Gould (for his memories of Behan in the US) Reginald Gray (for his memories of Behan and for his kind permission to reproduce his portraits of Behan and Cecil ffrench-Salkeld), Pete Hamill, Nuala Harris, Reggie Hastings (for his kind encouragement and hospitality in County Kilkenny when finishing the book), Anne Henderson (Irish Architectural Archive), Senator Dr Mary Henry, Seamus Hosey, John Hurt, Sharon Hutchinson (Irish Times Library), Margaret Hyland, Dr W.S. Jagoe (for his kind help with Behan's medical history) Conal Kearney, Paddy Kelly, Maire Kennedy (The Gilbert Library, Dublin), Irene Keogh, Lainey Keogh, Benedict Kiely, the late Humphrey Langan, John Lonergan (Governor of Mountjoy Jail), Brian Lynch (for his kind help in the RTÉ Archives), Count Randal MacDonnell KM, MacDomhnaill na nGleann (for his kind help in compiling the family trees), Dr David McCutcheon (for Behan's medical records in the Meath Hospital), Joe McGill Jnr., Cyril

McKeon, Desmond MacNamara, Rex Mackay S.C., Derek Mahon, Norman Mailer, Norris Mailer, Dr Philip Mansel (for his kind hospitality in London), Tom Mathews, Chesley Milliken, John Montague, Mary Moreton, Edward Mulhall, Dermot Mullane, Jarlath ffrench-Mullen, Nicholas Myers, Noel Nelson (Royal City of Dublin Hospital), Derek Newcombe (General Records Office, Dublin), Mary Rose O'Brien, Sister Peggy O'Gorman, Anne O'Neill, Paddy and Angela O'Neill, Lord Oranmore and Browne, the late Oonagh Lady Oranmore and Browne, Nora Owens and Sarah Owens, Pauline Parker, Roger Plant (Governor of Hollesley Bay), Poolbeg Press, Dublin, Dr Martin Purcell (for his help with Behan's medical history), Tom Quinlan (National Archives), Grace Pym, Alan Reid (Deputy Governor Hollesley Bay), Frances Redmond, Rev Fr Stephen Redmond, Anna C. Ryan, Maureen Ryan, Jean Rylands (US Embassy, Dublin), Tessa Sayle, London, Jerry Scanlan, Mrs Peter A. Sebley (Rae Jeffs), Sisters Louise, May and Veronica (The Sisters of Charity, Dublin), Patsy Sheridan, W.G. Simpson (Librarian of TCD), Isobel Smith, the late Paul Smith, Kelvin Smythe, Denis Staunton (for his kind help in Berlin), Rosamund Stevens (Steve Willoughby), Francis Stuart, Ian Stuart, Anthony Summers, Carolyn Swift (for her extraordinary generosity with material relating to the first production of *The Quare Fellow* at the Pike Theatre, Dublin), Random House, London, Beverley Tormey (St Vincent's School, Dublin).

Finally, I wish to express my gratitude to my editors Rosemary Dawson and Sheila Buckley, for their advice, encouragement and meticulous attention to even the most minute editorial detail of the book.

Introduction

Brendan Behan and The Mire of Mythology

In the years before his death and mainly for the wrong reasons, Brendan Behan had become a transoceanic legend. After he died, those who had known him – some well, some distantly and some hardly at all – combined to transform his life into myth. Writing thirty-three years after his death, the task of distilling the essence of the man behind the mass of anecdote, sensationalist press coverage and memoir is fraught with difficulties. In this attempt to objectify Behan's legacy, some myths have been destroyed and some have been rationalised, but the tragi-epic nature of his life, it is hoped, has been preserved.

The problems of unearthing the true facts, let alone the true man, are exacerbated by Behan's large and wilful personal contribution, through his deeds, statements, and autobiographical writings, to the mythologising process. He claimed, for example, that he 'was born on the Northside of Dublin in a great lord's house which had gone to ruin.' He was actually born on the more fashionable Southside of the city. This act of geographical sleight of hand helped fit his own story to the 'Broth of a Boy' image that he and his handlers wished to project. His very name gave rise to considerable confusion. During his life, various authorities searched in vain for a record of the birth of 'Brendan' Behan. No such record exists. He had, in fact, like his father before him, been christened 'Francis'. He revelled in this aura of enigma.

As a boy, he identified closely with the martyred heroes of republican history. In emulation of many of those heroes who had also been writers, he first took up the pen in defence of the emergent Irish Nation State. He also – albeit in a somewhat confused and ineffectual fashion – took up arms in its cause. Later, the theme of his writing would be personal liberation within the confining human condition, and it would also place a heavy value on the voice of the ordinary man. However, neither as a 'writer for the cause', nor as a

writer with a personal philosophical quest, did Behan resolve the issues which
he sought to address.

Time conspired against him, but his chief enemy was his confused sense
of self. Neither he, nor anyone close to him was ever able to fully harness the
force of his personality to productivity. His larger than life nature distracted
him from both the business and the art of writing. In his plays he found a
suitable vehicle for his talent, but, like Oscar Wilde, he reserved his genius for
his life. When he was young, his instinct for living and his desire for the heroic
life both placed him in situations which would become the raw material for
his best writing, and enabled him to survive those self-inflicted predicaments.
But his 'genius for life' was also the root of his later self-destruction, both as a
man and as a writer.

His inability to handle success, or to cope with the seriously debilitating
consequences of a combination of diabetes and alcoholism, created an
unmanageable monster which engulfed – either with love or with destruction –
everything in his path. Despite this, one is constantly struck by his ability to
inspire stalwart, sometimes instant, loyalty in people he met. Many of those
close to him were prepared to put up with behaviour from Behan that they
would never have tolerated in anybody else. Sadly, towards the end of his life,
the number of these loyal supporters dwindled.

Behan had very little time for the middle-ground. Although his many
internal conflicts – between his patriotism and his humanism, between his
wish for approval at home and his desire for success abroad – may have
occasionally forced him into a hypocritical stance, hypocrisy was a vice he
detested. Many well-intentioned guardians of his flame have, nevertheless,
resorted to it in the years since his death. Nowhere is that more true than in
relation to his sexuality. In a long-standing charade to conceal the fact of his
sexual inclinations from his native land, there has been a conspiracy of silence
mixed with outraged denial, with few notable exceptions. His attraction to his
own sex has remained largely the subject of innuendo. I have tried to redress
the balance here, not in order to titillate, but because an examination of
Behan's complex sexuality is an essential part of discovering the internal
individual within the carapace of myth.

One of the elements of his tragedy was his inability to fully face up to his
own sexuality. There is no doubt whatever that Behan had homosexual
leanings. Had he lived in a more forgiving age and nation, he might well have
embraced open homosexuality. As it was he had great difficulty in dealing
with this aspect of his personality, a dilemma complicated by his deep-seated
Catholic reflexes. He was a self-professed 'daylight atheist' who dreaded dying

without the Last Rites of the Roman Catholic Church. He himself admitted that his Catholicism gave him a great deal of guilt but very few of the answers he was seeking.

While some striking contradictions in Behan's life have emerged in this portrait, it has not been my intention to debunk the man or treat him with any meanness of spirit. On the contrary, removed from the mire of mythology, Behan emerges as an altogether finer man than the image promoted by popular legend. In an extraordinary choice of phrase, Iain Hamilton, his London publisher, described the Behan he first met in 1957 as 'God-Branded'. Talking to the dishevelled writer in The Shelbourne Hotel in Dublin, Hamilton felt he could have been talking to Coleridge's fated mariner.

If, like Coleridge's mariner, Behan ended his life, drifting and powerless, he began his career with a bullish determination. He was aware from early on of his potential as a writer and the ferocity with which he battled from behind prison bars to use that potential is a more important testimony to the kind of man Behan really was than the head-line making displays of later years. An important collection of official prison documents and correspondence have remained in files in the British Home Office and the Irish Military Archives and Department of Justice. The Irish records, in particular, record his tenacity in challenging the right of the state that imprisoned him to prevent him developing his talent and to block the publication of his prison writings.

His early mistrust of authority came from his prison experience: 'If there's a government,' he declared, 'I'm against it'. If Behan was against authority, he was for a great deal else. As a man who spent so much of his life in jail he was, above all, for the freedom of the human spirit. Yet he himself remained trapped. In life, he was trapped in a failed quest for unconditional love and by a sexuality he failed to come to terms with. However, his greatest failure came when he lost the physical and emotional ability to write. In public, he would make excuses for the tape-recorded books of his last years. 'If dictation was good enough for the Mycenean poets, he declared, 'it's good enough for Brendan Behan.' In private, to close friends, he admitted: 'I'm finished'. With that realisation came the death of his spirit. The rest followed quickly. A conscious decision to neglect his rapidly deteriorating health caused his early death at the age of forty-one. From the moment his coffin, draped in the tricolour of the Irish Republic, was brought through the streets of Dublin to its final resting place, the story-tellers and embroiderers were busy at work on his legacy.

When Behan returned to Dublin after the success of the London production of his play, *The Quare Fellow*, an anonymous *Irish Times* writer wondered whether 'the thin reflective man imprisoned in his lurid and showy frame' would ever be allowed to emerge. While this biographer doubts that, however far one dug, one would ever discover anything 'thin' about Brendan Behan, and while 'reflective' hardly seems the adjective to describe the life-celebrating ebullience and fury of his best work, I hope I have at least let a complex and unique humanity walk free.

Michael O'Sullivan
Dublin, 1997.

TABLE 1 - Behan Family

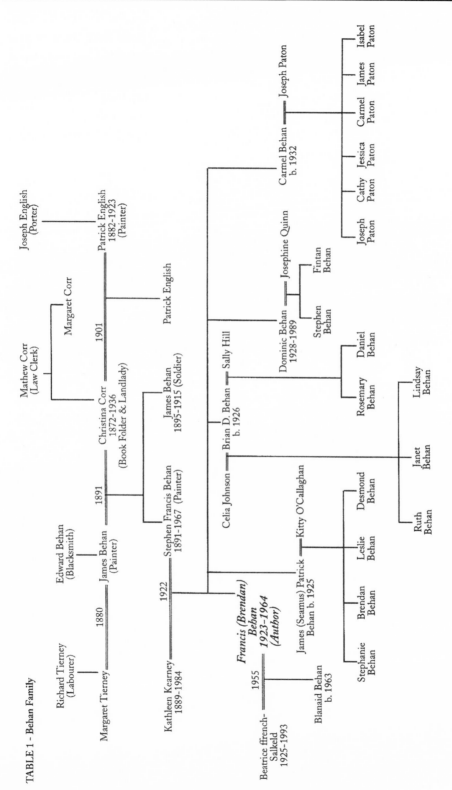

TABLE 2 - Kearney/Furlong Families

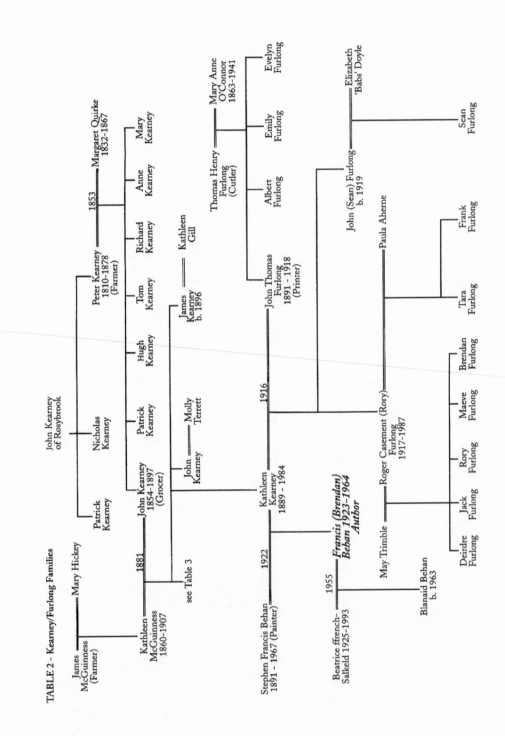

TABLE 3 - Kearney Family

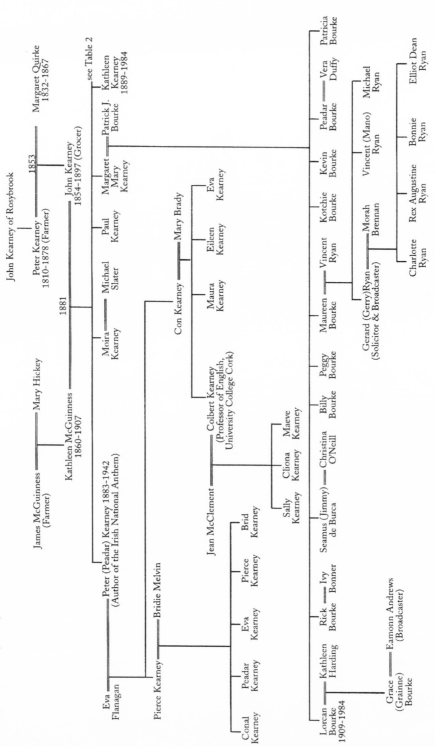

TABLE 4 - ffrench-Salkeld Families

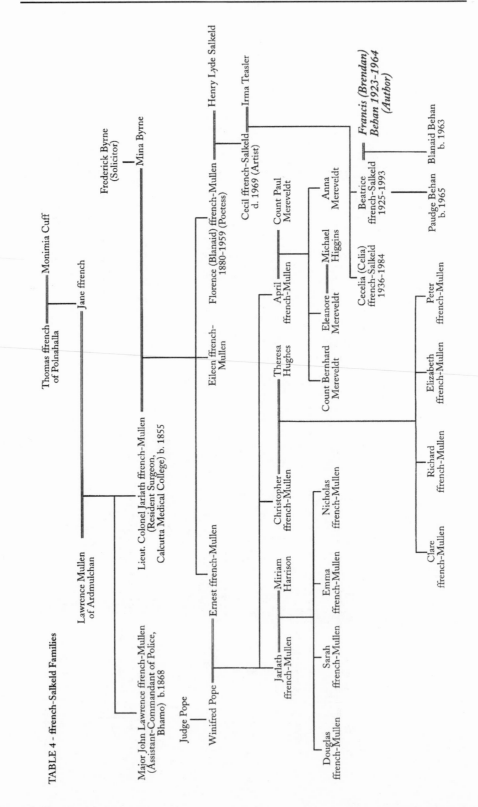

PART ONE

1923-1946

1

Granny's Boy

Late winter 1923; outside Kilmainham Jail, Dublin. A young woman, clutching a baby, strains towards the top row of cell windows. She is trying to attract someone's attention. At last, she sees the face she is looking for: a man comes to the window and catches a first glimpse of his new-born son. This stock-in-trade tableau of revolutionary melodrama was to prove prophetic for the baby in question. Brendan Behan was born to Kathleen Behan and her Republican-activist husband, Stephen, on the 9th of February, 1923, just six months after their marriage.[1] Brendan, a writer rich in talent, huge in personality and the stuff of extravagant legend, later drew much of his inspiration from prison life, with which he himself was to become intimately familiar.

Kathleen Behan, Brendan's mother, was a vivacious and strong-minded woman. She held her ideological convictions with a self-confidence unusual for a woman of her time. She was clearly attractive to men. Stephen Behan was not Kathleen's first husband. When she married him in 1922 at the age of thirty-two, she already had two sons by an earlier marriage. Kathleen, née Kearney, was born at 49 Capel Street, Dublin in September 1889. Both her parents were descended from prosperous, middle-class farming stock. Her mother, Katie McGuinness, came from a family of County Meath farmers in Rathmaiden, near Slane. Her father's family farmed a large holding and lived in a comfortable Georgian farmhouse at Rosybrook, County Louth. John Kearney, Kathleen's father, was established in the grocery trade in Dublin's Dorset Street out of income from the family lands. Later, when his fortune began to dwindle through a combination of negligence and bad luck, the business moved to the less salubrious Dolphin's Barn district. To the further detriment of his business affairs, he developed an obsession with the law and spent his days in the public galleries of the Dublin courts, absorbing the minutiae of protracted legal argument. He died in 1894, leaving his widow with seven children and with no means of support.

Kathleen and her sisters were sent to an orphanage at Golden Bridge Road, Inchicore. She remained there for seven years – a harsh experience but one that helped prepare her to deal with further hardships ahead, when like her mother, she too was later left to fend for her family as a young widow.

Kathleen's first husband, Jack Furlong, came from Belfast of a strong Republican background and worked in Dublin as a printers' compositor. They met in 1915 through their mutual involvement in the Irish independence movement; Kathleen's brother, the poet Peadar Kearney, introduced them at a dance hosted by Cumann na mBan, the women's movement of the IRA. Kathleen thought him shy but attractive. Above all, she valued his connection with the Irish Independence movement: 'He was a member of the Irish Volunteers with my brother Peadar ... and that meant we had everything in common,'[2] she recalled.

During the Easter Uprising of 1916, Jack Furlong was among the Volunteers who manned Jacob's biscuit factory in Wexford Street, one of the principal landmarks of the anti-British rebellion. Meanwhile, Kathleen was running dispatches to the Volunteer leaders in the General Post Office in Sackville Street. More than anything else, these shared Republican ideals drew the couple together. They married in August 1916. Kathleen later admitted to Cathal Goulding, a close friend of Brendan Behan's from boyhood, that within 18 months of marriage she had already become bored with Jack Furlong.[3] From her memoirs it is clear that, while Kathleen was physically attracted to her first husband, he failed to provide the intellectual stimulus and sense of excitement she desired and later found in her marriage to Stephen Behan.

Kathleen was Mrs Jack Furlong for less than three years.[4] Jack fell victim to the influenza epidemic that swept much of Europe in 1918. Kathleen insisted on nursing him at home at 32 North Great Charles Street, refusing to let him die in a hospital. She was ill-equipped to deal with the next four years of widowhood. While she may have found her husband unexciting, she had certainly imagined settling down to a long married life with him. His death at such a young age was the second serious blow dealt her in her first quarter century. She was left with one son, Rory, and pregnant again. She did not discover that she was carrying twins until she gave birth to two sons on 19 March 1919, only one of whom survived. She called him Seán. Sadly, the second one died.[5]

Left alone to support her children, Kathleen badly needed to find work. Fortunately, her solid Republican credentials connected her to a powerful and influential network. Through an introduction from the Countess Markievicz, a leading figure in the struggle for Irish Independence, she found a job in the

Dublin home of nationalist activist, Maude Gonne MacBride. Kathleen liked to describe her function in the household as that of 'receptionist'. She also performed light household duties. At Madame MacBride's house in St Stephen's Green – one of the grandest Georgian squares in Dublin – she met many of the leaders of the Irish Independence movement, as well as key members of Dublin literary society such as W.B. Yeats. The poet's long-standing, unrequited love for her employer was notorious and openly professed. Kathleen was amused at the way Madame MacBride kept him at arm's length and rebuffed his amorous attentions by calling him 'silly Willie'. On the other hand, she found Yeats' habit of calling her by the familiar nickname of 'Kitty' infuriating. She was equally irritated by his tendency to hold her in conversation in the entrance hall before he entered the drawing room. Kathleen recalled that she often paid dearly for these unwelcome chats with Yeats, the Nobel Laureate, because Madame MacBride scolded her for serving tea which had grown cold while she listened to Yeats' small talk.

While in Madame MacBride's service Kathleen also met the society portraitist, Sarah Purser, who asked if she might use her as a model. The ensuing portrait, *The Sad Girl*, is a study of her head. This rather melancholic image is a sympathetic record of Kathleen's troubled state at this point in her life.[6]

Kathleen's financial situation improved considerably when she took up employment as a clerk with Dublin Corporation, the municipal administration. During much of this time, Kathleen and her two sons, Rory and Seán, were living with her mother-in-law, Mary-Ann Furlong, at her house in Great Charles Street. In the basement of that house, Granny Furlong (as she was known to the family) had made uniforms for the rebels of Easter Week. In that house and at subsequent addresses in Dublin and in England, she gave refuge to IRA men who were on the run. Later, at the age of 77, she became one of the world's oldest political prisoners. Granny Furlong was an ardent nationalist who had no difficulty in reconciling her Roman Catholic faith with her own peculiar brand of Socialism. Bob Bradshaw, an IRA colleague of Brendan's, described her nature and beliefs thus:

> Warm and generous in her ways and manner, she was tolerant towards those who did not share her fervent belief in the IRA and accepted that there was more than one kind of Republican and, therefore, more than one kind of truth.[7]

Granny Furlong's philosophy was that God was good and Lenin wasn't a bad man either. It was a philosophy that her daughter-in-law also accepted and professed without reservation.

It was at Granny Furlong's house that Kathleen first met Stephen Behan. Jack Furlong had made Stephen's acquaintance through the Gaelic League, a popular movement that sought to revive Irish as a living language, and through Republican circles. He was also a friend of her brother, Peadar Kearney. Stephen Behan was 5ft 3ins tall, with a strong, stout build and a ruddy complexion that earned him the nickname 'Rosy' from his friends. 'I loved him the very first time I saw him', Kathleen recalled. 'Men don't marry women, you know, it's the women that marry the men – and we were married in no time.'[8] They wed in 1922, just three weeks after Kathleen had dismissed out-of-hand a proposal of marriage from her brother-in-law and fellow resident at Great Charles Street, Harry Furlong.

Stephen (christened Francis) Behan was the very quintessence of the native Dubliner. He was born at 34 Hardwicke Street on 26 December 1891 and derived much pride from the fact that both his parents were Dubliners, as, years later, did his son, Brendan. 'My father's people came from the cul-de-sac ... called "George's Pocket" at the back of St George's Church in Temple Street, which is the most beautiful bit of city anywhere,' Brendan wrote of his father's antecedents; '... and my father's earliest memories were of his grandmother, a hardy old sort from the lock-house on the Royal Canal above Mountjoy.' James Behan, Stephen's father, was a foreman house-painter, and his mother, Christina Corr, worked as a folder and gilder in Galwey and Co., a firm of printers in Eustace Street.[9] Her father was a law clerk, and therefore a member of the professional middle class. Later the family would jest that this position made her 'the first Behan in print'.[10]

Stephen received his early education from the Christian Brothers at North Richmond Street. He is believed to have spent a brief period in a Catholic seminary with the intention of becoming a priest. The details of this period of his life are somewhat sketchy, mainly, it seems, because of his own desire to obscure and mythologise his time at the seminary and his reasons for leaving it.[11] Stephen's own version claimed that he was summarily expelled for the seduction of a housemaid. The family, however, have tended to believe that a crisis caused by the death of his father and the remarriage of his mother to Patrick English, another house-painter, was the catalyst for Stephen's precipitate departure.[12] It now transpires that Stephen's mother remarried in 1901 when the boy was only ten years old.[13] Professor Colbert Kearney, a relative of Kathleen Behan's, believes the most likely explanation to be that Stephen was practical enough to realise he was constitutionally unsuited to the discipline of the priesthood and left of his own volition. Whatever the truth of the matter, for the remainder of his life, his family and his work-mates felt that 'the seminary left its mark, widening the scope of his mind and cultivating a delight in the subtle shades of thought and argument'.[14] Kearney's analysis of Stephen's later attitude towards his short seminary career provides valuable insight into the psychological stance of Brendan Behan's father:

> That he should advertise the expulsion and the attempted seduction is telling. The loss of vocation was not a topic for polite conversation, yet Stephen welcomed the double image of 'spoiled priest', the priest and the sinner, the sacred and the profane; that it had the power to shock people by seeming to look lightly on two taboo areas, religion and sex, suited him down to the ground.[15]

Later, Stephen was apprenticed to his step-father and from him he learned the house-painting trade. His relationship with Patrick English, who died of 'painters' colic' caused by white lead poisoning in 1923, never developed into anything more than that between master and apprentice. His relationship with his mother was always difficult. Christina English was a woman of gigantic personality. She ruled the Behan family with a despotic matriarchal hand until her death in 1936.

After their wedding on 28 July 1922, Kathleen and Stephen Behan set up an independent home in a flat at Inchicore, but they had little chance to enjoy it. The Irish nation was now brutally divided by civil war. Stephen took the side of the Republicans, who supported Eamon de Valera's rejection of the 1922 treaty that granted Ireland the partial independence of Dominion Status and took up arms against the new Free State. Within two months of his marriage, Stephen was arrested by government troops and taken to Kilmainham Jail. Alone again, Kathleen could no longer afford the Inchicore flat and was soon forced to move to 14 Russell Street, as a rent-free tenant of her mother-in-law, Christina English. The Behan family continued to live there for the next fifteen years, until they were forcibly re-housed in 1937.

Even before her second husband's death, Christina (Granny English to the family) appears to have marshalled sufficient resources to enable her to become a slum landlady of not inconsiderable size in Dublin's Northside.[16] Ultimately, her property holdings amounted to three substantial tenement houses at number 7 Fitzgibbon Street, and numbers 13 and 14 Russell Street, just north of Mountjoy Square. This once fashionable, but by then decaying street became the centre of Granny English's property empire.

The move to Russell Street was not an ideal solution to Kathleen Behan's housing problem, for Kathleen has made it quite clear that she and Christina were never the best of friends. The older woman thought the younger woman unattractive and said so within Kathleen's hearing. Kathleen thought her mother-in-law mean and her view of her was further coloured by the fact that Stephen made no secret of his dislike for his mother, with whom he had had a troubled relationship since his late teens. Kathleen remembered sharing as a confidence with her mother-in-law, an account of an attempted rape made on her when she was a young woman, and being rebuffed with the unsympathetic view that she 'must have encouraged it'.[17] For the rest of her life, Kathleen remained resentful of Granny English's domineering interference during the early years of her marriage.

Granny English's generosity was always exercised with strict conditions attached. Kathleen recalled that she had a battle on her hands when she tried to stake her limited claim on accommodation in 14 Russell Street:

> At first we had just one room, and it was no thanks to my mother-in-law that we had even that. Though she was keen enough for us to live with her, she didn't want us taking up rooms that she could get money for.
> So to begin with we had to make do with whatever space we could find.[18]

When Kathleen arrived with her children at Russell Street, she was given a key to a basement room by a woman who was just vacating it. Within hours of settling the children in, there was a knock on the door and another tenant who had been promised the room by Granny English demanded her right of occupancy. Kathleen's reaction was to threaten her with a sweeping brush and see her off the premises with the admonishment, 'What I have, I hold'.[19] When her mother-in-law visited on the following morning, Kathleen presented her tenancy as a *fait accompli*. Later, Kathleen acquired an upstairs room in much the same way, but in the fourteen years the family lived in Russell Street, those two rooms remained the extent of their accommodation. Christina English resented her daughter-in-law's decision to abandon her secure job with Dublin Corporation, and its guaranteed weekly pay-packet, in favour of looking after her children and setting up house for her imprisoned husband.

Dominic Behan, one of Brendan's younger brothers, claimed that his grandmother also resented her other tenants and 'thought she honoured them by allowing them to pay rent'[20] for houses where one lavatory served thirteen families. Granny English spent hardly a penny on maintenance and, after her death, the tenements were condemned and knocked down by the city authorities.[21]

Russell Street had been completed by 1803 and named after its builder, John Russell, and not, as sometimes claimed, after his namesake John Russell, the Duke of Bedford. Its houses formed a typical Dublin-Georgian streetscape. Most were three storeys over a basement with handsome cut-stone door cases and uniform fenestration. Their basement areas were protected by fine ironwork, which added to the overall sense of solidity. Within one hundred years of its completion, the fate of Russell Street was sealed by the passing of the Act of Union, which deprived Ireland of its parliament and Northside Dublin of the residential gentrification which once attended it.

The street became an odd mixture of residential and commercial usage. By the nineteenth century, it contained a ladies' seminary and the Mountjoy Brewery, which provided a major source of neighbourhood employment. Granny English's two houses had been in use as private homes until the end of the nineteenth century, but by 1905 they were listed in Dublin street directories as tenements. Dominic Behan described the site of the Behan's first family home as 'An island of tenements surrounded by petty middle-class respectability.'[22] When the Behans moved there, the aroma of 'alcohol brewed from carbolic'[23] hung over the street – the combined emanations of the Mountjoy Brewery and the Phoenix Laundry. Russell Street residences, Kathleen Behan recalled, could be divided simply into two types of dwelling: those with closed and those with open front doors:

> The houses in Russell Street were typical Dublin tenements with large windows. Some were shiny with clean curtains, others were dusty and grimy, hiding dirty rags of curtains. Some of the houses were the 'closed hall door' kind. They were lived in by people who had work and could afford bigger rents. Ours was the other kind, with doors that hung back into the gloomy hallway day and night.[24]

The street was populated by what are known in Dublin as 'characters', many of whom became fodder for Behan's pen in later years: Seanie Kirshaw, a poacher by trade, used to parade the street with a cigarette-smoking monkey on his shoulder and a bulldog by his side who ate the monkey's discarded cigarette butts; Maggie Riley, a woman of immense size, who was often seen on the street carrying her paralytically-drunk husband, Jack, back from the pub, wrapped in her apron; Mrs Farrell the coal-woman who kept her donkey indoors during the winter; 'Major' House, a retired sergeant major from the British Army, who blared out English songs from a horn gramophone to the annoyance of his Republican neighbours.

Today, the street is known principally for two things: its proximity to Croke Park, the headquarters of the Gaelic Athletic Association, and as the childhood home of Brendan Behan.

Behan's birth certificate gives his official first name as Francis, which was also his father's. But, like Stephen and according to a peculiar Dublin habit, he would be known to the world by a name other than that under which he was officially registered. Within a few days of his birth, the young Behan found himself planted at the centre of Granny English's Russell Street tenement kingdom.

Brendan's position as his grandmother's favourite grandchild, her adored 'Bengy' or 'poor little Bren', was secure from infancy. His early childhood was set firmly in the exclusion zone of Granny English's hegemony. She spoiled and indulged him to a point that made him quite often insufferable to his siblings and at times almost uncontrollable to his parents. It was a condition from which he would never fully recover.

Brendan would later describe his relationship with his grandmother in the autobiographical short story, *The Confirmation Suit*: 'My grandmother and Miss McCann (a character modelled on one of Granny English's tenants) liked me more than any other kid they knew. I like being liked and could only admire their taste.'[25] That story also gives a very precise sense of his grandmother's eccentric private world:

> ... my grandmother, who lived at the top of the next house, was a woman of capernosity and function. She had money and lay in bed all day, drinking porter or malt, and taking pinches of snuff, and talking to the neighbours that would call up to give her the news of the day. She only left her bed to go down one flight of stairs and visit the lady in the back drawing room...[26]

'Fat, black, and as powerful as any man,'[27] Granny English was a bedroom dictator. She ruled from the top floor of 13 Russell Street. Her rooms, furnished with heavy Victorian furniture, were a gathering place for her cronies who were known in the street as 'Mrs English's committee'. From the grand-matriarchal bed she received, in the eighteenth-century manner, the supplications of family and tenants. There, amid crumbling stucco and peeling paint, rents were paid and gossip exchanged. In sharp contrast to the Behan household, Granny English's urban demesne was free from 'economic constraint, spiritual commitment and radical ardour.[28] Like a Mark Twain character, 'she was not quite what you would call refined. She was not quite what you would call unrefined.' She proclaimed no particular allegiance to either political ideology or religious conviction. Her principal loyalty was to unbridled indulgence in her own simple pleasures. Part of her enjoyment of life was the pleasure she got from sharing her anecdotes and pleasures in a conspiratorial manner with her grandson, Brendan.

While Granny English conducted her business and entertainment from her bed, her heir apparent, the hapless Paddy English, her only son by her second marriage, often slept soundly beside her. He was usually wearing a cap to conceal encroaching baldness from the several female admirers who saw him as an ideal marital prospect. With his indolent disposition, Behan's uncle Paddy spent his days in the limited world of Russell Street, venturing only as far as the neighbouring retreat of Gill's public house. A girlfriend of Paddy's once cut her throat to get his attention, but even that violent act awoke nothing more in him than an urgent desire to visit Gill's bar.

The reclusive Paddy was of little practical use to his mother as she was quite reclusive herself, save for her passion for attending funerals. At the age of six, Brendan was already a much more reliable conduit and emissary to the outside world. He became her most trusted link to the world beyond Russell Street.

Kathleen Behan resented Granny English's unusual relationship with her son. She particularly disliked the fact that Brendan was introduced to alcohol by his grandmother while he was still a very young boy, and she saw this as the origin of Brendan's later problems. Kathleen was powerless to prevent Brendan's grandmother plying him with drink because, as she admitted in old age, Granny controlled the purse strings. Kathleen claimed that her mother-in-law was a furtive drinker who poured whiskey from a china teapot when her tenants and family were present. To maintain her secret, she enlisted Brendan to smuggle a constant supply of either whisky or, more usually, Guinness in a pint jug to her bedchamber headquarters from Gill's, the neighbourhood pub. If anyone dared complain about her encouraging Brendan to drink, she would dismiss them by saying it was 'good for the worms', and insist that if children were given alcohol when young it would prevent them developing a taste for it in later life. 'I never turned to drink,' Behan later claimed, 'it seemed to turn to me. I don't ever remember not drinking.'[29]

Brendan was rarely excluded from the circle of Granny English's female hangers-on, no matter how delicate or adult the conversation. But the result of allowing this child special status at his grandmother's bedroom-court was that, throughout his life, Brendan believed that his wayward behaviour would be excused, as it had been when he was his Granny's precocious and much-praised boy. Christina English idolised her grandson. Her family believed that she thus marked him for early destruction: 'To make a god of someone is to destroy them as surely as sticking a knife into their back,' says Brian Behan, another of Brendan's younger brothers. 'Our Brendan would brook no arguments as to what he did or where and when he did it.[30] Brian believes that Brendan had been spoilt from birth by an 'over-abundance of talk and flattery' and thus could deny himself nothing. In later years, Brendan acknowledged that he had been awarded 'most favoured' status in his early childhood. There was at least a tentative admission that such treatment might be harmful to a young boy when he wrote, 'I was reared a pet, God love me', but he continued to believe that Granny English was the only person who truly understood him. Her death, when he was thirteen, launched him on a lifelong quest for the understanding and the unconditional love he had found in his grandmother.

In popular memory, and by his own desire, Brendan Behan is inextricably linked with Granny English territory – the tenements of Dublin's Northside. As a boy he had been proud to be called a 'Russeller', as the inhabitants of Russell Street were known. It was an era when such tribal identification mattered a great deal to a young Dubliner's street credibility. 'But then we said more than our prayers in the slums of North Dublin where I was born – less than an ass's roar from Nelson's Pillar', Behan later wrote. He was taking a considerable degree of poetic licence, for which he would become well known, and more than an inch or two of geographic transposition, when he added: 'I was born in a Georgian House that had gone to rack and ruin as a tenement'.[31] That declaration was made in 1962, just two years before his death and at the height of his international fame. He was staking his claim to *bona fide* membership of the working-class clans of Dublin's Northside slums. He was actually born on the more fashionable southside, in The National Maternity Hospital, Holles Street, just a few hundred yards from the former family home of Oscar Wilde in Merrion Square. In working-class Dublin semiotics, the distinction between those born on the Southside and those born on the Northside was all-important, but Brendan chose to gloss over this detail. Later, he would allow no amount of literary and financial success to interfere with his cherished public image as a working-class hero. When he came to write *The Hostage*, he immortalised that urban environment with which he so wished to be associated.[32]

The Kearney/Furlong/Behan/English line had plenty of reasons to paint a rather different picture of their background. Granny English was not simply a tenement dweller – she was a property owner and a hard-minded landlady. Brendan's father, Stephen, was a man of unusual intellectual range. His mother was connected to the world of Dublin theatre. His parents were both part of a Republican network that tied the family into the aristocracy of the Independence movement, which included men who later became government ministers. Kathleen Behan's ancestors were middle-class farmers and merchants. But if, in real terms, the Behan family carried a certain bourgeois 'taint', Brendan never cared to acknowledge it. His mother might occasionally aver to the family's genteel origins when she gave newspaper interviews, but even though aspects of his adult history contradicted his self-professed working-class loyalties, for Brendan there would be no such admission.

The truth is probably nearer to the view expressed by his friend, the writer Anthony Cronin:

> If the realities of working-class life were known to him it is also true that he had never been among the great unacquainted submerged; there was plenty of acquaintance and tradition about in his growing-up; and indeed it was to some extent at least, the show business element in him that contributed to his destruction in the end.[33]

To his public, however, Brendan Behan the showman eschewed that inheritance of acquaintance and tradition in favour of the self-created myth of his emergence from the collective miasma of human indistinction.

2

Northside Childhood

Upon his release from Kilmainham Jail in April 1923, Stephen Behan joined his wife and baby son in their quarters at 14 Russell Street. He found it difficult to settle down to family life after the rigours of prison confinement. His position was made more difficult by unemployment and partial dependence on financial hand-outs from his mother. Former employers shunned the IRA man after his release from prison and it was over a year before any form of regular painting work came his way. To Kathleen's relief, a firm called Dockrell's eventually took him on as a painter. She had been concerned that he might take up more unorthodox employment. According to Kathleen, Stephen had been approached in their Russell Street flat by a cousin of hers who had made a fortune in the United States during prohibition. He had a proposal for Stephen. He was recruiting former IRA men to take to the US as gun slingers and guards for his bootlegging empire. It was an attractive offer and Stephen considered taking it until the combination of her persistence and the Dockrell's opening changed his mind.[1] Brendan Behan's earliest memory is of his father in painter's overalls, carrying brushes, paint and sometimes glazing tools.[2]

With Stephen employed, the Behan family settled into life in Russell Street. Between 1925 and 1932, Kathleen bore four more children: Seamus, Brian, Dominic, and finally, a girl, Carmel. Another child, Fintan, is believed to have died in infancy.[3]

It seems certain that Brendan's place in his grandmother's affections played a larger part in securing the family's rent-free accommodation than the blood ties between Stephen and his mother, Christina, whose relationship at the best of times bordered on mere civility. Christina had always preferred Stephen's brother, James, who had served in the second battalion of the Royal Irish Rifles. She had once rescued him from the recruiting officer's grasp by paying for his discharge from the British Army, only to find that he returned at the first opportunity. In September 1915, he was reported missing in action, presumed dead. Christina was inconsolable after his death. Brendan's younger brother, Seamus, remembers being severely scolded by his grandmother when she found him playing with his dead uncle's war medals. He also felt that she was distressed by his Christian name because it reminded her of her dead son.[4] *Seamus* is the Irish translation of James.

Although the family continued to live at Russell Street for fourteen years, Stephen was acerbic about his mother's generosity: 'She could live where another person would die,'[5] he said. Her view of him was probably best expressed by the fact that she left him nothing in her Will.[6] The children were aware from an early age of the enmity between their father and grandmother. Dominic Behan recalled the following exchange between his brothers Seamus and Brian:

'Did yeh hear Da last night?'
'No. Was he drunk? Was he?'
'Not drunk, yeh eejit. In a temper.'
'Over what?'
'Well, I don't know what it was over, but he said awful things about Gran. Himself and Ma were talkin'.'
'About what?'
'I don't know, I couldn't hear.'
'Then how d'ye know he was fightin'.'
'Because he was cursin' Gran an' callin' her a bloody oul' bitch.'
'Oh, that's terrible, he'll go to hell for that.'
'For what?'
'For callin' his mother a bloody oul' bitch.'
'Not if he tells it in confession.'[7]

Initially the Behans occupied the basement kitchen, with its black, flagstoned floor, dark, polished range, scrubbed deal table, and a dresser, which Seamus Behan recalled contained 'willow-pattern crockery, which was not for everyday use.'[8] On the walls, he remembered, hung several pictures including those of James Connolly, Patrick Pearse and a print of Fuchs' painting of the Blessed Virgin Mary. In the evenings, the family lived by gaslight, but the room, whose principal source of natural light was a small window giving onto the basement area, was dark by day.

Later, the family acquired a room on the hall floor which was used as the children's bedroom. It was separated from the next-door flat only by dividing doors. At night, the neighbours' fire cast shadows under the doors which seemed to the Behan children to resemble the 'flames of hell'.[9] The bedroom had a large, black, Kilkenny marble chimney piece, and it was from there the children believed that the souls in Purgatory, had they a mind to do so, would make their earthly return.[10] Their room was simply furnished with three iron bedsteads, and the floor covering was brown linoleum. Around the room ran a heavy cornice, a reminder of the house's former status as 'a great lord's town house,'[11] as Brendan liked to think of it. On one wall hung 'a picture of the Sacred Heart with its symbolic entrails looking like something out of a butcher's shop, and frightening the living daylights out of us', recalls Seamus Behan. Brendan himself remembered lying in bed in that room listening to distant trams braking heavily and 'avoiding the eye of the Sacred Heart in the picture on the far wall'.[12] The young Brendan derived more comfort from the familiar noises of the trams than he did from the room's religious icons: the trams had 'lights and people on them; old fellows, a bit jarred and singing, and fellows leaving their mots[13] home to Drumcondra after the pictures.'[14]

The Behans found themselves on good terms with most of their neighbours with whom they shared the unifying bond of a common poverty. Some saw Kathleen as standoffish because she chose not to spend her days on the doorstep, gossiping. They dubbed her 'Lady Behan' but that was more in friendly jest than serious acrimony. Stephen was affable to most of his neighbours. He is, however, recorded as having disliked one particular resident of 14 Russell Street: a one-time British Army soldier who, when drunk, shouted anti-Republican insults at him. The problem was at its most intense on Wednesdays, when the former soldier collected his pension. Stephen solved this intolerable domestic situation by giving the man a severe hiding.[15] The usually mild-mannered Stephen found the presence of a prostitute, who plied her trade from a neighbouring flat in Russell Street, and of another neighbour who kept a donkey in the house in winter infinitely preferable to that of the truculent ex-squaddie. The question of service in the British Forces was a vexed one in the Behans' immediate environment. It was not unusual for Irishmen to serve in the Crown Forces – 200,000 Irish men participated in World War I. Of the Behans, Brendan's Uncle James lost his life in the trenches and his brother, Seamus was to serve in the RAF during World War II. During the '20s and '30s, British Armed Services' pensions were an important source of income for many of the Behan's neighbours. However, although the IRA made good use of the military expertise of some returning soldiers, nationalist feeling tended to look askance at such a background.

As a child, Brendan had sometimes joined the weekly ale-fuelled meetings of local War veterans. He describes them in the collection of his writings from the *Irish Press* entitled *Hold Your Hour And Have Another:*

On Wednesdays and I a child, there were great gatherings of British Army pensioners and pensionesses up in a corner of the North Circular, in Jimmy-the-Sports.

When the singing got well under way, there'd be old fellows climbing up and down Spion Kop till further orders and other men getting fished out of the Battle of Jutland, and while one old fellow would be telling how the Munsters kicked the football across the German lines at the Battle of the Somme, there'd be a keening of chorused mourners crying from under their black shawls over poor Jemser or poor Mickser that was lost at the Dardanelles.[16]

But, as the scion of a family whose loyalties were ardently Republican, he was aware of a guilty sense of betrayal at attending such occasions:

My family would be shocked out of our boots listening to such loyalist carrying-on, but I – oh, woe to me in the times of Republican wrath – I lusted after false gods, and snaked in among the widows and orphans, and sat at the feet of the veterans, to sell my country for a glass of Indian ale and a packet of biscuits, and as Jembo Joyce would say, 'putting up me two hands to thank heaven that I had a country to sell'.[17]

Stephen Behan soon gave up worrying about which of his neighbours had served whom and turned his attention to bringing up his family. He had no particular desire to be seen as a model father. He could be selfish, sarcastic, intolerant, and regularly drunk, but he loved his children dearly and made no distinction between Rory and Seán, from Kathleen's first marriage, and his own children. Rory recalled that both sets of children were treated with the same 'sublime indifference',[18] a remark which pleased his step-father immensely. When a very young Seamus Behan asked his father why he took the older Furlong boys to the theatre so often, Stephen quietly replied that it was because he 'knew them first'. And when Seamus taunted Seán Furlong with the refrain 'you're not a Behan, you're a Furlong', his step-brother came back with a nonchalant reply: 'That's right, I'm a first edition' – an indication of the erudition and wit which, at an early stage, marked these children out. Whatever his faults, Stephen Behan gave his children a firmly-rooted belief in the value of the written word. This self-described ex-seminarian may have been reduced to slum-living, but he retained certain values. Chief amongst these was a passion for literature.[19] Stephen set an unusually high example of intellectual curiosity and accomplishment, and this offered to his children a route out of their tenement environment, should they wish to escape it. His pedagogical approach was benign, based on the pleasures of knowledge rather than its burden, and it was an approach that worked. Over sixty years later, his son Seamus would hail his father's methods as 'threatening us children not too seriously with the benefits of education.'[20]

Stephen read a great deal to the children, often acting out the parts. He loved simple ritual and theatricality. His readings were usually preceded by the ritual preparation and lighting of a pipeful of tobacco and the careful arrangement of the book – all elements in the thrilling sense of occasion that was part of his story-telling technique. He knew Latin and declaimed from the writings of Marcus Aurelius in the original, translating and acting as he went. Through their father, the children became familiar with Dickens, especially Stephen's favourite, *The Pickwick Papers*. The eclectic mix of family reading included Thackeray, extracts from Samuel Pepys' Diary, Fielding's *Tom Jones*, Charles Kickham's novel *Knocknagow*, the plays of Shaw, Synge and O'Casey as well as the poetry of Yeats, and works by Dostoyevsky, Zola and Maupassant, adding an international perspective.[21] On top of all this literary activity, Stephen sometimes regaled the family with snippets from a daily newspaper.

If he was not in the mood to read, Stephen played the violin for the children, making up in the gusto of his performance what he lacked in actual musical ability.

Music was a mainstay of the Behan household: Kathleen came from a family steeped in the nationalistic ballad tradition of nineteenth-century Ireland. Her sisters-in-law, the Furlongs, from her first marriage were accomplished pianists and often accompanied her while she sang. 'I could see my old man with the fiddle, standing beside the piano, and Aunt Emily playing the piano ...' Brendan recalled in the *Borstal Boy*.[22] His friend Cathal Goulding, says that Kathleen learned some of her songs from his grandfather, Charlie Goulding.[23] Many came from her own family, the Kearneys. She sometimes sang Brendan to sleep not with lullabies but with rebel songs:

> Come workers sing a rebel song,
> A song of love and hate,
> Of love unto the lowly
> And of hatred to the great.[24]

But she sang not just of hatred, her son Brian recalls, but of hope of better things to come. Her maxim was, 'It's better to sing your grief than to cry it'.[25] Amongst the songs she sang to her children were *Carrickfergus*, *When All the World was Young* and *The Castle of Dromore*.

Although she favoured Irish ballads, she also sang songs from music-hall, pantomime and light opera. The music-hall world was an integral part of

Brendan's upbringing. Kathleen's sister, Margaret, married P.J. Bourke,[26] the Dublin actor-manager who took an annual lease of the Queen's Theatre and made famous the role of Colonel O'Grady in Boucicault's play *Arrah-Na-Pogue*.[27] In plays like *The Northern Insurgents* and *For Ireland's Liberty*, Brendan's uncle presented not just strong men, who were willing to die for Ireland but strong women as well. Like Kathleen Behan, these characters shared the idealism of their menfolk and were not hesitant in giving voice to it. Brendan and his family rarely missed a production of the plays and reviews put on by Bourke. Brendan remembered being in the Queen's Theatre with his father and brothers and the pride he took in his uncle Paddy:

> See those three kids there, and see your man there, the O'Grady, the Colonel that's after telling off the other rat of an English officer on the Court Martial? Well, he's their Uncle.[28]

This was the hot-house home environment that produced the writer, Brendan Behan. His unusual parents, forced by unfortunate circumstances into tenement living, came from family backgrounds rather different to the majority of their near neighbours. From his father he got his love of literature. From his mother he got his love of song and his passionate hatred of England, a hatred that would become somewhat tempered with time and would rarely if ever extend to the ordinary English people he met.

Brendan was an attractive child, pale-skinned, blue-eyed, with dark curly hair, and small hands and feet. He kept up an incessant adult patter punctuated by blasts of intermittent nervous stutter. All the Behan children had accomplishments and talents exceptional for children of their social environment. But an extraordinary self-confidence and even arrogance marked Brendan out even among the sharp-witted Behan brood, as did his compulsion to put himself in the spotlight. Brendan's special relationship with his grandmother and her circle of cronies helped him to believe all his little performances were unique and invested with special status, more worthy of attention than anything his siblings may have done. He had a remarkable capacity, while still a very young child, to recite from memory vast quantities of poetry, prose and nationalistic political tracts. This he did, by all accounts, with a great facility to entertain his spell-bound elders. Brendan's first major party-piece was his memorised recitation of one of the sacred texts of the Irish Republican cause – the speech that Robert Emmet, the eighteenth-century nationalist martyr, made from the dock:

> Let no man write my epitaph; for as no man who knows my motives dare now vindicate them, let not prejudice or ignorance asperse them. Let them and me rest in obscurity and peace; and my tomb remain

uninscribed, and my memories in oblivion, until other times and other men can do justice to my character. When my country takes her place among the nations of the earth, then and not till then, let my epitaph be written.[29]

The IRA activist, Bob Bradshaw, was one of several witnesses of this early precociousness. When Brendan was ten, Bradshaw took shelter in the safe house that Brendan's other grandmother, Mary-Ann Furlong, provided in her Dublin home. One day her daughter, Emily, brought Brendan to meet Bradshaw and his colleagues so that he might perform for them. Bradshaw recalled a 'very bright-faced boy in short pants who trotted through the door at Emily's skirts' to recite a speech about O'Casey, Shaw and Wilde with quotations from selected works. Bradshaw noticed a pronounced stammer, through which the child battled on regardless until he finished his piece. The listeners, Bob Bradshaw remembered, were left 'with the feeling that we were at the wrong end of a little bit of "unconscious" iconoclasm.'[30]

Brendan was fiercely possessive of all this attention, especially that which came from Granny English. 'She's my Granny, not yours,' he yelled at his brother Seamus, as he pushed him down the stairs on learning that his younger brother had received a penny from her.[31] His behaviour left his brothers in awe of this threatening personality who could 'cut you up with his tongue or his fists, as he chose.'[32] Granny's darling boy, who lacked for nothing 'in a street where money was counted in halfpennies and pennies,'[33] could be ferociously selfish. 'Brendan was a very good-looking child and was usually very even-tempered', according to his father, Stephen. 'But he had another side. Because he was the golden boy, he always wanted his own way. There was a vicious streak in him side-by-side with the personality of a sensitive little boy.'[34]

When Brendan was not performing his set pieces or closeted in his grandmother's private world, his life was little different from that of any other tenement child. There were, quite literally, hundreds of children to play with. They organised themselves in gangs of twenty to thirty, according to street or other loyalties. The Royal Canal, which divided Russell Street, was the focal point for their games and intrigues. 'My family always had an interest – let me say a proprietary interest – in the Royal Canal ... so much so that the great-aunt gave us permission to swim in it,' Brendan said. Brian Behan recalled the importance of the canal in their young lives:

The eternal source of entertainment, we waited until the barges came either puffing on their little engines or pulled by huge, bony horses.

Then we would leap on to them from the bank and dive off the end, much to the annoyance of the bargees and the horror of our mothers, who were forever telling us about boys being sucked under and never seen again or having their heads chopped off by the propellers.[35]

This waterside world was Brendan's territory as much as that of any of the Russell Street toughs. He shared with the other children on the street a sense of being different from the neighbouring children, who came from the 'red brick respectability of Jones's Road, Fitzroy Avenue, Clonliffe Road, and Drumcondra generally'.[36] Those children, Brendan recalled, were 'despised, hated and resented,' because they lived in one-family houses 'which we thought greedy, unnatural and unsocial; they wore suits all the one colour, both jacket and pants, where we wore a jersey and shorts ... Furthermore, it was suspected that some of them took piano lessons and dancing lessons while we of the North Circular Road took anything we could lay our hands on which was not nailed down.'[37]

On 18 April 1928, this paradoxical six-year-old was presented to Saint Vincent's School run by the French Sisters of Charity of Saint Vincent de Paul at Dublin's North William Street.[38] The school was set in what Behan called 'Sean O'Casey land':

If you stood at the canal side of the school, you'd see, looking one way, the docks and cranes and gantries rising the far side of the North Strand, out past the barren space where shops and houses stood, 'till late one night the quiet of the late spring sky was rent by the crashing bombs [of World War II].[39]

The school buildings were red-bricked with 'castor oil plants in the windows'.[40] Nearby were the Royal Canal, Croke Park, and a girls' school where Brendan's female contemporaries shared classes with the girls of Saint Vincent's Orphanage. To Brendan they seemed 'the very model of mysterious and ladylike decorum'.[41]

The most dominant influence in Brendan's early school life was Sr Monica Gallagher from Roscommon. She had been in the North William Street school since the 1890s. After his grandmother and mother she was the most loved figure in his childhood. Sister Louise, who arrived at the school as a postulant two years before Brendan left, remembers Sister Monica as a 'tall and stately figure, yet she could appear very frail. She had an extraordinary magnetism that was felt and respected by even the toughest boys.'[42] She was especially fond of Brendan Behan. Some of the more favoured boys, including

Brendan, worked in a soup kitchen where, at lunch-time, the nuns dispensed nourishing broth to their hungry pupils. For many of them it represented their main meal of the day. For performing this duty, the favourites were given a daily ration of bread and jam as a special treat. One day, soon after Sister Louise arrived at William Street, Brendan and his pals gave the young postulant a severe ribbing. When she complained to Sister Monica the reply was, 'Surely not my boys'. Such was the boys' respect for the elderly nun that this mild admonishment was enough to ensure that the incident was never repeated. Brendan felt especially guilty.

Michael Coogan, a neighbour and boyhood friend of Behan's, remembers Sister Monica as 'a severe figure', constantly threatening the boys with the possibility of 'the hand of God falling heavily upon them'. According to Coogan, boys frequently checked the colour of their tongues in looking-glasses to see if Sister Monica's prediction that they would turn black after telling lies had become a reality. She would stand, he recalled 'at the head of a classroom twiddling her heavy brass crucifix in her bony hands as if she was trying to mesmerise you.'[43]

There were also lay teachers at the school but they held no interest for Brendan – not even the eccentric Miss Andrews, who rode a motor bicycle and marched the boys along to the tune of *Blaze Away* which she played on a harmonica. 'They say the nun is the apple of God's eye,' Behan wrote, 'and if so, North William Street had a whole orchard.'[44] Brendan himself was certainly the apple of Sister Monica's eye and she often overlooked his unruly behaviour because of his precocious intelligence. In school, as at home, Brendan was subject to different laws. In Sister Monica, he found a powerful female figure, who, like his Granny at home, was ready to brush aside his temperamental behaviour as a mere aberration. Sister Monica told Brendan's mother that she need not worry about her son's naughty behaviour because she had 'no doubt but he would go very far in life.'[45]

The school records support Sister Monica's view of Brendan's abilities. He received ten out of ten in all the subjects – reading, writing and composition, and arithmetic – in which he was tested during his final year at St Vincent's.[46] For the rest of his life, he would retain happy memories of Sister Monica who had been so long at North William Street she called some of the children by their fathers' names. Here is his affectionate portrait of her and of a schoolmate:

> The late Sister Monica, who taught generations of boys, including ...
> the present writer, at North William Street School, was encouraging a
> boy called Champers, who, even for that district, was considered a chaw

of some dimensions. Some doubted whether he was a human being at all, and by his shaggy looks and his taste for raw vegetables and chewing tobacco he might have escaped from a circus.

Champers by dint of some pen-chewing, finally produced a composition: *The Autobiography of a Mouse*.

'I was a muss. So was me mother and me father and we all et chees till the cat kem an et me da and me ma an me an all.'

'Now, Stanislaus Kostka' – this was Champers' real name – 'that is really very good indeed and most interesting, but,' and Sister Monica looked at him earnestly from under her big linen bonnet, 'if the mouse was eaten by the cat, how could he have written his autobiography?'

Champers looked at her scornfully, and asked with great patience, 'Listen, Sister, how could a mouse write his beeyografee anyway?'[47]

Sister Monica had told Brendan to sleep at night with his arms folded, so that if he died in his sleep he would have the sign of the cross on him. When in Borstal, Brendan, a confessed 'day-time atheist', acted on Sister Monica's advice.[48]

On 30 June 1934 Brendan left Sister Monica for the more uncertain world of St Canice's Christian Brothers School, on the North Circular Road. He would hold no such fond memories of its teachers. He was a pupil there from 1934 to 1937. Two of his teachers remembered him for lively intelligence and for being 'brassy bold'[49]. He regularly interrupted and corrected one master, Brother O'Donnell, especially on religious matters. One day, in absolute frustration, O'Donnell screamed out, 'And now Bishop Behan, if your Grace is finished with his sermon, may I proceed with my teaching?'[50]

Behan later wrote of his unhappiness at the school, where his inquisitive mind seems to have found insufficient stimulation. The deficiency manifested itself in a strong urge to give cheek to the Christian Brothers, which often landed him in trouble:

> My connection with the agricultural interest and with the backbone of the country was so slight, that when the teacher was explaining how much we owed the farmers of Ireland and asked me where our food came from, I replied, 'Summerhill',[51] and when that strapping Christian Brother moved towards me in a manner that behoved no good to Brendan Francis Aidan Behan, though I knew I had given the wrong answer, the only alternative that came readily to mind was 'Dorset Street'.[52]

By the time Brendan arrived at St Canice's, he had already developed reading skills and a degree of political consciousness that were most unusual for his age. His political awareness had developed through three principal channels: his membership of Fianna Éireann – the boy scout movement of the IRA that he had joined at the age of eight; his mother's Republican loyalties; and his family's general commitment to left-wing causes. The latter, in particular, brought him into conflict with the ruling ethos at St Canice's. There was one particularly memorable clash: During his third year, 1936, his religious instruction teacher, a Christian Brother, used to read aloud to Behan's class from James Hogan's *Could Ireland become Communist? The facts of the Case*. Hogan, Professor of History at University College, Cork who had expounded his Crypto-Fascist theories in *United Ireland*, offered a diet of heavy native piety in place of communism. His theories were the very antithesis of what Behan was hearing at home. Behan gave a solid 'yes' to the possibility of Ireland being overcome by the Red Scare he had been warned of by the Church. He was beaten for his opinion and this punishment was the subject of his first public letter. Soon after leaving the school, in November 1937, he wrote to the left-wing paper, *The Irish Democrat*, explaining 'For giving a very definite answer in the affirmative, I got a kick in the neck'.[53]

Although he had been marked out as a troublemaker at St Canice's for his endless stream of classroom impudence, his teachers also remembered him for his capacity to 'roar out' endless torrents in the Irish language; his inability to hold a grudge; and for his rapacious reading of 'everything from *The Catholic Herald* to *The Daily Worker*' – which presented him with the whole gamut of political opinion. His schoolmates, meanwhile, were struggling with material more suited to their age group. One teacher was surprised to find him reading *The Hidden Ireland*, by the nationalist writer, Daniel Corkery. The book is, among other things, an exploration of the literary testimony of an oppressed group of Irish language poets. To the teacher's surprise, when he quizzed Brendan on its subject matter, he turned out to have understood it thoroughly.[54] On another occasion, his father was once called to the school by Brendan's English master, who wanted to know if Brendan had had help in writing a certain essay. Stephen was 'astonished when he read it'[55] but was sure that Brendan's views on the *'French Influence on British Culture in the Renaissance'* were entirely his own. Though his teachers considered 'his thoughts ... mature beyond his years',[56] they did not accept Stephen's assurances and still questioned the authorship of the essay. Stephen later said that this interview had made clear to him the 'lack of rapport between Behan and the school in which he received most of his formal education'.[57] When that formal education came to an end at the age of fourteen, Brendan wrote with laconic dismissal of his experiences: 'After fourteen years ... I've come to the conclusion that it's a mad world, and one of the maddest things the inhabitants of this mad universe stand for is the rotten educational system imposed on us ...'[58]

Though a problem to his teachers, Brendan was hugely popular with his fellow pupils. His pointed wit and his skill at the Gaelic games of hurling and hand-ball made him an instant success with his peers.[59] The boys of a neighbouring Protestant school looked on him less benevolently. On Poppy Day he would lead a band of like-minded Republican youths to snatch the poppy emblem from the button holes of the Protestant boys, giving them a hiding in the process.

As a very young boy, Brendan had a special friendship with a girl, Teresa Byrne, who lived with her family at 8 Russell Street. She enjoyed teasing Brendan and attempting to deflate his burgeoning ego. One day, when they were out walking together, a rather sad and poorly-attended funeral procession passed by. Brendan, who had inherited an obsession with funerals from his grandmother, remarked to Teresa, that when he died, the mourners would come from all over the world. She replied that he would be lucky to have even the neighbours in attendance. Brendan retorted that the neighbours would be lucky to get in on the edge of the crowd.[60]

Teresa Byrne was also the recipient of some of his earliest letters. One was an apology for getting her into trouble with the nuns at her school, after writing a composition in Irish for her in which he made snide remarks about the nuns' morals, or lack of them. Teresa's fury caused a breach in relations and Brendan wrote his apology in verse:

> Oh, what can I do now, love,
> To restore our happiness?
> Will I go across to Gill's pub
> And to your Ma confess?
>
> Actually, Teresa,
> I've just got two and six
> So will you stop sulking in the parlour
> And go with me to the flicks?
>
> I'll take you to the Drummer
> To the ninepenny cushion seats,
> And that will leave me with a bob
> To get you oranges and sweets.
>
> To give this its proper ending
> I'll wind up yours for ever, Brendan.[61]

As he grew up, however, the diversions of the street and the friendships he made there began to take second place to an all-consuming passion: his total immersion in, and zeal for, the Irish Republican movement. The issues surrounding the Republican cause had been the main ideological influence of his childhood. He was already a member of Fianna Éireann, the boy scout wing of the Republican movement. 'We became members of the Fianna,' Behan later wrote, 'the way other kids became altar-boys'.[62] The organisation had been founded in 1909 by Constance, Countess Markievicz,[63] as a counter-balance to the 'Englishness' of Baden-Powell's Boy Scout movement. Markievicz feared that Irish boys who joined Baden-Powell's scouts would be natural material for the recruiting officers of the British Army and Police. Instead, Fianna Éireann was to be a potential 'reservoir of supporters'[64] for the recruiting needs of the Republican movement. The official magazine of Fianna Éireann, *Fianna: The Voice of Young Ireland*, exhorted the boys to attain physical fitness so that they would 'rise up strong and virile Irishmen fit to take a soldier's part in the national struggle of tomorrow'.[65]

In the year that Brendan joined the Fianna, the Government banned it, along with 11 other organisations, under repressive legislation aimed at weakening the Republican movement. However, the ban merely steeled the resolve of Behan and his fellow Republican scouts to fulfil the expectations voiced in the chorus to their marching song:

> *On for Freedom, Fianna Éireann!*
> *Set our faces to the dawning day;*
> *The day in our land, when strength and daring*
> *Shall end for evermore, the Saxon sway.*

After joining, there was a probation period in which the boys learned the skills that would enable them to take the Fianna test. The test was based on the ordeal that the ancient Irish warriors of legend, after whom the scouts were named, were required to pass through. Members were bound by an honour code that required loyalty to Ireland and absolute obedience to superior officers. Brendan had no difficulty with the first requirement, but he often found himself at odds with the second.

The year Brendan joined the movement, the Chief Scout was George Plunkett, a brother of Joseph Mary Plunkett, one of the seven signatories of the Proclamation of the Irish Republic in 1916. He was assisted by Seán Mooney, later stage manager of the Abbey Theatre, and by the writer and journalist Seamus G. O'Kelly.

O'Kelly described Behan's role in the movement as 'not only a decided asset [but] also a decided liability.'[66] Plunkett, a deeply religious man, found Brendan's bad language profoundly shocking. Brendan's choice of words,

O'Kelly recalled, 'would do justice to the toughest soldier in or out of uniform'.[67] Brendan was known in the Fianna as Mickey Behan because he thought his real name too effete for a young soldier of the Republic. His appetite for 'provoking fist fights and for falling out of trees', both activities that required constant first aid attention, earned him the nickname, 'Mickey the ointment' from his fellow scouts.[68]

In 1934, Behan was court-martialled and expelled from the Fianna for 'disorderly conduct whilst drunk'. The incident occurred at the annual commemoration for the martyred patriot, Wolfe Tone, at Bodenstown, County Kildare. Brendan was in charge of a squad of Dublin Fianna and proudly marched them from the graveside ceremony to Sallins railway station. When he found there would be a delay of over an hour for the connection back to Dublin, he decided to head for a village pub. On his way back to the station, the eleven-year-old Behan was seen by the scandalised Plunkett to be 'blind[69] drunk'. He was, Plunkett told the court-martial, a disgrace to the noble aspirations of Fianna Éireann. Brendan laughed off the lecture and the expulsion that followed and some days later brazenly lined up in a parade for recruits to the Dublin Brigade. Any officer who recognised him that day was silenced with a knowing wink. His ruse was successful and he rejoined.

Brendan's membership of Fianna Éireann allowed him to indulge his love of ritual. He adored dressing up in the scout uniform provided by W.J. O'Hara the gentlemen's outfitters of Francis Street. Most of all he loved the marching, flag-waving and the public bellowing-out of Fianna songs. Ritual was central to his upbringing. For Brendan, the formal ceremonial of the Latin Mass, funeral processions, and the drilling and marching of Fianna Éireann shared a common thrill. However, his activities in the Fianna were more than a game – they were a sign of his growing political awareness and of his innate tendency to view himself in epic, literary terms. Fianna Éireann was to be Brendan's direct route to full membership of the IRA and to the possible fulfilment of his desire to be a hero and a martyr. He finally graduated from scout to fully-fledged IRA member by the age of sixteen, but not before trying to hasten the day by offering himself, at the age of fifteen, for full membership. His offer was rejected on the grounds that he was too young and perhaps because he had already acquired a reputation for recklessness and attention-seeking – not ideal qualities for membership of an underground movement.

In the meantime, the Fianna provided him with an outlet for the talent for which he would become famous. In the pages of its national magazine, *Fianna: The Voice of Young Ireland*, Brendan made his debut as a writer. The magazine was essentially a propaganda tool for the indoctrination of young

Republicans. It contained practical information on the supply and pricing of
Fianna uniforms, notification of meetings and advertisements for books which
had the Republican imprimatur, but principally, it was a vehicle for reverential
pen portraits of Republican heroes. It gave its young readers a forum for letters,
poems, short stories and competitions. In June 1936, it carried thirteen-year-
old Brendan Behan's first published short story. *A Tantalising Tale*[70] appeared
under his name in Irish, Breandáin Ó Beacháin, and beside an advertisement
for Capt. Robert Monteith's book, *Casement's Last Adventure*. In his seven-
hundred-word piece, Behan models the central character on himself. Not
surprisingly, he casts himself as a Republican hero, J. Frank O'Brien, who had
escaped to America after the '67 Rising. He returns to Ireland as a wealthy oil
magnate who entertains his Fianna friends in the library of his 'large and
comfortable house'. There, after attending a Fianna Ard Fheis (the annual
convention), he is encouraged to tell something of his life and times since his
departure from Ireland. He recounts the story of the gift of a ring that he
received under puzzling circumstances in Paris, from a donor whose dying
words he is unable to understand. There is a tussle with the police, but the
protagonist escapes to the US where the ring mysteriously disappears. He
survives to tell his 'tantalising tale' back in Dublin.

There is nothing remarkable about either the quality of the writing or the
construction of the plot in this earliest piece of Behan's published juvenilia.
What is remarkable is the confident and almost adult voice in which he writes.
His own reading, and his father's, had exposed him to a wide variety of Irish,
English and European literary models. It is an indication of his mind-set at
the time that he opted to include aspects of Irish political tracts in his writing.
In the story, O'Brien describes his search, 'as he strolled along the Rue du
Bac', for the house in which Theobald Wolfe Tone, the eighteenth-century
Republican revolutionary, had stayed. The detail is from *Wolfe Tone's
Autobiography*.[71] Wolfe Tone remained a hero of Behan's all his life.

However, the story does stand out from his contemporaries' efforts in that
publication – the Republican literary influences in Behan's story are less
hackneyed. Even in his earliest efforts, Behan was seeking to establish his own
voice. In the last turbulent year of his life, he laid claim to having had literary
ambitions from the age of six:

> If I am anything at all, I am a man of letters. I'm a writer: a word which
> does not exactly mean anything in either the English, Irish or American
> language. But I have never seen myself as anything else, not even from
> the age of six ...'[72]

Behan is credited with having contributed quite frequently to the Fianna magazine but only the short story discussed above appeared under his name.[73] He may well have contributed unsigned articles, but at this remove it is almost impossible to establish which, if any, of these anonymous articles are by him.

The Fianna magazine ceased publication in 1936 – an extremely traumatic year for the thirteen-year-old Brendan Behan. In that year, two of the most important figures in his young life died: his Granny English and his old teacher, Sister Monica. The loss of one of these powerfully-influential women would have been a severe blow to the boy; the loss of both in the same year left him inconsolable. His grief at the nun's death he could share with the hundreds of Dublin boys whom she had educated; his grief for his grandmother he had to endure as a private trauma. Of all his family, even his father, he had been closest to her and of all his family he therefore would miss her most.

Christina English died on 5 February, 1936. Her body was laid out in her Russell Street flat and her family and tenants came to pay their last respects to the street's most powerful landlady. Her funeral, at Glasnevin Cemetery, was the sort of affair she would have approved of. By her instructions, her hearse was drawn by 'black, fat horses', suitably plumed. By the time the cortège reached Glasnevin, 'there wasn't a dry throat' in the funeral party and on the way back to the centre of Dublin, the mourners made the customary pit stop at a pub where the virtues of the deceased and the conduct of the funeral were discussed in great detail.[74]

Brendan assumed the role of chief mourner. Dressed in a three-piece suit and with his head turned slightly sideways, his shock of dark curls blowing in the cold February wind and his lower lip pouting, he cut a consciously-Byronic figure who was 'really sorry to be losing her'.[75] He watched as 'the priest stood on one side of the open hole, waving his left arm to and fro while his right one clutched a Prayer Book from which he was making the stock excuses for deceased persons'.[76]

His grandmother's passing brought not just a sense of loss to Brendan but also a sense of betrayal. His brother Dominic described the impact her death had on his older brother:

> He had lived by her and with her. He slept in our place but that was about all. A lot of his life died when she did, for his granny was everything in the world to him. 'Poor little Bren' she used to say 'loves his gran.'[77]

The strain of his grandmother's death took its toll on his health. He came down with an extremely heavy cold which developed into pneumonia and he was admitted to Temple Street Children's Hospital.[78] His reaction to the discovery that Granny English had failed to remember him in her Will has not been recorded.

His grandmother's uncomplicated, one-page Will was witnessed by her sister, Margaret Corr and by her nephew, William Bendal. She left her entire estate to her son, Patrick English. No other bequests appear in the Will and the only specific property named in the document is number 7 Fitzgibbon Street which was the most valuable of her houses. Christina English is said to have accumulated large amounts of money, besides her rental income, from the profits of life insurance premiums that she paid for some of her tenants. Once funeral expenses had been met for the insured party, the residue of the cashed-in insurance policy went to Mrs English. It was a not uncommon practice amongst Dublin slum landlords and those who engaged in it were known to the poor of the city as 'Kulaks'.[79]

According to family sources, Christina English left behind a considerable amount of cash, which she kept hidden in her flat, but all of it is believed to have gone to Patrick English.[80] Within a year of coming into his inheritance, Patrick English had dissipated it through drink. The Behans stoically dismissed their exclusion from Granny English's last testament. When neighbours taunted young Brendan about the family's disinheritance, and his uncle's wastrel habits, his father used to say, 'tell 'em wasn't it a good thing he didn't spend it on something foolish'.[81] Another favourite remark of Stephen's was to greet Paddy's return from the pub with the ironic dig: 'Ireland sober, is Ireland free'.

Before Granny English had been dead a year, the Behans' fourteen-year association with the street she had ruled came to an end. When Kathleen was clearing out her mother-in-law's personal effects, she found 'whiskey bottles behind the bed [and] a letter from the Corporation [which] surprised me because it said that most of the houses were condemned and that meant she wasn't entitled to charge a penny rent.'[82] Granny English's houses in Russell Street were marked for demolition before her death. She kept this news even from the family: she simply continued to charge her tenants for accommodation that the civil authorities thought uninhabitable. Very soon after her funeral, the authorities swooped. Her family and tenants were plucked from their familiar environment and transplanted to soulless suburban housing developments.

The Behans moved to 70 Kildare Road, Crumlin; 'A little cold dogbox of a house,[83] Brian Behan called it. Kathleen was eager to make the move, but

Stephen resisted it. For him, suburban Crumlin represented 'the country' and the country was 'a place where they eat their dead'.[84] Many of their neighbours also resented being rehoused in what was, to entrenched urbanites, an alien rural environment. Some of the Behans' Russell Street neighbours had to be forcibly removed by bailiffs, but Kathleen insisted on going quietly. Their furniture and other belongings were packed on the donkey and cart that belonged to their neighbour, Mrs Farrell, the coal vendor. Brendan and his brother Dominic went ahead as an advance party to light fires and air the rooms. Stephen was left behind in Dublin at his place of work. From there he was naturally drawn first to the pub and afterwards to Russell Street, where he found their two rooms deserted. His excursion must have been an exercise in wishful thinking, because earlier that day he had seen the departure of Mrs Farrell's cart laden with his belongings.[85] He was left to make his journey to the new family home alone. While he did so, he opined to himself that his choice, quite simply, was 'to Hell or to Kimmage' (Kimmage and Crumlin are adjoining surburban areas).

The Behans blamed the Fianna Fáil government, led by Eamon de Valera, for their cruel removal to the wastelands of Crumlin. Brendan, at the age of nine, had canvassed support for the party in the 1932 general election that brought it to power for the first time. After the move from Russell Street, he cursed his 'foolishness'. Brian Behan believes that 'de Valera pulled down [the] slums only to break up the anarchistic blocks of people who lived so communally that they oft times found themselves in one another's beds [something the puritanical politician would hardly have approved of]. Being such a solid crew they paid neither tax nor rent, but managed to live by helping one another the best they could, and when things got tight, a little robbing in the rich world outside would help to fill empty bellies.'[86]

Whatever the government's motives, it faced the hard fact that, between 1926 and 1936, the population of Dublin City had increased by 81,271[87]. There was a chronic shortage of housing for the poor. Dublin's Chief Medical Officer, giving evidence to a 1936 housing enquiry, told of slum houses where six families totalling 33 persons occupied six rooms in the most appalling conditions. The legislative solution to the problem, the Slums Clearance Order, decreed forced rehousing in the suburbs as a reflex reaction to the problems of an underclass whose condition was described by one visitor to Dublin as being on a parallel with that of the slum dwellers of Calcutta.[88]

The Behans had not endured such appalling conditions in Russell Street, and the move to Crumlin turned out to be a prescient indicator of bad times just around the corner. Soon after moving, a strike kept Stephen out of work for over nine months. With no help now forthcoming from Granny English, the family often found itself in difficult circumstances. Kathleen has described the traumas of poverty the family experienced during this period:

> We were so poor that the lads would go on to the Corporation rubbish dump and salvage apples or anything. One day they brought home a great box of chocolates. Then they would start digging for old coal and cinders in the hot ash ... You couldn't believe how poor we were. I tried to sell two old vases to a friend for a shilling, just to buy a bit of tea and that ... I always tried to send the children to bed full no matter how I did myself. But it was an awful time trying to manage on half nothing.[89]

Brendan was miserable in Crumlin. Again and again, he wandered back to Russell Street looking for his old companions and for the warmth and camaraderie of his first fourteen years. He found only desolation. The great hallways of the decayed houses where the mysteries of carnal knowledge had been revealed to generations of tenement children were abandoned. He would return, dispirited, to his mother who comforted him by telling him that cities, like people, must change; that they too must renew themselves. Kathleen believed Brendan never got over leaving Russell Street and that the move from there marked a fundamental change in him.[90]

He had been restless throughout 1936 and 1937, frustrated by his failure to gain full membership of the IRA and disappointed by his removal to the anonymous suburbs. In 1937, his formal education ended with his removal from the Christian Brothers to Bolton Street Technical College, where he attended the Day Apprentice School. He took a course in house-painting, sign-writing and decorating. The course was given by Charlie O'Byrne, whom Behan saw as an exotic, if somewhat reactionary, creature. O'Byrne had worked in Egypt, where he met and married an Italian woman. He lectured Behan on the value of physical culture and talked admiringly of the 'marvellous physique' of his son, Sylvester, who had spent some time in Mussolini's youth movement.

The trade of house painting was the only one Brendan would ever acquire by formal instruction. Attendance at Bolton Street also allowed him to escape the wastelands of Crumlin and be near his beloved North inner-city.[91] Cathal Goulding, who enrolled in the same painting course, remembers escaping from classes with Behan to 'go on robbing expeditions to Woolworths where I stole tools and he stole dictionaries'.[92] Behan and Goulding were regularly in trouble with the college authorities. They found the weekly subsistence of six shillings difficult to live on and resorted to doing illegal 'nixers' (i.e.

moonlighting). They were both expelled from the college before completing the full course of instruction.

During this period, Brendan attempted to join the Irish Republicans who were leaving to fight in the Spanish Civil War. His mother hindered his efforts by intercepting his correspondence from the recruiters and destroying it. Cathal Goulding recalls going with Brendan to a house on Ormond Quay to meet veteran Republican, Frank Ryan, who was organising Irish Republican recruitment to the International Brigade. Because of their age, neither boy was accepted by Ryan. They were told rather abruptly to go home. Later, Goulding and Behan worked with other Republicans organising clothing collections for the International Brigade. They also attempted to cycle to Belfast to join a ship leaving for the Spanish conflict. Their plan was to arrive in Belfast, sell their bicycles and hope that their enthusiasm for the cause would be welcomed when they tried to join the ship for Spain. The plan came to grief in Balbriggan, just north of Dublin, where Behan's bicycle got a puncture. The two returned to Dublin, tired and disappointed.[93]

In Ireland, the Spanish conflict was viewed as a head-on confrontation between Communism and the Church:

> All who stand for the ancient faith and the traditions of Spain are behind the present revolt against the Marxist regime in Madrid.
>
> *Irish Independent*, 22 July, 1936

The Behans had no problem with the defence of the 'ancient faith' but the views they held on the 'Marxist regime' in Spain were not those offered by the conservative press in Ireland. Nor did they support the Irish government's backing of the non-intervention principle and the introduction of legislation prohibiting the participation of any Irish citizen in the war in Spain, under pain of fine or imprisonment. Brendan heard the Spanish Civil War discussed at home. The Irish Left was not in a particularly strong position to publish its views on the war, following the demise of the periodical *Republican Congress* in February 1936. *The Worker*, a periodical which had a tiny circulation, was probably Behan's main source of printed information from a Left perspective.

Brian Behan took the family's unorthodox views to school with him. In an argument with one of his teachers, who was condemning the 'Red Scourge' in Spain as a 'menace to Catholicism', Brian said the Spanish Republicans were the lawfully-constituted government. The catechism taught that those whom God places over us should be honoured. Brian argued that the Republican position was thus inviolable and Franco was a mere rebel. He was slapped about the face for his pains.

Having failed to make his way to Spain and having been rejected for full IRA membership, Brendan now concentrated his efforts on writing for the Irish Republican cause. The main forum for his writing to date had been the Fianna magazine. When that ceased publication in 1937, he started to send contributions to the *Wolfe Tone Weekly* which had begun life in September 1937 under the editorship of the nationalist author, Brian Ó hUiginn. In an editorial he described the magazine's aim as 'the full freedom of a united, virile, self-respecting, happy, peaceful and prosperous Irish Republic.' It soon came under attack by hard-line Republicans for 'lacking punch' – perhaps because Ó hUiginn urged his contributors 'not to engage in the setting down in print of libellous statements about political opponents'.[94]

In the issue of 2 October 1937, Brendan launched an attack on H.B.C. Pollard's book *Secret Societies in Ireland*, which had disparaged the Fianna. As evidence of the absurdity of Pollard's belief that the Republican boy scout movement was by nature 'blood thirsty', Behan described the author's depiction of the Fianna song, *The Brave Boy Scout* as inflammatory:

The brave boyscout to the battle has gone,
In the ranks of death you'll find him,
His bandoleer he has girded on,
And his rifle slung behind him,
'I'll go where duty calls', he cried,
'Please God, no ill shall harm me,
But though for Ireland's cause I died,
I'll join the Republican Army.'

In the same issue, Brendan read the magazine's request to young poets that they send in no further contributions until they had 'studied carefully' the verse already published and formed an idea of what was required. What was required was praise of the achievement of Republican heroes of the past, and affirmation of a belief in victory for the Republican struggle ahead. Brendan seems to have hit the right formula before many other would-be Republican poets: his first published poem appeared in the issue of 8 January 1938. He wrote the untitled poem in response to – a pro-British piece praising Empire Day, published in the *Irish Press* on 31 December and entitled 'Resurgence':

'Éire' – O God! why do they mock me
With paper 'freedom' – under England's Crown?
Even while they forge another link to bind me,
Another traitor's chain to drag me down.
But God be praised! My lovers are not vanquished,

Their arms are strong as steel, their hearts are true;
Another day will see my armies marching,
To strike another blow for Róisín Dubh.

Aye, once again old Dublin will awaken,
To the tramp of marching feet of valiant men;
The rearguard will do battle once more for me
On the mountain, in the town and in the glen.
Their bayonets shall flash gladly in the sunshine,
And sycophants and slaves the day will rue,
When with Judas kiss they put the crown of tinsel
On the bowed and dear dark head of Róisín Dubh.

My children yet shall drive the foe before them –
Whether clad in khaki coat or coat of green –
And mercenaries will flee in droves ere vengeance
O'ertakes them for the insults to their Queen.
My flag shall fly o'er all my many counties –
From Antrim's hills to Kerry's mountains blue –
And my sons shall place the bright gold crown of Freedom
On the dear dark head of deathless Róisín Dubh.[95]

The poem, though accomplished for a fourteen-year-old, differs from Behan's first prose piece in that there is nothing of his own voice in it. It is a pastiche of the nationalistic ballad, exactly tailored to fit the editorial dictates laid down by the magazine. Brendan had first heard the evocation of *Róisín Dubh (Dark Rosaleen)* as Mother Ireland when his father read him James Clarence Mangan's 1846 poem *My Dark Rosaleen*. This poem is the least memorable of Behan's juvenilia.

Far more noteworthy is his next published poem, *Four Great Names*. He wrote it to mark the anniversary of the execution, on 8 December 1922, of four leading Republicans, Rory O'Connor, Liam Mellows, Richard Barrett and Joseph McKelvey, by the Free State government. They were shot, a government communiqué said, 'as a solemn warning' to those 'engaged in a conspiracy of assassination against the representatives of the Irish People'. Sixteen years after their deaths, the poignancy of their loss was still felt by young Republicans like Brendan, whose father, after all, was a fellow political prisoner with the executed men. Behan is best in the opening stanza, in which he sets the scene for the grim act at Mountjoy Jail, where he himself would be a Republican prisoner within a mere four years.

'Tis midnight, and the only sound the watching sentry's tramp,
December night, frosty, clear, enfolds Mountjoy's armed camp,

Then thunder-like it crashes forth, each word a cry of woe,
These four must die ere morning – Rory, Liam, Dick and Joe.[96]

The publication of *Four Great Names* gave a boost to Brendan's status within the movement. *Wolfe Tone Weekly* now described him as 'a young veteran' who had served his apprenticeship as a Republican boy scout, and as a 'scribe for the cause'. By mid-1939, the moment he had so desperately longed for finally arrived: he became a fully-fledged IRA guerrilla, ready and willing to serve the cause he believed in – with his life, if the occasion required it.

3

Boy and IRA Man

The most significant event in Brendan's teenage years was his acceptance into full membership of the IRA in 1939. That rite of passage had been the focus of all his ambitions and desires. At this stage he appears to have had no wish to do anything more with his life than to make an enduring impression as a successful IRA guerrilla fighter. Family and friends affirm his fanatical desire for hero status.[1] Now, in the last year of the decade he saw his destiny draw near.

The IRA that accepted him into its ranks was a dispirited and outlawed organisation. Circumstances made it vastly different from the IRA to which his father had belonged. As Taoiseach, de Valera did not wish to see any internal threat to his dream of an Ireland based on his personal notions of self-sufficient bucolic bliss. On the other hand, much of the IRA remained committed to the reunification of Ireland through violent struggle. De Valera's government declared the IRA illegal on 18 June 1936. Later that month, it banned the organisation's march to Bodenstown churchyard for the annual homage to Theobald Wolfe Tone. In 1937, de Valera's new Irish Constitution marked a decisive break with the neo-colonial Dominion status of the 1921 settlement. It laid claim to the whole island of Ireland but left no role for a guerrilla army that proposed unification by physical force. The IRA was further weakened by the arrest and internment of its leadership and large numbers of its rank and file. The Spanish Civil War also depleted the organisation of its many leftist idealists, thus leaving it under the control of the more ardent militants. This latter tag fitted none more appropriately than the new Chief of Staff, Seán Russell, who had been elected at the IRA Convention of April 1938.

His election sidelined the more politically-dexterous within the leadership, particularly Seán MacBride and Tom Barry. They disagreed with Russell's most radical initiative: a planned bombing campaign in England. This campaign would bring the sixteen-year-old Brendan Behan to the forefront of the Republican crusade.

On 12 January 1939 the IRA, claiming the authority of the 'Government of the Irish Republic', issued an ultimatum to the British government. It declared that, if Britain did not withdraw its remaining forces from Ireland within four days, the IRA would 'reserve the right of appropriate action without further notice'. The ultimatum was ignored and the bombing campaign in England began on 16 January. By the end of the year there had been nearly three hundred explosions, causing seven deaths and almost one hundred injuries. There was little support for the campaign in Ireland. The government worried about the effect it would have on Ireland's neutrality in the probable future war with Germany. De Valera strongly denounced the campaign and warned: 'These people may get the country into a mess that the whole Irish people might not be able to get out of. We sympathise with their ambitions, but we cannot allow that to blind us to the consequences of their deeds.'[2] The IRA leadership was conscious that it was losing popular support in Ireland to the democratic process. Fianna Fáil, the party that it helped to power in 1932, was claiming the moral high ground on the question of Irish Unification through Constitutional means.

While awaiting acceptance into the adult ranks of the IRA, Brendan had acted as a courier for the organisation. He operated mostly in and around Dublin, but there were a few trips to Belfast and one trip to London in April 1939. He took a package which he had been told to deliver to a man at an underground station near Tottenham Court Road. Brendan was to recognise his contact by the fact that he would be carrying a copy of *Picture Post*. When Brendan arrived, he failed to see any man carrying that publication, but he did approach a woman seated on a bench who was reading *Picture Post*. The alarmed matron thought the sixteen-year-old Irish boy was trying to make an audacious sexual pick-up. He moved away rapidly when she screamed for the police. In the confusion, he was rescued by his IRA contact who had witnessed the farce from a distance.[3] Brendan spent a few further days in London during which time he contacted several painters' contractors with a view to getting work there or in the North of England. It was an attempt to find a suitable cover for his next trip to England, when he would be on active service.

Cathal Goulding, who also joined the IRA with Brendan and was later to become Chief-of-Staff of the Official IRA, recalls that his friend was dissatisfied with his junior role of courier. Brendan wanted to get involved in what he considered more 'grown-up' activities. It was nevertheless a useful training and induction into the ways of a secret military organisation. It also allowed him the opportunity to meet and get to know the IRA men with whom he later worked.[4]

At Easter 1939, as part of their scouting activities, Brendan and Cathal Goulding confiscated a camera from a German tourist who was innocently photographing an IRA gathering at the Republican Plot at Glasnevin Cemetery. The German's pleas for the return of the camera went unheeded. IRA HQ feared that British Intelligence was planting photographers at IRA gatherings in Dublin, and using the photographs to identify Volunteers on their entry to Britain. The duo confiscated and smashed four other cameras that day.

Brendan, having served what he saw as a sufficient period of apprentice-ship, was keen to embark on the serious Volunteer activities he felt were his due reward for years of service in the junior ranks. Once accepted into the senior ranks as a full-time Volunteer, recruits had to undergo training in the tactics of guerrilla warfare and bomb-making at a secret IRA training camp in Killiney Castle, County Dublin. Chief-of-Staff Seán Russell had acquired the house through a mysterious 'Count' Heaney, who held the lease on the building. It was Russell who eventually agreed to allow Brendan's transfer to full Volunteer status. He was taken to Killiney in early May 1939. The training programme was run by the camp Commandant Michael Conway who later abandoned militarism to became a Roman Catholic monk. With his wit and happy disposition, Brendan almost immediately became a sort of favourite mascot for the older Volunteers. They were, however, alarmed at his fearless attitude towards the handling of explosives and appalled at the casual use of foul language in someone so young.

Brendan was not by nature suited to the rigours of the training regime. After rising at 6.30 a.m., there was an hour of tedious physical drilling. Breakfast was at 7.30 a.m., after which Pat McGrath gave instruction in bomb-making. This was Brendan's favourite part of the day. In what free time he had, he liked to swim in the nearby sea. The literary romantic in him delighted to find that the camp lay near George Bernard Shaw's cottage, looking out over the Irish Sea: 'Shaw said that no man was ever the same after seeing it. I know a good many besides myself that are not the same after seeing it, and some of them hung or shot, or gone mad, or otherwise unable to tell the difference.'[5]

Strict discipline was enforced at Killiney. As well as the exacting physical routine, alcohol was strictly forbidden. So was sex of any kind. When one Volunteer tried to bring a girl back to the camp, Mick Conway suspended him. Only the intervention of his colleagues and his solid record prevented his expulsion from the IRA. If Brendan was delighted to be undergoing training with full Volunteer status at long last, he was none too happy to be missing the regular drinking sessions which he had become accustomed to by the age of sixteen. His cocky attitude, and the familiarity his grandmother's drinking habits (especially after funerals) had given him with several of Dublin's better known public houses, made him an acceptable figure in the capital's drinking haunts – a milieu from which his age would otherwise have excluded him. The other Volunteers knew him as a lad who liked his drink, but he dared not risk the formidable ire of Commandant Conway and did his best to be on good behaviour while undergoing training. Even at this early age, the absence of alcohol was a considerable sacrifice for him. His letters to friends from Borstal[6] regularly referred to how much he missed drinking with them.

For the moment, however, he focused his attention on the manufacture of an altogether more lethal cocktail that he planned to employ in England before 1939 had run its course. Recruits were trained in the construction of both explosive and incendiary devices. French clocks (favoured for their near silent ticking) were used to make timers. The main base of the explosive was chlorate of potash and paraffin wax, a mixture known as 'Paxo' (after a popular brand of packaged stuffing for meat and poultry). Gelignite was stolen from building sites around Dublin. These incendiary ingredients were mixed together in saucepans, using wooden spoons to avoid any sparks. Brendan became particularly adept at the construction of an ingenious alternative to the alarm-clock detonator. It involved using acid-filled wax containers inserted into balloons or condoms. Some Volunteers, though already excommunicated by the Roman Catholic Church, balked at the idea of using condoms even for furthering the Republican cause. Brendan had no such reservations. The principle of this construction was that the acid corroded the rubber and then came in contact with the explosive 'Paxo'. He called these deadly devices 'me toy balloons'.[7]

He soon became so proficient at bomb-making that he was giving advice to more recent recruits, many of whom were several years older than himself. One of his methods of introducing the new boys to the use of explosives involved typical Behan bravado. While giving his little lecture, he would throw lighted matches at live explosives and wait until the last possible moment before calmly walking over and blowing the match out. On a visit home from Killiney to Kildare Road, he brought the tricks of his newly-acquired trade with him. While he was experimenting upstairs, he set off an explosion which, had luck not been with him, could have left him dead and his parents and brothers homeless. His uncle, Paddy English, who only rarely visited the Behans' suburban home in Kildare Road (an area that for an inner-city man represented uncharted territory) was once seriously shocked to be met by a portion of the upper part of the house falling down to greet him at the Behans' front door. It was the result of another of Brendan's blunders with his 'toy balloons'.[8]

Not long after that dramatic incident, Brendan felt himself sufficiently expert in the use of explosives to take his craft to England as part of the 1939 bombing campaign. The campaign had claimed its first English victim on 17 January, when an innocent civilian passed by an explosive device in Manchester. Earlier that month there had been seven explosions at major power installations across the country. On 24 June, a series of devastating explosions rocked the centre of London. The following day, Brendan joined the IRA men who defied the Irish government's ban on the parade to that most sacred of Republican shrines, Wolfe Tone's grave at Bodenstown, County Kildare. He was still undergoing training. The leadership at Killiney, aware of his hot temper, had warned him not to get involved in any fighting with the police. He heeded the advice and steered clear of a pitched battle that continued throughout most of the day.

In response to the bombing in England, the British government introduced the Prevention of Violence Act. The extensive new powers it brought into law were a serious obstacle to the IRA campaign. It also had profound repercussions for ordinary Irish people living and working in Britain. The Act provided for the screening of Irish immigrants, the registration of all Irish citizens, extended powers of detention and the hasty deportation of IRA suspects. It was a piece of legislation that was to cause Brendan Behan considerable inconvenience right up until the last years of his life.

On 25 August, the most terrible event in the bombing campaign took the lives of five people in central Coventry. Sixty people were injured. British public outrage against the Irish living in Britain became an almost palpable force. Most Irish homes in Coventry were raided and several innocent Irish residents were arrested along with known IRA members. By the winter of 1939, the IRA bombing strategy was virtually in tatters. It lacked more than financial and physical resources: numerous police raids had seriously depleted the pool of Volunteers available in Britain. The IRA leadership in London looked in desperation for new recruits from Ireland. The high level of co-operation between the British and Irish police made that almost impossible: known suspects were watched at ports and arrested soon after their arrival in Britain. Still the campaign spluttered on into December. Brendan decided his moment for decisive action had come.

The activities of his Granny Furlong had bolstered his resolve. She had instigated what amounted to a one-woman bombing campaign of her own. In May 1939, she sold her Dublin home and moved to Cliff Rock Road, Rendal,

Birmingham. From there she intended, with the help of her daughters, Emily and Evelyn, to process enough explosive devices to give the faltering IRA campaign a boost. A tenacious woman, she sometimes kept sticks of gelignite hidden in her underwear. Her efforts were undone when an explosion in her Birmingham house drew the attention of the police to her enterprise.

She and her two daughters, together with her lodger, Martin Patrick Clarke, were sentenced at Birmingham Assizes on Friday 14 July. The prosecution claimed that 52 sticks of gelignite, 175 detonators, 54 fuses, balloons and potassium chlorate were found concealed in an armchair in the house. Emily Furlong told the court she believed the sticks of gelignite to be sugar sticks which her sister had bought for her mother. Chief Detective Inspector Sanders told the Court that Mrs Furlong was known to members of the IRA as the owner of a very reliable house where they could go for shelter. There were four charges against the women, including possession of explosive substances and conspiracy with persons unknown to cause an explosion. Sentencing the 77-year-old woman, Mr Justice Singleton said to her: 'I could wish I did not have someone of your age to deal with, but the public must be protected'. She was sentenced to three years' penal servitude, making her, in Brendan's words, 'the oldest political prisoner in the world'.[9] Her daughters Evelyn and Emily were sentenced to three and five years respectively. As the women were taken below they shouted 'Up the Republic' and 'God save Ireland'.

The case drew an extraordinary amount of press attention in Ireland, Britain and the United States. In 1939, the pro-Republican *Irish Echo* in New York carried this leader:

War

We had better get our troops ready to defend the British Empire! A 77-year-old woman, Mrs Mary A. Furlong, has declared war on the Crown. She committed treason and was sent to prison for three years. Where are you Congressman Bloom and all other pro-Britishers who want Americans to go to war to defend the principles for which Britain stands?

Are you not going to defend the country you idolize against this attack? This vicious woman was aiding the IRA – are you sure three years is enough for her? Maybe she ought to be executed. Think of the voters, gentlemen. They will expect you to do your bit for the King in this national emergency. It certainly shows that Britain is a great democracy, anyway. No distinction is made, no partiality shown, between women in their old age and immature boys in their teens. The same fine democratic jail does for all of them.[10]

With 77-year-old Granny Furlong making world headlines and languishing in an English jail, sixteen-year-old Brendan felt any further inaction on his part was a betrayal of his duty. He made up his mind to follow her example by going to England to take as active a part as he possibly could in the bombing campaign. It has not been possible to establish with certainty whether the IRA command endorsed his decision to go. Most of the evidence suggests, however, that the decision was his and his alone and that it did not have the direct approval of the leadership. When he told his friend, the IRA veteran Bob Bradshaw, that he was going on active service to England, Bradshaw advised him that his plan was foolish in the extreme because the movements of all known IRA activists were being monitored by the police in Ireland and the information was being passed on to the British police.[11] The fact that Brendan brought his own bombing-making kit with him also indicates that he had no direct contact with IRA controllers in England. For reasons of security, the usual practice was to pick up one's bomb-making equipment at a named safe house after getting off the boat.

Stephen Behan claimed to have no idea of his son's immediate intentions, and that he and Kathleen believed Brendan had secured a painting job in Somerset. After his arrest in Liverpool, Stephen wrote to the British Home Office:

> His mother and myself were astounded to learn that he had been in trouble as we both understood from him that he had work to go to in Somerset.
> I was perfectly content and anxious to keep him at home but he convinced his mother he had work to go to and she prevailed on me to let him go.[12]

Stephen, of course, was all too aware of Brendan's activities with explosives in Ireland. He had warned him against using the family home as a halfway house between the Killiney training camp and wherever his next destination was likely to be. Father and son had a bitter row about Brendan's involvement with the IRA. Brendan accused his father of abandoning the principles he had held during his own involvement with the Republican movement in the War of Independence and the Civil War. So acrimonious were the exchanges that their relationship was never again to be on quite the same sure footing as it had been until Brendan was sixteen years old.[13]

On the evening of 30 November 1939, the atmosphere was extremely tense in the Behan household. Another bitter disagreement between Brendan and his father had soured the usually tranquil family atmosphere. He spent much of the day in his room packing his kit for his departure to England. Apart from his bombing kit, he took 2 pairs of trousers, 2 shirts, a pullover, a waistcoat, a change of underwear and a pair of painter's overalls.[14] In the early evening, the family gathered around the kitchen fire. In his memoir, *Teems of Times and Happy Returns*, Dominic Behan recalled his father attempting to break the feeling of tension in the house by reading aloud from his beloved book, *The Pickwick Papers*:

> '... Dismay and anguish were depicted on every countenance, the males
> turned pale and the females fainted, Mr Snodgrass and Mr Winkle
> grasped each other by the hand and ...'
> 'Danced the walls of Limerick,' interjected Brendan. Da turned on him
> fiercely:
> 'You keep yer witty remarks to yourself and carry on with whatever yer
> doin'.

Suspicious of his son's intentions but probably unaware of their exact nature, Stephen put down his book. At one of the most important moments of his life, Brendan asked Dominic to fetch him a length of string to secure his few belongings in a parcel. Dominic was loath to leave the comfort of the fire and refused to budge. This was to be a bone of contention between Brendan and Dominic thereafter.

By the time Stephen had Mr Pickwick snug in his bed, Brendan had left Kildare Road in a huff. He made his way to the docks at Dublin's North Wall, his departure point for his journey to Liverpool. It was not the first time he had attempted to take this route to Liverpool.[15] The police presence at the port had hampered his travel plans on at least two previous occasions. On this occasion he boarded the *S.S. Inisfallen* for its overnight sailing to Liverpool without any apparent problems.[16] But the stolen Travel Permit he presented to immigration authorities, with its altered photograph and date of birth, proved to be his undoing. The Department of External Affairs had originally issued this document to a Peter Russell at an address at 109 Poplar Row, Ballybough, Dublin. Russell had intended travelling to England to find work but due to lack of funds was unable to go. The Permit went missing from Russell's overcoat pocket at the L.C.R. Football Club premises in Russell Street. When the police interviewed him about the loss of the Permit, he told them that he believed Brendan Behan had stolen the document while his attention was distracted during a game of billiards.[17]

The British police tailed Brendan to his lodgings at 17 Aubrey Street, Liverpool, where he had taken a room in a house owned by an Irish woman with no known IRA involvement. Within ten hours of landing on English soil, Brendan found himself in police custody. He has left two later accounts of his arrest, one of which was published in 1952 in *Points*, a Paris-based magazine. The other is a more polished version of the same account which later became part of *Borstal Boy*. However, a less dramatic but certainly more accurate account of the arrest is to be had from a series of letters he wrote at the time to family and friends. Sadly, many of them never reached their intended recipients – instead the British prison censors intercepted and suppressed them. The letters remained buried in Home Office files. They were due for destruction in 1967 and would have been destroyed but for the vigilance of one astute civil servant who recognised the Behan name. These letters are a particularly valuable source, since few of the Borstal letters that were allowed to reach their destination have survived. The following account of Behan's prison years draws heavily on this newly-discovered material and other Home Office files.

Behan was taken quite by surprise by the arrival of the police at Aubrey Street. He claimed his landlady shouted up the stairs that there were some gentlemen to see him, but it is unlikely that the police would allow time for such a warning. In *Borstal Boy* he described how he attempted to escape.

> I grabbed my suitcase, containing Pot. Chlor. Sulph Ac, gelignite, detonators, electrical and ignition, and the rest of my Sinn Féin conjuror's outfit, and carried it to the window. Then the gentlemen arrived.[18]

The arresting officers searched him and found some money, Peter Russell's altered travel papers, and a letter written in Irish. There were no instructions from IRA headquarters or other incriminating documents of any nature, again suggesting that he was on a solo mission of his own initiative. One officer asked him how he would like to see a woman cut in two by a plate glass window as a result of his bombing activities. Unusually for Brendan, he resisted the temptation to recite the catalogue of British atrocities which his mother had taught him to recite – 'Bloody Sunday, when the Black and Tans attacked a football crowd in our street; the massacre at Cork; Balbriggan; Amritsar; the RAF raids on Indian villages.'[19] The arresting police asked if he had a gun, to which he replied, 'If I'd have had a gun you wouldn't have come through that door so shagging easy.'[20] He was then searched, his trouser buttons were loosened to impede escape, and he was marched, he later claimed, through an angry loyalist mob which had gathered outside the house.

At Lime Street CID Headquarters, he told the desk officer his name was Lord Rosebery and that he worked as private secretary to the Aga Khan. He said he was forty-nine years of age and had been three times arrested for bigamy! He also admitted he had intended to seek out employment as a painter at Cammel Laird's shipyard in Liverpool.[21] He refused to answer any further questions, but he reveals in *Borstal Boy* that he agreed to make a statement in order to propagandise the IRA cause. It was characteristic of this literary-minded and self-aware young terrorist that he also thought it would make good newspaper copy to be read by his friends and relations in Ireland: 'I often read speeches [made] from the dock, and thought the better of the brave and defiant men that made them so far from friends and dear ones.'[22]

In *Borstal Boy*, Behan claimed to have announced the following to the Lime Street Police:

> My name is Brendan Behan. I came over here to fight for the Irish Workers' and Small Farmers' Republic, for a full and free life for my fellow countrymen North and South and for the removal of the baneful influence of British Imperialism from Irish affairs. God save Ireland.[23]

He felt the left-wingers in the IRA would be delighted with the Communistic references and 'the craw-thumpers could not say anything against me because I was a good Volunteer, captured carrying the struggle to England's doorstep – but they would be hopping mad at me giving everyone the impression that the IRA was Communistic. The 'God Save Ireland' bit made me feel like the Manchester Martyrs, hanged amidst the exulting cheers of 50,000 fairplay merchants, and crying out with their last breath:

> 'God save Ireland,' cried the heroes,
> 'God save Ireland,' cry we all;
> 'Whether on the scaffold high,
> Or the battle field we die,
> Sure what matter when for Ireland dear we fall.'[24]

On 4 December, he was transferred from police custody to H.M. Prison, Walton, where he was held on remand. A memo from the police Chief Inspector to the Prison Governor warned that 'Brendan Behan, committed to your custody, is not in possession of a Gas Mask, he states that he came over from Ireland two days ago and was never issued with a Gas Mask[25]. Britain was, of course, at war with Germany by this time. The Roman Catholic chaplain at the prison, Father J.T. Lane, talked to him on the afternoon of

5 December. It would be a matter of serious understatement to say that the meeting was not a success. Brendan's account in *Borstal Boy* makes it quite clear that it was nothing short of disastrous. His opinion of Father Lane has entered the canon of his more famous descriptions. The Priest was to become one of the most despised characters in his writings: '... to hell with you, you fat bastard, and to hell with England and to hell with Rome, up the Republic ...'[26] Fifty-six years later, the priest's official report of his encounter with Brendan reveals the feeling was entirely mutual:

> A determined member of the IRA who came over last weekend to take part in the IRA operations. He has come under very evil influence and produces with great fluency the communistic and IRA arguments against Church and State. He is very much older than his years and will be a centre of anti-English and anti-social agitation wherever he finds himself.[27]

The chaplain began his interview by asking Brendan when he proposed to 'give up this business', meaning his membership of the IRA. He reminded him that the Bishops of Ireland had denounced the IRA time and time again, and that he was automatically excommunicated until he repented of his sin. Brendan then embarked on a full-scale lecture on how the clergy had consistently proven themselves to be against the cause of Irish freedom and in sympathy with the British Empire. He began at the Synod of Drumceatt in 1172 which ordered the excommunication of any Irishman who failed to acknowledge the King of England as his ruler, continued on through the details of the excommunicated Fenian leaders until he came to the excommunication of de Valera and his own father for IRA membership. Uproar followed his outburst. The priest dismissed him and two warders dragged him back to his cell where they gave him the only severe beating he was to receive while in custody. He was punched in the ribs, slapped, and repeatedly hit in the face with a bunch of keys until his lip was split. He was sent sprawling to the floor of his cell with a series of kicks and told 'a half-starved Irish bastard had no right to insult a minister of religion'.[28]

A medical examination at the prison on the same day showed he had sustained a fracture of the left clavicle and, most likely as a result of the beating, he suffered a deflection of his nasal septum which caused obstruction to the breathing in his right nostril. This last was later surgically corrected. The report described his general health at this time as 'fair' and recorded the fact that he stammered and that 'his family has no history of fits, insanity or alcoholism'. True to his characteristic relish of the tall tale, Brendan told the

Medical Officer that his father had been in prison for murder. The report made no reference to any other evidence which might indicate a beating had been administered, but it would have taken some time for bruising to show.[29]

The physical severity of the beating mattered less than the psychological damage caused by his excommunication: he was ordered to be deprived of the rites, rituals and sacraments of the Roman Catholic Church. He was, as he constantly repeated throughout his life, 'a day-light atheist'. When he was in health, he was not at all religious but when sick was very religious indeed: 'In religion my family has always been Catholic – and anti-clerical. I don't know of one priest in any generation of the family and I don't know of one member of it who has died without a priest. Deo Gratias'.[30] Yet, as a child, he had been extremely devout, rarely missed Sunday Mass and was a weekly communicant:

> ...The day I made my First Communion I had prayed to God to take me, as Napoleon prayed, when I would go straight to Heaven. I was a weekly communicant for weeks after, and in spasms, especially during Lent, a daily one. Then I had difficulties, when I was thirteen or so, with myself and sex, and with the Church because they always seemed to be against the Republicans ... and it seemed the Church was always for the rich against the poor'.

According to his brother, Brian, Brendan's relationship to Catholicism remained troublesome throughout his life. He would often reject the ministrations of priests, but never freed himself from the constraints of his faith: 'It gave him all of the guilt but none of the answers. His father broke free of the church's influence but he did not.'[31]

In the loneliness and darkness of an English prison he longed for the ceremonial comforts offered by his faith. In his biography of Behan, Ulick O'Connor wrote that Behan was 'deprived of a support that had been bred into him; something that was part of his upbringing, part of his country, part of his city, his home, his instinct. He was a religious animal, and to take it from him was in a way to pervert his nature. In the back of his mind he had always felt that he could slip from the confines of Walton and England into ritual that was part of something known to millions of other worshippers. Now this solace had been taken away from him by an Englishman'.[32]

> I had never given up the Faith (for what would I give it up for?) for now I was glad that even in this well-washed smelly English hell-hole of old Victorian cruelty, I had the Faith to fall back on. Every Sunday and holiday, I would be at one with hundreds of millions of Catholics, at

the sacrifice of the Mass, to worship the God of our ancestors, and pray to Our Lady, the delight of the Gael, the consolation of mankind, the mother of God and of man, the pride of poets and artists, Dante, Villon, Eoghan Ruadh O Sullivan, in warmer, more humorous parts of the world than this nineteenth-century English lavatory, in Florence, in France, in Kerry, where the arbutus grows and the fuchsia glows on the dusty hedges in the soft light of the summer evening. 'Deoríní Dé' – 'The Tears of God' – they called the fuchsia in Kerry, where it ran wild as a weed. 'Lachryma Christi' – 'The Tears of Christ' was a Latin phrase, but in future I would give Him less reason for tears, and maybe out of being here I would get back into a state of grace and stop in it – well, not stop out of it for long intervals – and out of evil, being here, good would come.[33]

On 7 December, Brendan's father responded to a questionnaire about his son's background sent to him by the prison authorities. It was the first communication to the prison from the family and is quite revealing in its frankness. It was here Stephen Behan stated that neither he nor Kathleen had any idea that Brendan was on a bombing mission to Liverpool.[34] In Stephen's finely-formed handwriting – he wrote in exquisite English which surely must have impressed the officials who read it – the details of his son's education, employment and recreational interests are laid out. Stephen admitted, with notable honesty, that Brendan had been dismissed by three employers for 'slackness'. In response to a question about the likelihood of Brendan being employed in Ireland, should he be released, he said his own employer would very possibly give Brendan a job.[35] Stephen's account of his son was attached to Brendan's file and would have been seen by most of the prison administrators with whom he came into contact until his release in 1941. This obvious example of the Behans' family's literacy, coupled with Brendan's own precocious intelligence, left the more perceptive of them, as we shall see, with the feeling that they were dealing with no ordinary sixteen-year-old.

In the meantime the Governor of Walton, J. Holt, reported him to be:

A precocious and conceited lad – who finds in political fanaticism an easy rationalisation of wild and undisciplined impulses and who is sustained in his anti-social attitude by the designs to show off as a hero and a martyr. He needs deflation and discipline.[36]

At Walton there was no shortage of the Governor's prescription. On 16 January, Brendan was reported to the Governor because his cell slate 'had been scratched and defaced with IRA propaganda', an offence for which he had been previously warned.[37] However, Brendan once again demonstrated his ability to adapt to prevailing conditions. He immediately accepted his lot with stoic reserve as a suppressed letter written to his brother, Seán, just nine days after arriving at Walton, shows:

> My treatment could be much worse. Rise 6. Breakfast: Bread, Marg and Tea. 8.30-9.30. Exercise (Physical training, no speaking). 9.30-10.00. Smoke (Cigarette, no speak. Walk round in circle. 10-12. Work (mailbags) 12-2. Dinner (not bad). 2-4.30 Work. 4.30. Supper, locked up for night. Eat all meals in cells. No speaking anytime. I am about as popular here as a dose of V. disease but my fellow-prisoners, with some exceptions, treated same as anyone else. As for the exceptions you and I know I have every dirty trick in the bag.[38]

In the same letter, he asked for a Penguin anthology of English poetry and a copy of Shakespeare's plays, and wrote:

> Jesus help you if you don't send some Irish papers as soon as you get this. They'll cost you a few coppers. ... For the love of God send them now.

He boasted to his brother that if he had had a gun, 'I would never have been pulled though I was booked the minute I landed'. He was anxious to know how the news of his arrest was received in Dublin. He especially wanted to know how Bob Bradshaw and Cathal Goulding reacted to the fact that he had become 'the pride of the 2nd Battalion' and if a report of the remand hearing had appeared in the Irish newspapers. What bothered him most was the possibility that the version of the statement that the police claimed he had made at the time of his arrest would be taken seriously by his IRA colleagues in Ireland. He wrote to Seán that:

> I didn't at any time make any verbal statement to the police and tell everyone back home the statement: 'I came over to take the place of Chris Kinneally, [sic] Crompton, etc.' is a lot of lies. The police made it up out of their heads. I did however make a statement (for the sake of my landlady) in which is: 'My aim has been a free independent Workers Republic etc. but for the other stuff it's only a frame-up.'

He begged his brother to make this point very clear when speaking to his IRA comrades. Kenneally and Crompton, two other Volunteers on active service in England, had been arrested and imprisoned in Portland Jail in connection with their part in the bombing campaign.

The style and content of Brendan's letter to his brother reveal a curious mixture of adult and adolescent. Through Seán, he attempted to send a message to his fellow-members of the Second Dublin Battalion of the IRA in the voice of Brendan the man: 'For the sake of your comrades held in British jails let every man at home redouble his efforts to secure the complete independence of our country and release of our captured Volunteer'. A line or two later, we get the voice of a sixteen-year-old boy away from home: 'Write and send papers as soon as you get this. Send a few bars of chocolate as well.' The letter was written two days before he made an appearance in court. He told Seán that he expected to be sentenced to five years' detention – 'see you in 1945(maybe)'. The letter shows him to have been in remarkably good spirits considering his situation. He told his brother:

> We may be down but we're never bloody well out ... Nobody could be bubbling over with joy among people who regard you as a potential assassin. But still it takes a hell of a lot to get me down and my hair has not gone grey nor do I look very woebegone.[39]

On 14 December he wrote to a family friend, a Mrs Fitzsimons of Avonmore Terrace, Cabra in Dublin. The censors never sent it on. From the tone of his letter, she seems to have been far better acquainted with his activities than his parents were: 'I'm afraid it didn't work this time,' he informed her, 'as I was picked up 10 hours after I landed. The Broy Harriers[40] had sent my name, age, home address, full description two weeks beforehand. Well, I hope you won't do too much moaning over me as I can do enough for both of us'. After enquiring for a number of friends and IRA colleagues, he told her he expected to get five years Borstal detention and asked her to have the table ready for him in Cabra in 1945. And, just as he had in the letter to his brother, he begged her to 'tell everyone that I did not say the ridiculous things I was supposed to have said' to the police. 'I did write a statement as they had pinched my landlady and I wanted to get her out,' he added. This is oddly at variance with the disparaging description of his landlady in *Borstal Boy*. According to that account, he was untouched when one of the arresting officers said he would not be surprised if angry loyalists in her area wrecked her house:

> This landlady was mean and as barren as a bog. Her broken windows would be a judgement on her for the cheap sausages and margarine she poisoned her table with, for she was only generous with things that cost little in cash, locking hall doors at night time and kneeling down to say

the Rosary with the lodger and her sister, who always added three Hail
Marys for holy purity and the protection of her person and modesty, so
you would think half the men in Liverpool were running after her,
panting for a lick of her big buck teeth.[41]

As ever, Brendan was faced with a dilemma when it came to portraying
certain people for the wider audience. In other words, he tended to exaggerate.
Perhaps he felt it better to speak well of his landlady to the devout Mrs
Fitzsimons, who had given him religious medals to protect him as he went
about the business of preparing to plant bombs in Liverpool:

> The medals you gave me are in the hands of the police. I am very sorry
> to have to say that the RC Priest here treated me very badly. I cannot
> go to the altar unless I confess that it is a sin to be an Irish Republican.

Later, when he was famous, he was able to reap the literary benefits of
portraying his Liverpool landlady as a demonic, tight-fisted, old harridan who
deserved everything she got at the hands of her loyalist neighbours.

His main concern was not the fate of his landlady nor even the length of
sentence he was expecting but that the IRA should think he made a statement
to the police which might be incriminating in any way. He assured Mrs
Fitzsimons he did not regret his actions in coming to Liverpool:

> [I] will gladly pay the price of striving to be a good soldier of the
> Republic. If I got the chance I would do it a 1000 times over what I am
> now in English convicts cells for doing.[42]

'It might interest you to know that you are one of the most talked of prisoners
in England', his brother Seán assured Brendan in a letter dated 20 January
1940. If Brendan had actually received this letter it would, without doubt,
have interested him: there could have been no more powerful self-vindication
for the young prisoner than to receive confirmation that he had, by the age of
sixteen, achieved the notoriety he had so desperately desired. The letter
contained much news of fellow IRA Volunteers, of their arrests and of their
daring prison escapes. It also contained the distressing news that his Granny
Furlong was in poor health. Seán promised that if two horses he had received
reliable tips for ran to form, he would use the winnings to visit him in
Liverpool: 'Well Brendan, since you have returned to your "former
superstitions" pray hard for my two nags next Saturday.'[43] Before signing off,
he mentioned that Albert Wood, a leading Dublin barrister had been sent to

England to conduct the appeal of Peter Barnes and James McCormack, IRA activists who had been sentenced to death on 14 December 1939 for their part in the Coventry explosion. While both were known to be IRA Volunteers, there was no substantial evidence to link them to the Coventry explosion. In Ireland, there was absolute outrage at the sentence: in public opinion the hand of perfidious Albion was raised once again against two willing Irish martyrs. Their appeal failed and, on 5 February 1940, 5,000 people turned up at Dublin's Mansion House to protest against the decision to hang the two Irishmen at Winson Green Jail in Birmingham. Two days later, on 7 February, the death sentence on Barnes and McCormack was carried out. On the following day, Ash Wednesday, newspaper accounts of the execution appeared side by side with the story that Brendan 'Beham' (his name was misspelled in all the Irish newspaper accounts of the trial) had been sentenced in Liverpool to three years' Borstal detention on explosives charges.

4

Behan in Borstal

Brendan Behan's trial was set for 8 February, at Liverpool Assizes. Since he had been caught with bomb-making equipment, he expected to be found guilty. The question of whether the court would accept his minority and thus be obliged to exercise the more lenient sentencing that applied to offenders still under 17, hung in the balance.

As the date of his trial drew nearer, the anger Behan felt against the English prison system since his arrest appears to have given way to a sense of resignation to his fate. A letter that he wrote to his brother, Seán, shortly before his trial, demonstrates a jocular acceptance of prison conditions:

> There's nothing new to report here. I go to trial on Monday at Liverpool Assizes and I am told by experienced lags here that I may be moved to Wormwood Scrubs before going to Borstal. This is not official and the sooner I get to Borstal the better. ... If we had a bookies and a pub here I'd never go home. One chap says 'The screws aren't here to keep us in — but to keep the riff-raff out'. If half the people outside knew what this was like they'd have to fill vacancies by election. ... It's better than the Union. I have a private suite.[1]

The dour Governor Holt also appears to have undergone a change of attitude in the period immediately preceding Brendan's trial: on 25 January, he had noted that his young Irish charge was 'conceited' and in need of 'deflation and discipline'. By the time he came to write a further memo on 6 February, the same boy had metamorphosed into 'an honest youth who will have time in Borstal to think of his many problems'.[2] Except for the brutal beating administered after his interview with the chaplain at Walton, Brendan was, on the whole, treated very fairly by the English prison and Borstal systems. This treatment radically altered his attitude towards England and the English that he had acquired principally through his mother's unbridled hatred of that nation and race.

Brendan's thoughts were naturally concentrated on his trial, but in all his letters home he never failed to ask after the welfare of his family and friends in Dublin. Much has been made, principally by Brendan, of his row with Dominic on the eve of his departure for Liverpool. But the register of his outgoing letters from prison, which records several letters to Dominic, contradicts his claim that he did not communicate with his younger brother while in Borstal. It was only later, when Dominic began his own writing career that the relationship between the two brothers began to falter.

Brendan was very distressed when he heard that his brother, Brian, had been sentenced to four years detention in an approved institution for 'mitching' from school. 'Keep your heart up', he wrote to his younger brother, 'The darkest hour is before the dawn'.[3] His interest in affairs at home helped him keep his mind off his circumstances and his letters show his hunger for news from Ireland:

> I suppose all the boys are on the run. Who has been pulled in? ... How are the Furlongs doing? ... Send them my regards. I still hope Rory makes the night hideous with his howls. ... Is Da toiling and Rory and Seamus? ... What's going to win at Leopardstown? I fancy Jack Chaucer as a good thing if he's not carrying too heavy but I suppose you're tipping Royal Danieli to anyone foolish enough to listen.[4]

Brendan never became a hardened 'lag', but he revelled in the hard man image which serving time in prison gave him. He relished the secret language of prison life and would pepper his speech with it for the rest of his days:

> [I've] picked up the vernacular pretty well. Stir (jail) Screw (warder) lag (convict) snout (tobacco) flowery (cell) lagging (sentence).[5]

He adopted a rather cocky tone when writing to IRA friends and tried to pass off his situation lightly. He had planned to meet his old Fianna Éireann friend, Mick Whelan, the night he left for Liverpool. From Walton he explained why he missed the appointment:

> As you see from [the] papers the pitcher has gone to the well once too often and so I am enjoying a rest cure. If you remember I [was] to see you before I skipped town but as I had to seize a suitable opportunity when there was no watch on the North Wall I couldn't do it. ... I am expecting to get away with three years and that's not here nor there. ... I was caught while making up a few 'lucky bags' for the decent people here.[6]

Before he appeared in court for sentencing, Brendan was already aware from Walton's 'jailhouse lawyers' that, being under 17, he would be sent to Borstal and not to an adult prison like so many other IRA activists caught during the bombing campaign. The British authorities made every effort, through contacts in the Irish police, to obtain a Birth Certificate for him to verify his age. It proved to be an impossible task because the official document carried only his given name, Francis, and the searchers were looking for a Brendan Behan who had no official existence in Dublin.

Brendan Behan's trial date fell just one day before his seventeenth birthday, and he was in an upbeat mood as he faced the prospect of sentencing. 'Monday before the Hanging Judge!' he wrote to Seán Furlong. 'See you in Church. Felon of our land. They'll have to get me out by force I won't leave peaceably.'[7]

In several letters written in the few days before his trial, he expressed his concern for the fate of Barnes and McCormack as they awaited execution in Birmingham. While he considered it good fortune that Albert Wood, a barrister of distinction, should be handling the appeal, he correctly felt the case was lost even before it was heard.

On the night before their execution, he sat in his cell reading Elizabeth Gaskell's *Cranford* and wishing at that moment for nothing other than to survive the night peacefully. Brendan knew that when IRA prisoners were executed, Irish prison inmates were likely to vent their feelings through violent disturbances. He was alarmed when another Irish prisoner – not jailed for IRA activities but for the theft of Sir Harry Lauder's overcoat – screamed through the ventilation shaft, exhorting him to join in a protest. The chant of 'U-u-u-uup the Rep-u-u-u-u-u-ub-lic!' came booming through the prison wing. Only too conscious that a severe beating might follow if he joined in, but unable not to participate at all, Brendan whispered meekly down the ventilator 'Up the Republic and to hell with the British Empire.' The next sound he heard was that of his fellow Irishman's moans as he was beaten in his cell. Brendan was not usually one to err on the side of caution. On this occasion, however, he showed an uncharacteristic instinct for self-preservation. He was later grateful that he had been sensible enough to muffle his tongue: 'I thought it better to survive my sentence and come out and strike a blow in vengeance for them, than be kicked to death or insanity here.'[8] He returned with a guilty conscience to *Cranford* and Miss Betsy Barker's inane concern about how tipsy she felt after eating damson-tart.[9]

'Dublin Boy Goes to Borstal'; 'Speech From Liverpool Dock'; 'Dublin Boy On Explosives Charge In Liverpool'; 'Three Years For Boy On Explosives Charge'. When it finally came, Brendan's trial made gratifying headlines.

Most of the Irish newspapers carried quite extensive coverage of the trial and even *The Times* of London did not allow the occasion go unmarked.

The Hon Mr Justice Hugh Hallett, Kt. MC, heard the case. Mr Eric Errington, MP, who pleased Brendan by appearing in court wearing his British Army uniform, was the prosecutor. Brendan's declaration that he had 'no interest in the proceedings' was construed as a plea of 'Not Guilty'. A Detective-Sergeant Earps gave evidence on Brendan's alleged statement at the time of his arrest. He claimed that Brendan had said 'I have been sent over to take the places of Chris Kenneally, Nick Lynch and the others who have been arrested. I was to reorganise further operations in Liverpool. I intended to put bombs in big stores, Lewis and Hughes, I think they call it ... I would have put one in Cammell Lairds [the shipyard] if I had the chance. I am only sixteen and they can't do much with me'. At this point in the proceedings, Brendan interjected from the dock 'that's a lot of damned lies'. The judge told him to be quiet or the case would be heard in his absence. An Inspector Tilley told the court that the boy came from a Republican background, had joined Fianna Éireann when still very young, and that in his teenage years he had joined the IRA. He claimed that Brendan had been in London early in 1939 and was then also engaged in bomb-making. Brendan had made this story up, but it suited the policeman's purpose to take it as a fact. Tilley also told the court that all efforts to trace Brendan in the records in Ireland had failed. The judge then asked him if he was under seventeen. Brendan replied that he was. Sentencing him to three years Borstal detention, Mr Justice Hallett remarked that the British Parliament had taken an extremely lenient view of what ought to be done with young persons found guilty of major offences. The maximum penalty for an adult in Brendan's position would have been fourteen years. From the tone of Mr Justice Hallett's remarks it seems that had the option of handing down a longer custodial sentence been available to him, he would have done so. And indeed, by comparison, on the same day in Dublin, a teenage boy received a sentence of three years for petty crime – the theft of a half crown – Brendan's punishment does seem rather light.

Aware that his moment of glory had come, Brendan then delivered a Robert Emmet-style nationalist address from the dock. The words recorded by the court correspondents differ to the version Behan gives in *Borstal Boy*. The rendition that the newspapers printed is less polished but more honest. By the time he came to write *Borstal Boy*, Brendan was incapable of resisting the temptation to embellish the past. Such embellishment was unnecessary – the original version was more touching. Here is the court reporters' version:

> It is my proud privilege and honour to stand in an English court to testify to the unyielding determination of the Irish people to regain

every inch of our national territory and to give expression to the noble aspirations for which so much Irish blood has been shed and so many hearts have been broken and for which so many friends and comrades are languishing in English gaols.[10]

As he was taken below to the cells he shouted 'Up the Republic', in the traditional IRA fashion. He was removed to Feltham Boys' Prison where he remained until 21 March awaiting placement in a Borstal institution.

In a letter to his mother, written the day after his sentencing, he tried to allay any fears she might have about his condition. He made light of his predicament and assured her that he was lucky to have escaped a more onerous sentence. He did, however, tell her that the situation he now found himself in was 'entirely attributable' to her. By this he meant that Kathleen's hatred of England and the English had been at the root of his Republican ideology. He was now having second thoughts about that entrenched position.

Dear Mother,
As you read last night I was sentenced to 3 years Borstal yesterday at Liverpool Assizes by Mr Justice Hallett. Well, I can't complain of the sentence because if I was over 17 I would have got 14 years penal servitude. I will say however that never have I seen such barefaced perjury on the part of the police. I don't deny I had the stuff but I never made any of the alleged statements I was supposed to have made. I was listening to the detectives suavely lying until I could no longer control myself & I shouted out 'It's a lot of lies'. I must in justice admit that the police in the course of their investigations treated me very well, almost as well as if I were a guest of Sir Mark Byrne at Oriel House.[11] But even if I was treated like Davy Nelligan[12] O'Ballyseedy I would not have stated the Record they gave me. On my own admission I was supposed to have planted bombs in London, Southport, Fleetwood and Blackpool and as you know I wasn't away from home for more than a fortnight last year. The judge compared me (on the basis of these statements) to the chap in Synge's *Playboy* who boasts of patricide. He evidently wished to show his clear insight into the Celtic temperament (as interpreted by J. M. Synge). He slayed me unmercifully – he criticised the Acts of Parliament which let me away with 3 yr[s] B. and stated to me, 'While indulging in such mock heroics it is quite clear that you took a cowardly advantage of this fact'.
In the course of the evidence a cop stated that I told him (among other things such as [that] I was making bombs all over England) I was born on Feb 13 1923 – my birthday is the 9th and the reason he told him the 13th was that it enabled him to get an assurance from the Dublin

Registrar that there was no person of my name (the proper one F.B.)[13] born on that date in Dublin from 1921 to 1925 – thus casting a doubt as to whether I was really a juvenile or not. But the judge, though he did not accept that I was 16, could get no evidence to prove I was more. This [was] clearly an attempt to treat me as an adult and get sentenced accordingly. In sentencing me he said 'I am very sorry it is not in my power to sentence you to penal servitude. I trust however 3 yrs B. may cure you of both your precocity and conceit.' I said, 'Thank you, my lord – God Save Ireland'. Well I had a great day all the same for the warders in charge were very good skins & I got a smoke off them. Also my favourite dish – coffee & beef sandwiches. I must say I had a great time. Now 3 yrs B. does not mean locked up all day, etc. It's miles better than any institution of the same sort in Ireland. It has more of a reforming influence, 'Reward for virtue rather than Punishment for vice'. That's what [had] the judge so mad. I hope you won't worry about me as I am OK myself, never felt better in my life (I have just eaten my dinner). In any event it is entirely attributable to yourself that I am here and you don't want to believe $^1/_2$ what you hear about prison. So long as you don't swim against the current you're alright. I may get another letter in lieu of a visit before I get to Borstal but ask Seán to deny for me that [I] made the ridiculous statements about causing explosions in London etc. A person would want to be buailte suas[14] to say such things. Also I shan't do any more than about 2 years or maybe 21 months as there is remission allowed up to $^1/_2$ the sentence.

So really you see I got off nearly scot free. I have made 15/-[15] making ammunition sacks during the time I was awaiting trial and I will ask the Governor to let me send it home.

I hope Da got my letter OK.

See you in church – ever your mad son.

Brendan.[16]

Being 'mad' stood Brendan in good stead during his time in the British penal system. His sheer exuberance and almost manic bonhomie made it certain that he did not go unnoticed in that netherworld. But at Feltham there was no particular pressure on him to try to impress his fellow inmates. He was there on licence awaiting transfer to a suitable Borstal and felt he was merely marking time.

Our days in Feltham were the same every day except Sunday. We got up at seven, washed, and went to a big hall with tables each seating about twenty where we had breakfast. This was a great and happy

surprise to us after Walton. It consisted of any amount of bread, a piece
of margarine, and wonder of God! a rissole, and a big bloody rissole at
that. There was a big pot of tea to each table, and you could usually get
three mugs, if you wanted them.[17]

The Feltham interlude lasted for just under five weeks. Particularly interesting
is an assessment made of him there by the prison medical officer, Dr A.P.
Lewis. The document is a curious mongrel – it is half the invention of
Brendan's frenetic imagination and half the product of the doctor's shrewd
powers of observation. No doubt aware of the fact that Dr Lewis was assessing
him for Borstal placement, Brendan tried to make himself appear as
interesting as possible. The word going around Feltham was that only
'interesting' candidates received places at the new, experimental open Borstals.
Again, Brendan spun a yarn to his interviewer: he claimed again that his father
had been in prison for murder and that an older brother was killed in the
Spanish Civil War. He said his two older brothers had influenced his political
thinking and that he had been connected with the IRA since the age of six.
The latter was at least correct. He said he had given up his last job to come to
England to take part in the bombing campaign. He was chosen, he said,
because 'I was supposed to be above average intelligence for my age and suited
for the job'. Dr Lewis found him to be only of 'quite average' intelligence. He
also found him to be 'unreliable in as much as he withholds various little
details about himself until he realises that the interviewer already knows all
about them. In some measure he is compensating for a feeling of inferiority
which has developed into an attitude of conceitedness'. Lewis felt Behan's
understanding of his position was good; he did not carry rationalisation to
extremes and though he talked a great deal about his beliefs, he was not a
fanatic. Lewis's ultimate assessment was penetratingly accurate:

> Now that he has been sentenced, I think he feels that like an actor in a
> play who makes a stage exit early, he has finished his job and can now
> wait and simply look on. Whilst it is unlikely that much impression will
> be made during his training, his political ideas and outlook I think
> would respond more satisfactorily at an open institution than
> elsewhere.[18]

There were only two such open institutions for young offenders in England:
North Sea Camp in Lincolnshire and Hollesley Bay, near Woodbridge, in
Suffolk. These open Borstals were the product of a rehabilitative approach to
penology that was creeping into the British prison system. At these
institutions, boys had considerable freedom of movement and were

encouraged to develop new skills and abilities. While Brendan was awaiting trial, he heard much talk from other boys of the relative merits of various institutions for young offenders. To be sent to a closed institution such as Portland or Sherwood was considered a disaster. Feltham and Rochester were bad, but not so bad. North Sea Camp and Hollesley Bay, with their laxer regimes and seaside locations, were the most desirable places. Hollesley Bay, which was the newest of the two, was the Holy Grail. Competition for places was intense.

In mid-March Brendan was interviewed by a three-man selection committee. It consisted of a member of the Prison Commission, the Governor of Feltham and the Governor of Hollesley Bay, Cyril Alfred Joyce. The latter was to have a profound influence on Brendan, who was to develop absolute and almost reverential respect for 'the old man', as he called Joyce.

Brendan remembered the Governor's physical appearance from that first meeting – 'a stout gentleman with his hair split in the middle ... and the look of a British Army officer about him'. In his youth, Joyce had considered taking Holy Orders and had already begun his religious training when the First World War intervened. He served in the Army, and after the war, briefly joined the new Army Education Corps. Joyce left the armed forces to take a degree at University College, Southampton. It was during this period that he decided to take up a career working with young offenders. He joined the Prison Service in 1922, at a time when new, humanitarian ideas were beginning to influence the British penal system, both in adult and young offender institutions. Joyce was to be at the forefront of that movement. He served first at Portland, a former prison converted to a Borstal, before becoming Governor of Camp Hill Borstal Institution on the Isle of Wight.

In 1938, Joyce established Hollesley Bay Colony. His plans for a progressive open Borstal met with resistance from conservative officials. They considered that the idea created a dangerous and unacceptable precedent and favoured a more heavy-handed approach than Joyce proposed. He overcame these objections with the powerful support of Sir Alexander Patterson of the Prison Service, who was eager to overhaul the Borstal system with the aid of men like Joyce.

Joyce believed that prison only served a useful function if it instilled in the prisoner the belief that his capacity to reform himself is greater than the capacity of the institution to reform him. Joyce took the English public school system as his administrative model for Hollesley Bay. The colony had four 'Houses', each with a House Master, a House Captain elected by the boys, a Matron and other trappings of public school life. The buildings lay in farm lands of 1,400 acres. Hollesley Bay inmates spent much of their time outdoors.

Joyce decided that the first participants in his new project should be staff and boys he knew already from Camp Hill. Fifty boys volunteered to go with him, even though it meant a prolongation of their sentences.[19] The whole party departed on an epic march to the new institution on the Suffolk coast. There was great respect among the inmates at Hollesley Bay for 'The Squire', as they called Joyce:

'He was known to be a fair man, and, though they were afraid of him to an extent, they knew that, no matter what they did, he would do anything rather than send a bloke to Sherwood Forest or Wandsworth'.[20] His real skill lay in his ability to win the boys' respect through his enlightened, and for the time, unusual approach to their personal predicament. 'In the attempt to reclaim the people whom we call criminals', he wrote, 'there is only one answer: the relationship of two individuals who recognise in each other a genuine desire to help one another, or at any rate not to do one another an injury.'[21] If Joyce was fair, he was certainly also firm. He had a well worked-out theory of discipline. He believed that punishment was only justified if the victim understood it to be a matter of cause and effect – chastisement being the natural result of the original infringement. He preferred a situation where the boys realised that it was more acceptable for them to punish themselves than for him to administer it to them. He believed that restitution – being made to replace, with interest, the thing you had stolen or broken – was the most effective form of discipline. Dietary punishment was sometimes used. Although it has not been possible to establish whether he employed corporal punishment at Hollesley Bay, he did, by his own account, resort to beating boys at Cotswold Approved School, where he later became Headmaster.[22]

Brendan's admittance to Hollesley Bay was passed by the selection committee and, on 21 March 1940, to his immense satisfaction, he was transferred there from Feltham. Within half an hour of his arrival, he was brought to Joyce's office. Joyce informed him of his notions of mutual co-operation between prison officials and inmates:

> To my astonishment he asked: 'Well, now, would you mean that I am to be treated fair?'
> And I answered, 'I hope so.'
> 'Then,' said he, 'would it help you to know that I haven't any inhibition and me complexes is all in order?'
> 'Who the devil taught you that jargon?' I exclaimed.
> 'Sure,' he said, 'I've been examined till I'm sick of it, and I thought it would save you the trouble and me going through it all again.'

On arrival, Brendan was allocated a place in St Michael's House, which was one of the older of the Colony's buildings. He relished the architecture of the open Borstal:

> The buildings were big, rambling and timbered like the headquarters of The Horse Show or the Phoenix Park Race Course buildings in Dublin. There were dormer windows and a clock tower. They were built about 1880 or 1890 ... to imitate a Tudor great house.
> I'd learned about building, all my people being in that industry, and I was not reared to that style of building at all. I was reared to Georgian, Regency or modern, but I liked these buildings because they were more unlike a jail than any place could be.[23]

He was to spend time in three of the four Houses at Hollesley Bay and took to the system with ease. St Michael's was a vast timbered space with beamed ceilings supported by wooden pillars. It was freezing cold in winter and hot and stuffy in summer. There was a well-stocked library with an open fire. It had, Brendan liked to think, something of the atmosphere of a London gentlemen's club, 'with old bishops and colonels and other manner of tail-waggers discussing a letter to *The Times*'.[24] On his first visit to it, he was thrilled to see the room 'jammed to the doors with fellows sitting at the tables reading'. He was too shy to venture further than the door but, on his next visit, he saw on the shelves, books by Shaw and O'Casey and he thought that little discovery as good as a visit home to Dublin. In the library, he met a fey young man of about nineteen who wore a rose-coloured silk tie and smoked through a cigarette holder. This young man was reading a copy of Frank Harris's *Oscar Wilde, His Life and Confessions*. He explained to Brendan, in a 'languid elegant accent', exactly why Wilde had been jailed. This revelation was meant to be disturbing, but Brendan responded sharply: 'Every tinker has his own way of dancing, and I think that if that shocks you, it's just as well ordinary people didn't hear about it. Because, bejasus, if it shocked you, it'd turn thousands grey.' This pointed remark won him another friend and the young man promised to lend him the Wilde biography. From that moment on, Brendan spent a great deal of his spare time in the library reading amongst others, Dickens, Somerset Maugham, Shaw, D.H. Lawrence and a book which introduced him to rugby – *The Silver Fleece* by Irish international Robert Collis. He tells us in *Borstal Boy* that he had always thought of rugby as having nothing to do with Ireland or Dublin. Collis' book transformed his view of rugby from something 'played by bank clerks' into something fit for any class of

Irishman. Collis' description of an Irish forward rush put him in mind of *Fontenoy*, by Thomas Davis.

> And standing in his charger, the Brave King Louis spoke,
> 'Send on my Irish Cavalry,' the headlong Irish broke,
> At Fontenoy! at Fontenoy! 'Remember Limerick,
> Dash down the Sasanach!'

'Reading Collis' book was like meeting someone from home, and I could see rugby football not as a winter meeting of cricketers, but as a battle fought in the churning mud, and myself in the forward line charging for Ireland.[25] He took the game up with a passion that surprised even himself. He played as an enthusiastic and competent hooker for his House against the colony's other Houses and once against the Highland Light Infantry, who were billeted nearby.

Once Brendan had settled into activities like rugby playing, Governor Joyce was struck by his constant good humour and quite unusual intelligence. 'His intelligence', Joyce recalled, 'showed itself mainly in his approach to problems; his extraordinarily sharp and quick wit and the colourful choice of words in his ordinary speech. In ways he was so refreshing, so out of the ordinary'.[26]

There were other boys at Hollesley Bay who were also out of the ordinary. Most were working-class but some came from public school backgrounds; all were chosen by Joyce for their capacity to respond well to his reforming methods. One of Joyce's failures was Neville Heath who was hanged in 1950 for the brutal murder of two women. Brendan liked to claim that he used to shock Heath by his use of bad language. There were several boys who had served in the British ArmyBritish Army and Navy, amongst them a Cockney naval rating, 'Charlie Millwall' in *Borstal Boy*. He arrived at Hollesley Bay with Brendan and was his closest friend there.[27] Brendan believed that it was a shared working-class background that made him so instantly acceptable to the majority of English boys at Hollesley Bay. He warmed to the Londoners' colourful use of Cockney rhyming slang and they in turn enjoyed his adroit use of 'Dublinese':

> I had the same rearing as most of them, Dublin, Liverpool, Manchester, Glasgow, London. All our mothers had all done the pawn – pledging on Monday, releasing on Saturday. We all knew the chip shop and the picture house and the four penny rush of a Saturday afternoon, and the Summer swimming in the canal and being chased along the railway by the cops.[28]

He was also proud of the fact that his Dubliner's sense of classlessness allowed him to mix comfortably with the public school boys. When his friend 'Charlie' saw him giving one such boy some tobacco, he chided Brendan: 'What did you give that Kensington puff a bit of snout for?' But Brendan felt compassion for the boy, whose family background and education alienated him from his fellow inmates: 'I couldn't help being sorry for him, for he was more of a foreigner than I, and it's a lonely thing to be a stranger in a strange land'.[29]

Hollesley Bay offered a number of vocational courses. On 1 April, Brendan enrolled for the course in painting and decorating under the instruction of F.E.J. Curtes. Since Brendan had already acquired these skills in Dublin, he made rapid progress and Curtes thought him 'reliable when left alone and expected him to earn £2/15-00 a week when released'.[30] What little money he did make from his painting work while still in Borstal he spent on newspapers.

He fell ill with suspected tonsillitis on 19 June 1940 and was removed to the Borstal hospital, where he remained until 24 June being fed on a diet of pudding and marmite.[31] Later that summer, he entered an essay competition for the colony's Eisteddfod. His essay on Dublin, rich in references to Joyce, Shaw and O'Casey, took first prize and his stock rose several more points amongst his fellow inmates. 'Paddy Behan', as they called him in Hollesley Bay, had established his literary credentials and enjoyed the kudos enormously.

Though in later years Brendan got out of the habit of letter writing, favouring the telephone instead, he kept up a very regular correspondence while at Hollesley Bay. Letters from Seán Furlong kept Brendan informed of developments at home and abroad.

> There is a Corporation strike on for the past 2 weeks, the majority of people in Dublin are against the workers. ... As I write the USSR has just won the Finnish War ... Da is still idle ... I mentioned about your case in my last letter, it got a great bust in all the Dublin & English papers.[32]

In early November 1940 he was deeply upset by the news that his Granny Furlong had been taken ill in prison. He wrote to her from St Michael's House on 10 November. It appeared that she was to be released on the grounds of ill-health:

> Dear Gran,
>
> You will hardly believe how happy it makes me to be writing this. I have written to Seán and told him that my congratulations must be offered

to you first. As you know your illness has been a trial to us all. But thanks be to God you have come through successfully. As you may know I was arrested in Liverpool last December and was sentenced to 3 years Borstal by Mr Justice Hallett (deputising for Singleton[33] who was fortunately ill) at Liverpool Assizes in February. As I was actually found preparing a bomb there was no question of getting off. Considering the charge (possession of explosives) I [did] very well. The maximum sentence under the Act of 1883 being 14 years

P.S. I was held some 3 months in prison and have been 8 months here. Although I went through the mill a bit in prison, I cannot speak too well of this place. It is at times really very hard to realise this colony of ours has any connection with Walton Prison Liverpool. My mother has a photo of it. I['m] doing very well, in great form could jump over the Dublin mountains with the greatest of ease.

Seán told me the air raids are worrying you. Jerry doesn't worry us a great deal. I was often thinking of the times we used have in 32 and Clontarf. Do you remember all the fuss there used be on Easter Sunday & Bodenstown. The night you went away you thought, I think, it would be the last you'd see of me. The night I get out, I'll prove you wrong. I'll be as large as life and twice as mad. I'm sorry I cannot meet you at the North Wall to congratulate you. I could say so much better. Still 'till we meet again, Slán leat.[34]

I am proud of you, love to Em. and Ev.[35]

Yours ever,
Brendan.[36]

'I cannot speak too well of this place,' he tells his grandmother. Stories peddled in Dublin pubs in later years depicted Brendan as an ungovernable rebel during his time at Borstal. There is no evidence to support this view. Brendan made no secret of the fact that he was extremely happy at Hollesley Bay and that he willingly conformed to the rules. There were occasional minor infringements but nothing of a very serious nature. Indeed, he became a bulwark of the Hollesley system when he was appointed House Captain at St Patrick's House. The position brought with it both responsibility and privilege. The principal advantage was a private cubicle in which the House Captain slept and entertained his coterie of mates, or 'chinas' as Borstal intimates referred to one another. In the opinion of Joyce, Behan was one of the most lovable characters that ever passed through Borstal, no matter what he did you could not help liking the man'.[37] Before he met Brendan Behan, Joyce had had the opportunity to observe generations of Borstal boys at close hand. His assessment of him must therefore carry considerable weight, although it has to be noted that Brendan, with his easy charm and wit, had an intuitive sense of the need to impress the right person at the right time. It was an important lesson he had learned at an early age at Granny English's all-powerful court in Russell Street.

The day after Brendan wrote to his Granny Furlong, Governor Joyce wrote his first full assessment of Brendan's progress at Borstal. Joyce believed – wrongly as it turned out – that he had had a change of heart about his IRA activities:

> Many contacts with this man leave the impression that he is either a super snake or a very straight forward person. I think he is the latter. He is much in favour of his cause in the IRA but says now that their methods were and are wrong. It is not his present intention to return to such activities on discharge and he is clearly and outspokenly pro-English for the duration of the War. This lad is a good-hearted loyalist whose misdirection is tragic.

Three days later, on 16 November, Joyce expanded on that view.

> Has a more detached view of being used by [the] IRA - his loyalties however are strong and it is possible his martyrdom may be used by his family. Says he will not be coerced or flattered in the future.[38]

The turnaround in Brendan's feelings about the English as a people, which lasted for the rest of his life, was observed by a Scottish inmate who accused him of liking the English despite their behaviour in Ireland. Brendan replied that it was the imperialist system and not the English that persecuted the Irish and that some of that system's most ardent supporters were Scots and Irish. In terms of his former attitude towards the English, this represented a quantum leap.

By December 1940, Brendan's relationship with Joyce was on a very firm footing. He was impressed above all else by the Governor's sense of fair play, something he came to associate with English people generally. Mrs Joyce, an accomplished sculptor, also took a great interest in Brendan and offered to sculpt his head. She was struck, as was her husband, by his intense interest in religion. They were impressed that he did not wear his religion heavily but seemed instead to possess a deep-rooted spirituality. He discussed his excommunication with Joyce and told him how distressed he was about not being able to attend Mass. The Governor appealed to the colony's Roman

Catholic chaplain. The priest was sympathetic, but could not ignore his Bishop's ruling on excommunicated IRA men. So as not to disappoint Brendan, Joyce said he would take him to the chapel and there, he a Protestant and Brendan a Catholic, they could pray together: 'Sometimes we would go into the chapel together when nobody was there. I would play the organ for him. We sang *I'll Sing a Hymn to Mary* and *Sweet Sacrament Divine.*'[39]

On one occasion, however, the Chaplain made an exception to the ban. One day, the usual altar boy was unable to serve at Mass. Brendan's knowledge of Church Latin made him an ideal replacement. In his desire to escape the tedium of everyday life, Brendan took all the routes available to him but none pleased him more than being back in the comforting embrace of Mother Church. He bellowed out the responses he had learned by heart in the churches of Dublin:

> 'Introibo ad altare Dei.'
> 'Ad Deum Qui laetificat juventutem meam.'

Brendan also developed a close relationship with the Matron of St George's House, Ann Halfpenny[40]. She was a well-read English Catholic who lent him books and encouraged him to take the part of one of the Wise Men in the nativity play at Christmas. So loved was the Matron by the boys that there was intense jealousy among them for her attention. Brendan had already snaffled a great deal of it for himself. He regularly took tea with her in her rooms in the long lazy summer afternoons when he was free from work. She was devoted to her dog, which she called 'Bran'. Brendan told her it was the name that a character of Irish legend, Fionn Mac Cumhaill, had given his dog. She became quite susceptible to the charms of his Irish banter. She was fond of the poetry of Yeats, and Brendan told her how his mother had known the poet at Maude Gonne's house in Dublin. When he remarked to her that Woodbridge lacked any literary association of note, she countered with the information that Dickens drowned James Steerforth just up the beach, and Edward Fitzgerald translated Omar Khayyam only a few miles away.[41] He quickly pronounced Fitzgerald to be an Irishman.

From the end of summer to the end of autumn, the boys at Hollesley Bay were released from all other work duties to pick the institution's fruit crop. With its huge acreage of farmland, gardens and orchards attached to it, the Borstal was self-sufficient. Brendan enjoyed the fruit-picking as a release from the tedium of digging the garden or painting windows:

> After the berries came the first apples, the Worcesters, and after that
> the first plums, the Early Rivers and, in the high season, the Victorias,

till we started on the pears, and in the last days of September we were all, everyone in the place, brown and tanned from working in the fields and orchards. On the face, and chest, and arms and legs ... It was a great summer and we were sorry in a kind of a way to see it finished, and the first cold of mornings, and the first shortening of the day.[42]

Winter was another matter:

The autumn got weaker and beaten, and the leaves all falling, and a bloody awful east wind that was up before us and we on our way to work in the morning, sweeping down off the top of the North sea, which in the distance looked like a bitter band of blue steel out along the length of the horizon, around the freezing marshes, the dirty grey shore, the gun-metal sea, and over us the sky, lead-coloured for a few hours, till the dark fell and the wind rose, and we went down the road from work at five o'clock in the perishing night.[43]

The boys spent much of the pre-Christmas period preparing the nativity play. They were ecstatic when the attractive young wife of one of the prison officers agreed to play the Virgin Mary. Keen to get close to this rare phenomenon, one boy offered to play the Holy Ghost and another the Infant Jesus.

The adolescent inmates of Hollesley Bay were almost totally deprived of female company. The only woman they regularly saw was the Matron. Not surprisingly, there was a certain amount of homosexual activity. In an unpublished twelve-page manuscript, probably written about a year after his release from Borstal, and serving as a sort of work-in-progress towards *Borstal Boy*, Brendan talks openly about sexual practices in Hollesley Bay. It represents Behan's most frankly-written discussion of his attitude to homosexuality:

I loved Borstal boys and they loved me. But the absence of girls made it that much imperfect. Homosexuality (of our sort) is not a substitute for normal sex. It's a different thing, rather similar to that of which T.E. Lawrence writes in *The Seven Pillars*. The youth of healthy muscle and slim-wrought form is not the same as the powdered pansy (who I hasten to add, as good as anybody else, has every right to be that and a bloody good artist or anything he wants to be). Our lads saw themselves as beautiful and had to do something about it. About a third of them did. Another third, not so influential or less good-looking, would have liked to. As I say however, without women it could not be a pattern of life, only a prolonging of adolescence – it was as beautiful as that.[44]

It is important to remember that though the fragment remains an unpublished part of the Behan œuvre, he wrote it with a view to publication. Brendan qualifies his admission that he engaged in homosexual practices in Borstal with the assertion that these activities were merely a 'prolonging of adolescence'. However, the statement is unusually considered for a nineteen-year-old boy and shows an extraordinarily enlightened attitude towards a sexual orientation for which there was absolutely no tolerance or understanding amongst the general public in Ireland in his lifetime.

This manuscript presents the earliest evidence of Behan's bisexuality. In *Borstal Boy* he alludes to homosexuality principally in the person of 'Joe', who avails of any opportunity to suggest fulfilling his fancy for homosexual sex. Otherwise the book contains only rather vague homoerotic references, such as when Brendan's friend, the irrepressibly butch sailor 'Charlie', asks him to soap his back in the shower. In later years when he referred to sex in Borstal he would simply say 'it was no worse than being in boarding school'. That Brendan could distinguish, however, between 'the good-looking and the less good-looking' and between 'the pansy and the youth of healthy muscle and slim-wrought form' at the age of nineteen, suggests more than a literary interest in the male form. It was an interest he would continue to develop in later life.

In *Borstal Boy*, Brendan disposes of 1941, his last year at Hollesley Bay, in only seven pages. It was not a happy period for him. A drawn-out bureaucratic wrangle over his possible early release had him in a state of suspended expectation through most of the year. As early as August 1940, when he had been just five months in Borstal, the question of his discharge was mooted by both Governor Joyce and at least two Prison Visitors. One possible method of securing an early discharge was to join the Navy. An entry on his file for 20 December 1940 shows that he agreed to the condition, albeit with a degree of reluctance:

> He wants to be expelled to Ireland for all his relations are there. He feels that the expulsion order will clarify the position and help him. He would go to sea if this were insisted upon, but he says he is always sea-sick, and being a good Irishman, he had a good deal of respect for Wellington but none at all for Nelson![45]

The Irish authorities informed the Home Office that they had no objection to Brendan's repatriation. Two officials of the Prison Commission, W. H. Waddams and R. Bradley, took up his cause. Throughout 1941, they engaged in a lengthy correspondence with the Home Office supporting his expulsion to Ireland. Their view was that he was no ordinary IRA bomber and his exceptional intelligence and positive response to Borstal made him worthy of special treatment. Bradley had seen Brendan in mid-January 1941, and discussed with him the likelihood of his early release. He later wrote to Joyce because he was concerned that he might have given the boy too much hope. In that letter, he worried that Brendan 'would feel cheated' and that he had fooled him, even though inadvertently. In late January, Governor Joyce asked him how he felt about serving two to two-and-a-half years of his sentence and offered him the position of his 'right-hand man amongst the colonists'. Brendan told him he was happy enough to soldier on if the question of his early release could be resolved in a definite fashion. 'He is quite prepared to face the whole sentence in manly and reasonable spirit', Joyce noted in a letter to Mr Bradley. He also said that Brendan believed implicitly in Bradley and himself and that 'coloured his attitude considerably'.[46] By the end of January, Joyce was convinced that Brendan no longer 'showed signs of subversive tendencies' and was willing to give up his IRA activities. However, despite the best efforts of Joyce, Waddams and Bradley, the Home Office postponed any decision on his release for six months. The delay upset Brendan a great deal. His best mate 'Charlie' had been discharged in March. Quite suddenly, Hollesley Bay Colony was no longer the happy place it had been for him. He became extremely restless and at times uncooperative for much of his remaining time in Hollesley Bay.

Joyce had accepted another post within the prison system and was due to leave in July. The impending departure of the 'old man' was a further cause of distress to Brendan. On 13 July, just three days before Governor Joyce departed and his replacement, C.T. Cape arrived, Brendan threatened to go on hunger strike. He had been placed in detention at seven o'clock that evening by the Deputy Governor. In *Borstal Boy*, Behan gives a fictional reason for this punishment, choosing to make himself the victim of a heroic gesture in giving tobacco to a boy already in detention. Home Office records, however, show that he was locked up on suspicion of obtaining money under threat from another inmate named Lightning. He was also accused of carrying on a money-lending business in the Borstal. The Governor saw him at eight o'clock. Brendan adamantly protested his innocence. Joyce did not accept his word on this occasion, believing that he was 'involved somewhere' in the extortion of money and the money-lending charge.

The Deputy Governor felt that Brendan had been so unsettled during the year that there was a chance he might abscond. As he was an IRA prisoner, the reputation of Hollesley Bay would suffer. Joyce knew Brendan was unlikely to do that: on one occasion he and his wife left Brendan waiting in their car as they went shopping and he was still sitting there when they returned. The Governor's view was that he should be transferred or discharged.[47]

On 17 July, Joyce left Hollesley Bay for his new posting at the Cotswold Approved School, Ashton Keynes, in Wiltshire. Hollesley inmates had planned to make some form of protest at his departure. He asked the boys not to make a fuss – he felt it would be a mark of disrespect to the new Governor. Brendan was devastated at the loss of this man he had grown to respect so deeply. Joyce was sad that his last dealing with him had been a rather negative one, but for the rest of his life he remembered Brendan Behan fondly. In 1955, when he came to write his memoirs, *By Courtesy of the Criminal*, Joyce singled Brendan out as one of the most impressive and memorable Borstal boys he had met in his long career.

The Home Secretary finally signed Brendan's Expulsion Order from Britain on 18 October 1941. He had given Governor Joyce a verbal undertaking not to take part in any IRA activity against England 'till we've finished that [bastard] Hitler'.[48] On 24 October, he went one step further for Governor Cape. As part of the conditions of his release he signed the following declaration: 'I, Brendan Behan, hereby undertake not to take part in any of the activities of the IRA.'[49]

On 1 November, he left Hollesley Bay. When the actual moment of leaving arrived, a terrible sense of sadness and loss overcame him. The emotion of departure wiped out any bitterness there had been in his last months:

> I'd have thought our Matron would have been there, and was disappointed that she was not, but, all of a hurry, just as we started the car, she came rushing to the doorway and waved a half-knitted sock, and I waved frantically back, and that was the last I saw of Borstal. Though she wasn't given a chance of saying good-bye to me not a bad picture was our Matron, to carry away with me.[50]

Police officers escorted Brendan to *S.S. Hibernia* at Holyhead and the ship sailed for Ireland at 5 o'clock. His complex recollection of the physical landscape as he sailed into Dun Laoghaire is one of the most moving passages in his writing. There, in all its permanence, was the familiar topography of his childhood walks:

> There they were as if I'd never left them; in their sweet and stately order round the Bay – Bray Head, the Sugarloaf, the Two Rock, the Three Rock, Kippure, the king of them all, rising his head behind and

over till they sloped down to the city. I counted the spires, from
Rathmine's fat dome on one side to St. George's spire on the North,
and in the centre, Christchurch. Among the smaller ones, just on the
docks, I could pick out, even in the haze of morning, the ones I knew
best, St Laurence O'Toole's and St Barnabas; I had them all counted,
present and correct....[51]

When he disembarked, he gave an immigration official the Expulsion Order
as an identification document. The man scrutinised it carefully, handed it
back, and welcomed him home with the words, 'It must be wonderful to be
free'. With studied irony, Brendan replied, 'It must', as he moved past a silent
Special Branch detective and made his way to the train for Dublin, uncertain
of what awaited him.

5

Six Months of Freedom

When he stepped off the boat train in Dublin on 1 November 1941[1], Brendan was still, in his own mind, a Republican soldier on active service, despite his declaration to the contrary prior to his release from Borstal. Governor Joyce's faith in his success in turning his favourite charge's political attitudes around had been misplaced. Within six months of his release from Hollesley Bay, Brendan was back behind bars for the grave offence of attempting to shoot two Irish police officers.

Brendan was unprepared for the Ireland he arrived back to and disappointed by the reception he received from his IRA colleagues. The returning hero of the bombing campaign in Britain, as he saw himself, did not receive quite the ecstatic welcome he had dreamt of in Borstal. The more senior figures in the IRA saw him as something of a liability and did not take him seriously. It was mostly his close comrades from the Fianna and Killiney training days who made a fuss of his return.

In 1941, the Republican movement was fragmented as never before. While Brendan was in Hollesley Bay, relations between the Free State Government and the IRA had deteriorated drastically. With the outbreak of war, de Valera's government found itself in a complicated position. Ireland had declared neutrality, but nevertheless found itself sitting in a pincer. A rampant Germany might find the island a convenient 'back door' to England, and the British Government might respond to such a threat by invading the country itself. Ireland was not just in a sensitive position regarding enemies from without. From the government's point of view, the IRA (elements of which might conceivably support a German invasion), represented a threat from within. The Minister for Justice, Gerry Boland, felt drastic measures were needed because the dilemma threatened the very existence of the state.[2] While Behan was in Borstal, several such measures were introduced in Ireland. On 4 January 1940, the Dáil approved internment for IRA suspects. On 6 June it established a Military Tribunal, known as the Special Criminal Court, to deal with the IRA in a more stringent manner than might be expected from the normal judicial process.

On 1 June 1940, British intelligence informed Dublin that an IRA-supported German invasion was a distinct possibility. A month earlier, shortly after the German invasion of the Low Countries, the Irish police had found intelligence reports, a used parachute, maps, a wireless transmitter and over US$20,000 in a house in the Dublin suburb of Templeogue. The house belonged to a German, Stephen Held. The haul found there, coupled with plans for a German airborne attack on Ireland found by Dutch police on a captured SS officer, deeply alarmed the government. A Cabinet committee on internal security was established in September 1940.

There were certainly many German sympathisers among the general public in Ireland at this period, but few of them were particularly influential. Prominent sympathisers included Iseult Stuart, the daughter of Maude Gonne MacBride, Kathleen Behan's old employer. Iseult Stuart found herself arrested, detained and brought before the Special Criminal Court for aiding, however unwittingly, the German spy Herman Goertz who landed in Ireland in May 1940. On 1 July 1940, the court cleared her of any involvement in intelligence activities. Her husband, the novelist Francis Stuart, had moved to Berlin in 1939 to take up a university post. From there he wrote propaganda broadcasts for transmission to Ireland and his activities were closely monitored by Military Intelligence. There were others, including the diplomat Charles Bewley, who took a more doctrinaire pro-Nazi line. As a result, Bewley was dismissed from the Irish diplomatic service. With the possible exception of Francis Stuart whose connection with the contemporary IRA was limited, most of the better known Irish Nazi sympathisers were not supporters of the IRA. Nonetheless, there can be no doubt that a pro-Nazi faction did exist in the IRA at this time. For the Irish government, this added a new and quite sinister dimension to the threat already posed to internal security by that organisation.

Behan was reasonably well-informed of what had been happening in Ireland during his years in Borstal. On his return home, he was anxious to hear the news in greater detail. He heard with considerable delight from his brother Seán how, in the early months of the War, IRA men successfully blasted their way out of Mountjoy Jail. He was told of a daring IRA raid, just before Christmas 1939, on the Magazine Fort, the Irish army arsenal in Phoenix Park, Dublin. Over a million rounds of ammunition were stolen in a most audacious and cunning manner. Other more alarming news included the arrest and execution of two IRA activists for shooting dead two detectives in Dublin. Hundreds of Republican activists were rounded up for questioning under the Offences Against the State Act. Internees began hunger strikes and before the end of the war the government allowed three of them to die. Six others were executed.

After a round of visits to family and friends, Brendan threw himself back into the IRA cause with renewed fervour. Again, his activities lacked both direction on his part and guidance from his superiors. Cathal Goulding confirms that, after his return to Dublin, Brendan failed to establish solid links with the IRA leadership and that this accounted for his somewhat erratic behaviour.[3]

Irish Military Intelligence, however, took Brendan's terrorist potential seriously. The organisation, known as G2, had opened a file on Brendan while he was still in Borstal in England. The first entry was a note stating that he appeared as a suspected member of the Communist Party of Ireland on a list forwarded to the Garda Síochána[4], the Irish police force, (he was never, in fact, a card carrying member of the CPI.[5]) Within a month of his return, G2 was keeping records of his outgoing telegrams. On Christmas Eve 1941, he sent the following telegram to the Matron at Hollesley Bay, which clearly shows that he continued to think affectionately of many of the people he had left behind in Borstal.

A. Halfpenny, c/o Governor Hollesley Bay

Regards, yourself Padre Mac
Shoemaker Chief Carberry
Ruggerteam Cads Atkinson
Parcel Customs Stopped.

PADDY[6]

He also sent a telegram to his aunt Emily who was still in Aylesbury Jail, Buckinghamshire, wishing her and the other Irish political prisoners with her a happy Christmas.[7]

A G2 memo of 20 March 1942 shows that an informer, known to his controller in Military Intelligence as 'S', was monitoring Brendan's movements. Such sources cannot be considered entirely reliable, although much of 'S's' reporting of Brendan's doings and sayings carries the authentic Behan stamp. 'S' informed Commandant Harrington of G2 that Brendan had recently been in the home of fellow Republican, George Parnell, at 20 North Great George's Street. He was carrying a large suitcase and 'S' saw that it contained '50 detonators, Chloride of Potash, Aluminium powder, Weed

Killer, 23 Fuses, Small cylinder of Gas, Paraffin Wax and revolver ammunition'. He asked Behan if he 'was back on his old methods' and Brendan replied that he was and that he had '8 tons of stuff [explosives] to shift'. 'S' also claimed that he heard Behan discussing the possibility of blowing up the HQ of the Local Defence Force in Dublin. Another memo, dated 28 March, states that 'S' knew Behan and had served with him in England during the bombing campaign. This seems unlikely since we know that Brendan went to Liverpool alone.

The memo describes a public meeting addressed by Brendan at O'Connell Street, on St Patrick's night. Significantly, 'S' told his handler that Brendan had spoken to him of the cleavage in the IRA leadership.

One section was advocating a policy of inaction and the other was anxious for a display of militant activity. Behan had told him that the active section was contemplating seizing the weapons of their more passive colleagues and that he firmly supported that move. The informer says that Brendan advocated reprisals for the execution of George Plant on 5 March. Plant had been convicted of the murder of Michael Devereux, the IRA's quartermaster in Wexford, whom he believed to be a police informer. This was another example of the bitter fissures that were dividing the IRA.

The G2 file contains a transcript of Brendan's speech to the O'Connell Street Republican meeting. It gives a very clear picture of his opinions at this point and shows his firm resolve to remain an active part of the more militant wing of the Republican movement:

> 26 years after Easter Week, Ireland is still part of the British Empire. Today, St Patrick's Day, 1942, you are marching in a Gaelic procession. You are shouting of your loyalty to Ireland. You are protesting that you want to achieve a Gaelic Nation. You say you love Ireland. But do you? If you do, why do you tolerate the Ireland in which you live?
>
> What are the facts? You parade to a Gaelic meeting. You talk of reviving the Irish language, but do you ever stop to consider that a partitioned British Dominion can never revive Irish; can never build a Gaelic Nation. Do you realise that the man who said 'Not merely free but Gaelic as well' died for an Irish Republic, not for a Partitioned Free State. If you stand for Ireland within the Empire, and yet say you want Gaelic culture you are frauds and hypocrites.
>
> Whilst you stand here, talking of reviving the Irish language, over 2000 young men and women are suffering in the jails of England, Northern Ireland, and the so-called Sovereign Independent State of Éire. They are suffering because they stand for more than you.
>
> They stand for Ireland, not merely Gaelic, but free as well. Today

Ireland is partitioned. British and American troops have invaded our territory [Northern Ireland]. The British fifth column is openly showing itself all over Ireland. Young men and women are wearing British emblems. Economic privation is driving our young men and women in thousands into the war industries of England. Hundreds are joining the British Army. What are you doing to stop it?

Only a week or so ago a man who fought for Ireland from 1918 till 1942 was put up against the wall and butchered by the Free State Government. We refer to George Plant. He was murdered because he stood for Irish Freedom. Before him, Paddy McGrath, of Aungier St. was murdered. Thomas Harte of Lurgan was by McGrath's side. Bernard Casey of Longford was murdered in the Curragh Camp. John Joe Kavanagh was shot dead in Cork. Sean McNeela and Anthony Darcy died on hunger strike rather than suffer persecution from the Free State Fianna Fáil butchers. What did you do to stop all this? Are you going to prevent a repetition? ... When are you going to wake up? When are you going to cease fooling yourselves? When are you going to smash British Propaganda? When are you going to achieve the Republic?

We issue this call to you. Continue your work for the Irish language but add to it the work for Irish Independence. Do away with the Free State and Northern Ireland Colonies. Do away with the Free Mason Gang and all the British war mongers. ... Join the IRA and prepare for the day which is approaching when Ireland will again be gripped with the fervour of 1916 and Irish rifles will again spit defiance at Ireland's enemies.

Arise from your knees and stand as free men before the world. Do not any longer cringe as slaves. Take to your hearts the slogan of Pearse, 'Not merely free, but Gaelic as well, not merely GAELIC but FREE as well'. Arm and equip yourselves to meet the British enemy at the barricade so that history cannot say of you that you are the meanest, most slavish, and most cowardly of all Irish generations. LONG LIVE THE REPUBLIC.'[8]

This speech is peppered with the sort of Republican oratorical clichés that Brendan had been exposed to since the cradle, and had perfected in quiet moments at Borstal. It is, however, an accomplished piece of rhetoric, considering that Brendan was only 19 when he made it. More importantly, it shows him aligning himself openly with the most militant wing of the IRA. His tragedy was that this wing of the movement did not take him seriously. His mother recalled him saying that the IRA leadership suspected him of being a Communist. Although he would not have been alone amongst IRA men in holding that political outlook, it certainly damaged his credibility in the eyes of the movement's militant leaders.[9]

Brendan is also said to have belonged to the pro-German school of IRA thought. That this is in direct contradiction to his statements to Joyce during his time at Hollesley Bay is not necessarily conclusive evidence that reports of Behan's pro-Nazi sympathies are untrue. However, the real weight of his position regarding Hitler's rise to power is probably best measured in a remark made by the poet, Máirtín Ó Cadháin. He said that in political debates in the Curragh detention camp, where he was imprisoned with Brendan in 1944, there were three factions – those who were pro-Hitler, those who were against him, and Brendan Behan.[10]

G2's director, Colonel Dan Bryan, kept a particularly close watch on the activities and opinions of the pro-Nazi element in the IRA. If the nineteen-year-old Brendan had ever been known to have spouted pro-Nazi opinions, G2 did not think them worth recording.

On 5 April 1942, Brendan committed the most reckless act of his IRA years – the attempted shooting of two policemen. The desperate piece of bravado was an ill thought-out attempt to prove himself to his peers. The shooting confirmed the leadership's view of him as a loose cannon and had terrible repercussions for his own life. A combination of factors triggered this act of folly. He was disappointed that he had not been acclaimed as a hero on his return to Ireland. His positive sentiments about his Borstal experiences, the reduction of his sentence for good behaviour, and his new inability to detest the English race *en masse* caused disturbing personal doubts about his commitment to the Republican cause. His inner agitation came to a head on Easter Sunday when he assembled with IRA colleagues at St Stephen's Green to march in a parade for the annual commemoration of the 1916 insurrection. It was an occasion attended by a range of Republican groups. Their destination was Glasnevin Cemetery, pantheon of Irish Republican heroes and the place where James Joyce set the 'Hades' episode in *Ulysses*. The turn-out of IRA members was disappointingly small. Brendan lined up in a group of thirty to forty for the march to Glasnevin.

The events that followed changed the course of his life. Behan has left a highly unreliable and romanticised account of them in *Confessions of an Irish Rebel*. The oral myth of Behan in Dublin has further contributed to the confusion about the details of the day and its immediate aftermath.[11]

The police had kept a close watch on the marchers following their departure from St Stephen's Green. Brendan had observed the police earlier and sensed that a confrontation was likely. 'I looked around and saw the squad cars and inside them sets of fugh-faced bastards intent on nothing less than grievous bodily harm'.[12] The actual intention of the police was to attempt to disarm and arrest known IRA members. Behan, one of the least senior of the IRA men present, was not the focus of their attention that day. They were more interested in Lazarian Mangan, Andrew Nathan and Joseph Buckley – all of whom, though approximately the same age as Brendan, were senior to him in the IRA. They knew Mangan and Nathan to be armed and also believed that Buckley was also carrying a gun (it was later discovered that Buckley was carrying only six rounds of ammunition). It was not until after midday, when the graveyard ceremony was over, that the police began to move in. The crowds were departing along Finglas Road when armed officers descended on the IRA marchers to arrest Mangan and Nathan.

Brendan would later describe the general hysteria that exploded on Finglas Road, with both the police and IRA men shouting wildly. According to him, he was the only one present who remained calm. In reality, the opposite seems to have been the case. Mangan managed to get out of the grip of the police and produced a revolver from his raincoat. He took aim but hesitated to fire. Behan then came running towards him in an excited state and repeated the words 'Use it, use it'. When that had no effect he shouted, 'Give it to me and I will shoot the bastards'. Mangan, losing his nerve, threw him the gun. Brendan stripped off his jacket and waistcoat and backed off towards de Courcey Square, while firing two shots at officers Martin Hanrahan and Patrick Kirwan. He was approximately fourteen yards from his targets but missed them both. The police returned fire, but were hampered by their reluctance to harm the crowd of innocent civilians, which included several children. Behan fired one more shot before escaping through the crowds.

Considering the incidents of serious violence involving the police and the IRA that occurred so frequently during these years, the skirmish on the Finglas Road amounted to a fairly minor incident. For Brendan, however, his impetuous behaviour could have had the most serious consequences. He was lucky not to have been shot down on the spot or sentenced to death by the Special Criminal Court. In later life, he described the brief exhilaration of those minutes on Finglas Road: 'short and sweet like an ass's gallop but in those few moments I lived a full life's span, and in the years that followed I was never to forget them'.[13]

The few days between his escape from Glasnevin and his arrest by the police on 10 April were intense and crammed with incident. In his *Confessions of an Irish Rebel*, Brendan refers to a companion on his escape, whom he names 'Cafferty'.[14] As in so much of his writing, the truth of his account comes into question here. IRA sources consulted for this book maintain that he made his escape alone. After the shooting, he evaded the police by jumping over the garden wall of a house not far from the scene of the incident. He crouched in the shrubbery while attempting to regain his composure and work out the next move. Behan recalled how frightened he was:

> My hands were trembling, and I would have liked to see if my voice was still with me but I knew the effort of holding my breath to stop my stammer would have made me nearly pass out in a weakness.
> It was about one o'clock in the afternoon and winter had made way for spring.[15]

The back door to the house was open. He entered only to be confronted by the owner who resisted his attempts to bully him and his family. The householder insisted that he would not have his wife and children frightened by a 'gun touting pup'. Behan later wrote of the guilt he felt about disturbing the lives of this quiet, suburban family. A daughter of the house, who seems to have had Republican sympathies, saved the situation. She calmly led him out through a side entrance to Glasnevin Cemetery. Before they parted, the girl gave him cigarettes and chocolate, a gesture that touched Brendan.

> And I nearly fell out of my standing, for this girl handed us two packets of cigarettes, a box of matches and several bars of chocolate, which shows a kindness and an understanding that you'd not be meeting every day. I felt the lump come up in my throat, swallowed back hard, for I am not a hard man and these things touch me.[16]

During that Sunday afternoon, the fugitive hid out in a cornfield awaiting the cover of nightfall. Making his way through the suburbs of Dublin next day, Behan spotted a pitch-and-toss game, a popular form of street gambling. He chanced his luck before deciding to make his own by removing the entire 'pot' at gun point. By early evening, the ill-gotten gains were spent in Belton's pub in Santry.

> The bells out in the city rang a quarter past seven, and I knew the pubs would be closing soon for the day, such were the licensing laws in Ireland at the time. However we felt our standard of living had gone up with a bang, and we had another smoke and finished off the chocolate when I remembered some relations of mine who were living nearby and who might be persuaded to help us to the tune of some clothing at any rate.[17]

Fortified with several rounds of drink, Behan made his way to the house of his aunt, Maggie Bourke, in Iveleary Road, Whitehall. There he was fed and was given a cap to conceal his shock of curly hair. When he insisted on showing his cousin Patsy his revolver, his aunt asked him to leave. Later that evening, he pitched up at the home of another aunt, Maura Slater, where he received a rather cold reception.

Brendan then made his way to the Northside slum flat of a family friend, where he got a bed on the floor. He read the *Sunday Independent* before falling into a deep sleep. When he awoke on Monday morning, he found he was one of the main news items on the radio news bulletins.

Brendan spent much of Monday 6 April wandering gingerly around his old stomping ground of the north city slums. He spent part of the day at 20 North Great George's Street, the home of George Parnell, his old friend from Fianna days. The house was known both to Military Intelligence and the Special Branch. Behan's decision to stop off there nearly proved to be his undoing. Special Branch officers raided the house late on Monday afternoon, but he managed to get away through the coach house at the rear of the building.

The next sighting the police had of him was on Thursday 9 April, when they spotted him at Parnell Square, not far from where he had had his narrow escape on the previous Monday. Luck was with him again. When the detectives moved to arrest him with revolvers cocked, a group of school children got in the way, thus foiling their efforts. It was to be Brendan's last day of freedom. He holed up in houses in Hollybank Road, Drumcondra and in a house in Blessington Street[18], which was near his old family home in Russell Street.

Again, Behan's account of his capture is very unreliable. He maintained that he was taken by surprise in his bed at his Blessington Street hideout.

> The door flew open as if the devil himself was behind it, and a lot of mean-faced bastards grabbed me as I made for the window. I was treated to a piece of verbal abuse by Gantly and his minions, but I was not physically assaulted as I had been in Liverpool when I was last arrested. One of the detective officers slipped me a packet of cigarettes and a box of matches, some would say for to soften me up to give information, but I am always prepared to look upon these things as manifestations of human charity. They searched me, putting their hands along the seams of my trousers where they found the gun.
> 'You wouldn't have come in here so shagging easy,' I said, 'if I had the time to use it.'[19]

His claim that he was still armed is one of the more outrageously untruthful statements in his account of his escape and arrest. The police report on his arrest records that he was unarmed and Ulick O'Connor has clearly established that two of his IRA colleagues, George Dempsey and Ultan O'Neill, had removed his revolver on 8 April. That his colleagues saw fit to disarm him gives credence to the view that, within the IRA, his rash nature was seen as the very antithesis of what was expected of a reliable Volunteer.

In fact, he was not arrested indoors, but on Blessington Street where he was out taking a stroll. The arresting officer was a Detective Doran, assisted by a Detective Donegan and not, as Brendan has claimed, Chief-Inspector Gantly of the Special Branch. This error might be explained by the fact that Brendan developed something of an obsession with Gantly, whom he later heard had wanted him shot on sight. In truth, Gantly had no special interest in the case of Brendan Behan. His attitude towards him was no more malign than the feelings he held for any IRA man who shot at his officers. It was general knowledge at the time that the police did not hesitate to shoot IRA men who shot at them during an attempted arrest.

According to Cathal Goulding, it was Brendan's father who approached the IRA and asked them to remove his gun; he believed that his son stood a better chance of being taken alive if he was unarmed.[20] Seamus Behan recalls that his father, who no longer identified with the contemporary IRA, acted quickly to ensure that Brendan would not be shot by the Special Branch. Stephen had shared a cell in Kilmainham Jail with Seán T. O'Kelly, later to become Minister for Finance in de Valera's government.[21] It was to their cell window that the young Brendan was held up by his mother in February 1923. Now Stephen went to O'Kelly's Dublin house to call in a favour from his old friend. The Minister acted quickly to make sure that, if it was at all possible, Brendan should be taken alive. Stephen also called on the Minister for Defence, Oscar Traynor, and made a similar plea to him.[22] There could, of course, be no guarantee that this action would afford sufficient protection to his son. The police did not know that he was unarmed. They were aware of Brendan's trigger-happy disposition. They knew that it was IRA policy in such situations to go out with all guns blazing, shooting as many of the arresting officers as possible.

Brendan's claim that he was willing to engage in a shoot-out with the arresting officers fits in with his behaviour throughout this whole incident. However, he lacked the physical means to sustain a dramatic ending to his ordeal. In the end, Brendan's capture was a rather calm affair. He was approached in the street, overpowered, and went quietly with the arresting officers.

In the Behan pub mythology, the whole Glasnevin episode has often been laughed off as nothing more than a wild and Behanesque escapade. Jokes are made about his inability to handle a gun and it has also been claimed, even by Behan himself, that he was drunk at the time.

The stark reality of the whole affair is that in the dark mood of the times in Ireland, he very narrowly escaped with his life at Glasnevin and during his period on the run. As we shall see, he was also fortunate when he appeared before the Military Tribunal.

After his arrest on 10 April, Brendan was taken into police custody, where he was charged and detained overnight. In the loneliness of his detention cell he confronted the seriousness of his position. There he was, in the city of his birth, detained not by the traditional enemy but by his fellow countrymen and facing a possible sentence of death. The following day he was transferred to the 'C' wing of Mountjoy Jail, where he was held while awaiting trial. The Special Criminal Court fixed the date of his trial for 24 April.[23] In the meantime, the waiting battered his bare nerves. 'All I could do with the sickness in my stomach was to lean over the side of the bed and wish that the waiting would end. Except, God look down on you, it could be the end.'[24]

The Special Criminal Court sat in a rather grim upstairs room at Collins' Barracks. Three officers, seated on a raised dais, their caps and dress swords placed on a wooden table before them, passed judgement on the belligerent young men and women hauled before them. IRA policy was to refuse to recognise the jurisdiction of this court. Tony Gray, then a young reporter, covered the court for *The Irish Times*.

> There was usually a scuffle as the young men in mackintoshes were dragged in, and usually another scuffle as they were hauled out, some to be shot, more to be interned or imprisoned, but it was a doddle for the reporters because the prisoners did not attempt to defend themselves or offer any evidence beyond a formal statement, usually in Irish, to the effect that they did not recognise the competence of the court to try them. I'm ashamed to admit that it didn't impinge on me at the time that these men were motivated by the same ideals as all the patriots who had gone before them and that their sacrifice, sealed in that dreary, dusty upstairs room now renamed after Michael Collins, was every bit as significant, from their own point of view, as Patrick Pearse's or Robert Emmet's.[25]

Col. John Joyce, known to the IRA as 'Hangman Joyce', and two other officers presided over Brendan's case. R.J. Feely, the Commandant Registrar of the Court, recorded the proceedings. The charge was the attempted murder of Detective Guards Martin Hanrahan and Patrick Kirwan and the possession of firearms. Nathan, Mangan and Buckley were tried at the same time on charges of possession of firearms and ammunition, membership of an illegal organisation and possession of incriminating documents. M.D. Murnaghan, Barrister-at-Law (instructed by the Chief State Solicitor) prosecuted. Various Detective Guards gave evidence to confirm the case for the prosecution. Shortly before his death, Behan recalled that moment:

> The police told their story and, with one exception, told it without any venom, and I reflected on the sadness of Irishmen fighting Irishmen or men fighting women or women fighting anywhere, because at heart I'm a pacifist.[26]

Since Behan refused to recognise the Court, it entered a plea of 'Not Guilty' on his behalf. Before sentencing, Col. Joyce asked him if he had anything to say. He decided to use much the same statement he had delivered to the judge at Liverpool. Joyce, who had heard many such statements, though perhaps few as well-delivered as Behan's, remained impassive. He sentenced him to fourteen years penal servitude. Mangan, Nathan and Buckley received lesser sentences. Behan was deeply shocked as he heard the reality of that sentence delivered in the tiny, makeshift court room.

> My guts twisted up inside of me and I could feel the stomach muscles snarl and stiffen. Fourteen years' penal servitude ... That the devil may choke you and the Republic, but leave me out of the shouting for the cause all on my own.[27]

Characteristically, it struck him as quite unfair that he should have received the heaviest sentence. It is difficult to fathom exactly what he meant when he said that of the four involved in the Glasnevin incident, he was 'the least guilty in the eyes of the Irish Republic.'[28] It was he, after all, who took the lead in shooting at the police. The most likely explanation for the remark must be that, twenty years later, he believed that the impulsive nature of his act deserved lenient treatment.

After the conclusion of the trial, he found his mother waiting outside the courtroom with the mothers of some of the other boys. As he struggled to give her his hand he tried to speak but for once words failed him. Kathleen Behan was left in tears as he ran down the steps and into a waiting prison van, which took him to Mountjoy Jail.

Mountjoy Jail

Mountjoy Jail is one of the holy places of Republican martyrdom. Generations of participants in the struggle for Irish freedom were incarcerated there. As the Black Maria sped towards it, taking him back to imprisonment after such brief liberty, Brendan comported himself in characteristically extrovert fashion. He peered through the ventilation slits of the van and gave his fellow prisoners an upbeat running commentary: 'We're going past the Plaza now, the picture house,' on their whereabouts. He kept up his patter as the unhappy bunch made their way up Blessington Street, round Berkeley Road and down the North Circular Road to the gates of the jail.

The new arrivals lined up in the prison yard under the scrutiny of officers and inmates. Brendan gave his name to a warder, who wrote in the Convict Register that he was 19 years of age, 5 feet 7 1/2 inches tall, had blue eyes, dark brown hair, a fresh complexion and that his 'make' was proportional. His religion was recorded as Roman Catholic, his profession as 'painter'. The entry stated that he could read and write. His convict number was F662. The report of the Medical Officer who examined him on admission shows that his general health was good. The doctor recommended that because he was 'a growing youth' he was to be allowed extra daily rations of half a pound of bread and half an ounce of jam.[1] The new prisoners were dispatched to the bath house. Brendan was very proud of his physical appearance at this time. He was a strikingly handsome and fit young man.

> I felt good after the bath and holding the towel away, I looked down at myself. Jesus, it must be a terrible thing to get old, I thought, with bent old legs and twisted buniony toes, and the crinkle in my belly would straighten out in this kip without the aid of porter, for it was the drink that did the most damage.[2]

He was assigned to a cell in 'B' wing, as were Nathan and Mangan. On his way there, he surveyed his surroundings. He noted the steel galleries where warders stood sentry and, towards the bottom of 'D' wing, a red metal door with a barred gate covering it. This was the door to the hang-house that was to become so potent a motif in *The Quare Fellow*, the work that brought him international fame.

The oppressive reality of his situation hit him when his cell door slammed behind him. Half of the cell window was below ground level. Its dim light revealed the maudlin iconography that almost obliterated the fading whitewash of the walls – the usual inscriptions of undying love for some girlfriend or wife, indecipherable names and entwined hearts. He walked the ten paces that the room's length afforded and contemplated the amount of exercise he might get if he did this for the next 14 years.

Soon after his arrival, Brendan wrote a defiant note to a fellow Republican inmate, Jim Savage. It was the sort of note IRA prisoners wrote to bolster morale:

> 15 April 1942
> Red Front![3]
>
> Brendan Behan 3501 H. M. Prison Liverpool 1939-41[4]. Re-arrested Mountjoy Prison. Attempted murder (amongst other things) of Broy Harriers 5th April '42. 'The great only appear so because we are on our knees. Let us rise.' J. Connolly.
>
> Brendán Ó Beacháin
> Dublin

Brendan's 'tough guy' reputation preceded his arrival at Mountjoy. He came under particularly close scrutiny from the prison warders, who expected this twice-convicted young terrorist to give considerable trouble. So, initially, did the governor, Seán Kavanagh. But in fact, as Kavanagh later recalled that Brendan in person produced a very different impression:

> ... meeting this mild-mannered boy gave one a feeling of anti-climax; surely this was no desperado, no trigger-happy gunman. Even the fact that a sentence of fourteen years' penal servitude was imposed on him ... by the Special Criminal Court for attempted murder did not lessen this feeling. The better one grew to know him the more the impression grew that basically he was a very gentle person who in his senses would not hurt a fly.[5]

The recollections of fellow prisoners and prison records, which show that on the whole he was a well-behaved prisoner, support Kavanagh's view. Again, he fell in easily with the daily grind of prison routine. It is one of the paradoxes of his life that this anarchic individual, whose behaviour was so notoriously uncontrolled and impulsive while at liberty, was able to deal so well with the regimented institutionalism of prison existence. One explanation of this apparent contradiction must surely lie in his unusually-developed social skills, his desire to charm, and his power to enlist the sympathies not just of his fellow inmates but of those in authority over him. It was that very vitality that marked him out from the other prisoners in Mountjoy. To his jailers and his fellow prisoners, he seemed to possess an irrepressible spirit. 'It was in those days that we who lived with Brendan came to know the real loveable character that he was', recalled Seán Ó Briain, an Irish language scholar interned for IRA activities at the same time as Brendan. 'He was at his best in those years, and I can affirm that he did not need drink or fame to make him a fine character and a fine writer. Day by day we "punched in our time" – there was no complaining or no whining.'[6]

The regime at Mountjoy differed little from Brendan's experience in English jails except that, since in Ireland he was considered a political prisoner, he had certain privileges not available to the common criminal. For example, he had the dignity of wearing his own clothing and greater freedom of association. Of more importance to his emotional resilience, however, was the sense of special status that he derived from belonging to the fraternity of Republican prisoners. The IRA prison brotherhood, at least in this early stage of his imprisonment, made him feel part of a prison aristocracy.

The government had come under intense pressure to move the IRA prisoners from Mountjoy. Josephine Mary Plunkett, mother of executed 1916 leader, Joseph Mary Plunkett, wrote to Cardinal McRory, seeking his support for the removal of the IRA men from a jail 'where sexual degenerates are also imprisoned.'[7] As a writer, however, Behan was to benefit greatly from this opportunity to mix freely with the type of prisoner from whom Mrs Plunkett wished to protect him. When he came to write *The Quare Fellow* his fellow Mountjoy inmates proved an invaluable source of inspiration. 'I have nothing against criminals', he wrote, 'except every criminal I know is a Tory and a bore.'[8]

IRA prisoners occupied an ambivalent position. It was only just over 20 years since the organisation had played a vital role in securing Irish independence. Now, the government found itself in the uncomfortable position of treating men who formerly would have been hailed as national heroes as enemies of the State.

Through his family, political internee F662 was closely connected to the national legend of the Republican movement's heroic past. His uncle, Peadar

Kearney, wrote the lyrics of *The Soldier's Song,* which became the Irish national anthem. On 24 November 1942, Brendan learnt from Governor Kavanagh that his uncle had died. He immediately applied for parole to attend his funeral. On 25 November, he wrote to his cousin, Pearse, Peadar's eldest son:

Mountjoy Jail
Dublin
25 11 '42

A Phiarais, a Chara Dhílis,[9]
Yesterday morning the Governor told me the news that at six o'clock that morning my Uncle Peadar died – needless to say it came as a very great shock to me – and a great blow. I know that it has been a terrible sorrow to yourself, Aunt Eva and Con.[10] I would be pleased if you would besides accepting this token of my most sincere sympathy yourself, convey to Aunt Eva & Con my condolences. It would be presumption on my part were I to compare the deep sorrow uncle Peadar's death caused me to the devastating blow that it was to Aunt Eva, & to you and Con, who had lost your father.
But I know that you will understand that I have lost a very dear friend – merely being my uncle would not have caused the deep affection in which I held him – after all you choose your friends but you can't help your relations – But my uncle Peadar was the one, outside my own parents, who excited the admiration and love that is friendship. I tell you this so that you may understand this is not merely the usual and conventional expressions of sympathy from a relative.
True I was proud that the same blood ran in our veins – the proudest moment of my varied existence was on Christmas Night 1939 when in the stillness of an English prison, after a night in which the Christian doctrine of Peace & Goodwill was battered into Irish heads with truncheons, an Irish voice rang out in defiance – 'You may laugh in your castles and hovels' – it was a soldier of the Royal Engineers reciting Peadar Kearney's *To England.*[11] ... I have written a rather poor tribute to one who will forever rank as a National Poet and I thought you might like to have a look at it so I enclose a copy. I have applied to the Government for parole to attend the funeral – so far I have received no reply – if I am not allowed to attend it please tell my mother that I will write next week.[12]

In his letter to Gerry Boland, the Minister for Justice, he asked to attend the funeral of uncle and 'very dear friend'. The Minister knew Kearney personally. He also knew that Peadar Kearney fought alongside Thomas MacDonagh during the 1916 Rebellion and that he had been interned during the War of Independence. Although his uncle was such a distinguished Republican figure, Brendan was not granted parole for his funeral. Gerry Boland was later said to have claimed that he 'wouldn't allow Brendan Behan out on a chain'.[13]

The elegy to his uncle that Brendan sent along with his letter to his cousin may have lacked the accomplishment of later poems. It is in the poetic tradition of laments for dead Republican heroes. If there is an echo of anything more substantial, it is of Yeats's roll-call of nationalist dead in *To Ireland In The Coming Times*.

Peadar O'Cearnaigh

The voice that spoke so clear for you is silenced
His praising song is stilled, your squire of words
Has fled the sweet yoke of your service,
Muted his harp and scabbarded his sword.

The blood that ran red-hot in Easter's gladness
In the fiery veins of blazing youth is chilled
No more that loving heart beats for you,
His eyes, their tender glance is dimmed.

In the company of your lovers long departed,
Sweet patterns of your praising are being woven
With Donncad Ruad, Mangan, Rooney, Davis,[14]
He's singing still the graces of his love.

Despite the sadness of missing his favourite uncle's funeral, Brendan received consolation throughout his imprisonment from the outstanding support he got from family and friends on the outside. Between 27 April 1942 and 3 September 1946, he received 82 visits and on some of those visits up to three people attended. His brothers, his mother, and his father visited regularly, as did his cousins and friends.[15] While in prison, Brendan also attracted a remarkable level of encouragement from the wide spectrum of influential people whose sympathy and admiration he had gained in his teenage years. C.A. Joyce, the former Governor of Hollesley Bay, did not forget his favourite charge despite his recidivism. Early in the New Year of 1943 Brendan received a letter from him. He had sent a New Year's card to Joyce informing him of the circumstances of his arrest and detention in Dublin. Joyce wrote to the Governor of Mountjoy enclosing a letter for Brendan.

The Cotswold School
Ashton Keynes
Nr. Swindon
Wilts.
5 Jan 1943.

Dear Sir,
Re. Brendon [sic] Behan

I received a New Year's card from the above-named man and the enclosed reply is submitted for issue to him, if you approve please.

May I explain that my own connection lies in the fact that until a year ago I was Governor of Hollesley Bay Colony Borstal Institution, in which Behan was serving a sentence of three years B.D.[16]

I had no knowledge of the fact that he had been re-convicted but in his card he informs me that he was sentenced to fourteen years P.S.[17] by a Military Court last April.

I should be grateful to know whether he is allowed the letter and the photographs enclosed.

Yours faithfully,
C.A. Joyce
Headmaster. [18]

Brendan's most exotic supporter was composer Frederick May, Musical Director at the Abbey Theatre, who was one of his earliest visitors. May, who was 12 years older, had befriended him when he was 15. He remained one of his most loyal and devoted friends. A highly intelligent and sensitive man, Freddie May was homosexual. His almost obsessive devotion to Brendan at this time is just one indication that he was in love with him.[19] Brendan felt unable to fully return his love but he did feel a strong sense of friendship and loyalty. The relationship would never be what Freddie May wanted it to be but, after his release, Brendan did allow limited sexual contact to take place. 'After all', he was to tell a friend of Freddie's. 'It's only sex'.[20]

To the prison authorities and the Minister for Justice, whom May petitioned for Brendan's release just six months after he had been sentenced to 14 years penal servitude, this friendship must have seemed quite odd to say the least. As Musical Director of the Abbey, Freddie May was well-known in Dublin society. He was educated at Trinity College Dublin, in London and Vienna and his 1936 composition, *String Quartet in C Minor* brought him international acclaim. The bearing of this highly intelligent aesthete, with his exquisite manners, finely-tailored clothes and habitual white cotton gloves, could not have failed to make a striking spectacle against the grim background of prison visiting facilities.

May remained Behan's most regular correspondent and visitor during his confinement. On 15 October 1942, he made what must have appeared a very strange request to the Governor of Mountjoy. He wrote from his home, 38 Marlborough Road, Donnybrook, asking the Governor to release Behan for a day, so that he could attend a concert in the Olympia Theatre, where a new work of his was being played. Freddie May's infatuation with Brendan appears to have been strong enough to blind him to the most basic realities of his friend's position. He couched his letter to the Governor in language suited to an invitation to a vicarage tea party:

> A Chara,
> I should be most deeply obliged to you if you would have the extreme kindness to set certain necessary machinery in motion with the object of securing the release on parole of Brendan Behan for the afternoon of Sunday, November 1st.
> I wish you to do this so that he may attend the final Oireachtas concert, to be given on that afternoon in the Olympia, and at which a piece of mine, entitled *Scherzo* will be performed.
> I may add that we intend engaging a box or two into which we hope to fit Brendan (DV) and, if at the same time you and your wife cared to come along too, we should feel highly honoured.
>
> Mise, le meas,
>
> Fred. May.[21]

The notion that a prisoner convicted of attempted murder might join the Governor of Mountjoy, his wife and the composer for an evening of musical entertainment seemed scarcely credible to the Assistant Secretary of the Department of Justice, Peter Berry.[22] He did, however, pass the request on to the police authorities who naturally refused parole.

Despite this disappointment, Freddie May pursued his relentless efforts to have Brendan's sentence mitigated. Just after Christmas 1942, Brendan wrote to the Minister for Justice seeking authorisation for a special open visit from May. He wanted to be able to discuss the composer's efforts to have his sentence lightened out of the hearing range of prison officials.

Mountjoy Prison
29/12/42.

A dhuine uasal,
I wish to make application to receive a special open visit from my friend
Frederick M. May, 38 Marlboro [sic] Road Donnybrook. May has
been interesting himself in seeking a mitigation of the sentence
imposed on me and has had an interview with Chief Superintendent
Sean Gantly of the Special Detective Branch regarding my case. He
feels that it would be as well if the conversations could be
communicated to me and as he is slightly deaf (left ear almost totally
so) and other ordinary visits were found to be unsatisfactory, that it
would be almost impossible to transact this important business on an
ordinary visit. I may also add that May is not in sympathy with or has
any connection with any illegal organisation and that his only interest
in this business is an interest in my welfare. He is a member of the
Local Defence Force and is a man of impeccable character. I trust that
you will understand that this application has been made only because I
believe the matter to be discussed at this visit is of the highest
importance (to me) and that it would be quite inexpedient to discuss it
by letter.

Is mise,

Brendan Behan.[23]

Freddie May's efforts, while touching as a display of loyalty to a friend, can
only be seen as naïve in the extreme. To visit Chief Superintendent Gantly
and attempt to set the official wheels moving to have the sentence reduced was
a triumph of hope over desperation. It was not rewarded. Peter Berry of the
Department of Justice scribbled a note on Brendan's letter that reads: 'No
matter what Mr. May has to say, Behan will not get out'. On 30 December,
permission for the open visit with May was refused and Brendan settled down
to what he then thought would be another thirteen years in jail. In *Confessions
of an Irish Rebel* he captures the sense of the passing seasons marking time:

Now the days began to shorten and the autumn got weaker and weaker
and then beaten into winter and there was an awful east wind that was
up around the jail and we were on our way to Christmas. Instead of
embroidery, now, the fellows were making Christmas cards, but I
didn't have anything to do with it as I was too busy reading and

smoking and having an occasional drink, by the courtesy of a warder
who made a few pennies shopping in drink and cigarettes and shopping
out letters, until he was caught and given his cards.[24]

If Freddie May's main interest in Brendan's release was personal, his two
other major champions among Dublin's literary élite were more concerned
about the future of his literary talent. Brendan had attracted the attention of
Peadar O'Donnell, the Republican socialist and a writer of repute. He had
first met Brendan in 1937 when, together with Frank Ryan, he was organising
volunteers and supplies for the International Brigade for Spain. It was
O'Donnell who first suggested to Seán O'Faoláin, then editor of Ireland's
most distinguished literary periodical *The Bell*, that he should look at Behan's
writings for possible publication. O'Faoláin, the short story writer, novelist,
and biographer, had just brought out *The Great O'Neill* (Hugh O'Neill was the
author of a seventeenth-century rebellion against English power in Ireland
and much admired by Brendan). O'Faoláin took the Republican side during
the Civil War and became Director of Propaganda for the First Southern
Division of the IRA. He was the sort of man who would have had every
sympathy for a Republican prisoner seeking to advance his career as a writer.

These two men, internationally renowned, and deities of Irish literature at
home, applied all their influence in a sustained but very partially successful
campaign to persuade the authorities to allow publication of Behan's writing
during his incarceration.

That two such distinguished men of letters should take such passionate
interest in the writings of a boy who, before his arrest in 1941, had published
little of outstanding merit might seem unlikely. However, the men shared a
strong Republican idealism with Brendan, (O'Donnell himself was in
Mountjoy during the Civil War). Both men knew Behan's father, Stephen,
and his uncle Peadar Kearney. Brendan's writings for the *Fianna* magazine
had already given him claim to be a writer for the cause. Most importantly,
O'Faoláin had already seen Brendan's *I Become A Borstal Boy*, the
autobiographical account that developed into his much later novel *Borstal Boy*.
Started in 1941, this was Brendan's finest piece of writing to date. O'Faoláin
printed it in *The Bell* in June 1942, two months after Behan's arrest. It was the
first time he received payment for his literary work.[25]

Encouraged by the interest of his literary seniors, and eager to benefit from
Seán O'Faoláin's critical evaluation of his writing, Brendan made a written
application to the governor for permission to write and send out work for
publication from prison. His first request was made on 18 August 1942:

Mountjoy Prison
18 August 1942.

A dhuine uasal,
I wish to apply for permission to write and publish from this place
articles, short stories etc. Mr Seán O'Faoláin, the well-known writer
has expressed his willingness to accept material from me and to place
any articles I may write with various editions.
I agree to accept any conditions laid down by the Department of Justice
in this (as for instance, if it be expedient to write under a pseudonym).
You will appreciate that it is not my intention to send out material of
political colouring. Quite apart from the financial aspect (and this too
is of some importance!) you will no doubt understand that it would be
a means of keeping my mind fresh and keen and would also give me an
added interest and perhaps the feeling, in later life, that my period of
detention was not altogether misspent.

Is mise,
Brendan Behan.[26]

The governor recommended to the Department of Justice that Behan's
request be granted. On 25 August, a memo from the Department informed
the governor that Behan was free to write and send his novelist manuscripts
out on condition that they went through the governor's office and thence to
the Department for further evaluation and censorship.

Behan felt he could now begin to perfect his craft, assured that his work
would benefit from the critical judgement of one of Ireland's most
accomplished writers and that it stood a good chance of being published. We
have a clear picture of his writing methods at this time from a description left
by his friend and fellow internee, the Kerry school-teacher, Seán Ó Briain. He
remembered him writing a great deal in prison. Lying on his bed with a
blanket wrapped around him he would finish a page, dispatch it into the air
and let it land where it might. He rarely bothered to collate the finished pages
and Ó Briain often did this task for him.[27]

Just days after he received authorisation to send his writings out, Behan
began to submit manuscripts to the governor for approval by the Department
of Justice. Memos show that the Minister for Justice saw all of Behan's
manuscripts sent to the Department for review.

Gerry Boland was a veteran of the 1916 Uprising and a long time associate
of de Valera's. As Justice Minister from 1939-1948, he implemented the
stringent legislation introduced during this period with the aim of crushing

the IRA. If de Valera's resolve on the matter needed bracing, it was Gerry Boland who had the steel to brace it. He was unlikely to take a sympathetic view of the literary aspirations of an IRA man convicted of the attempted murder of two of his police officers. For Boland, the essential issue was the preservation of the legitimacy of the state he helped found. Taking a lenient approach to people like Brendan Behan was not high on his priority list. Furthermore, he is not likely to have welcomed the chore of acting as censor to a bombardment of literary efforts by a nineteen-year-old, whatever their worth.

On 28 August, Governor Kavanagh handed over an unknown number of Behan manuscripts for approval by Boland. Three days later, on 31 August, he submitted a further quantity of manuscripts. On 9 September, the Justice Department informed Kavanagh that, having examined the works, they would sanction their publication. On 25 September, Kavanagh presented more manuscripts to the department. On 10 October, the Justice Department rescinded its permission for Behan to publish altogether. He was, however, allowed to continue his writing.[28] His manuscripts were returned to him, but his request for a reason for the Department's refusal to allow publication went unanswered.

Unfortunately, these early memoranda give no description of the works and there is no other record of their nature and content. The original manuscripts returned to Brendan at Mountjoy have not survived.

Despite his early indications of support, Governor Kavanagh did little to promote Brendan's urgent wish to appear in print. Kavanagh, an ex-Republican prisoner himself, liked Behan from the moment he met him, but his relationship with him was never to be as close as that which he enjoyed with Governor Joyce at Hollesley Bay. Just over a month after advising Boland that Behan should be allowed to publish his work, Kavanagh changed his mind on the matter. If Boland had even the slightest doubt about what to do with Behan's writings, his decision might have been influenced by Kavanagh's advice. Before finally withdrawing authorisation for the publication of the work, Boland consulted Kavanagh, who warned him that any further writings by Behan let out for publication would carry the tacit approval of the authorities. He advised the Minister that the privilege should be withdrawn altogether.[29] Had the governor fought Behan's corner a little more stoutly, even as uncompromising a man as Boland might have relented. Governor Kavanagh later wrote that when Brendan looked for facilities for his writing he gave him all the help he could.[30] He certainly provided the physical tools necessary for writing, but he took the mistrustful official line when it came to the possibility of the work appearing in print.

Of Behan's Mountjoy writings, only four manuscripts or recorded descriptions remain, namely: three short stories and a play. One story, The Green Invaders[31], a highly autobiographical piece, tells the story of an IRA volunteer being sent to England to take part in the bombing campaign. It includes character portraits of men such as the IRA boss Seán Russell. Brendan had plans for developing it into a novel, but it has not been found in either form.

The eponymous heroine of another short story, 'Tasharoon Kate', is witness to a bombing in England but refuses to identify those involved. One of the bombers is the brother of a nun who is rearing Kate's child in Ireland. These two stories have been lost and the details survive only as short accounts of their content contained in a memo in Behan's G2 file. Both the stories share the subject matter of the IRA's 1939 bombing campaign in which Behan had played a part, however questionable the wisdom and effectiveness of his actions. In a letter to his friend, Bob Bradshaw, he said:

> Then of course since I was sixteen all but a few months I've been in jails and Borstal Institutions. I don't regret my time in England. (IRA prisoners in Ireland I've discovered are an uninteresting and boring lot.) It provided me with material for a book on Borstal which I'll get fixed up after the war and with material for numberless short stories, one of which, 'Borstal Day', you may borrow from Seán[32] ... I had some other stuff I'd like you to have seen. Some short stories about the '39 campaign and the beginning of a long novel I'm doing on it, title 'The Green Invaders'.
>
> Traynor, Adams[33] etc, have apparently accepted me as a sort of official historian of it and it's with their assistance I'm doing it. (I mean in the line of verifying facts, etc. – the impressions noted and conclusions drawn will of course be mine.)[34]

Those impressions and conclusions appeared to make little impact on the official in Military Intelligence who examined them for possible subversive content. A note appended to the description of the stories states that if published 'they would do more discredit to the IRA than anything else'.[35]

Despite his description of himself as an 'official historian' of the IRA, a third, surviving short story from the Mountjoy period shows that Behan's literary talent was already driven by something more than the desire to propagate the doctrinaire views of Militant Republicanism. The G2 official logged this tale as 'The Executioner' and described it as giving 'details of the execution of an IRA informer'. The story came out after Behan's death as 'The

Execution'.[36] This short story is an early example of Behan's ability to empathise across factional, national and ideological divides regardless of his own political loyalties. His non-discriminating power to understand the human predicament was to be a major feature of his later writing. The narrator of The Execution vividly describes how an IRA party carried out its orders to shoot a young man who had betrayed the location of an arms dump to the police. In terse, pared sentences, Behan shows great sympathy for the unfortunate victim while stressing the need for the maintenance of discipline in a secret organisation. '... we couldn't let people give away dumps on us or there'd soon be no respect for the army'. During his training as an IRA Volunteer and during his years locked up with other IRA men, Behan would have heard many stories of the elimination of informers. He describes the execution of his character, Ellis, with touching humanity. None of the execution party has a stomach for the deed. When they stop at a pub to give their victim his last drink, which is a whiskey, the narrator thinks of how, in France, the condemned man gets a glass of rum and a cigarette.

> We stood at the spot.
> Kit was lighting a cigarette – his hand cupping the flame.
> Ellis looked around him, just a little wildly - 'not yet, lads', he moaned.
> He began to cry not wildly but softly – the way a child cries. The tears streamed down his cheeks.
> Kit Whelan patted his shoulder.
> I wondered what to say to comfort him.
> I could hardly tell him it was quite painless – we'd be sure to get the heart – after all he wasn't having a tooth out.
> He knelt down and began to pray.
> We knelt down with him.
> I tried to pray for his soul. I couldn't. It seemed awful to think of souls just then ...
> We put him in the grave. He felt quite warm.
> I told the lads to be careful not to get bloodstains on their clothes.
> We began to shovel in earth.
> I moved a big stone off my shovel – it might smash in his face.

Death was seldom to be absent from his writings. 'Alone in his cell he had ample time to ponder his own escape at Glasnevin and the precariousness of that vitality which was his chief characteristic'.[37]

As Behan's literary abilities developed apace in the confines of Mountjoy Jail, his friends outside became increasingly active in their efforts to persuade the authorities to allow him to take a fuller part in Ireland's public literary life.

In January 1943, Peadar O'Donnell began to lobby Boland intensively in an attempt to get Brendan's work published. He was also anxious that his protégé should have the best possible advice available to him on the development of his writing career. To that end he enlisted the aid of Seán O'Faoláin.

O'Donnell's pressure on the Minister bore fruit in February. 'As a result of further representations made to the Minister for Justice', Peter Berry noted on Behan's file on 20 February, 'a special open visit has been granted to Seán O'Faoláin'. Three days later and just fourteen days after Brendan's twentieth birthday, O'Faoláin arrived at Mountjoy. Acknowledging O'Faoláin's importance, the authorities allowed the visit to take place in the Governor's office. 'They had a long chat during which Brendan was assured that he had undoubted talent and was strongly encouraged to persevere to continue with his writing'.[38] O'Faoláin remembered Brendan as a slim, dark curly-haired man. He reminded him of Dylan Thomas in Augustus John's portrait, a quiet, gentle creature. O'Faoláin saw nothing of the flamboyant Behan of popular legend.[39]

Seán O'Faoláin's visit was a major turning point in Brendan's life. For him it represented a laying on of hands by an acknowledged master of the short story. So encouraged was Brendan by O'Faoláin's visit that on the next day, 24 February, he wrote to the Minister for Justice seeking permission to send his manuscripts to O'Faoláin for critical analysis.

Mountjoy Prison
24-2-'43

A Chara,
I had a visit yesterday from Mr Seán O'Faoláin, who is interested in my literary work. He expressed a wish to read and criticise anything I may have written in here. As can be understood his expert opinion and advice would be of tremendous value to me. Therefore, I should like to be allowed send out any MSS I may have written and any I may write in the future. Both Mr O'Faoláin and myself clearly understand that anything sent out shall not be published. I will give my word that your wishes in this matter will be respected and that anything sent out to Mr O'Faoláin shall be returned here when he has read it and criticised it. Actually, in a nut-shell, the idea is more or less that I get a sort of correspondence course on short story writing from Mr O'Faoláin.
Let me again say that we both fully understand that these MSS cannot be published unless the permission of the Minister is granted and that I have no intention of abusing the concession if it's granted.[40]

Opinion was divided within the Department about what to do about this request. On the face of it, the application was quite reasonable. An interesting note on Behan's file, from Peter Berry to the Secretary of the Department, indicates the strength of the pressure which Peadar O'Donnell was exerting for his manuscripts to be allowed out for O'Faoláin's criticism. The note demonstrates the strength of the two Irish writers' belief in Behan's talent and future prospects:

> Peadar O'Donnell told me that he and Seán O'Faoláin regard Behan as the most promising writer produced in this country in recent years. He said that Behan has the unmistakable hallmark of genius and he pleaded that Behan should be allowed to develop his writing powers and have his efforts directed into the right channels by having his MSS vetted by O'Faoláin. Behan is a nephew of Peadar Kearney who wrote the National Anthem and all his parents' relatives have fought for the National cause.
>
> O'Donnell says that Behan's IRA activities so far were just a process of growing up, that he is now matured and is ready to develop into a good citizen. For this reason he suggests that the prisoner should be allowed a little latitude.[41]

As O'Donnell was privy to the views of those still active in the organisation, his assessment of the insignificance of Brendan's juvenile IRA activities might be expected to have carried some weight. But the record shows that, when advising Boland on the matter, a senior Justice Department official did not share this view of Brendan as a harmless, ideological prankster. He saw him as 'a reckless and dangerous young fellow, addicted to pulling a gun'. He felt it was correct for him to be 'made to understand that he must suffer for his misconduct and one of the penalties is the lack of facilities for developing his talent'.[42] He said the situation called for 'a little old fashioned rigidity'. Reflecting the paranoia of the times, this senior civil servant informed the Minister for Justice that there was 'a danger of codes being used for conveying information either in the MSS sent out or in the criticisms sent back.'[43]

For the moment, at least, that draconian view was rejected and Brendan was allowed to send his manuscripts to Seán O'Faoláin. The Secretary, however, qualified his indulgence with a stern warning to the Governor of Mountjoy that 'the articles, etc. should be carefully scrutinised to ensure that no information involving the breach of any Prison Regulations is permitted to issue to or from the convict'.[44]

Brendan now busied himself with the composition of work to send to O'Faoláin. O'Faoláin, in turn, thought sufficiently highly of what he received to write to the Governor of Mountjoy, indicating his wish to have it appear in *The Bell*.

The Bell
43 Parkgate Street
Dublin
23 March 1943

Dear Mr Kavanagh,
Would you be so good as to tell me whether I may take it that Behan's manuscripts are now officially out for criticism? That is to say, may we approach the Minister for permission to publish?

Yours sincerely,
Seán O'Faoláin.[45]

The Governor replied by return letter, requesting that Behan's manuscripts be sent back to Mountjoy and adding, 'the manuscripts of Brendan Behan cannot be published while he is serving imprisonment'.[46] This situation obtained for the remainder of his time in prison, although the ban on publication did not discourage him from writing. As we shall see, he persisted in his efforts to have that ban lifted right up until his release in 1946.

Quite soon after his arrival in Mountjoy, he began work on a play called *The Landlady*. It drew its material from the happenings and characters that enriched the world that revolved around Granny English's tenement flat in Russell Street. The landlady of the title is Mrs Clarke. She has a son called Jacko Clarke, of whom she is inordinately fond. The play opens with Mrs Clarke talking to a Mrs Keane in a tenement building in Dublin. Mrs Keane's daughter has had an illegitimate child by a character called Moran. During their conversation Mrs Keane lets it slip that Jacko Clarke is having an affair with Nora Creedon, whose family (tenants of Mrs Clarke's) are described as 'canvas caravan Tipperary tinkers'. Jacko refuses to abandon his love and she eventually cuts her throat – much as the lover of Behan's uncle Paddy had done in Russell Street. We also meet Meg Mahon who makes shrouds for the dead. She was later reworked as Miss McCann in the short story, *The Confirmation Suit*. Behan devised the play in three acts. He asked his cousin Seamus de Burca, son of the actor manager P.J. Bourke and himself a budding Dublin playwright, to type the manuscript:

I agreed to type the manuscript. It was rather a long play in three acts of more than a hundred quarto pages, double spaced. There was the original, a carbon copy and Brendan's holograph; and the three I wrapped up in a parcel and returned to the author.

I soon regretted doing this; Brendan was an extremely careless man about his scripts.[47]

De Burca regarded the play as simply an exercise in the craft. His principal criticism was that it lacked action. He suggested that Behan devote his talents to writing a novel or short stories. Mindful of the active discouragement he himself suffered at the hands of Dublin theatre administrators, he did not give that advice lightly – he was attempting to save his cousin the pain of rejection at this early stage of his career.

A number of people saw the script at this time, amongst them Bob Bradshaw. In a letter to Bradshaw, who had sent him some welcome criticism of the play, Brendan says the landlady and the play's other characters are real Dublin people known to him.

I don't mean to say that any of them are exactly and in every detail as I described them (and I painted them, didn't photograph them). I even go so far as to claim that they are as genuine as any of O'Casey's battalion – maybe more so, because O'Casey was born a Protestant and that means a big lot. Therefore, three cheers and many huzzas for your statement that them that says they're not true to life, are illiterate. They definitely are, and I hope you'll tell them so.[48]

A planned production of the play by the Republican prisoners at Mountjoy was abandoned because many of them found its coarse language and references to prostitution unacceptable. A production was also suggested when Brendan was transferred to Arbour Hill, but was abandoned due to lack of interest amongst the inmates.[49]

During his fifteen months in Mountjoy, Brendan met several characters whom he would later draw on for inspiration for his writings or just for their conversational entertainment value. Few, however, would remain so vividly in his mind as did Bernard Kirwan. A pork butcher by trade, Kirwan was under sentence of death for the murder of his younger brother, Lawrence. He had disposed of the body by filleting it so skilfully that identification was impossible. One of Brendan's less tasteful jokes was that Kirwan sold his brother as fresh pork to the Jesuit fathers at Tullabeg, County Offaly.[50]

The murder was one of the more gruesome crimes of the time and caught the public imagination through quite considerable coverage in the national press. The facts of the case, according to newspaper accounts, were these: up to 1936, Kirwan had been living with his mother and brother on their small farm not far from Tullamore. In February of that year, Kirwan received a seven-year sentence for armed robbery. While he was in prison his mother died, leaving the farm in equal parts to her six children. Four of the children had no interest in the property and made no claim on it. Lawrence remained in sole possession while Bernard was in prison. On his release in 1941, Bernard returned to live on the family farm but relations with Lawrence were far from cordial. On 22 November 1941, Lawrence Kirwan vanished without trace. Six months later, in May 1942, workmen found part of a dismembered body in a bog about a mile from the Kirwan farm. Bernard Kirwan was taken into custody and after a 17-day trial was condemned to death for the murder of his brother. It was the first time in an Irish murder trial that the judge's summing-up was broken off twice, having taken three days to deliver. Kirwan protested his innocence to the end.

In Mountjoy he was seen as a calm, intelligent and cheerful fellow. Brendan talked with him on several occasions and was impressed by just those qualities. Kirwan's execution date was set for 2 June 1943.

If, as Dr Johnson assured us, the fate of a man about to be hanged 'concentrates his mind wonderfully', so too does it concentrate the minds of those in prison with him. 'Nobody spoke of it of course,' Behan recalled, 'but there was an air of tension about the place as we had heard that a prisoner in "D" wing ... was due to be topped shortly.'[51] The night before his execution, he rushed up to Brendan and told him; 'Tomorrow, at ten past eight, I'll be praying for you in heaven'. Friends who had organised a fruitless petition for his reprieve visited him in his last days and were astounded at how calm he appeared. A warder told Brendan that just before Kirwan went to the gallows, he balanced a cup of water on the back of his right hand to show his executioners that he was not nervous. Some prisoners thought him brave, at that point Brendan thought him mad. The executioner, brought over from England, was the notorious hangman, Albert Pierrepoint. On the morning of the hanging about fifty men and women gathered outside the prison on the North Circular Road and recited the Rosary and prayers for the dying. When Behan came to write *The Quare Fellow*, it was Kirwan and the reaction amongst the other prisoners to his death, that he largely drew on for his inspiration.

On 15 July 1943, shortly after that grisly event, the political prisoners in Mountjoy were slopped out earlier than usual – an indication that something significant was about to happen. After breakfast a list, on which Behan's name appeared, was read out. He was told to assemble his kit and prepare for transfer to the military prison at Arbour Hill, where he spent the next eleven months.[52] He left Mountjoy feeling somewhat apprehensive about what lay ahead, for on the prison grapevine he had not heard encouraging reports about his new place of detention.

Arbour Hill and The Curragh

The removal of IRA prisoners to military detention at Arbour Hill was a partial response to pressure from Republican supporters to separate political prisoners from those whom they considered to be the common criminal class. In practical terms, the move to this new place of internment made only a marginal difference to the lives of the Republican prisoners. For Brendan it mattered little. He had nothing against 'common criminals' and had found them both diverting and a useful source of material for his writing. His greatest worry was that the Arbour Hill cells were smaller than those at Mountjoy. He also feared that he might not be allowed to write as much as he had done.

Arbour Hill was another shrine to the struggle for Irish freedom. The British had begun to build Arbour Hill Prison in 1845 and imprisoned many Irishmen there during the Fenian troubles, including James Boyle O'Reilly, the Fenian writer, who was transported to Australia in 1867. Brendan knew O'Reilly's writings well and could quote them from memory. The executed leaders of the 1916 Rising were buried at Arbour Hill.

> ... I also knew that beyond the boundary wall of the exercise yard were the graves of the men who had been executed in Easter Week, 1916: Thomas J. Clarke, Padraig H. Pearse, Thomas MacDonagh and the rest. I knew their names and all belonging to them as well as I knew my own.[1]

Even closer to his heart, was the fact that Theobald Wolfe Tone, whom Behan considered to be the architect of Republican thought, had died nearby in 1798. Tone had cut his throat upon being refused a soldier's death by firing squad. The court martial that convicted him of treason had sentenced him to hang.

Brendan had been a model prisoner in Mountjoy, but quite soon after arriving in Arbour Hill his behaviour became quite erratic. Brendan's cousin points out the stress he was under as his sense of his vocation as a writer contended with his sense of loyalty to the Republican cause:

> There were growing pains. He was uncomfortably aware of contradictions within himself, between his Republican idealism and his own experiences in England, between his duties as a soldier and his ambitions as a writer.[2]

In December, he was fined for tearing up three blankets in his cell. When the Camp Commandant, Michael Lennon, questioned why he had done this, he said he was 'trying to make a getaway'. Lennon rejected this explanation, and rather curiously decided that what Brendan had been doing was 'trying to make himself a couple of pairs of trousers'. In a memo to F.J. Henry, the Provost Marshal at the Department of Defence, Lennon noted that Brendan 'considers himself an intellectual but from my observations of him I am of the opinion he is suffering from some mental kink'.[3]

Lennon's opinion was important to Brendan. He was now very anxious that the prohibition on publication imposed by Gerry Boland be lifted. Seán O'Faoláin's critical appraisal of his work and Peadar O'Donnell's encouragement had convinced him of the commercial possibilities for his writings. O'Faoláin confirmed his interest in Behan's writing when he visited him at Arbour Hill on 5 September. In December, just ten days after the Commandant had made a note of his 'mental kink', he appealed to Lennon to allow his stories out for publication.

Arbour Hill Military Detention Barracks
31.12.1943

A Chara,
I wish to make application for permission to send from here short stories and articles for publication. Apart from the financial angle (which is not without its importance) writing provides a great interest for me.
While in custody, some people glue matches to pieces of card board and make Celtic Crosses or Round Towers, others do leatherwork. Unfortunately for me I have no handicraft. I am a house painter and signwriter by trade, but not by inclination. And handicrafts have no attraction for me. Therefore from that point of view I should be glad if you could accede to my request.
Another reason is, that there is a big market open just now for short stories, particularly in England, due to the fact that many pre-war

writers are now serving in the armed forces etc. As I intend to adopt the profession of letters, whenever I shall return to normal existence, it would be of great help to me if I could get 'dug in' so to speak, while stories are in demand and cannot be supplied by well-known authors. Messrs Peadar and Seán O'Faoláin are willing to act as my agents outside in this matter. Both have expressed the view that my stories are marketable.

Lastly I should like to say that I am agreeable to any condition, that you may see fit to make (such as the use of [a] pseudonym) and my stories and articles will not deal with any controversial matters (politics, Irish prisoners, etc).

Hoping that you may see your way to grant this request.

Is mise,
Brendan Behan.

This is a significant letter. For the first time, we find him distancing himself somewhat from the other Republican prisoners. He scorns the handicrafts that Arbour Hill thought suitable for political prisoners – like the painstaking carving of romantic Celtic symbols – in which the majority of his fellow Republicans happily engaged. And the submissive tone of his undertaking not to write about 'controversial matters' such as politics or Irish prisoners is certainly not what his superior officers in the IRA would have expected from the self-styled 'writer for the cause'. Permanent defiance, in public and in private, was what they required. But in this letter, Behan puts a greater value on the opportunity to practice his profession as a man of letters than he does on trumpeting the struggle. We may place the beginnings of his disillusionment with the movement from the date of this letter, which shows that by now his paramount ambition was to establish himself as a writer.

In the same month he confided to his friend, Bob Bradshaw, that he found the majority of the IRA prisoners he met in Ireland 'an uninteresting and boring lot'.[4] Twenty years later, he confirmed his reassessment of most of his fellow inmates when he described the futility and tedium of their hours of labour over sentimental objects of reverence:

They sat there on their chairs in silent rows, embroidering mostly monuments to misery, 'In Memory of Our Lord Jesus Christ,' and 'The Sacred Heart' and 'To the Soldiers of the Republic Executed from 1939 to 1942.' And one more ambitious hungry-faced little bastard gave a list of those who were hanged or shot or killed. Jesus, Mary and Joseph, it put years on me, and there wasn't man or boy among us who didn't make these Celtic crosses from matches in memory of some bloody thing or another. After a while some of the fellows became really handy at it, and they would stick together pieces of used matchsticks and make them into all sorts of things ... I used to collect their rejects and send them out to friends of mine who would say, 'Brendan Behan made this up in Mountjoy Prison.'[5]

Alienated by his lively intelligence from the makers of Round Towers and Celtic Crosses, Brendan drew closer to a minority group of highly educated political prisoners. At Arbour Hill, there were a handful of intellectual internees: teachers, professors, writers, historians and linguists. To these men, he could confide his desire to be a writer without risking derision. On the contrary, he received every possible encouragement. Much has been written about the notion of the 'internment camp university' – Behan was one of its most distinguished graduates.

While he found himself growing apart from the majority of his fellow internees, he also found a common bond that kept him united with them – the Irish language. Many IRA men, through lack of education, were only able to pay lip service to the Irish language, but most Republicans gave wholehearted support to the notion of its revival. Behan's parents had only a limited knowledge of Irish, but his mother insisted on using her stock of the language at every possible opportunity.

One of the men who played a role in Behan's prison education was Seán Ó Briain, a native Irish speaker and school teacher from Kerry. They had met in Mountjoy, where the older man had formed a master/pupil relationship with the boy from the Northside slums. Ó Briain was instrumental in helping Brendan to develop his schoolboy Irish into a literary medium:

> Brendan loved 'the old Tong-u', as he used to call it. He used to recall singing an Irish song for a few 'oul wans' sitting on the steps in Russell Street and one of them says to the other, 'That's a lovely boy and Mrs Jewel the darlin' and isn't the Oul Tongu-u very sweet.'[6]

Ó Briain believed that the Irish Brendan acquired while in prison, and his written use of it, amounted to more than a case of 'wise words on the lips of a fool'.[7] According to Ó Briain, Behan took his study of Irish and Irish literature more seriously than his bumptious demeanour suggested. But Ó Briain insisted that, above all, Brendan's understanding of the language was instinctual – his fine ear made it easy for him to achieve a vernacular facility in the language. Brendan loved to hear Ó Briain's stories of life in places like the Blasket Islands, Dun Chaoin, and Ballyferriter – Irish-speaking enclaves on the West Coast. Later, his visits to these places were probably some of the happiest times in his life.

Ó Briain had part of a copy of Bryan Merriman's *Cúirt an Mhean-Oíche (The Midnight Court)* with him at Arbour Hill. The comic epic, written in 1780-81, was the masterpiece of the County Clare-born poet. The uproarious, bawdy verse tale was a deflation of Irish puritanism and paved the way for a great deal of modern Irish language writing. Brendan borrowed the 1,000 or so lines of text and within a surprisingly short space of time he had committed the lot to memory. During his time in various prisons between 1942 and 1946, Brendan began writing poetry in Irish.

Behan the writer, now in his 21st year, was in full literary swing in the confines of his cell, from where he was making every possible attempt to establish literary contacts that might benefit him in the future. Frustrated by the adamant refusal of the authorities to allow his works to be published, he continued to press Lennon at Arbour Hill to have the ban lifted. On 19 January 1944, the Provost Marshall wrote to Lennon saying he had no objection to articles being sent out for publication, provided they were censored by the Commandant's office before being passed on. The following day, Behan wrote to Seán O'Faoláin at *The Bell* and in mid-February to the novelist and playwright, Maura Laverty, at Jury's Hotel in Dublin. His excitement, however, was short lived. Within a month of receiving the extremely good news that he could now go about finding a market for his work, Lennon informed him that permission to publish had been withdrawn again. He was ordered to 'store his manuscripts until his release'.[8] The G2 and Department of Justice files contain no particular explanation for the withdrawal of the privilege on this occasion. However, a letter about Brendan from Justice Minister Gerry Boland to his colleague, the Minister for Defence, Oscar Traynor, suggests that in granting permission, the Provost Marshall, based at the Department of Defence, acted without the knowledge of the Department of Justice. Brendan's outgoing correspondence with established writers and literary editors had not found favour with the Department of Justice. The paranoia and distemper of the times are apparent in the final paragraph of Boland's letter:

> There may be a certain amount of danger in allowing documents to pass in and out of a prison as they may contain codes which would assist the escape of prisoners. The censorship of such documents throws a rather unfair strain on the prison authorities.
>
> On the other hand, I feel that industry and hobbies should be

encouraged amongst the prisoners and if their minds are kept occupied they are likely to prove more amenable to prison discipline. Behan was granted permission to submit his manuscripts to a well-known author for criticism but not for immediate publication. I felt that there might be a certain objection to having stories printed, and, perhaps, advertised as printed by a man serving a sentence of penal servitude. It would look to the police generally and to the public as if we were carrying leniency very far. Another consideration which weighed with me in prohibiting publication was that some of Behan's stories contained rather indelicate language and I visualised the possibility of his writing something really offensive which might bring him up against the Censorship of Publications Act.

It is ironic that the Minister for Justice should wish to protect him at this early stage from the Censorship of Publications Act, an instrument under which his most famous work, *Borstal Boy*, would later be banned in Ireland.

The prohibition on publication did not prevent Brendan from applying himself to his craft. He started work on a play about the life of Wolfe Tone, based on Tone's autobiography, as an entry for a play competition at The Abbey Theatre. The play opens in Tone's house in Irishtown in Summer, 1790. Tone, his wife, Matilda, and his close friend Thomas Russell, are the three main characters. He described the play as 'a perfectly innocent little thing', which he expected to run to about ten to fifteen minutes.[9] He had written the first scene of the play, which alas like so much of his prison writing has been lost, when it struck him that he should adapt the Tone material to a radio script. He began it in early May. Tone's birth date is June 20th, and he hoped Radio Éireann would accept his script as an anniversary piece. He envisaged it beginning with Tone's first birthday in 1763. It would include extracts from the autobiography and a summary of the principal events of Tone's struggle for Irish freedom, and end with Patrick Pearse's famous oration at Tone's graveside at Bodenstown in 1915.

It was the sort of material which Radio Éireann would have readily accepted for broadcast. The subject matter was entirely unobjectionable. Believing this to be the case, he appealed to the better nature of the mandarins at the Department of Justice in May 1944. The letter, which for the first time in his correspondence with officialdom mixes reasonableness with an outrageous, Behanesque cheek, shows how angry he had become with the department's stonewalling:

Bhoil, A Chairde,

Here we go again as the chorus girl said to the bishop. I've no doubt that you (whoever you are – one of the difficulties of carrying on a discussion of this sort is that I have no idea whom I direct my pleadings to – and this is a matter of great importance as I will show you later on) when you see this will say to the underling who brings it to your notice – 'What [–] that bloody fellow in the Hill at us again over his blasted scribbling – doesn't he never take "no" for an answer – or does he think our typists have nothing better to do but write "The Minister cannot see his way et seq". Ten times a year – and for the next $8^1/_2$ years too – that's if he gets his four years remission – tell him again and this is final "No, No, a thousand times NO!" and if [he] doesn't give over drivelling at us we'll reduce his bread ration'. But gentlemen, be patient.

I'm not at you over the short stories, the articles or the plays, all I'm looking for is to be let go on the radio. 'What!' I hear you say. 'My God the poor fellow's gone nuts altogether – er, Jack, ring up Dundrum will you and see if they have e'er a vacancy for a poor nit-wit – and er Jack tell them on no account to leave pen and ink within his reach or he'll leave us bad as himself'. But no it's not as bad as all that. I suppose I better come to business.

It's this way: The Abbey are running a historical play competition. I decided to enter (after I get your permission of course, and I won't be looking for that until about August) ... Gentlemen, what is there in that that could be in any way objectionable?, and here I can fully appreciate your viewpoint – that my name should go over the air and as for that, sure we can tell the radio people (if they take it) that the programme is to be anonymous, so far as the scriptwriter is concerned.

The only thing I ask, gentlemen, whether you can grant this application or not and even if you can't, I'll know it's not your hearts that stop you, is that you notify the governor as soon as possible because the radio people need at least three weeks notice for anything of this sort and it's only a month 'til 20th June. If I may digress for a moment, it is a strange thing, but since our Radio Station begun never has anyone written anything to let Tone know that we still remembered him and to let Pearse know that his glorious panegyric didn't fall on deaf ears. There have been programmes written to commemorate them all, even O'Connell but never one word in commemoration of him but for whom we wouldn't have [a free] radio station.[10]

His pleas on behalf of the memory of Wolfe Tone and his pledge of anonymity – even though, from Behan's point of view, public knowledge that the play was by an imprisoned IRA man would have increased its impact – had no effect on his censors. The Department of Justice remained as intractable as ever and the opportunity to have a commemorative piece on a founding father of Irish Republicanism by Brendan Behan was lost. The letter is a touching affirmation of a young man's desire to have his work recognised. It shows great resilience on his part in the face of the authorities' constant refusal to grant his wish to gain a first footing on the literary ladder he so wished to ascend.

After his Tone project was scuppered by officialdom, he became restless and unhappy at Arbour Hill. A Corporal Culliton registered a complaint against him. When ordered into his cell by Culliton, Behan rebelled. 'He told me to come in and put him into it and not to come single-handed and not to bring the Construction Corps', a distressed Culliton told his superior officers.[11]

In his isolation, the visits Brendan received became increasingly important to him. He found the opportunity to talk to people from outside the prison system so exhilarating, that his visitors rarely got the chance to speak. His cousin Seamus de Burca recalled going to Arbour Hill with Brendan's brother, Seán, the ever loyal Freddie May and Freddie's sister, Sheila:

> This time when Brendan caught sight of us, he did stammer in the beginning, but once started he gave what I can only describe as a tour-de-force. Apart from the greeting: 'Hello, Jimmy! The soul man Freddie. And Sheila, how is every bit of you? Hello, Seán, me oul china,' each of us got barely time to acknowledge the greeting before Brendan was pouring forth a torrent as if he had been kept in solitary confinement, or he had been in a monastery where the rule of silence is rigidly enforced. It was like a holiday to him to talk, and he enjoyed every word that came from him. I will say this for Brendan Behan, he had the gift of making you feel ... the most important person there.[12]

Brendan now had less than a month to spend at Arbour Hill before his transfer to his final place of long-term detention. In the remaining days, he busied himself with a flurry of literary correspondence. He wrote to the manager of The Gaiety Theatre, Hamlyn Benson, to Seán O'Faoláin at The Bell, to Charles J. Connolly at *The Irish Echo* in New York and to M.J. McManus at the *Irish Press*.[13] At the same time, he mentioned work in progress or work completed in letters to fellow internees at the Curragh Military Detention Camp, where he was soon to be moved.[14]

On 12 June 1944, he was taken to the Curragh Camp, having served over two years of his fourteen-year sentence. As he left Arbour Hill for the thirty-mile drive to the Curragh, he assumed he would serve out the greater part of his fourteen-year sentence on the plains of Kildare.

The Free State government had used the former British military base to intern its opponents during the Civil War. Now de Valera's government used it in an attempt to break the will of those Republicans it had themselves imprisoned. Though many internees, including Brendan, retained reasonably happy memories of the Curragh Camp, it was a tough station. As many as forty men lived together in cramped, primitive wooden huts that were freezing cold in winter and insufferably hot in summer. The main advantage of being there was free association for Republicans, and a better chance to exercise than was available at Mountjoy and Arbour Hill. Despite the hardship, Brendan made the best of the situation. He told Lazarian Mangan, soon after their arrival, to count his blessings because he believed the Curragh to be 'a good kip'.

Besides the Republican prisoners, the Curragh also held German and Allied servicemen, mostly airmen caught in neutral Ireland. One hundred and forty-one Allied and sixteen German planes made forced or crash landings in Irish territorial waters between the beginning of the war and the end of June 1945. The German and Allied internees had a much better time of it than the Republican prisoners. They were allowed parole to go racing at the nearby Curragh race course, swim in the local baths, attend the cinema in Newbridge; and even venture as far as Dublin. There, the better-heeled of the officers enjoyed the culinary delights of Jammet's restaurant. Indeed, so good a war did many of them have that quite a few stayed on in Ireland when the conflict ended.

When it came to interning foreign airmen, the Irish government drew a distinction between operational and non-operational flights. The Republicans in the Curragh, Brendan pointed out, drew no such distinction: 'Though I suppose the Canadians thought we favoured the Germans, and the Germans thought we inclined towards the Allies, in actual fact we were in favour of only one side: that was our own'.[15]

In keeping with established Republican tradition, the IRA men in the Curragh divided into factions described by Behan as 'those who supported the official IRA, those who supported the unofficial IRA, and those who didn't agree with either side and formed a group of their own'.[16] He dismissed the notion that differences between those who supported Germany and those who supported the Allies, or questions of right-versus-left wing inclinations, were a basis for factionalism. He believed that 'in every prisoner-of-war camp there is a barbed-wire psychosis that makes outside judgements truly ridiculous'. He saw the cross-currents at work as unfathomable and tiresome, and flitted between all three groups with frolicsome abandon.

His co-defendants at the Glasnevin shooting trial moved with him from Arbour Hill, and he was now re-united with one of his closest friends, Cathal Goulding. The two immediately teamed up and exchanged news and gossip, played handball, remembered their days in Fianna Éireann, poked fun at their jailers and looked forward to better days ahead. It was a usual practice in the camps to keep a book of jottings in which prisoners exchanged sometimes frivolous, sometimes serious views on a variety of subjects. On 4 July 1944, Brendan made an entry in the little book kept by his friend and fellow internee, Christy O'Neill. The message was addressed to Christy's younger brother, Seán, and it carried all the fire of Brendan's early beliefs in Tone as the father of modern Republicanism:

> I have no doubt that Seán appreciates as well as I do, that from time to time leaders arise in a nation whose every heart beat is the lessened murmur of the pulse of that nation, whose rejoicing is in the nation's joy & whose sorrow is the sorrow of one who suffers a thousandfold in sad union with his people – who crystalises a nation's being into a formula – who sees with an almost spiritual vision the way that lies to national peace and national happiness. These men are not the property of the age in which they live nor the land of which [they] are the living symbol (still living because as I say they don't belong to the age in which they die any more than the age in which they live).
>
> Thus, we in Ireland in 1944 still remember the prophets who led Israel centuries before Christ. We have by heart the ordinances they transmitted for the guidance of their people – we know them as the Ten Commandments. In the same way our own land has its prophets – Connolly and Pearse, Lalor and Mitchell. But looming largely in the background overshadowing the others stands a figure in lace ruffles and knee breeches – not a giant by reason of his height – not a handsome man by ordinary standards – a smallish slight figure with left
> cheek touched by smallpox – his face twisted in the sociable smile of a friendly man – so sociable as to look upon all men as members of his family and all Irishmen as bloodkin – It is the figure of Tone.
> ... The best advice I could give any young Irishman is to study [his doctrine] from its source, his own book, and such as I am, I offer this advice to you hoping it brings you as gas a time as it brought me and takes you to as many interesting places.
>
> Brendan Behan, Irish Republican Army.[17]

Of the new friends Brendan made in the Curragh, the most important was Máirtín Ó Cadháin, considered by many to be the outstanding writer in Irish of his generation. He had already published *Idir Shúgradh agus Dáirire*, stories based on the life of his Gaeltacht community in Connemara, and was working towards his masterpiece *Cré na Cille*. Ó Cadháin's unrivalled mastery of Irish and several other languages, his absolute dedication to the writer's craft, and his unpatronising willingness to share his knowledge with less educated prisoners impressed Behan. He encouraged and advised Brendan in his choice of reading and told him to continue his writing and ignore the authorities' ban on publication. Máirtín Ó Cadháin believed that Behan possessed a remarkable talent for the composition of Irish verse.[18] However, his output in the medium was, as we shall see later, limited. Behan was aware early on that he would not find the popularity he sought through Irish verse. As Colbert Kearney points out : 'the writer who chooses to work in Irish rather than in English is seeking something other than popularity: he may write great verse, but he must leave it to a little clan'.[19] According to Dr Aidan Doyle, the Gaelic scholar authorised by the Behan estate to make the official translation of Behan's Irish language play *An Giall*, the market for Irish language literature was and will remain 'a fixed market that will not go up and down because it is ideological.' The number of genuine native speakers in the '40s and '50s, who mainly came from the Gaeltacht areas of the West, was probably less than 30,000. Of these, few were regular consumers of high literature. Irish revivalists, who numbered among them some of the most intellectually and politically influential Irishmen of their day, did much to encourage writers to use the Irish language. Parts of educated society, whose Irish was usually a learnt tongue, were rightly prepared to laud the output of these writers for emotional reasons, and to appreciate works of genuine merit.

In one sense it is sad that most of Behan's major literary successes were not written in the language of his ancestors, of which he was so proud. On the other hand, it is unlikely that he would ever have found the freedom to manipulate language and bend its traditional boundaries in a tongue he had not spoken daily from infancy. It was this unfettered linguistic elasticity and inventiveness that marked out his talent, as it did that of his predecessor, James Joyce. Doyle supports this view. While Behan commanded a wide vocabulary in his written Irish, his work contains words that are simply untranslatable by Irish language scholars. In English, Behan was capable of creating a word like 'capernosity', which he uses to describe his Granny English. In context, this word, which existed in no dictionary, has meaning for any native English speaker. Because it wasn't his first language, his attempts to stretch and invent words in Irish did not and could not have the same success.

In August 1944, Brendan sought permission to send the script of what was described as a 'comedy' to M.J. MacManus, Literary Editor of the *Irish Press*, who that year wrote the official biography of Eamon de Valera. Sanction was not forthcoming and the manuscript was handed back. The official correspondence does not describe or name the play but this was, presumably, a version of *The Landlady*, which underwent several transformations, including translation into Gaelic, while Brendan was in jail.

Throughout most of 1945, Brendan settled down to the drab routine of life at the Curragh. He took little interest in the progress of the War. In moments of despair, and in his case they were few, he found great support in his friend Cathal Goulding. For the most part, he concentrated on his reading and writing. At Easter 1945, he took part in a concert held in the camp to mark the annual anniversary of the 1916 Rising. The prisoners managed to distil some lethal poteen, the first three drops of which were offered, according to tradition, to the fairies, a gesture Brendan thought a terrible waste of good drink. He was in splendid form and delighted the gathering with his singing of James Clarence Mangan's *My Dark Rosaleen*.

The death of Hitler caused a bit of a stir in the Camp when the announcement came on the wireless. It was, of course, of most concern to the interned German and Allied airmen, but the Republican prisoners also believed that the end of the war, and thus of the state of Emergency in Ireland, would affect their sentences. Brendan did not share the general optimism. He thought it likely that he would have to serve out most of his fourteen-year sentence. In fact, he had little more than a year left in prison.

His outgoing literary correspondence tapered off during 1945. He wrote a letter, the contents of which is unknown, to Howard Spring of Collins Publishers in London, in November 1945. Presumably he was offering a manuscript for publication. Unfortunately, the letter was not allowed out and was returned to Brendan. It has not survived. He also wrote to his friend Neil Gould about the progress of his work that year.

> For myself, I am pretty well. I do very little except for a translation of *Cúirt an Mheán Oíche* on which I'm working and have practically finished. I also write an odd short story, sometimes in Irish – there is much searching for some MSS of mine which have gone astray in *The Bell* office. Harry Craig[20] is last said to have had them – it doesn't matter very much because I can publish nothing anyway.

By early 1946, Freddie May, realising the futility of his attempts to have Brendan's sentence mitigated, abandoned his efforts. He continued to visit him at every possible opportunity. This sometimes annoyed Brendan, especially on the occasions when he wanted to be alone with a particular family member or friend. In January 1946, Freddie wrote a letter to Commandant Lennon expressing his desire to be allowed to visit Brendan alone:

> I was wondering whether you ever grant the favour of allowing an internee, whose conduct has been satisfactory out on parole for a few hours, and if so, whether you would consider doing so on this occasion. Naturally, I have not seen Brendan alone since his arrest and, if it is at all allowable I should much appreciate the privilege of having a few hours with him, you understand yourself that one can talk more freely with a person when one has him entirely to oneself.[21]

In 1946, Brendan again renewed his attempts to have his work published or performed. On 14 May, a memo from the Provost Marshal to the Governor of the Curragh notes a request from the Abbey Theatre 'that permission be awarded to prisoner Behan to submit the script of a play in Irish for review by them'. The authorities granted the request, which came from The Abbey's Managing Director, Ernest Blythe. On 18 May, Brendan explained to Blythe, in a letter, what he was sending.

> Dear Sir,
> I enclose the first Act of my play – *The Landlady* – you might, perhaps, also be interested in the bilingual sketch '*L' o Lion*. If I don't get word from you that it is not worth continuing with, I will go on with rewriting the other two Acts, and I will send them to you next week. As regards *The Landlady* – I had two acts written of a play in English and one of a play in Irish – they both had a fault – the characters of the two plays should be in one play, for they came from the same period of my life and from the same house – I decided to bring them together – that's what I did in *The Landlady*.[22]

He went on to tell Blythe about a work in progress, *The Twisting of Another Rope*, which eventually became *The Quare Fellow*.[23] He remarked to Blythe that he was not sending the work just then because he felt 'it would scare the Department of Justice'. Nothing came of the work submitted to the Abbey, and it would be many years before it produced a play by Brendan Behan.

A month later, he wrote to Blythe again asking his advice about his rather daft notion of entering a translation into Irish of *Finnegans Wake* for the Oireachtas literary competition. This was the premier Irish language cultural festival. It was founded in 1897 by the Gaelic League along the lines of the Welsh Eisteddfod but went into decline after 1918 and was revived again in 1939. Blythe's reply to his request for a £100 fee for the translation sadly does not exist, but it was no doubt strongly worded enough to put the ambitious project on permanent hold. Brendan asked the Commandant's agreement to enter the Oireachtas competition because 'large money prizes are offered for original works in Irish'. He rather over-reachingly planned to enter for 'novel, drama or short story competitions, or if possible for all three.'[24] The Department of Justice ultimately refused him permission to enter for fear that the prisoner's work 'would be published in the papers.'[25]

Brendan had been moved to another part of the Curragh detention complex known as the 'glasshouse'. During the transfer there, he had a scuffle with some of the German and Canadian airmen who had hurled insults at the Republicans during the move. Once settled in, he thought the 'glasshouse' a great improvement, principally because the Army cooks did the cooking and not the prisoners themselves.

Soon after arriving at the Curragh in June 1944, Brendan was admitted to hospital. He had heard that patients received two bottles of Guinness a day, so he feigned some form of convincing illness. On his arrival, a party was given for him by the other patients who had saved up their ration of stout for the purpose. They saved the drink in chamber pots under the bed. When the party was in full swing, a prison guard looked in the window but when he saw Brendan raise the piss pot to his head and drink deeply, he fled in horror. The festivities went on uninterrupted:

> A happier hospital I've never seen in my life. The singing got well under way, and us throwing out from the roots our rich tenor voices, increasing in volume with the intake of stout. The sergeants of the 'Linseed Lancers', as we called the Medical Corps, came in to sing an aria from *Lucia di Lammermoor*, and one from Gounod's *Faust*, and I contributed a couple of numbers myself.[26]

This particular visit to hospital may not have been the result of medical need, but it is clear that prison life took a toll on his general health. It may have been a factor in his early death at the age of forty-one. During his imprisonment in Mountjoy, Arbour Hill and the Curragh, he made sixty-seven visits to prison Medical Officers. His complaints varied. He was twice hospitalised in Mountjoy after coughing up blood. His chest was X-rayed at the Curragh in July 1944, but no signs of active disease were found. He was plagued by problems with his teeth, of which he was inordinantly proud. The only implement of vanity he carried in his possession was a toothbrush that he used at all times of the day. He was released under supervision from Mountjoy and Arbour Hill for ten visits to the Dental Hospital in Dublin. The authorities, concerned that he might make a dash for freedom, instructed the accompanying officers that 'special care should be taken to ensure [the] safe return of the prisoner'.[27]

In the Curragh, he became extremely upset about the condition of his teeth and lived in dread of losing them. In a rather sad letter to his father, which the censor refused to allow out, he complains bitterly about the lack of proper dental care and asks his father to use his influence with his former IRA colleagues, who were now in Government, to get him treatment:

> I suppose you'll say I must be looking for something when you see this, the first letter I've written you in months. Well it's this way – I am being treated in the most lousy manner by these people (I don't think it's the actual prison staff, who are quite decent, – but some of my higher captors anyway) in regard to dentistry – they absolutely refuse to give any but the most primitive treatment for teeth – I was being treated in the dental hospital before we left the Hill and was to return for a filling – I came down here and was dogmatically informed that 'we don't fill teeth in the Curragh Command' ... now the teeth are rotting in my head and I suffer from neuralgia ...You know I am not the sort that broods over trifles and truly in this case I have a legitimate grievance – go and see the fellow[28] from North Strand – tell him from me I'm not asking him or his associates for any favour but for the treatment I'm entitled to ... I'll make protest as best I can and if I go down well sure I'll have to put up with it.[29]

Later that month he made a formal protest to the prison Medical Officer and demanded that his teeth receive attention:

> There are holes in my eye teeth and I suffer from neuralgia. I am afraid my jaw-bone will become diseased if they are not attended to.
> I have been refused dental treatment every time I asked for it, which in my opinion is not legal. It is my right to have treatment and attention and not a privilege or pleasure.[30]

His worries about his teeth were soon replaced with worries about his mother's health. He received word that she was seriously ill and wrote to the Governor on 9 September requesting 14 days parole to see her. A request for parole that he had made in October 1944, after his brother Rory Furlong informed him that his sister-in-law, May Furlong, was seriously ill in the

Meath hospital, had been refused. This time, to his astonishment, he was granted parole two days later from 11 to 25 September, 1946. He signed an undertaking not to take messages, verbal or written, out of the prison camp, not to speak to the Press and not to take part in any subversive activities. He was issued with a wartime food and clothing ration book. He signed a docket to acknowledge receipt of 'a copy book, a bundle of loose written sheets, six magazines, a copy of *World News*'.[31]

At 4 p.m. on 11 September, he was searched, and at 5.05 p.m. in possession of bus pass number 394431, Republican prisoner, F662, Behan, Brendan (Francis), left Co. Kildare to return to Dublin. He could scarcely believe his good fortune as he took leave of his IRA colleagues.[32] His parole was soon extended to January 1947, by which time a General Amnesty for political prisoners was in place. He had served four years and five months of his fourteen-year sentence.

PART TWO

1947-1955

Adrift in Dublin Bohemia

The post-war Dublin in which Brendan Behan now found himself at liberty has sometimes been romanticised as a kind of northern Tangier, favoured by an international presence. Ireland was briefly a refuge of plenty in a ration-strapped Europe. Much has been made in memoir and in fiction of the endless quantities of red meat and claret, served up in establishments such as Louis Jammet's and The Dolphin Hotel to hoards of delighted visitors from England, and the occasional American undergraduate from Trinity College. But the city's moral climate was staid, and its handful of acceptable well-stocked restaurants made it only a very temporary pleasure ground for foreigners with money to spend. Many of its well-heeled natives sought their pleasures elsewhere.

Dublin was still an intact Georgian city, but the architecture of its principal streets had begun its steady decline. The smell of peat smoke hung heavily in the air. Cattle were still driven down the streets on their way to the docks. Children ran barefoot even in winter and the main method of private transport was the bicycle. Her ordinary citizens lived with deprivation as severe as the rationed inhabitants of the neighbouring island in its period of post-war recovery.

Culturally, Dublin emerged slowly and painfully from the isolation and social decline imposed by neutrality and by years of exposure to the stultifying effects of 'Gaelic Irelandism', de Valera's pious philosophy of cultural and economic self-sufficiency. Many Irish writers felt oppressed by the combination of isolationism and moral piety. Few expressed this more caustically than Behan's mentor, Seán O'Faoláin. He wrote of a city where 'The quality of life is weak ... weak for a capital ... Politics, journalism, conversation is generally tawdry, and sometimes far worse'.[1] In the pages of *The Bell*, he attacked the hermetically sealed attitudes of 'Little Irelanders, chauvinists, puritans, stuffed-shirts, pietists, Tartuffes, Anglophobes, Celtophiles, et *alii hujus generis*'. However, while there was no shortage of Irish writers who sympathised with Samuel Beckett's opinion that he preferred to live in France at war than in Ireland at peace, not many of them rushed to join him. Most stayed and suffered the debilitating effects of a censoriousness that was to survive for nearly twenty years before the wind of liberal change began to blow with any noticeable results.

What Dublin lacked in liberal official culture, it made up for in the abundance of that human phenomenon known to Dubliners as a 'character'. John Ryan, artist, publisher and author of *Remembering How We Stood*, the classic account of bohemian Dublin in the mid-twentieth century, believed the essential quality required in a 'character' was complete unawareness of being one. Brendan Behan might be thought to fail that particular test. But it was to the mastery of this role that Brendan, now twenty-three and moving about Dublin with a reputation as an ex-Borstal boy and IRA 'hardman', set his attention.

Dublin provided role models for this endeavour in great prodigality. The eighteenth and nineteenth centuries had had no shortage of eccentrics. These ranged from a wealthy member of the Ascendancy who walked to Jerusalem for a bet, to the less affluent street balladeers who pilloried the flaws of their 'betters' for a couple of pence and made a colourful nuisance of themselves. In the age of Yeats and Lady Gregory, the outlandish fops of the literary salon appeared on the scene. Other pre-World War II personalities were more energetic. There was the irrepressible 'Bird' Flanagan, who imitated the antics of his eighteenth-century predecessor 'Buck' Whaley by jumping into his carriage from the upper floors of Georgian buildings, and managed always to land gracefully. A man known as Endymion, a fringe member of Dublin Bohemia, bought a ham at an Italian emporium, left it for a month, returned in the pretence of stealing it, was arrested and acquitted, with much judicial embarrassment, when the truth emerged.

Such antics had become somewhat subdued in the post-war era. However, one could still see the curious sight of the barrister, Eoin 'Pope' O'Mahony, in the full robes and decorations of a Knight of Malta, flapping about the city on a bicycle. This distinguished 'Pan-European wandering aristocrat manqué', as John Ryan dubbed him, held court in the great houses of Ireland proposing the restoration of the Irish monarchy. His first choice for king was the handsome Irish Catholic peer, Lord Gormanston. Failing him, he suggested the Rev. The O'Conor Don, a Jesuit priest who was directly descended from the High Kings of Ireland.

By the late 1940s, Dublin's characters were mostly aspiring writers like Brendan himself. The public manifestations of their wit and talent were confined mainly, though not exclusively, to a coterie of Dublin public houses and late night drinking dens. These men included established figures like the poet Patrick Kavanagh, the novelist Flann O'Brien, and the painter Seán O'Sullivan. Others were on the rise, like American student J.P. Donleavy; novelist, Benedict Kiely; the poet, John Montague; novelist, Anthony Cronin; critic John Jordan and many others. It was Brendan Behan who emerged from this tribe as the Dublin 'character' *primus inter pares.* In his early twenties, Brendan began the heavy drinking for which he became legendary. Only too late would he discover and neglect the diabetes that, coupled with his manic drinking, caused his early death. The caricature he created for himself in these Dublin drinking establishments became, unfortunately, the image for which he is most widely remembered.

Dublin has long been associated with alcohol in popular imagination, and not without cause. A Select Committee of the House of Lords on Intemperance, reporting in 1878, described Dublin as 'saturated with drink, it is flooded with drink, it is the staple manufacture. Every kind of drink which the people care to consume is manufactured in unlimited quantities in Dublin, every third or fourth house deals in drink.' The committee concluded, not surprisingly, that there was a connection between intoxication and poverty. In a world of deprivation and hardship, the public house provided a refuge for the poor in Dublin just as it did in London. In the 1940s, Dublin was still 'flooded with drink'. The Dublin pub was a safe haven with a clubbish atmosphere for writers and artists who, in the past, might have aspired to the more sedate environment of the vanished literary salon.

Different pubs attracted the loyalties of distinct types of customer. There were working-class bars, which Brendan often frequented in the company of the working Dubliners, whose champion he always claimed to be. The better-off professional type – civil servants, lawyers – drank in The Dolphin Hotel. The Palace Bar in Fleet Street was the watering hole of journalists and presided over by *The Irish Times* editor, R.M. Smyllie. His corner was known as the 'intensive care unit'. Others, like Davy Byrne's in Duke Street, had powerful literary associations – Joyce had immortalised it in *Ulysses*. John Ryan bought its near neighbour, the Bailey. Apparently, he had attended the sale with the intention of buying an electric toaster. Under his ownership, The Bailey also underwent a revival as a literary drinking spot. It established its credentials by acquiring that most potent of Joycean literary symbols, the door of number 7 Eccles Street, home of Leopold Bloom. But among the city's literary pubs, one stood out – Dublin's literary Mecca, McDaid's in Harry Street, just off fashionable Grafton Street. It was here that Behan made his initial impact in Dublin's wider artistic circles.

McDaid's was a plain, high-ceilinged pub with little of the Victorian or Edwardian grandeur of many of the neighbouring establishments. The building was reputed to have been a prayer house for some sect. In its new, altogether different function, it served a mainly working-class clientele, mixed with the city's classless literati. These were the individuals who, as Brinsley MacNamara, the novelist, observed, 'walked straight out of the pubs and into our novels and plays'. They were to become an important part of Behan's own creative stock.

Anthony Cronin, one of its most distinguished *habitués*, remembered the pub's catch-all ambience:

> McDaid's was never merely a literary pub. Its strength was always in variety, of talent, class, caste and estate. The divisions between writer and non-writer, Bohemian and artist, informer and revolutionary were never rigorously enforced. The atmosphere could have been described as Bohemian-revolutionary.[2]

Paddy O'Brien, the then head-barman, credits John Ryan with transforming McDaid's into a literary landmark.

> He's the man who made it a literary pub. It just happened. He got this thing called *Envoy* [Ryan's influential journal] going and he'd come over to McDaid's and have a drink. And then, bit by bit, it all came into a circle, all types of literary people, poets and story writers and you name it. From that on it just mushroomed. Then McDaid's became the 'in' place if you wanted to find somebody. When the literary people took over there was always something happening. You had Behan, Paddy Kavanagh, Brian O'Nolan and Gainor Crist. There was this great blend. They all seemed to live in the one time.[3]

They did not, however, live in one harmony. Where such enormous egos strutted, sensibilities were easily offended. Conflict was rife, and quite often Behan was the catalyst of trouble. Much of it centred on his arguments with Patrick Kavanagh. They started out as friends, but ended up disliking one another and eventually appeared in court on different sides of a sordid libel action of a type that Dublin specialises in. The presence in any room of the hefty, bullying figure of Behan and the gangling, fragile frame of Kavanagh was a potentially explosive situation, though confrontation remained merely verbal.

It would be incorrect to give the impression that Behan did all his drinking in McDaid's. Many Dublin pubs – some with considerable justification – claim to have been his favourite. But he did do a lot of his drinking in McDaid's. The head barman, Paddy O'Brien, was well placed to observe the effects of drink on Brendan's behaviour in those years. He believed that his capacity to hold his drink was not at all as good as he claimed, or as was sometimes claimed for him. O'Brien remembered that he got drunk very quickly, and that his mood could swing just as rapidly. Noel Gill, whose father was proprietor of another pub which Granny English frequented, witnessed the same traits:

> His voice would be head and shoulders over everybody and his fucking would be twice as loud and that'd be the way he emphasised a point whether it was politics or football. And he'd give a thump, stamp his authority on the subject. We treated him as a character but he could be tricky and boisterous. But he was quite lovable. Brendan would get excitable quite quick and he'd get into hectic arguments. Anyone who picked an argument with him got the worst of it 'cause he was quick at putting them down.[4]

While establishing himself in Dublin's non-conformist literary clique, Brendan also had to deal with the necessity of making a living. Writing professionally as a free man was a different matter from pouring out words in time-heavy confinement and battling with the prison authorities to have his manuscripts passed for publication. From his sixteenth to his twenty-third year he had spent most of his time in Borstal or in prison for political offences. It shaped him completely and left an indelible mark. It was not – principally due to his sense of equanimity – without its compensations for him. He had become accustomed to, indeed conditioned by, the routine of prison life. It had afforded him the chance to meet writers like Ó Cadháin at close quarters. It also gave him the leisure to write without distraction from his drinking or anything else to which he easily fell victim. His status as a Republican internee meant that his writings from prison attracted a special interest outside. This, together with a ready audience for his work among fellow inmates and free bed and board, meant that prison was not so onerous for Brendan as it might have been.

In many ways, the reality of the freedom he emerged to was much harsher. The winter following his release was one of the coldest on record. By the beginning of 1947, rationing of food and fuel had begun to bite deeply, reaching levels far worse than anything experienced in Ireland during the war. Basic foodstuffs like bread, sugar and tea were rationed and the bad weather caused havoc with the turf harvest, on which so many depended for fuel. The larger cities were hardest hit, and an active black market developed. A Crumlin neighbour of the Behan's, Gertrude Gahan, was jailed for a month for stealing gas by bypassing the meter through the skilful use of a bicycle tyre tube. It was a sign of the times.

After a few days of intensive celebrations to mark his release, Brendan quickly accepted that, to make ends meet, he needed a source of income other than the very small sums he could make by writing. His parents allowed him to live at home but he had little option, for the time being at least, other than to go out to work:

> For days following I drank everything that was to be found in the line of porter, though I kept off the hard stuff, until my mother suggested I go out and do a bit of a job and knock out something for herself and the family. I looked out of the window and shuddered but she was adamant.[5]

Though resentful of the waste of his writing time, he knew from the moment he heard he was to be released he had no alternative but to find a job or face poverty.

> When I knew I was going to be free again, I knew I was going to be free again to hunger and poverty and to no kind of pyjamas, not even Free State Army ones. But I knew also I was free to the lights of my native city, which are very large and welcoming.[6]

House painting was the only job he knew anything about. Through his father's contacts in the painting business, he found a number of jobs in the trade. One of his first jobs was in County Kerry. He was engaged as foreman painter to restore the home in Caherdaniel of Daniel O'Connell, the man who initiated the popular campaign for Catholic Emancipation in the early nineteenth century. Brendan enjoyed the job because he had very little to do apart from savouring the local pubs. He did sack one painter – not for inefficiency but for ratting to Foreman Behan on his workmates, who were drinking during working hours. The informer was not a species beloved of any IRA man. While in Caherdaniel, he befriended the local Catholic priest, a namesake, Father Behan. He spent long hours talking in his company. One night the priest got him out of his bed to assist him in cutting down the body of a beautiful young local woman who had hanged herself. The priest gave her the last rites of the Catholic Church and Brendan was deeply moved, as this was usually denied in the case of a suicide. 'Who are we to judge? Maybe it was an accident', the priest told him. This incident went some way towards restoring his estimation of the Catholic clergy. His faith in the Catholic clergy had taken a severe battering in the English prison, where he came to believe 'that religion of any description had nothing to do with mercy or pity or love.' This incident went a long way towards restoring it.[7]

Over the next few years he came to depend on house painting for a living. He moved quickly from job to job around the country, more because of a lack of dependability than a lack of skill. Meanwhile, he continued to write for publication, but met little success. The few works published in the year or so after his release continued his earlier, heavily Republican themes. Three of his Irish language poems appeared in print in 1946 and 1947, only the third of which, 'The Return of McCaughey', merits much attention. In December 1946, the Irish language magazine *Comhar* published this poem by Behan to commemorate the death of IRA leader, Seán McCaughey. McCaughey died on 11 May, 1946 after 23 days on hunger and thirst-strike in Portlaoise Prison. Brendan wrote the poem during his last months in the Curragh. It concentrates on the spiritual nature of McCaughey's self-sacrifice. 'The Return of McCaughey' does not have the metrical control that he achieved in his later Irish verse compositions. He was obviously influenced by the heightened sense of emotional loss felt by one IRA internee at the death of another:

> His journey today will bring him to Milltown,
> Surrounded by thousands paying their respects,
> He'll pass like a prince in the old days of freedom
> Slowly and stately, through the host of his friends;
> The Fianna, young props of the Irish Republic,
> Men and women, all soldiers of our land,
> Young girls all dressed in their bright Irish costumes,
> Great banners being carried to the sound of the band.
> Thousands will humbly follow the coffin
> Of the darling of Ireland, the Lion-heart so bold,
> Welcoming McCaughey back to his homeland,
> For his death in the end is stronger than their force.[8]

In January of 1947, Brendan joined family and friends in the funeral procession of labour leader Jim Larkin. Larkin, born in Liverpool of Irish parents, arrived in Ireland in 1907 and became the messianic leader of Irish trade unionism and an inspiration for Brendan's much admired Sean O'Casey. In March 1947, *Comhar* published an elegy he wrote on the occasion of Larkin's death. Like the McCaughey poem, his commemoration of Larkin is rich in sentimental cant. Like the earlier composition, it is none the better for it.

I was him – every mother's son of us was him.
Ourselves – strong as we wanted to be,
As we knew how to be.
And he threatening the powers and bringing relief,
Following his coffin through the mouth of the city,
Amid great shouts of anger.
Following his coffin through the mouth of the city last night,
Was it us who were in the coffin?
No! we were marching along the street,
Alive – grateful to the dead man.[9]

During the last week of January, Brendan attended a meeting of IRA men who were planning a commemorative concert for their executed comrades Barnes and McCormack. They wanted to raise funds for the cause by touching the emotions of Republican supporters who were still enraged by the executions. Some of the men proposed a one-act play on the theme of the 1798 Insurrection. Brendan objected strongly and demanded a play on the theme of Barnes and McCormack. When it was pointed out to him that no such play existed, he offered to write one within forty-eight hours. The concert was scheduled for 7 February in the Queen's Theatre, a place resonant with memories for Brendan. No one believed he could produce a work in that time but, as promised, within forty-eight hours, he delivered the required script to the waiting players. It was the first of his dramatic works to be publicly performed.

The play, *Gretna Green*, was in one act.[10] It had three characters, two men and a woman, and was set outside a prison on the eve of a double execution. No one attending the first night could be in any doubt as to the prison and the executions involved. The script has not survived, but the players remembered that it had very little action and consisted mostly of dialogue. Brendan was to play one of the male roles but turned up drunk on the evening. By good fortune, there was a young understudy who muddled his way through the text. The concert and the play were a total disaster because of poor attendance due to bad weather.

Unhappy that his progress towards becoming accepted as a writer in Dublin was so slow, Behan became a familiar sight at public meetings, especially if they had even a slightly unorthodox political flavour. When the Dean of Canterbury, the Rt. Reverend Hewlett Johnson, known as the 'Red Dean', addressed a meeting in Dublin organised by the Irish-Soviet Friendship Society, Brendan was engaged as a bouncer. Scuffles with protesting students disrupted the meeting, and Brendan moved with another

IRA colleague to protect the Dean on stage.[11] The meeting broke up after several of those present suffered injuries. Some days later, when the Literary and Historical Society debated a motion supporting the students injured at the Dean's meeting, Brendan was given permission to speak against the motion. Ulick O'Connor, who was present, described his performance in a potentially hostile environment as 'a *tour de force* which lasted twenty minutes. It ended with the audience cheering him loudly for five minutes after he sat down'.[12]

In 1947, Behan's intemperate Republicanism again landed him in jail. He was arrested in Manchester on 15 April. He had entered Britain using the service identity document and pay book of Liam Dowling of Leighton Road, Crumlin. The police files describe Dowling as 'an RAF deserter'. Dowling was known to have IRA sympathies and his documents were reported lost in Dublin a month before Behan used them. Upon his arrest, he refused to give an account of his movements except to say that he had been there for five days. The reasons for his trip to England remain obscure. The Home Office files refer only to the fact that he was in England contrary to the terms of the Expulsion Order that banned him from British soil after his release from Borstal. In his *Confessions of an Irish Rebel*, however, Behan claimed that he had gone to Manchester to take part in the escape of Dick Timmins, an IRA bomber serving a fourteen-year sentence in Wakefield Jail. His account of his role in the springing of Dick Timmins is highly fictional and must be disregarded. Timmins himself denied that Behan was actively involved in his escape from Wakefield.[13] He may have gone over as a courier with money for the project, but even that is not certain.

Brendan appeared in court on 16 April and again on 1 May 1947 when he was sentenced to four months imprisonment in Strangeways Jail, Manchester.

The week before he was sentenced, he received a rather curious telegram from Dublin. It read simply: 'I'm flying to defend you. The Pope'. It came from the eccentric Dublin barrister, Eoin O'Mahony, but caused quite a stir in the Governor's office at Strangeways, where Brendan was on remand at the time. Behan's account of his interview on the subject with the Governor is probably his truest account of the entire Manchester episode:

> 'How well do you know the Pope, Behan?'...
> 'I know him fairly well,' I said, which was the truth, though not His Holiness Himself. 'I have a friend, Eoin O'Mahony, a Cork barrister, and he must have read of my case in the newspapers.'
> 'I don't believe you,' said the Governor in a stern voice.
> 'I don't care whether you do or you don't', says I, 'but you can read for yourself that the Pope is coming over to help me.' [14]

The genial and erudite lawyer from Cork did go to Manchester to help him. Despite his grand designs for the restoration of the Irish Monarchy, and the time he spent in the company of what remained of the Anglo-Irish aristocracy, O'Mahony had considerable sympathy for Republican prisoners. He spent much of his time defending them free of charge in the courts of Britain and Ireland. Indeed, his Republican Prisoners' Release Committee became quite a thorn in the side of Britain's Labour Home Secretary, Chuter Ede. It was due principally to the Pope's sterling defence of Brendan that he got off with a four-month sentence.

At no point during his imprisonment in Britain or Ireland, had Brendan felt as dejected and alone as he did in Strangeways. He spoke of it as 'loneliness without peace'. He spent much of his time in solitary confinement. When he did mix with the other prisoners, it was quite often with British soldiers, some of whom were serving time for rape in Germany near the war's end. Others were deserters from the Eighth Army found guilty of murdering their officers. Brendan felt these British Army men to be entirely acceptable – a tolerance he could not have achieved had he not undergone that almost Pauline conversion in his attitude towards the English while he was at Borstal.

During his time in Strangeways, he reflected on the vicious circle of hope, political action, imprisonment and despair in which he was trapped and which had prevented him from realising his literary ambitions. He put his thoughts in a poem written in Irish, the title of which translates as *Repentance*. He scratched it out with a mail-bag needle as if he were etching its meaning so deep into his consciousness that it might never be erased. The work is a turning-point in his œuvre – his voice is unhindered by the need to pay lip service to any political ideology. The poem is couched as a point-of-death realisation of the terrifying consequences of a lifetime of sin. It has a strong emotional honesty. Colbert Kearney has interpreted this imagined death as 'a correlative of another doom which haunted him at the time – the death of the writer within him, dissipated in the aimlessness of his life'.[15]

> My misdeeds are visible like a pack of hounds
> And my memory summons them to howl at me;
> My life's course has run, here's death on horseback,
> Scaling the ditches of my years;
> I await the kill, my breath draining out,
> The bloodsweat of the hunt is dark on my face,
> I tremble as the red-eyed baying draws near,
> O Virgin, have mercy and forsake me not.[16]

It was with the dark sentiments reflected in this poem that, on the evening of 23 July, he boarded the *S.S. Longford* under police escort at Liverpool. It sailed for Dublin at 10.10 p.m.

Back in Dublin, Brendan failed miserably to establish a productive literary routine. He submerged himself again in the unproductive mire of his old Dublin drinking haunts. The Behan household remained beset by economic difficulty. There was little sympathy for a member of the family sitting around at home in a routine of writing, recovering from a hangover and cursing his bad luck. Kathleen Behan was nothing if not a practical woman. She had suffered the early death of her mother; several years in an orphanage; the death of her first husband and the loss of two children. She insisted that the boys go out and find work to supplement the family income. Seamus had already left to join the RAF and establish a life in England. Rory had served in the Irish Army during the Emergency. Seán was immersed in the politics of labour organisation. Dominic took whatever work came his way. Carmel was still the baby of the household. Although Stephen disliked being out of work, he endured regular periods of joblessness. Brendan rose with a daily curse on the misery of being reduced to the 'death without dignity' imposed on him by the type of work he despised, while his mother harassed him during what the family called 'the Goebbel's hour'. By 1948, the pressure on him to find regular employment as a house painter became too much for him. Brendan began to spend less time at home and more and more as a Bohemian *peregrinus*, moving between pubs and the flats of friends who were willing to give him a bed for a night or two.

He had already become a familiar landmark in the louchest late-night drinking den in the city. On his return from jail in England, this world took on a more significant role in his life. The Catacombs was a warren of basement rooms beneath a Georgian house at number 13 Fitzwilliam Place. It opened after pub-closing and stayed open as long as the drink lasted, which might mean until the next morning. Behan did not hesitate to soak up the solace it offered him at a time when he was wracked by serious doubts that he would ever succeed as a writer.

The guardian of this subterranean retreat was a good-looking English homosexual called Dickie Wyeman, who had abandoned a career as a night club manager in London after the wartime death of his boyfriend. He pitched up in Dublin and soon became a focal point for the city's literary and sexual demi-monde. He had acquired the basement lease at a peppercorn rent and quickly realised the premises' potential as part of the new dynamic of post-war Dublin social life. The clientele of The Catacombs crossed over with that of McDaid's. Alan Simpson and Carolyn Swift, who were to play an extremely important part in Behan's rise to fame, were occasional visitors. The novelist J.P. Donleavy, was an *habitué*, along with Gainor Crist, on whom Donleavy later modelled the character of Sebastian Dangerfield in *The Ginger Man*. Other regulars were the poets Pearse Hutchinson and Patrick Kavanagh, the author and critic John Jordan, Michael Heron an assistant editor at *Envoy*, A.K. O'Donoghue (O'Keefe in *The Ginger Man*), and a host of students, revolutionaries and free loaders. They all carried the only invitation the owner required – a supply of bottled Guinness or other drink. The return money on the empties formed a substantial part of Dickie Wyeman's rather shaky personal economy.

It is difficult, even with the benefit of so many first-hand accounts, to understand why the damp, dreary basement became a focal point and intellectual stimulus for a generation of writers whose understanding seems, at least in retrospect, to have been enriched by the place.[17] For most, it was an opportunity to prolong a night's drinking in a city where the licensing laws were stacked firmly against the consumer. For others, it provided an occasional opportunity to make homosexual contacts in a country where such activity remained illegal until 1993. For a handful of people, it provided cheap temporary accommodation. Anthony Cronin lived in The Catacombs for a period:

> The whole place smelt of damp, decaying plaster and brickwork, that smell of money gone which was once so prevalent in Ireland. Off the corridor leading out of the kitchen were various dark little rooms. Mine had, I think, once been the wine cellar. There was hardly space for a bed in it, and none for anything else except a few bottles and books. The other rooms were variously occupied and people came and went according to need and circumstance, but our host was a great stickler for the rent, so one had to preserve some sort of affluence or go. There was never any difficulty about gatherings, however, for he lived partly on the proceeds of the bottles that the revellers brought and left behind.[18]

Dickie Wyeman disported himself in the detached manner of an English gentleman and, though effeminate in his behaviour, could quickly dispatch his detractors with his tongue or a well-placed fist. He was nearly six feet tall, slim, and had piercingly beautiful grey eyes. He took laudanum to soothe the pain of the loss of his boyfriend – a British Army officer – whom he referred to as 'the faithful heart'. Brendan did not endear himself to Wyeman by calling his late lover 'the Sacred Heart'.

The Catacombs had a reputation as a place where, mainly because of the sexual orientation of the owner, homosexuals and lesbians could freely gather and have sex without incurring the wrath of the law or the censure of the prudish. Brendan perceived it as just such a place. 'There would be men having women, men having men and women having women. A fair field and no favour. It was all highly entertaining'.[19] Other *habitués* rush to defend its memory against such claims. Perhaps the reality was that in the stygian darkness and Rabelaisian drunkenness, nobody was really sure of what exactly anybody else was up to.

To say that homosexuality was frowned on by Irish society at large during Behan's lifetime is an understatement. Ireland was a deeply puritanical place. Public morality was still so oppressive that, in the middle years of this century, the elders of Dublin Corporation refused a gift of Rouault's *Christ Crowned with Thorns* as unsuitable. When a reproduction of Manet's *Olympus* was hung in the Waddington Gallery in Dublin's Anne Street it was denounced as an immoral work. Most trying of all for the artistic community was the relentless invocation of the 1929 Censorship of Publications Act in order to ban the work of certain Irish writers. Few of any merit were left untouched by the puritanism and xenophobia exercised by the Censorship Board. Reasonable protests by writers such as Yeats, Gogarty, Beckett, O'Faoláin, and even Ezra Pound writing from Italy to the letters' page of *The Irish Times*, were ignored by the law makers. The new generation of writers, which was to include Brendan Behan, would suffer a similar fate. Kate O'Brien's novel, *The Land of Spices* was banned in 1941 because it contained a harmless reference to homosexuality: 'she saw Etienne and her father, in the embrace of love.' Eric Cross's largely anthropological work *The Tailor and Ansty* was banned because of its earthy language and Patrick Kavanagh received a visit from the police because his masterpiece *The Great Hunger* was thought to be obscene.

John Ryan, who attempted to undo the damage being done in the name of false morality, marvelled at the tenacious survival of creativity in the face of such opposition:

> That it did not die was no thanks to priest, politician or technocrat, but to poet and painter. It was these, without physical roots, and the dreamers, who finally hurled themselves against that green density of gombeen men, crawling hack, bogus patriot and pietistic profiteer, that found this humanity stimulating in Ireland's green and unpleasant land.[20]

A young, working-class homosexual in 1940s Dublin seeking models for his orientation faced a desert. There was a certain amount of clandestine homosexual contact among a coterie of middle-class professionals and theatrical types. The most public representatives of this clique were Micheal MacLiammóir and Hilton Edwards, founders of the Gate Theatre and domestic and sexual partners. Though quite often MacLiammóir spent his winters in Ireland, he rarely lost his Riviera sun-tanned patination which he achieved with the none too subtle application of make-up. There was a civilised tolerance of such behaviour in most quarters of Dublin because MacLiammóir could carry it off with the sheer force of his personality. He also had the excuse of his profession.

Freddie May, the musical director of the Abbey Theatre, was a character in the same pattern. His manner of dress and gesture suggested, to say the least, a sexual ambiguity, but the general Irish public gave no indication of noticing. Freddie May had championed Brendan while he was in jail in Ireland and remained totally infatuated with him after his release. He sometimes accompanied Brendan on his visits to The Catacombs. To some in that group, May made no secret of his sexual attraction for Brendan.

Brendan's feelings towards him remained unchanged. He continued to be very fond of Freddie and grateful for his loyalty during his years in jail, but he did not reciprocate the older man's sexual passion.[21] Friends of Freddie and Brendan believed that their sexual relationship went no further than Brendan occasionally allowing Freddie to kiss and fondle him. One friend who saw them together on many occasions believed that, had Freddie been a younger man whom Brendan found physically attractive, the situation would have been quite different.[22] What especially attracted Brendan to Freddie was his unqualified love for him. It was the sort of love with which his Granny English had spoiled him and which he would continue to seek throughout his life.

The question of Brendan Behan's sexuality has been a contentious one. Ulick O'Connor's 1970 biography dealt briefly with Behan's sexual tastes. He wrote that Behan was known to have bisexual leanings, picked up in Borstal, and that 'for the rest of his life he was to be bisexual. The type of boy or man he admired sexually was the type he had met at Borstal – clear-skinned, athletic and fair'. According to him, Brendan might occasionally brag to his friends about his 'Hellenism', but he was not unduly troubled by it because 'he was equally attracted to girls'. He quotes the shock felt by an unnamed IRA acquaintance of Brendan's when he caught his comrade kissing a man they both knew well who was 'a composer with left wing sympathies'. The IRA man told O'Connor that he found this confusing because he had recently been engaged in trying to get Brendan out of trouble with a woman who claimed he had made her daughter pregnant. O'Connor later refers to Brendan's interest in other men, particularly black youths, in New York, but does not mention any actual sexual activity. O'Connor believed that when Brendan became famous he started to be very worried that knowledge of his sexual tastes would ruin his popular 'hard man' reputation.

The publication of O'Connor's book, with its very tentative exploration of Behan's sexuality, caused a furore in Ireland. There was a heated exchange of correspondence in *The Irish Times*. Seán Ó Briain, Brendan's mentor from his Mountjoy and Arbour Hill days, Seán Kavanagh, and Beatrice Behan, the writer's wife, all wrote to object to O'Connor's claims that Behan was bisexual. One newspaper flagged the fracas with the headline: 'Quare Fellow; Queer; Query?'

Only one individual has ever come forward with a public admission that he had engaged in homosexual acts with Brendan – a sailor-cum-aspiring actor who wrote an account of his relationship with Behan in 1960s America. Only once, in *The Courteous Borstal*, an unpublished fragment and precursor to *Borstal Boy* did Behan write about homosexual activity in an autobiographical context. But the writings and comments of many of his friends present strong evidence that Behan's sexuality was, at the very least, ambiguous.

In *Dead as Doornails*, Anthony Cronin's account of bohemian literary life in Dublin, Cronin writes that, while in his twenties, Behan talked openly of his 'homosexuality'. Cronin, however, believes that he delivered such statements mainly for effect, that in them there was 'an element of picaresque braggadocio which was meant to suggest cynicism and villainy on his part'.[23]

> Mostly when he spoke of it, it was not as a difficulty but as a distinction. Sometimes he averred to it simply to shock. In the presence of a bishop and a curate for example, if that unlikely eventuality can be imagined, he would declare that he fancied the curate, or perhaps even the bishop, in order to shock the one or embarrass the other. He used to say wryly that de Valera's housing reforms had ruined his ordinary sexual development; that the move from the slums out to the windy spaces and semi-detached houses of Crumlin had come at a crucial age and had been disastrous. On the landings and the dark hallways of the tenements you could always get a grope or a squeeze and at fourteen he was just getting the hang of things ... when the move came along.[24]

Cronin claims that Brendan admitted total bewilderment about the physical side of homosexual relationships. As a very young man, he was so perplexed by the mechanics of it that a reference in Enid Starkie's biography of Rimbaud sent him to the National Library for several days, researching the trial of Oscar Wilde in the hope of discovering precisely what Oscar got up to in bed.[25]

But if Brendan admitted ignorance about what men get up to together in bed, he also complained to Cronin of 'strange ... naïveties where "ordinary" sex and the female were concerned; and was bitter about those who, not being privy to his real preferences, prescribed more orthodox sex as a corrective to our way of life. When reproached once by a progressive lady we knew for not having a regular girlfriend, Brendan replied that it was every bit as un-Marxist to reproach a man for not having a fancy woman as it would be to reproach him for not having a motor car. For a long time afterwards he used to refer to her suggestion that all his ills and malaises would disappear if he had more sex as "Dr So-and-so's remedy to the human condition".[26]

Cronin had no recollection of ever seeing him strike up a homosexual liaison, nor did he recall him giving any surface impression of being homosexual. On the contrary, his outward appearance was often so dishevelled and unkempt that no such interpretation of his sexual orientation could be attributed to it. He once made a drunken pass at Cronin but the matter was lightly dismissed and 'cheerfully disposed of'.

John Ryan, the editor of *Envoy* and Behan's close friend, recalled his omnivorous sexual appetite and that he made no great fuss about casually admitting his bisexuality to his friends.

> I think that even apart from the years of enforced confinement with other men, he might have considered homosexuality as simply another tasty morsel or savoury on the smorgasbord of the Bohemian running buffet. But only as 'afters', so to speak, following the main course. Booze, as always took precedence over all ... The definition of an Irish 'queer' is supposed to be 'a man that prefers women to drink'. He certainly did not come into that category.[27]

Ryan remembered that he was openly ribald about his sexual tastes, 'just as he was derisive and blasphemous about most of the things that ignorance wraps in a cocoon of modesty and piety'.[28] He makes the important point that though Brendan had many faults and flaws, intellectual dishonesty was alien to him and therefore he was incapable of lying to friends about something as fundamental as his sexuality.

There is other testimony to Brendan's frankness about his proclivities in the years before he achieved international fame. At a Dublin party, he was standing at the foot of a staircase talking to his friend, the author Benedict Kiely, when an extremely handsome man passed by on his way upstairs. Looking after him, Brendan turned conspiratorially to Kiely and asked 'Given the choice, who would you prefer to shag, him or Eleanor Roosevelt?' Once, while attending a performance by a French ballet company in Dublin, Brendan claims to have felt sorry for the boys dressed up as sailors because 'their pants were so tight I began to be concerned as to their physical well-being. When they began to dance, for a tender youth of my age, this was too much'. From his gallery seat he shouted 'Up sodomy'.[29]

That he took an unusually non-judgmental attitude towards homosexuality for his time is evident in several places in his published writings. His comments on Oscar Wilde in *Borstal Boy* are one example. Another is a passage in *Confessions of an Irish Rebel*. While awaiting transfer during his period in prison in Manchester in 1947, he noticed a bunch of particularly glum-looking prisoners, ranging in age from seventeen to fifty. He heard they were a group of coal miners who had been sentenced for sodomy or 'screwing each other down the pit' as he put it. 'Look,' I said to one of them, 'nothing that you have done, except you interfere with a little child, is shameful.'[30]

When among friends, however, he often used to boast drunkenly of his 'Herod Complex', or preference for young boys.[31] This led to serious misunderstandings on at least two occasions in later years, when he was accused of sexually interfering with young boys. Both incidents happened in County Wicklow and both were in the houses of Anglo-Irish aristocratic friends of Brendan's. The first occurred in Uplands, the home of Ralph Cusack, a painter and novelist who often held open-house for writers and artists. During one such house-party, Brendan disappeared for some time with Cusack's 14-year-old son. The boy later returned to his parents in floods of tears, unable to articulate what had happened. Brendan's own boasting about his 'Herod complex' led Cusack to believe he had molested the boy. Brendan protested his innocence and it later became clear that the whole episode arose because Brendan had rather too adult a conversation with the boy about the existence of God. The child was so severely shaken he burst into tears and fled.[32]

The second time Brendan had problems over his alleged taste for boys was at Luggala, the Wicklow home of Oonagh Lady Oranmore and Browne, where he was a regular house guest from 1955 until his death. Lady Oranmore and Browne's partner of the time, an extremely dubious figure, accused Brendan of sexually interfering with her son, Tara. No one else in the family believed the accusation.[33]

The extent and exact nature of Brendan's homosexual activities cannot be ascertained. *The Courteous Borstal* mentions only vague homoerotic contacts. His sexual encounters with Freddie May are thought to have been limited to 'kissing and fondling'. The sailor, Peter Arthurs, with whom he took up in

America claims that their sexual contact was limited to fellatio, with Behan as the active partner. The sailor Peter Arthurs, also claims that, when Brendan requested that he bugger him, he refused. Behan did brag about having had anal intercourse with a woman (see page 143), but said he found the experience displeasing. But, although the evidence is contradictory and mainly hearsay, its combined weight leaves little doubt that Behan had a sexual interest in men and, at least on occasion, indulged it in a variety of ways.

His younger brother, Brian Behan, also a playwright, is convinced that his brother engaged in homosexual sex, first in Borstal, then in Irish prisons. According to Brian Behan, the absence of female company during Brendan's imprisonment in adolescence and early adulthood 'made his sexual relations difficult. He didn't really understand women because he hadn't associated much with them'. After his brother got out of jail in 1947, Brian decided to introduce him to heterosexual sex. He took his brother to visit a group of prostitutes who traded in Phoenix Park. They were run by a Mrs Power, who had a wooden leg. The brothers decided that, for the novelty, she should have charged double. Brendan did avail himself of the opportunity offered by his brother (although not, it seems, with Mrs Power).[34]

Brendan once told the poet Allen Ginsberg that his favourite sexual scenario was two men sharing a woman.[35] But if hard evidence for his sexual relations with his own sex is somewhat thin, it must be noted that there is also an extraordinary shortage of accounts of sex with women in the otherwise fulsome Behan legend, whether oral or written; by his account or in the accounts of others. In her memoirs, Beatrice Behan mentions the satisfaction of their physical relations in the early years of their marriage. But unlike other famous figures, literary and otherwise, no woman has come forward to claim an extra-marital sexual relationship with the late Brendan Behan. His name has been linked in vague rumour with three or four women from Dublin's literary and artistic circles. He is said to have had an affair in New York with Valerie Danby-Smith, Ernest Hemingway's assistant. But close friends of his during the period between his release from the Curragh in the late '40s and the onset of his international fame in the late '50s insist that he had no regular girlfriends and cannot recall even minor affairs, although his brother Seamus has a vague recollection that there was a girlfriend in Dublin before he got married. His interest in women is certainly not something for which he is well-remembered.

Brendan Behan's sexuality was clearly paradoxical. Brian Behan believes that it was his complicated relationship to Catholicism that prevented him from ever finding a sexual balance.[36] Another analysis, and one that may be equally true, is Anthony Cronin's belief that Behan's bawdy boasting was part of the bravura public persona that was nearer his heart than any physical passion. Given the quantity he drank, this mooted disinterest may well have had a physical cause.

The Catacombs milieu embraced ambiguity, decadence, degeneracy, and outrageous show. It gave Brendan an important stage on which to play out the perplexities of his personality. In *The Ginger Man*, J.P. Donleavy captures the essence of Brendan's physical presence and something of his bisexual boasting in the Fitzwilliam Place warren.

> A man, his hair congealed by stout and human grease, a red chest blazing from his black coat, stumpy fists rotating around his rocky skull, plunged into the room of tortured souls with a flood of song:
>
> > Did your mother come from Jesus
> > With her hair as white as snow
> > And the greatest pair of titties
> > The world did ever know.
>
> Mary tugged at Sebastian. 'Who's that? It's a shocking song he's singing.' 'That's the son of the rightful Lord Mayor of Dublin. And his uncle wrote the national anthem.' Mary appreciative, smiling. This man swept across the red tiles wildly greeting people on all sides, telling the room: 'I loved the British prisons. And you lovely women. The fine builds of ye. I'd love to do you all and your young brothers.'

Amongst his literary peers, in the freedom of The Catacombs, he could play the sexually-ambivalent buffoon with a mixture of 'ironic confusion, humorous self-disparagement, mock surprise, combined of course with a satiric savagery about the pretensions of other people.'[37] His deflationary attacks extended way beyond the range of his immediate acquaintances, to politicians and other writers and artists. His most regular performance was *The Childhood of D.H. Lawrence*, in which he humorously attributed Lawrence's personality-defects to his childhood relationship with his father. *Pater* Lawrence arrives home to find his son reading a book and launches into a stream of verbal abuse at the lad while ordering him to scrub his back in the bath. Brendan played torturing father, supplicant mother and wimpish son in a variety of English accents acquired from listening closely to his mates at Borstal. He sometimes performed another favourite, *The Boyhood of John Ruskin*, as a companion piece to Lawrence. It was a bawdy parody of Ruskin and his parents on the grand architectural tour of Europe. Brendan would have them argue endlessly on aesthetic matters in pedantic detail, making all the rows sound ridiculous in the extreme. Even the sacred icons of the Republican cause became part of the fabric of his cabaret intime. He did 'Maude Gonne at the Microphone' in the crackling voice of the great matriarch. She would muse on the sexual fantasies of Yeats and on her hopes for the new Ireland. For this role, he wore a tea towel on his head and drew dark lines on his face with burned match sticks to mark the famous *Quattrocento* finger-fashioned image of Yeats's poem. He wittily ridiculed de Valera's slum clearance of the late 1930s and the sacred cow of his Gaelic Ireland. When he tired of all that, he occasionally chanted long sections of the Latin Mass, swinging incense at his congregation with an imaginary thurible, for which he substituted the simple prop of a lighted cigarette.

All of his antics were ornamented and accompanied by song. His fine tenor voice would swell above the most crowded room with 'an enormous theatrical sense, whether for the rendition of scurrilous comic pieces or passionate patriotic and left-wing ballads – often the two merged into one. According to what was needed by the song, the lips would curl, the eyes flash and roll and the tiny, sensitive hands clench or unclench in passion, or reach out in mock unavailing yearning and despair'.[38] Later on, when he tried to command an indifferent audience with the impact of his fame rather than win it over with his talent, his gestures sometimes became contorted and angry. For now, he was confident in the affection of an audience that welcomed his ephemeral performances. They relished the sight of him down on his knees acting out the brothel-crawling antics of Toulouse-Lautrec, and singing from his extensive repertoire of ballads. He, in turn, accepted their adulation on those simple terms.

He consolidated some important friendships during The Catacomb years. Perhaps the most important of these was his friendship with John Ryan. Ryan was two years younger and from an entirely different social background, but to Brendan he was more than just the editor of a magazine who would be willing to publish his work. Educated at James Joyce's old school, Clongowes Wood College, and the National College of Art, Ryan had the benefit of considerable family money, much of which he placed unstintingly at the disposal of impoverished writers. He allowed Brendan the use of *Envoy's* Grafton Street office and its typewriter. Above all, he gave Brendan the conviction that he had the talent to succeed as a writer. They probably first met in the studio cum apartment of the sculptor and set designer, Desmond MacNamara, at 39 Grafton Street. MacNamara and his wife Beverly Huberman welcomed their artistic friends. The MacNamaras also played a key role in establishing Brendan's belief in his abilities, simply by making him feel part of an intellectual community. At their flat he met people like Erwin

Schroedinger, a colleague of Einstein's, who was a refugee in Dublin from Nazi Germany. The MacNamaras entertained amid papier-maché stage set-constructions in various stages of completion. Desmond once began work on a statue of the then-unknown Brendan, planning to place it on St Stephen's Green without the blessing of the municipal authorities, but the project was never completed. All civilised callers and a few who were not so civilised were welcome at the MacNamaras, and the cast from McDaid's and The Catacombs often did their dress rehearsals here before moving on. Indeed, so complete was the MacNamaras welcome to Brendan that he regularly stayed overnight rather than trekking out to Crumlin. The MacNamaras had several cats and, being vegetarians, had to buy meat specially for the animals. They once asked Brendan to feed the cats while they were out visiting. He thought that feeding good steak to a cat a terrible waste, so he fried it up and ate it himself. As he was finishing the meat, he heard the MacNamaras coming up the stairs. In a flash of inspiration, he stuck the cats' faces into the fat in the frying pan. When their owners came in, they were gratified to see what they presumed to be two well-fed cats licking their chops.

Mingling in literary Bohemia was all very well as a night-time activity but it did not put food on the table or drink on the counter. Brendan continued to work sporadically as a house painter until the early 1950s. He was also a competent sign-writer and traces of his handiwork were still faintly visible in the capital many years after his death, most notably a no-parking sign in Merrion Row.

He also claimed to have earned a crust in a less orthodox way. He used to boast to friends that he accepted the regular patronage of a suburban matron who enjoyed being buggered. He said he found the work distasteful, but it presaged a future career opportunity in the sex trade that came his way in Paris in the future.

He spent much of 1948[39] as a deck-hand on board a freighter, the *Sir James*, which plied its trade between Newry, County Down and Glasgow. Its owner was Eddie Chapman, from Sunderland, who had bought it at the end of World War II to carry 'mixed' cargo – mostly of the contraband variety – between Ireland and Scotland. Chapman had a prosperous pre-war career as a safe-cracker who specialised in robbing the Odeon cinema group, until his luck ran out. He became a somewhat unsuccessful double agent during the war, working for the British and the Germans until his Nazi masters slapped him in a concentration camp to await liberation by the US Army. Brendan met him through John Ryan, who had made his casual acquaintance over a drink while waiting for a flight from Dublin Airport. After the *Sir James* entered Carlingford Lough, it headed for the lock-gates and in Newry in

County Down, Brendan headed for the local pubs. In many of them he became as well known as he was in their Dublin counterparts. After six months of their working association, Chapman and Behan had a disagreement over money and parted ways; they both returned to Dublin and were soon drinking companions again.[40]

The charms of bohemian café society had begun to wear thin even before Brendan embarked on his short sea-faring career. The literary clique were showing signs of growing bored with their latest interloper. His writing talent was not receiving the recognition that the poet, John Montague, for one, believes it already deserved. When Brendan returned to Dublin, he became increasingly restive and his dissatisfaction led him down the familiar path of binge-drinking and inevitable trouble.

On 30 July, matters got out-of-hand after a day's heavy drinking with two friends in several pubs in the city centre. At their last port-of-call, The Pearl Bar in Fleet Street, Brendan, John Daly (a house-painter), and James Carmichael (a metal worker), met a rather loud Englishman to whom they took exception. There are many versions of the remark that sparked the incident, but it ended in a street brawl that extended from Fleet Street to nearby Trinity College. By the time the police arrived, the porters at Trinity had become involved. Brendan and his friends tried to get away through Trinity's grounds by barging past a worried porter at the front gate. Brendan prolonged the disturbance by holding on to the college railings and lashing out with feet and fists at the arresting officers. Eventually all three were brought to Pearse Street station and charged with assault, resisting arrest and using abusive language. The case was heard before District Justice Lennon on 14 August and Brendan was sentenced to a month in jail and a fine of forty shillings. The ever loyal 'Pope' O'Mahony defended the three. He told the court that they had been provoked by a man who had spoken offensively about Ireland and, in particular, its neutrality during the war.[41] Brendan found himself in Mountjoy once more under the care of Governor Kavanagh.

This was the first time he had been imprisoned for a non-political offence and he felt very sore about it. He could no longer enjoy the glamour of being jailed for his convictions – he was in jail as a mere drunken street-brawler. The obligation to wear prison clothing and the attitude of the other lags depressed him.

During his latest jail experience, he began to think of his native city, much as he loved it, as a place where he had 'conviviality, but no friendship'; a place that gave him 'loneliness, too – but no solitude.' He was released from Mountjoy on 13 September and later that month, he decided to move to Paris.[42]

9

Between Paris and Home

When Brendan Behan decided to follow the lead of other Irish writers like Wilde, Joyce and Beckett, and seek his literary fortunes elsewhere, England was his first choice of destination. He hoped that the British Home Office would have softened its position on him by 1948. But it had not. That year a police note was added to his file: 'There is no evidence that Brendan Behan has changed his attitude towards this country and it is strongly recommended that the Expulsion Order be maintained.' One can understand why the British took this view, but it thoroughly misrepresented Behan's sentiments. So altered was his attitude towards the English and England by 1948, that he had hoped to live and work there. In February, he wrote what must have been for him an embarrassingly grovelling letter to the Home Secretary:

> I ask that you, considering the altered conditions nowadays, and that I was only sixteen when first imprisoned, will permit me to go to England. I would be a liability to no one as I am a house painter and signwriter of competence ... I trust in reading this application that any deficiencies in style, taste or proper respect will not be allowed to detract from the message I seek to convey [–] that of an honest artisan seeking an opportunity denied him through economic conditions at home, of earning a living in your country, despite that which is now past, and I should hope forgotten.[1]

It was not forgotten as far as the British authorities were concerned and would not be until January 1954, when the then Home Secretary, David Maxwell Fyfe, rescinded the Expulsion Order. Until then, the Order remained a considerable obstacle for Brendan because, at the time, it was very difficult to travel to any foreign destination from Ireland without passing through Britain. The moment Behan set foot on British soil he was vulnerable to arrest.

Blocked by the Home Office, Behan made up his mind to go to Paris instead after an accidental meeting in a bar with a like-minded acquaintance. He took a train from Dublin to Cork and a boat from Cork to France.[2] He was seen off with an Irish wake, a tradition that goes back to the emigration of the famine years when people who left the country almost never came back. Desmond MacNamara, John Ryan, Seán O'Sullivan and several others who wished him well in his venture, attended. In fact, he did not move permanently to Paris, but he made several lengthy trips there over the next five years, and the city became his second home.[3]

On future journeys abroad, he would risk travelling by way of Holyhead, Newhaven and Dieppe. He travelled on his own passport which carried only his official name, Francis Behan. He was fortunate to escape detection of his presence on British soil on some occasions; on others he was less fortunate. On this first trip, because of the route he had chosen, he could afford to relax about such matters and he reached Paris in high spirits. When he arrived he made his way to a small hotel on the Rue Dauphine in St-Germain-des-Prés.

The talk of literary Paris when he arrived was the petition to the President of France to have Jean Genet totally absolved of his past criminal record. Jean Genet decided to forsake the world of prison in favour of the literary alternative in 1943, the same year that Brendan, in his prison cell, made up his mind to become a professional writer. Genet's resolve was stronger than Behan's, but then the reasons for his imprisonment were different – he spent much of his youth in jail as a common thief. Only three writers refused to sign the petition for Genet. One of them, Albert Camus, became a friend of Brendan's. Brendan was fiercely defensive of the Algerian-born Camus. He admired him as a man of action and Resistance hero, womaniser and heavy drinker. Camus delighted in Brendan's interpretation of Joyce's Dublin – the shameless use of which won him many other friends in literary circles in Paris. Camus's dislike of Genet, based largely on his jealousy of Sartre's championing of him, totally coloured Brendan's own opinion of Genet, with whom he might otherwise have had much in common. Brendan was intensely loyal even to new-found friends and his friends' enemies were his enemies. Of Genet, he wrote, 'In a less civilised country he would have been engaged in the production of mailbags, four stitches to the inch ... I had extracts of his autobiography read to me, some of which rose the hair in my head. And, as my mother once remarked, that which would shock Brendan Behan would turn thousands grey.'[4]

Post-war St-Germain was still a veritable incubator of literary coteries. While Brendan prowled all over Paris at any hour of the day or night, he wisely chose the two most important kilometres of literary Paris as his base.

The area, bounded by the Boulevard Saint-Michel on the east, the Rue des Saints-Pères on the west, the *quais* along the Seine on the north and the Rue de Vaugirard on the south, became his familiar beat. The clearly marked borders of the *quartier* gave Brendan the same reassuring feeling that he had had in the familiar ambit of his Dublin city-centre patch.

> The atmosphere in the Latin Quarter at this time was quite extraordinary. Nobody gave a fiddler's for your connections, who you fought for or why you fought. All they wanted was a drink, a smoke and that, and were totally uninterested in any army or arms.[5]

Brendan described the Flore and the Deux Magots, the famous literary cafés of St-Germain, as 'The twin cathedrals of existentialism'. The Deux Magots had lost the ascendancy it had held in the inter-war years but it was still an influential gathering-place for writers and artists. Brendan was a regular in both. Sartre, who due to his fame, had had to move his base from the Café Flore by this time, observed that even in this literary Bohemia, certain conventions were observed. It was not considered good form to table-hop or to scatter greetings as one entered, no matter how well one knew those gathered. Brendan broke all the rules and made a pest of himself amongst those who used the cafés as a place to write in, as well as a place to meet friends.

Brendan also used the Studio Bar, which was near his hotel, and the Pergola Bar at the Odéon Metro station. There he watched the antics of a Chinaman whose only reading material was a bilingual furniture catalogue from which he read aloud: 'three-piece Chesterfield suite, twenty pounds ten, oak double bed, eleven pounds ten: mattress, best flock extra'. Also on Brendan's street was Raymond Duncan's Akademia, the centre of his eccentric Hellenic cult. His disciples greeted the dawn each day near his hotel – 'elderly ladies and gentlemen in sandals and a sort of kilted costume that bore as much resemblance to the clothes of the ancient Greeks as the uniform of the Fintan Lalor Pipe Band to that of Brian Boru'. In the Studio Bar, Brendan met the winner of the French National Lottery, a despondent Swede who had nobody to celebrate with him. Brendan and a companion soon had the champagne flowing and were happily making inroads into the unfortunate man's winnings.

Outside of his drinking bouts, Brendan pursued the literary circuit with some diligence. If Dublin had lost its great literary salons, those of post-war Paris flourished. They were hosted by aristocratic women sure of their social position or by middle-class women considered to be social climbers, vying with one another to collect the most sought after literary prizemen. But this was a world closed to an unknown young Irishman, and one in which Brendan was not particularly interested. There were more public salons in the city where he was able to shine on his own terms. He spoke very little French when he arrived in the capital. He had acquired some from his father and some in the Curragh 'academy' and did not hesitate to throw himself into ungrammatical conversations in the reassuring world of the café.

He made several new friends on that first trip to Paris. They came mainly from the expatriate community and at least half a dozen were Americans enjoying the benefits of the GI Bill in Paris. They included Milton Machlin who later became the editor of *Argosy* magazine. Apart from his friendship with Camus, Brendan made the acquaintance of one other important writer, the American, James Baldwin. Baldwin's circumstances were similar to Brendan's. He arrived in Paris with holes in his socks, little money and great ambition. He came from a large poor family and, like Behan, had stumbled from one badly paid job to another while attempting to write. They fell into friendship with considerable ease.

Brendan sought out, but did not find fellow Dubliner Samuel Beckett on this first Parisian trip. He knew Beckett's cousin, John Beckett, in Dublin, but did not have an introduction from him. Beckett was busy at work on *En Attendant Godot* when Behan arrived in Paris – the date '9 octobre 1948' appears on the first page of the French manuscript. The two writers finally met in 1952, when, very early one morning, Behan turned up drunk at Beckett's apartment. For three hours, he held forth in raving monologue until Beckett finally off-loaded him in the offices of *Merlin* magazine where he introduced him to Christopher Logue. Beckett told Behan that Logue would be fascinated to hear about his writing. Numerous acts of kindness from Beckett followed. He bailed Brendan out after a drunken brawl landed him in jail. Beckett gave him a substantial sum of money and a lecture on the evils of drink. On another occasion, Beckett paid Behan's overdue bill at his hotel. After a few meetings, however, Beckett began to find Behan tiresome in the extreme. There was much in Brendan's make-up that reminded Beckett of the life he had fled in Dublin and having it brought to his doorstep in large drunken doses did not please him. Beckett had no time for hammy Paddy-whackery and Behan, who, even at the best of times, lacked confidence, made up for his shyness in an extrovert show of 'Oirishness'. But no matter how appalling Brendan's behaviour was, Beckett always remained impeccably polite to him. Other friends did not maintain his civilised reserve. Even the most outrageous of the Americans sometimes found his drunken behaviour went beyond tolerable limits, and it was not unusual for him to find himself turfed out of their apartments for misbehaving. He regularly coupled insolence with ingratitude, but Parisian willingness to put up with such behaviour was not quite as generous as Dublin's. Sinbad Vail, editor of *Points* magazine, whose patience was often tried by Brendan's behaviour, recalled:

> ... he frequently got terribly drunk, and I'm no puritan when it comes to booze or most things for that matter, but he was awfully boring and abusive, insulting his friends, smashing their furniture and destroying pictures on the walls. In the end, most of us thought he was just a bloody drunken show-off Irishman, the sort that is caricatured, and I think now he must have wallowed in it.[6]

However, Brendan was fortunate to connect with Sinbad Vail in Paris. He was to publish some of his earliest prose works. Vail was the son of Laurence Vail and the heiress Peggy Guggenheim who had been Beckett's lover for a short time. Brendan later met Peggy Guggenheim when they were fellow guests at a party in Luggala in County Wicklow. The magazine *Points* was established with Guggenheim's backing, and her son became its English language editor. Vail, indulged and supported by his mother, had a reputation as a playboy who loved fast cars, playing billiards and heavy drinking.

His editorial methods were at best haphazard. 'I've been told', Vail claimed, 'to try and be original for once and not write an editorial; but then I do so little writing and it is so nice to see one's name in print, even in one's own magazine'. One contributor recalled that he waited until he had enough manuscripts to fill eighty-four pages and then took the lot off to the printers. His bewilderment at his involvement in the publication of a little magazine is clear from an editorial he wrote to mark the fifth anniversary of *Points*.

> It was in the summer of 1948 that I first thought about starting a magazine. I was in Venice on holiday, a holiday from God knows what as I was not doing anything anyway ... I vaguely thought about opening an art gallery in Paris, but I knew even less about art than literature ... I often wonder why anyone ever starts a little literary magazine in the first place. There are vague ideas running around that they are created to publish writing that never has a chance in the commercial press, 'new' writing, 'experimental' writing and even 'good' writing ... but I think the real reason is to give the editor and his pals an outlet for their own work plus an egotistical desire for 'fame' or 'notoriety' which in other circles are achieved by eating goldfish in public.[7]

Vail favoured prose over poetry. He paid authors 3,000 francs for a story – not a great deal of money but many of the little magazines paid contributors nothing at all. Brendan began appearing at Vail's office, in the Rue Bernard Palissy, bearing wads of manuscript. *Points* eventually published two. The first was a short story called *After the Wake* and the second an extract from what later became *Borstal Boy*.

Three Behan lyrics, written in Irish, were inspired by his association with Paris. Two have Irish writers who lived in the city as their inspiration. Behan quite literally dined out and drank out on the strength of his knowledge of Joyce or perhaps more correctly, Joyce's Dublin. He recorded his gratitude to him in this poem.

> Here in the Rue St André des Arts
> In an Arab tavern, pissed,
> For a studious Frenchman I constRue you,
> Ex. G.I.'s and a Russian, pissed.
> All of those things you penned I praise
> While, in France, I swill Pernod in return:
> Proud of you as a writer we are
> And grateful for the Calvados we owe to you.
>
> If you were me
> And I were you
> Leaving Les Halles
> Holding all this cognac,
> On a full belly bawling,
> You'd write a verse or two in my praise.[8]

His poem on Oscar Wilde conveys a sense of the terrible waste Behan perceived in Wilde's lonely death in the Hotel d'Alsace. It became almost a sacred shrine for him and whenever he passed it he paused to pray for the repose of Wilde's soul. He visited the Hotel and asked to see the room where Wilde died. Later he stayed in the hotel, when, like Wilde, his financial affairs became severely tricky. Behan's sexual ambiguity allowed him to empathise with Wilde and that empathy is reflected in the poem's ending.

> After all the strife,
> That, alive, he caused,
> Ravaged with fear,
> In the half-light stretched,
> The gay spark's body
> Lies dumb in the dark,
> Silent, the funeral
> Candles guttering.
> The graceful body,

The firm gaze, spent
In a cold bare room
With a concièrge spiteful
From too much attendance
On a foreign tippler
Who left without paying
The ten per cent service.
Exiled from the Flore
To a saintly desert,
The young prince of sin
A withered churl,
The gold jewel of lust
Left far behind him,
No Pernod to brace him
Only holy water,
The young king of Beauty
A ravished Narcissus
As the star of the pure Virgin
Glows on the water

Envoi

Delightful the path of sin
But a holy death's a habit.
Good man yourself there, Oscar,
Every way you had it.[9]

Another poem from his Paris period is a satirical look at what went on in those 'twin cathedrals of Existentialism'. Careless negation of the ponderous abstractions introduced in the poem reveals Behan's casual attitude to the intellectual arguments measured out in endless cups of coffee at the Flore and Deux Magots.

Watchman, walking the wall –
of an empty hall.
What is the chase after?
a grave matter.
A journey to hell?
Of course, but your mind as well?
What was before our time?
Dunno. I wasn't alive,
amn't yet.
Evil our fate?
too lazy
to say.

Virtue, not a gleaning,
nor pain, nor even meaning,
nor truth in what I posit -
nor in the opposite.[10]

Brendan's capacity for alienating those who might be influential in helping
him in Paris did not deter many of them, especially Sinbad Vail, who
supported him with cash, food and most important of all, placement for his
work. Vail was selective enough not to publish everything thrust at him by
Brendan. He did feel guilty about this and, in a few instances, paid for
unsolicited manuscripts. Despite Brendan's best attempts to damage his
reputation by playing the drunken Irish buffoon, Paris accepted him as a
writer, something which Dublin still did not fully do. This did not mean he
was financially secure. He was still forced to do menial jobs that he despised,
but in the evenings, when he sat at the café tables, he was joined by other
writers who were in the same position.

To be afforded the status of writer mattered more to him than material
advantage. In Dublin, he had neither but it was there he returned in late
December. He arrived back in time for Christmas. When he entered 70 Kildare
Road his father looked up from his newspaper and said, 'Ah! You're back', as
if he had just gone down the road to the shops. Brendan launched into an
enthusiastic litany of the joys of life in France. His brother Seamus, who had
served with the RAF there during the war, quickly deflated him by telling him
he was not the first Behan to go to France. Brendan looked deeply wounded
by the remark and no sooner had Seamus said it than he regretted it. He felt
Brendan desperately wanted to have his travels approved of by the family and
instead he was put down by Stephen's well-practised 'sublime indifference'
and his brother's quick tongue.[11]

He spent more and more time away from home. The pressure was on again
for him to return to his old trade; 1949 began, as so many other years had,
with the quest for painting work. His abhorrence of the trade knew no bounds
by this stage. '... I am allergic to painting', he told his friend Paddy Collins,
'not to paint, mark you, but to its application through physical labour'. He
found employment with the firm of Panton Watkinson of St Stephen's
Green. They had a profitable contract to paint The Gaiety Theatre that year
and needed extra men. Brendan was given the unenviable task of working on
the ceiling. During a rehearsal for *The Winslow Boy*, he deliberately splattered
the precocious young lead with a bucket of white paint. He caused further
havoc for Panton Watkin's administration by filling in his time-sheets in

Irish. At every opportunity, he nipped across the road to Sinnott's public house. Eventually his foreman, his patience in tatters, sacked him.

'The Salvation Army came to my rescue in 1949', he used to joke. He was employed on the decoration of their hostel in York Street until April and then went painting lighthouses in Northern Ireland for the summer period. By August, he was itching to return to Paris. His feelings of disappointment with the Dublin literary scene, expressed in a letter to Sinbad Vail, were published in *Points*.

> Cultural activity in present day Dublin is largely agricultural. They write mostly about their hungry bogs and the great scarcity of crumpet. I am a city rat. Joyce is dead and O'Casey is in Devon. The people writing here now have as much interest for me as an epic poet in Finnish or a Lapland novelist.[12]

In the same letter he told Vail: 'Sometime I will explain to you the feeling of isolation one suffers writing in a Corporation housing scheme'. He was caught in a terrible dilemma. While he dearly loved the working-class Dubliners among whom he was reared, he found being a writer put him outside their tribal bounds and that was painful. The writers in the literary pubs did not take him seriously, and he believed them to be middle-class. 'The literary pubs are not much good to me', he wrote to Vail. In fact, class-distinction did not operate in Dublin's literary pubs. If Behan was wearing sufferance as his badge at this time, it was entirely of his own making. He was feeling sorry for himself, because so many of the writers he associated with in Dublin were tiring of his constant attention-seeking and his refusal, when drunk, to cede the floor to a more interesting voice. Brendan had no cause to complain about what he saw as his unfair treatment at the hands of the Dublin literary establishment. John Ryan, Seán O'Faoláin, Peadar O'Donnell and others were still championing his cause. What he needed was confidence in his own literary talent, a confidence that Paris seemed to provide.

He passed through Newhaven on his way to Paris, on 19 August, 1949. He was fortunate to go unnoticed by the British police. They had information that he was due to return on 2 September. He did not.[13] Instead, he stayed on in Paris where he set up base again in St-Germain-des-Prés. His routine varied little from his previous Paris visit. He did, however, make several new friends, among them two Irish people, Desmond Ryan, *The Irish Times* Paris correspondent and Kathleen Murphy, a young sculptress studying ecclesiastical art in Paris. The Studio Bar became his social head-quarters – it was his office, meeting place and lender of last resort.

The art of making a living through literary endeavour still eluded him. He found it difficult to place his work in suitable publications, though a number of his short stories and poems were published in 1950 in Paris and in Dublin. In January 1950 *Envoy* published his poem, 'Loneliness'. It is a spare, impressionistic work that recalls the loneliness of his years of confinement.

> The tang of blackberries
> Wet with rain
> On the hill top.
>
> In the silence of the prison
> The clear whistle of the train.
>
> The happy whisperings of lovers
> To the lonely one.[14]

In August, *Envoy* published his short story, 'A Woman of No Standing'. It takes as its theme a broken marriage. The mistress hovers in the background as the man she has had the affair with is dying. The story is told by a female friend of the spurned wife who is eager to see what she assumes to be a glamorous prostitute turn up at the funeral. She is disappointed to see a haggard, middle-aged woman dressed in cast-off clothes.

> I had some idea of a big car (owned by a new and tolerant admirer) sweeping into the cortège from some side street or another, or else a cab that'd slide in, a woman in rich mourning heavily veiled in its corner.

The 'woman of no standing' is reduced to hiding behind a tree at her lover's funeral while his family gloat. The narrator, though she is a friend of the wife, has a more compassionate attitude and pities the 'pale hunted look in her eyes'.

While producing finely crafted work such as this, Brendan claimed he was also writing pornography for publication, in French translation, in magazines including *Points*. He excused himself by retorting, 'Hunger makes pornographers of us all'. He may well have written pornography, but nothing he published in *Points* can be regarded as that. *Points* restricted itself to more serious literary output. The writing of pornography may have reflected Brendan's desire to cast himself in the same mould as Frank Harris or Henry Miller, who did write that sort thing in Paris. One piece of Behan's so-called pornographic writings briefly emerged in Dublin. In the early 1950s, two sisters were shown a short story he published in a Paris magazine. It was a steamy piece concerning the exploits of two Dublin prostitutes who serviced the sexual needs of soldiers after the War. The sisters claimed they were defamed by it, and consulted Dublin solicitor Con Lehane. He advised them not to proceed with an action against Behan. Mr Lehane's view was that if the case went to court Brendan's reputation would attract a great deal of attention in the press and the women, who by that time had become respectable ladies, would be severely embarrassed by the publicity.[15]

When he talked of producing pornography, Behan may also have been referring to the short story 'After the Wake', published in *Points* in December 1950. He wrote it during this second, lengthy stay in Paris. It is arguably his finest short story. Sadly, it remained abandoned in the relative obscurity of *Points* until it was rescued in 1978.[16] The story was not given a wider audience during his lifetime because it had a homosexual theme which did not accord with the tough-man image created by Brendan and his handlers. He showed it to a handful of people in Dublin but swore them never to mention its existence to anyone. It would, however, be disappointing to think he regarded this story as pornography, because it shows an accomplished handling of the tragi-comic elements of sexual ambivalence, which Behan understood so well. It could not have been written by a man with exclusively heterosexual sensibilities.

He sets the story in a Dublin tenement, where the male narrator plans the seduction of a married man who lives in a flat in the same house. He establishes a friendship with the husband and the wife and enjoys the misplaced jibes of neighbours, who tease him about his sexual designs on the woman. So devious is his plan of seduction that he even gives the couple a book on homosexuality. The wife, an ordinary uncomplicated woman of twenty-one, thinks she would recognise a homosexual if she saw one: 'A woman can always tell them – you kind of smell it on a man – like knowing when a cat is in a room'. The husband is the same age as his wife, but he is worldly-wise, with 'pretensions to culture', and understands about the love of one man for another. They are both 'tall and blonde, with a sort of English blondness'; although the object of desire is intelligent, it is his physical charms that bewitch the narrator. The story is suffused with understated homoeroticism:

> Once we went out to swim to a weir below the Dublin Mountains. It was evening time and the last crowd of kids – too shrimpish, small, neutral cold to take my interest – just finishing their bathe. When they went off, we stripped and watching him I thought of Marlowe's lines – which I can't remember properly:
> 'Youth with gold wet head, thru' water gleaming, gliding, and crowns of pearlets on his naked arms.'

I haven't remembered it at all, but only the scene of a Gaelic translation I've read. When we came out we sat on the towel, our bare thighs touching, smoking and talking.[17]

They talk of the inconveniences of tenement living, and how they had hated sleeping with their brothers. The married man had also disliked sharing a bed with his father but felt remorseful when a seizure took the old man one night.

'I don't mind sleeping with a child,' he said, 'the snug way they round themselves into you – and I don't mind a young fellow my own age.' 'The like of myself,' and I laughed as if it meant nothing. It didn't apparently to him. 'No, I wouldn't mind you, and it'd be company for me, if she went into hospital or anything,' he said.[18]

His wife does go into hospital for a cancer operation. Then the narrator 'opened the [seduction] campaign in jovial earnest'. The operation proves unsuccessful and the wife dies. Her wake involves a great deal of drinking and late into the night, when the mourners have all gone, the narrator helps the husband into bed.

I had to almost carry him to the big double bed in the inner room. I first loosened his collar to relieve the flush on his smooth cheeks, took off his shoes and socks and pants and shirt from the supple muscled thighs, the stomach flat as an altar boy's and noted the golden smoothness of the blond hair on every part of his firm white flesh. I went to the front room and sat by the fire till he called me. 'You must be nearly gone yourself,' he said, 'you might as well come in and get a bit of rest.' I sat on the bed, undressing myself by the faint flickering of the candles from the front room.[19]

Another of Behan's colourful claims about his Paris life, apart from that of writing pornography, was that he worked as a pimp in Harry's Bar. In *Confessions of an Irish Rebel* he writes that, on his return to Paris, he took up an offer of pimping work, made to him on his first trip by a prostitute whom he called Jenny Étoile. The offer was made in the Studio Bar, and later confirmed by the master pimp 'Tony' who wined and dined Brendan in Le Nouveau Siècle. 'Tony', according to Brendan's account, ran a brothel – a mixed establishment that served the sexual needs of men seeking women, women seeking men and men seeking men. It seemed just the sort of place an old Catacombs hand would be at home in. The girls worked out of Trois Quartiers and Brendan's job was to find customers, mostly Americans, in

Harry's Bar. He did quite well for several months until the manager twigged his activities and told him to move on.

With his career as a pimp already at an end, he had to return to the painting trade yet again. With the help of the Confédération Général de Travail, he secured a union card and some work, painting a house in Saint-Gratien, west of Enghien. He struck up a friendship with the owner, M. Monti and with his son, François, to whom Brendan taught the art of enamelling. He seems to have spent more time drinking the contents of the Monti's cellar than applying his painting skills to their walls. When the job was finished he took various other painting and sign-writing jobs, including the one for which he is best remembered. A Parisian café owner asked him to do a sign to attract English-speaking tourists. The finished product read: 'There is but one Au Fait Café in Paris and this is fucking well it.'

Having asserted that establishment's primacy over its rivals, he travelled by bus to the South of France, arriving in Cannes somewhat dazed:

> ... I fell to wondering how it is that the Parisian worker goes little on the beautiful Côte d'Azur on account of it's being the playground of a gang of international millionaire loafers, [until] long before we came to Cannes I noticed camped along the road the tents of quite obviously ordinary French families.[20]

From Cannes he travelled onward to Speracèdes. His movements from there are not known, but he was in Paris again by late autumn and back in Dublin by Christmas 1950. Looking back on the year, he could take considerable pride in his literary achievements. Apart from the work mentioned above, he also had two poems published in an anthology of contemporary Irish verse, *Nuabhearsaíocht*, that did much to establish his reputation. *The Prayer of the Rannaire* (versifier) has all the caustic qualities of a Merriman satire and can also be read as his farewell to writing poetry in Irish. He wrote very little Irish after this. There was the question of reaching a wider audience but there was also his annoyance with the majority of those who wrote in the language. He found he had very little in common with most of them whom he saw as hypocritical and self-seeking. In *The Prayer of the Rannaire*, Behan castigates the narrow-mindedness of the Irish speaking Irelanders, including the civil servants who have used the Irish language to push themselves up the promotional scale. Such types were to be found at all levels of Irish society and he had even come across some in the IRA. He wanted nothing to do with them:

If some grown-up guy, with fluent Irish,
Wrote of people and things in a civilised style,
Of moods and opinions in the words of today,
Impudent, easy, expansive, au fait –
I'd happily hear what he had to say.
A poet with punch, with power and plenty,
A burgeoning bard, blazing and brazen,
Pained, impassioned, pagan-penned.

But Jesus wept! what's to be seen?
Civil servants come up from Dun Chaoin,
More gobdaws down from Donegal
And from Galway bogs – the worst of all,
The Dublin Gaels with their golden fáinnes,[21]
Tea-totalling toddlers, turgid and torpid,
Maudlin maidens, morbid and mortal,
Each one of them careful, catholic, cautious.

If a poet came and inspired some spirit,
I'd go home, my job finished.[22]

Behan's poem *Grafton Street* sums up his feelings about being back in Dublin.
The poem is, in his cousin's view, 'Behan's most jaundiced vision of his native
place and gives some idea of the difficulty he had in returning to live in Ireland
in 1950'.[23] The opening and closing stanzas capture that dark mood:

Saw last night the living
On death's island,
Heard talk in a place
Devoted to the silent.

Whisper as one must,
Of love in this sour land
Before they go in
To dance in the Classic.[24]

If he was despondent about being back in Dublin, he was happy to be at work
again on the book that would eventually, on publication as *Borstal Boy*, put the
cornerstone on his critical stature as a writer. In June 1942, he had published
I Become a Borstal Boy in *The Bell*. It dealt with his bitterly unhappy memories
of Walton Jail. Towards the end of 1943, he had sent his brother Seán a short
story called *Borstal Day*. In December of that year, from Arbour Hill, he wrote
to his friend Bob Bradshaw of his 'book on Borstal which I'll get fixed up after

the war'. That book would not appear until 1958 and, though its gestation was a tortuous process, it gave him the feeling that he was working towards a significant milestone in his literary career.[25] Now that he was back in Dublin, he had set his heart on making his living, not by the paint brush but by the pen.

Pursuing Honour In His Own Country

Except for a few odd jobs, by the middle of 1951, Brendan was supporting himself, however shakily, on his literary earnings. Dublin's wider literary world, which he had blamed for blocking his progress in the 1940s, would soon, however grudgingly, have to accept him as one of themselves.

The Irish language magazine *Comhar*, which had already published a number of his poems, was his main source of patronage in 1951. Its Westmoreland Street office became for him in Dublin what the office of *Points* had been in Paris. 'You could never be in any doubt as to who was coming', Riobárd MacGoráin, who became editor that year, recalled. 'You would hear him singing at the bottom of the stairs, stopping on the way to talk to anyone he'd meet, then singing again. He'd burst in the door ... He knew the *Comhar* office was the one place where he wouldn't be turned away and he appreciated this.'[1] Brendan proposed a book in Irish on his IRA and prison experiences in return for a weekly stipend of £4. MacGoráin agreed and even sponsored a three-month stay on the Gaeltacht island of Aran, so that Brendan could improve his Irish. The book project proved useful in gathering material for *Borstal Boy*, however, although he submitted drafts of a few chapters, he never completed this version of his prison memoirs. It was not the only, and certainly not the most spectacular occasion on which Behan was to fail to deliver goods already commissioned and sometimes paid for. Despite the non-appearance of the book, his relationship with the magazine remained solid and he continued to pressure MacGoráin for advances for future projects.

With the idea of an Irish language book discarded, MacGoráin suggested to Behan that he should write something about his IRA experiences for the magazine. Brendan began a series of six articles that covered his early training at Killiney Castle and the Republican tradition from which he and his family came.[2]

Brendan entertained the other writers drifting into the offices of *Comhar* with the rich anecdotal material he had gathered during his extended stays in Paris. One of his most riveting tales was the story of a journey through France he and Anthony Cronin had made in 1950. Their destination was Rome. Brendan suggested to Cronin that they travel during the Marian Holy Year. He believed the populace along the way would shower them with bountiful generosity when he proclaimed in broken French that they were 'deux Irlandais en *pèlerinage* à Rome'. Brendan's imaginative grand plan envisaged marching on Rome by way of Czechoslovakia. Cronin, whose sense of geography was more acute than Brendan's, thought this a daft notion and he objected to that leg of the journey. Nevertheless, the two set out through Chalons-sur-Saône, Macon, Villefranche, Lyon, Grenoble, Briançon and onwards to within a few miles of the Italian border where they quarrelled and parted ways. Cronin later wrote an account of the trip, including an assessment of Behan at the time, in his memoirs, *Dead As Doornails*.

Behan published a little known Irish language short story – 'Na hOilithrigh' or 'The Pilgrims' – in *Comhar* in April 1951. It was loosely-based on the same journey. Along the route Brendan had taken a liking to drinking large quantities of Ricard which he pronounced 'the nearest thing to absinthe you can get'. This put a severe strain on their finances and on their friendship. In 'The Pilgrims', Brendan captures this tension to his own disadvantage.

> 'Always drink! Drink! Drink! You think of nothing else.'
> 'I do,' said I, eager to list the other subjects of my contemplation in self-defence.
> 'O, you're the great fellow. The big man of the Studio Bar, the big man of McDaid's in Harry Street, the life and soul of the Mabillon roaring round the place like a drunken bull. You'll introduce me to the writers, the crowd in the Café de Flore, you'll take me drinking with the boys of the Beaux Arts. And in the heel of the hunt who are you? An ignorant animal from a Dublin back-street with nothing to distinguish you from the other thousands of them except that your tongue is more obscene and your lungs stronger.' [3]

Behan, the raconteur, was about to emerge from 'the other thousands' to a general Irish audience through regular broadcasts on Radio Éireann. Again, personal patronage played an important role in his early success. Micheál Ó hAodha, Productions Director at the station, was the first to recognise Behan's potential as a broadcaster. He was able to make a distinction between his literary talent and the rollicking image Brendan projected in McDaid's and elsewhere. In his view, in the early '50s Brendan bore little resemblance to the raddled, heavy-fleshed brawler of the colourful newspaper copy and drunken television appearances of later years.

> He seemed to me a shy and diffident fellow at heart. Beneath the swagger he remained a kind of altar boy whether in prison garb or in house painter's overalls. He was the kind of acolyte who having served wine at the altar would take a few swigs out of the bottle when he got back to the sacristy. He could kick up a rumpus from time to time ... but the rough-house tactics seemed no more sinister than that of an unruly youngster kicking the door because he had been locked out.[4]

Ó hAodha first invited Behan to broadcast in December 1951. The talk, 'On the Northside', described his childhood in Russell Street. It went on air on 29 December 1951. *The Irish Times* signposting of the programme was the first indication that Brendan Behan was metamorphosing from a pub 'character' into a public personality:

> Brendan Behan who has had a colourful life both at home and abroad, may be heard on R.E. (Radio Éireann) tomorrow evening, giving an account of his childhood on the north side of Dublin city ... Mr Behan is a house-painter by trade and a poet by inclination, writing both in Irish and in English.[5]

His natural talent as a story teller came across in these early broadcasts: Philip Rooney, the *Irish Press* columnist, devoted his entire review to Behan's first radio performance, which he eulogised as a new departure in the use of radio in Ireland.

> Mr Behan seized with both hands the opportunities which radio offered him ... Mr Behan's broadcasting technique has all the virtues of its defects. He has so much to tell that he races the clock to tell everything at pell-mell pace. Where another broadcaster would have spun out his talks to make half a dozen broadcasts, this indefatigable conversationalist crammed a boy's lifetime of pithy tales, pungent comment, vivid memories and racy songs into 30 minutes of broadcasting time.[6]

The reviewer, like so many others, believed Brendan's chief talent was as a conversationalist. That talent found expression without let or hindrance on radio. 'He is as free as the air', Rooney observed, 'and considerably more breath-taking'.

When Daniel Farson, the London-based author and photographer, telephoned John Ryan, to ask if there was a 'character' in Dublin who would suit a colour piece for *Picture Post*, Ryan recommended he should meet Behan. The result was a romp around Dublin that produced some of the best photographs of Behan ever taken. Sadly, they were rejected by the new editor of *Picture Post*, who felt Behan was not well known enough. Within four years Behan was making headlines in the British press and within eight his name blazed a trail across a thousand international headlines.

By 1952, his stock was already rising rapidly on his home territory. Early that year, Micheál Ó hAodha invited Brendan to be a regular contributor to a series of reminiscences and songs called *The Ballad Maker's Saturday Night*. He asked Behan to compile a series of programmes of Dublin street ballads. This did not pose a challenge – he possessed an almost inexhaustible stock of songs learned from his mother and from his uncle and it gave him a paid forum for something he had been doing gratis in Dublin Pubs. In one of his early *Ballad Makers* broadcast, he described evenings on Russell Street when the street lights were lit and local children began to sing:

> Often of a winter's evening after tea, all the kids on the street would stand round the lamp on the corner, watching along the road for Billy the Light to reach our lamp. You could see for a mile up the Circular Road, the lamps going on, one after another, as he came nearer and nearer. Then at last he was at ours and the little light that never went out, either by day or night, at the touch of his long stick, would burst the mantle into an orange flame and then the singing would start. Songs that were never made on paper, but grew out of the stories of the pavement, passed on from one generation of children to the next, songs that were as old as *Zoodlum Zoo*, that sang before Daniel O'Connell, when he was well-thought of.[7]

In the very first programme in ballad makers' series, Brendan sang a song that was to become synonymous with his name and later became the theme song from *The Quare Fellow*.

> A hungry feeling came o'er me stealing
> And the mice were squealing in my prison cell,
> And the old triangle went jingle jangle
> Along the banks of the Royal Canal.

It has been believed for many years that Brendan wrote that famous prison song but Micheál Ó hAodha says he never laid claim to authorship. Indeed he asked him to send a copyright payment to another Dubliner, Dick Shannon.

The newcomer's broadcasts were so successful that he was asked to share a double bill on radio with his old mentor Seán O'Faoláin. O'Faoláin had been one of the first to nurture Brendan's talent through his visits to him in Mountjoy and it must have given him pleasure to see his good opinion vindicated. On 29 March 1952, O'Faoláin gave a talk on land division in Italy and later that evening Brendan gave a talk on his life and times in Paris. *The Irish Times* primed his audience with a positive advance notice:

> As most of you are probably aware, Mr. Behan is a young Dublin writer who is rapidly winning a reputation as an accomplished broadcaster with an original style of approach. Those who have heard his memories of a childhood spent in the O'Casey country, north of the Liffey, or his programmes of Dublin street songs, will not need to be told that an account of a visit he paid to Paris ... is likely to be well worth a hearing.[8]

Although Brendan had insisted that the copyright payment for *The Old Triangle* be paid to another man, he could be extremely difficult about his own fees. For his newspaper piece, he often demanded immediate payment. At the Henry Street offices of Radio Éireann, he made a regular pest of himself to the administration staff. He sometimes used to turn up half-cut from an early morning drinking session in the market pubs and demand payment for recent broadcasts. On one such visit, Micheál Ó hAodha, in the presence of a US Embassy official, was auditioning for a quiz sponsored by the Irish American Association. The first question asked was, 'Who spoke the words, government of the people, for the people, by the people?' Brendan burst into the studio shouting, 'And what about the fucking niggers?' Brendan thought the incident hilarious, until he next applied for a US entry visa. The embassy demanded an apology for the intemperate remark.

There were conservative elements in the radio service who believed that the earthy vernacular performances of Brendan Behan had no place on national radio. They would gladly have kept him off air had they been able to do so. But as soon as his first broadcast was transmitted, it was too late for the quibblers at the station to put a stop to him. By now the critics who really mattered had taken up his case. The support they gave a relatively unknown individual was unusual in a small city like Dublin where internecine bitterness had so long been the order of the day in the artistic community. *The Irish Times* radio critic was particularly well-disposed towards this new talent and seems to have been aware of the tensions Behan's unconventional work and behaviour was causing in Radio Éireann.

... with reference to the station's swift and altogether praiseworthy recognition of his gifts as a broadcaster, I have heard it murmured that R.E. (Radio Éireann) now has a 'Behan in its bonnet.' Let us hope that he remains there, and continues to hum as happily as heretofore for a considerable time to come.[9]

Ó hAodha, encouraged by this critical success and firm in his belief in Behan's talent, asked him to write a weekly serial play for radio based on the Dublin characters of his youth. Behan produced only two pieces, *Moving Out* and *A Garden Party*,[10] both produced in 1952. It became the shortest serial in the history of radio drama, but both plays testify to Behan's growing skill at characterisation.

Moving Out is a totally autobiographical piece, based on the Behans' move from the Russell Street slum to the modern Crumlin housing estate. The action centres on the incident, told earlier here, of Stephen Behan's reluctant departure from the familiar environs of Russell Street for the 'wilds of rural Crumlin'. The Behan family become the Hannigans, and Kildare Road becomes Ardee Road. In the reassuring atmosphere of his local pub, Jim Hannigan is recovering from the shock of reading a note from his wife informing him that the family had moved. When the barman asked where his wife has moved to, Jim replies:

> Some place they call Ardee Road. It might as well be in Jiputty for all I know. The deceit of her. There I was this morning, going out to my hard day's work, little dreaming that before the day would be out, I'd be an ... an ... an orphan. And what nicer am I nor an orphan, an exile with no place to lay my head?[11]

The second instalment, *A Garden Party*, finds the Hannigans settled in Crumlin in their new corporation house. Again, Behan based his plot on a real life event. Kathleen had ordered a cart load of manure for the garden and pestered the reluctant Stephen to dig and fertilise the patch at the rear of the house. Brendan tended to gloss over the fact that his mother's family had owned large tracts of land in the most fertile part of Ireland.[12] Brendan used to tell people that 'All the Behan land came in window boxes'. The deeply urban Stephen may have married a woman whose family came from the land, but he had no intention of becoming a son of the soil. The battle between Kathleen and Stephen over the tiny plot of garden in Crumlin provided Brendan with the source material for his second radio play. Alan Simpson later combined the two short plays for his Pike Theatre to form an entertainment called *The New House*.[13]

Behan's success in broadcasting moved in tandem with his success in journalism. Robert (Bertie) Smyllie, the genial, pro-Unionist editor of *The Irish Times*, had taken a great liking to the Republican Behan when he first came across him up a ladder touching up the façade of the paper's offices. In October 1952, he asked Brendan to travel to Paris to do a colour reaction piece, from the French view point, of an international soccer match between France and Ireland in Dublin.[14] It was a plum journalistic assignment. Smyllie decided to fly Brendan to Paris because of the risk that he would be arrested for breaching the Expulsion Order if he landed on British soil. Rather than handing him a ticket, Smyllie foolishly agreed to give Brendan the air-fare in cash. The outcome of placing such a wad of money in hands so prone to temptation was predictable. Assisted by a former Irish boxing champion, Ernie Smith, he drank the majority of it in a few favourite Dublin pubs.

With time not on his side, it was now impossible to reach Paris without travelling through Britain. He arrived in Newhaven on 26 October and a vigilant immigration official spotted him immediately. Brendan has left an elaborate and heavily embellished account of the incident in *Confessions of An Irish Rebel*. The facts are simple enough. He was arrested at Newhaven and taken to Sussex Police Headquarters at Lewes. There he was remanded in custody for a week. The Special Branch questioned him on the subject of his current relations with the IRA. A police report attached to his file and relating to this incident suggests Brendan had switched his loyalties from the IRA to the Communist Party, and that he had 'the ear of MacBride'. Neither piece of information was correct. Behan had no special access to Seán MacBride, who was a prominent Republican and Minister for External Affairs in the inter-party government that fell in 1951 – a position the British police appear to have believed he still held. Brendan's mother had worked for MacBride's mother, Maude Gonne MacBride. MacBride, as a former IRA, chief would naturally have had a great deal of sympathy for Brendan's predicament, but that was as far as it went. That misleading report may, however, have accounted for the civil treatment he received while in custody.

On the morning of 4 November, a diplomat from the Irish Embassy in London visited him and told him he had secured the services of a barrister named R. J. Carter. His case was heard that afternoon before the magistrates at Lewes Magistrates' Court. While he was waiting in the holding cell, he met a railway worker charged with sexually assaulting two teenage male twins. He tried to comfort him but was discouraged by the police. That was the second time he is known to have shown courageous and open compassion for men charged with homosexual offences, in England in the post-Wilde pre-Wolfenden era. The man was in an extremely distraught state, both ostracized and insulted by his fellow prisoners and by his custodians. Brendan asked the police if he could go up to listen to the hearing of the man's case, but they refused him permission and told him to mind his own business.

At Behan's hearing, the police said they believed that he was no longer active in the IRA. His counsel told the Court that his client was a regular contributor to newspapers and radio in Ireland, and was establishing a reputation as a playwright. The chairman of the magistrate's panel, Mr A. Goldsmith, imposed a fine of £15 plus costs for illegally entering Britain. When imposing the fine, he added that Brendan was 'a man dangerous to this country'.[15]

At Newhaven the following day, under police guard, he boarded the *S.S. Worthing* bound for Dieppe.[16] The officer who accompanied him to the ship was a Dublin man named Finley. Brendan despised this man and likened him to the vindictive type of Dubliner he most resented:

> He was an Irishman, of the variety best known to me, who would be happily absorbed in the problem of seeing whom he could do next.[17]

The crowded *S.S. Worthing* sailed at 10.45 a.m. Searching his pockets on board, Brendan discovered that the only money he had on him was an Irish threepenny piece.

His friends Desmond Ryan came to his rescue once he reached Paris. He found him a bed in a small hotel behind the Luxembourg Gardens. The next day, Brendan listened to the match on the radio in the hotel bar. An incomprehensible commentary did not help his article for *The Irish Times* and the ungracious hostility of the French losers in the bar did not improve his humour. The match took place in Dublin's Dalymount Park. In Paris the following morning, Brendan read in a local newspaper that 'the Dalymount roar frightened the French team so much that they lost their nerve and also the match'. Dispirited and broke, he headed back to Dublin to face what he believed would be the formidable ire of R.M. Smyllie. To his surprise, Smyllie took his story of the débâcle well. Perhaps, it was because for once Brendan decided to tell the unadorned truth. The Editor sympathised with the longterm problem posed by the Expulsion Order. He took the incredulous Brendan for a drink and gave him £10 for good measure. During their chat, Smyllie told Brendan to try to control his drinking or it would be his ruination. Smyllie was one of the very few people in Dublin who could speak to Brendan like that, and his concern touched him though, of course, he chose to ignore it and carry on as before.

As a result of his arrest at Newhaven, diplomatic efforts were intensified to have the Expulsion Order lifted. That the case reached this high level was a sign that Brendan had achieved a certain public status in Ireland. F.H. Boland, the Irish Ambassador at the Court of St. James's, took up the cause. He raised the matter with the Commonwealth Relations Office in October 1952. On 23 October, the Irish Department of External Affairs brought the question up with the British Embassy in Dublin. The British police still considered Behan an undesirable and that opinion delayed the lifting of the Order for another two years.[18]

As his reputation gained stature, the expulsion order became an increasingly serious obstacle to his need to travel to promote his career. In 1953, in an indication that his reputation was now spreading abroad, the Irish novelist and broadcaster, Francis MacManus, told students at New York University to watch out for the Irish writer, Behan. Brendan always preferred to think that, like Athena, he emerged fully formed from Zeus's brow. But, for all his complaints about lack of help from Dublin's establishment, MacManus's comments demonstrate the kind of support he was already receiving from a diverse group of influential and established people.

In 1953, Behan published 'The Confirmation Suit', a masterly short story. It was broadcast on radio before it appeared in print.[19] It is told in the first person narrative in the voice of a twelve-year-old boy, unnamed but based on Brendan himself. The setting is clearly the Russell Street domain of his Granny English. The characters are drawn from people he knew and many of them are named, including his teacher, Sister Monica and his brothers Rory and Seán.

His grandmother is the subject of the improving attentions of Aunt Jack who suggests the adoption of more wholesome domestic and personal habits to the tyrant of Russell Street:

> Aunt Jack made terrible raids on us now and again, to stop, snuff and drink, and made my grandmother get up in the morning, and wash herself, and cook meals and take food with them. My grandmother was a gilder by trade, and served her time in one of the best shops in the city, and was getting a man's wages at sixteen. She liked stuff out of the pork butchers, and out of cans, but didn't like boiling potatoes, for she said she was no skivvy, and the chip man was better at it. When she was left alone it was a pleasure to eat with her.

One of Aunt Jack's improving notions was the regular ingestion of sheep's heads:

When she took it out of the pot, and laid it on the plate, she and I sat looking at it, in fear and trembling. It was bad enough going into the pot, but with the soup streaming from its eyes, and its big teeth clenched in a very bad temper, it would put the heart crossways in you. My grandmother asked me, in a whisper, if I ever thought sheep could look so vindictive, but that it was more like the head of an old man, and would I for God's sake take it up and throw it out of the window. The sheep kept glaring at us, but I came the far side of it, and rushed over to window and threw it out in a flash. My grandmother had to drink a Baby Power whiskey, for she wasn't the better of herself.[20]

The main body of the story deals with the selfishness of the central character, the young grandson, and his hurtful treatment of an old woman and his subsequent regret. Miss McCann, a maker of funeral habits, lives in Russell Street and is one of Granny's confidants. She offers to make a suit for his Confirmation day. He is horrified at the result – she produces an old fashioned suit of blue serge with 'buttons the size of saucers'.

He is so ashamed at having to wear this creation, that, on the Confirmation day, he covers the suit with his overcoat. Thereafter, he fools Miss McCann each Sunday, by briefly putting on the suit to visit her. The boy's mother, angered by his dishonesty, tells the old woman. Miss McCann is deeply upset. Soon afterwards, she dies. To expiate his sense of remorse, the narrator walks behind her coffin in the pouring rain, wearing the suit for all to see. The story is a powerful account of the pains of childhood, and it placed him in the first rank of writers of the modern Irish short story.

His other piece of 1953 fiction has less merit. On 19 October, the first of thirty instalments of a serial called *The Scarperer* appeared in *The Irish Times*. The work was a showpiece for Brendan's knowledge of the French and Irish underworld and it is resonant with the atmosphere of the places he knew intimately in both countries. At the core of the convoluted plot is a plan to spring a prisoner from Mountjoy Jail in Dublin and transport him to France by way of the Aran Islands. Coincidentally, the prisoner bears a strong resemblance to a leading French criminal. The Frenchman offers to pay a fortune if the Irish escapee's body is found washed up on a French beach. The story rips along at a great pace until the dénouement, when the scheme is undone by well-meaning Irish women, members of the 'The Irish Committee for the Defence of the Horse', who are campaigning against the export of live horses to France. Their intervention leads to the comical conclusion to the story.

Brendan did not want his name associated with the pot-boiling serial. It appeared under the pseudonym 'Emmet Street', a name he took from a street near his boyhood home. He later claimed that this disguise was essential, because the literary intelligentsia in Dublin was not prepared to accept him as a serious writer and would pounce on any excuse that allowed them to dismiss him as a mere hack and a pornographer. *The Scarperer* was the product of financial necessity and Brendan was not pleased that he had to set aside his Borstal memoirs, which he considered his great work, to engage in bread and butter activity.[21]

The serial was mostly written on the Aran Islands. Brendan had begun to spend time in the Gaeltacht regions of the West in 1947, when he visited the Blasket Islands in County Kerry. He considered these Irish-speaking districts a spiritual home. Kerry, the middle island of Aran, and the coast of Connemara became as important to him as Dublin. They were places he went for personal renewal and to escape the frenetic world of his Dublin drinking haunts. There was drinking done on Aran, but it was of a gentler kind. One evening, he locked the island police in their own barrack cell because they tried to stop him singing outside a pub. He had first become interested in this most Irish part of Ireland through IRA friends like Seán Ó Briain and Máirtín Ó Cadháin. He knew it through literature too, from books like Maurice O'Sullivan's *Twenty Years A-Growing*. He resented the changes which prosperity was bringing to these areas. He particularly resented films like *Man of Aran*, which he felt gave the islanders false hope that good times were just around the corner. The title of his poem 'A Jackeen says Goodbye to the Blaskets', published in *Comhar* in 1948 may sound like a renunciation, but, long after he had abandoned writing in Irish, he continued to visit the Irish-speaking districts. The poem is a testament to his love of the bleak beauty of the Gaeltacht fringe:

> In the sun the ocean will lie like a glass,
> No human sign, no boat to pass,
> Only, at the world's end, the last
> Golden eagle over the lonely Blasket.
>
> Sunset, nightshadow spreading,
> The climbing moon through cold cloud stretching
> Her bare fingers down, descending
> On empty homes, crumbling wretched.
>
> Silent, except for birds flying low
> Grateful to return once more;
> The soft wind swinging a half-door
> Of a fireless cottage, cold, wet, exposed.[22]

At the beginning of 1954, Behan again pressed the British Home Secretary to lift his Expulsion Order. In Ireland, he liked to give the impression that, except for his promise to his Borstal governor, he never gave any form of undertaking to the British authorities about his IRA activities. Describing his deportations in a letter to the Dublin *Evening Mail*, he claimed: 'On neither occasion did I give an undertaking to this man Ede,[23] or to anyone else, about my behaviour or about anything.'[24] He was not just being economical with the truth – he was telling a bare-faced lie.

In the 1954 letter, he stressed to the Home Secretary that he was not a member of the IRA and that he had not been one for a number of years.[25] It was one of several plaintive appeals he made to the Home Office and he had signed at least one undertaking not to have anything further to do with the IRA.

To be fair to Behan, the lifting of the Expulsion Order was a matter of the first importance in the consolidation of his burgeoning career as a writer and a hack, which required overseas travel. From 1952 onwards the Irish police had no objection to the lifting of the Order and they conveyed this to their British counterparts. On 20 January, 1954, the British police finally relented, but added that they still considered him 'undesirable'. On 25 January the Order was officially lifted, and he was at last free to travel to and through Britain.

In early February 1954, Behan became embroiled in one of the most acrimonious libel actions Dublin had seen for years. Patrick Kavanagh sued *The Leader* magazine, which had published a snide but at least partially accurate portrait of him. It portrayed him holding drunken court in McDaid's, and was in many respects a brilliant send-up of the more curmudgeonly aspects of his personality. Kavanagh and his brother Peter felt that those behind the article represented 'the most evil elements in Irish society'.[26] The piece was unsigned, and Kavanagh's theory of its authorship varied almost by the hour. He suspected the academic Desmond Williams, the poet Val Iremonger, but, above all, he believed the hand of Brendan Behan was at work. Kavanagh thought that, by taking action, he would win a handsome settlement and a vindication of his reputation. In the end, the case destroyed his health. He never forgave Brendan for his part in the unfolding drama.

Although he never claimed authorship, Brendan the showman was naturally keen to get on the most sensational literary libel case of the decade. He told John Ryan he was willing to give evidence for Kavanagh. Kavanagh rejected the offer and Brendan was furious at the snub. That rejection proved to be a serious error on Kavanagh's part. When asked by Defence Counsel John A. Costelloe (a former Irish Prime Minister then back practising at the

Bar) if he knew Brendan Behan, the poet launched into a diatribe on how he loathed Behan and all he represented. The next day Mr Costelloe produced a copy of Kavanagh's novel *Tarry Flynn* inscribed, 'To my friend Brendan Behan on the day he painted my flat'. The poet wrote the inscription after Behan had decorated his Pembroke Road apartment before a visit from a rich American lady whom he hoped to interest in his work. It turned out to be a rather expensive paint job: in the jury's eyes the inscription undermined Kavanagh's credibility, and lost him the case. They found for the publication, but later Kavanagh's Supreme Court appeal against the decision was successful. The victory came too late. Dublin's literary circles were riven. Brendan's friend Anthony Cronin refused to speak to him for some time. Cronin mistakenly believed Brendan to have supplied the defence team with the book. He had not. It was Brendan's brother, Rory Furlong, who, angered by Kavanagh's description of Brendan in the witness box, produced it. Brendan tried to effect a rapprochement with Cronin, but his friend was intractable. The situation deteriorated to the point where Brendan physically attacked Cronin on the street not long after the Kavanagh trial.

Brendan gloried in the publicity that arose from the case (including a photograph in *The Irish Times*), but he did feel sorry for Kavanagh. In later years, he would never allow any criticism of Kavanagh's poetry in his hearing. However, even after Behan's death, Kavanagh continued to damn him as 'evil incarnate'.

For a year that had started auspiciously for Brendan, 1954 had a rather stormy middle. His career as a journalist did not keep him out of trouble with the police, and sometimes the mere sight of a policeman's uniform was enough to trigger an angry response from him. On 2 April, he was fined ten shillings and sentenced to a week's detention in Mountjoy Jail for drunk and disorderly behaviour in Robert's Café in Grafton Street after a fracas with the police at nearby Anne's Lane, during which he injured his leg. J.M. McGoldrick, his solicitor, told the court that his client's political persuasions might not be popular just then, but at one time he would have been an Irish political hero.[27] It was Behan's last time as a guest of the nation in this famous Dublin prison. Brendan was released from Mountjoy on 8 April by Governor Kavanagh from whom he had borrowed *War and Peace*. Kavanagh found Behan's corpulent and dissolute appearance shocking in comparison to the slim, handsome youth he had first seen in 1942.

In mid-April, life returned to some semblance of normality, and Behan acquired a degree of financial security when Jim McGuinness, the editor of the *Irish Press*, commissioned him to write a regular column for the paper and offered him the attractive weekly fee of £5. McGuinness, like Brendan, had taken part in the 1939 bombing campaign in England. He too had been arrested and tried. Though just old enough to have received the full sentence which Brendan escaped, he was lucky that one of the jurors blocked the verdict of guilty. Instead of going to prison he was deported back to Ireland. The journalistic brief Brendan received from McGuinness was wide. The editor wanted him to write about what he knew best – his native city and its personalities.

His Saturday feature did for his print career what *The Ballad Maker's Saturday Night* had done for his radio persona. He wrote on contemporary affairs, Northern Ireland, Paris, the Dublin slums, and sport. The importance of his newspaper ephemera rests mainly in its evocation of a city and a society that was about to undergo radical change with the approach of the 1960s. His column featured his creations, Mrs Brennan, Maria Concepta and Mr Crippen. Through them, he was able to put his opinions into the mouths of ordinary Dublin characters readily accessible to the majority of his readers. The column became a show-case for the Dublinese he had been brought up on. He mixed phrases like 'he had a face like a plateful of mortal sins' and 'your blood's worth bottling', with Mrs Brennan's malapropisms and mispronunciations: 'Brending Behing.' 'Mrs Brennan.' 'How's Londing?' 'Who?' 'Londing. Didn't you come home from the Contingent be Londing?' He dashed off the majority of his pieces in pre-deadline haste, but this did not affect their public impact. The then London editor of the *Irish Press*, Donal Foley, believed his column to have been 'the best thing of its kind to appear anywhere at that time'. Foley had an opportunity to observe Behan's working methods at close quarters. One day, Brendan ambled into his London office and demanded an advance of 20 guineas for four articles that he promised to submit. Foley contacted his editor in Dublin who insisted that the articles be delivered before any money changed hands. An enraged Brendan went off to a quiet corner of Lincolns Inn Fields. A few hours later he returned with four articles totalling 7,000 words. Nearly ten years later, Foley remembered reading them again when Brendan's *Irish Press* articles came out as *Hold Your Hour and Have Another*.[28] He was astonished at how well they had stood the test of time.

Brendan craved fame and recognition. He wanted it in the 'timeless now' rather than when he was too old to enjoy it. Above all, he wanted the respect of his Irish literary peers. However, his success with the *Irish Press* did not endear him to certain up and coming elements of Dublin's small literary world. He had blotted his copy-book by going head to head with the revered Patrick Kavanagh. And there was a cohort of young Dublin literati who resented Behan. Most of them had been to university. They disdained the uneducated jailbird. In particular, he was resented by the aspirants at *Envoy*, who felt that their work merited publication before that of someone they considered to be a parvenu. According to the poet, John Montague, that Brendan had the support of O'Faoláin and O'Donnell was immaterial to this crowd. They saw themselves as the young Turks of Irish writing and felt that the sway of these older men was spent. Meanwhile, many others had repeatedly witnessed his pub performances and were long tired of his antics. Some were still reeling from the shock of his unabashed attention-seeking during the Kavanagh libel trial. The more haughty among the McDaid's folk chose not to acknowledge the impact that Brendan's journalism was making. They felt that *The Irish Times* and the *Irish Press* were their domain. But they could not deny Behan's access to the pages of these journals and, in the end, they had to accept these organs' own positive view of the young writer.

Piqued by the reaction of some of Dublin's literary Olympians, Brendan again felt the urge to travel. Soon after the Expulsion Order was rescinded, he began to make regular trips to London, a city where he felt free of the petty literary jealousies that haunted him in Dublin. His drinking dictated his London beat. He spent his early mornings in the Billingsgate and Covent Garden markets where one could buy a drink at that hour. He became as familiar a sight to the porters there as he was to the street traders in Dublin's Moore Street. Ward's Irish House in Piccadilly, The Cheshire Cheese in Soho, and The French House, the celebrated hangout of 1950s Soho bohemians, were his most regular drinking stops later in the day.

The year 1954 began with good omens. It closed with a blessing. *The Irish Times* announced on 16 November that:

> Brendan Behan, who has appeared to the public as journalist, novelist and poet – in Irish and English – emerges in yet another role this week. He has written a play, *The Quare Fellow* which is to open at the Pike Theatre on Friday.

He was thirty-two years old. His first major play was about to be produced in Dublin and the prophet was on the verge of honour in his own country.

Brendan (Francis) Behan's first photograph. Born 9 February 1923.

Kathleen Behan, Brendan's mother and her small sons by her first marriage, Seán and Rory Furlong.

Brendan, his parents Kathleen and Stephen Behan and brother Dominic attend the production of Dominic Behan's play *Posterity Be Damned* in London, 1960.

Rory Furlong, with a friend,
outside 14 Russell Street,
1932.

Kildare Road, Crumlin,
where the Behans moved in 1937.

The ground floor apartment, Herbert
Street, where Beatrice and Brendan lived.

Cúig.
No. 5 Anglesea Road, the first and
only home owned by Beatrice and
Brendan. Beatrice lived on here
after Brendan's death.

To the Dep't of   Brendan Behan
Justice.   Mountjoy Prison
                    26   24-2-43.

A Cara,

    I had a visit yesterday from Mr. Seán Ó Faoláin, who is interested in my literary work. He explained a wish to read & criticise anything I may have written in here. As can be understood his expert opinion & advice would be of tremendous value to me. Therefore I should like to be allowed send out any MSS I may have written and the any I may write in the future. Both Mr Ó Faoláin and myself clearly understand that anything sent out shall not be published. I will give my word that your wishes in this matter will be respected and that anything sent out to Mr Ó Faoláin shall be returned here when he has read it & criticised it. Actually in a nut-shell the idea is more or less that I get a sort of correspondence course on short-story writing from Mr Ó Faoláin: Let me again say that we both fully understand that these MSS cannot be published unless the permission of the Minister is granted & that I have no intention of abusing this concession if its granted.

                  'S mise
    F.662.   Brendan Behan

Ref.B.18/5468.

Submitted. ✓

                        Gobharnoir.

Letter dated 24 February 1943 from prisoner Brendan Behan to the Govenor of Mountjoy Jail, seeking permission to send out manuscripts of his work to Seán O'Faoláin. Courtesy of Department of Justice, Dublin.

Memorabilia from Brendan's prison years.
Courtesy of The British Home Office and *The Irish Times.*

The Wedding Party.
Beatrice and Brendan after their informal wedding with her parents and friends
outside the Morehampton Hotel, Donnybrook.
Courtesy of Cathal Goulding.

Homage to Cecil ffrench-Salkeld
Brendan's father-in-law by the artist Reginald Gray, 1960.
Courtesy of Reginald Gray.

Luggala, Co. Wicklow, the country residence of
Oonagh Lady Oranmore and Browne.
Courtesy of Kieran Conroy.

Oonagh Lady Oranmore and Browne, Brendan and Beatrice Behan in convivial
mood at Luggala, 1961.
Courtesy of Oonagh Lady Oranmore and Browne.

Miguel Ferreras, Oonagh Lady Oranmore and Browne's former partner, who brutally beat Brendan up shortly after this photograph was taken at Luggala, 1961.
Courtesy of Oonagh Lady Oranmore and Browne.

Brendan proposes a toast after dinner at Luggala, Christmas 1960. Courtesy of Oonagh Lady Oranmore and Browne.

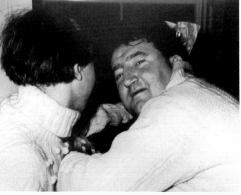

Brendan and the 'camera shy' Garech Browne at Luggala, Christmas 1958.
Courtesy of Oonagh Lady Oranmore and Browne.

Dr F. H. Boland, Irish Diplomat (the man responsible for clearing Brendan's Exclusion Order from Britain), Beatrice, Brendan and Mrs Boland, at the opening of *The Quare Fellow*, The Comedy Theatre, London, 1956.
By kind permission of *The Irish Times*.

The Playright.
Brendan and Beatrice with the artist Seán O'Sullivan in his
Molesworth Street Studio, late 1950s, viewing a portrait of Brendan.

A bruised and battered Brendan Behan arrives in Dublin Airport after his appearance in Bow Street Magistrate's Court, 1959.

Brendan and Beatrice on O'Connell Bridge, 1960.

Under Littlewood.
Brendan having a drink with his producer Joan Littlewood.
By kind permission of *The Irish Times*.

Brendan arrives to attend a performance of his play *The Hostage*
at London's Wyndham Theatre, accompanied by Beatrice.
By kind permission of the Associated Press, London.

Brendan Behan with a bruised left cheek after being fined
at Bow Street Magistrate's Court. Behan's play *The Hostage*
was then running in the West End, 1959.
By kind permission of the Associated Press, London.

Brendan on the phone at 5 Anglesea Road, Ballsbridge,
August 1960.

Brendan and Beatrice at Anglesea Road planning their first
trip to New York in 1960.

Brendan and Beatrice in New York.
Brendan and Beatrice at the height of his career, after
attending a performance of *The Hostage* on Broadway.
By kind permission of the Associated Press, London.

On the Wagon.
Brendan Behan, arriving in Idewild Airport, New York, September 1960, for the
première of *The Hostage* says 'it wasn't easy to smile while drinking milk'.
By kind permission of the Associated Press, London.

Placid Waters.
Beatrice and Brendan prepare to depart L.A. with Brendan imbibing
nothing more than tea, after a boisterous stay which included the L.A. lockup.

Unscheduled guest appearance, New York 1960.
Brendan Behan makes one of his impromptu forays onto the stage in New York during
a performance of *The Hostage*.
By kind permission of *The Irish Times*.

Brendan Behan, sharing a drink and good times with his actor friends,
Jimmy O'Dea and Cecil Sheridan.
By kind permission of *The Irish Times*.

Peter Arthurs, the man who has given the
most frank account of his understanding of
Behan's sexuality, 1961.

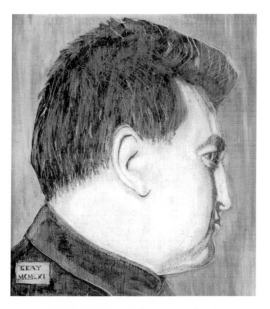

Portrait of Brendan by Reginald Gray, 1961.
Courtesy of Reginald Gray.

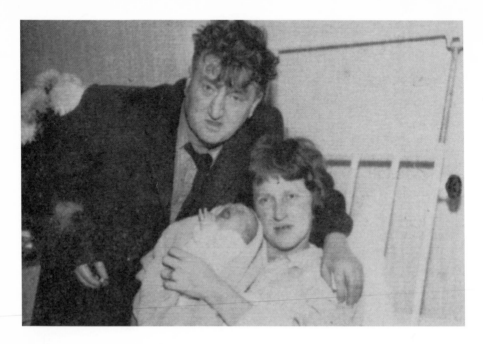

Beatrice, Brendan, baby Blanaid in the Rotunda Hospital, Dublin, 1964.

Beatrice.
Brendan's young widow at his funeral in Donnybrook Church, 1964.
By kind permission of *The Irish Times*.

The Rise Of The Quare Fellow

The Pike Theatre Club, founded by Alan Simpson and his wife Carolyn Swift, opened its doors on 15 September, 1953, with a production of Chesterton's *The Surprise*. Just over a year later this ground-breaking new theatre produced *The Quare Fellow*, Behan's prison drama – a work he had begun more than eight years previously. After the first night of The Pike Theatre production, no one would be able to call Brendan a hack – it turned him into one of Ireland's most celebrated young playwrights.

Carolyn Swift, who acted as the script doctor and producer of the Pike partnership, had abandoned a career with the British Council in England to work in theatre in Dublin with Anew McMaster and others. Alan Simpson was the son of a Protestant clergyman, and an engineer by training. He had served as an officer in the Irish army during 'the Emergency', as World War II was euphemistically known in Ireland. He continued his army career for some years after the War while also working in the theatre in Dublin. By the early 1950s, he was developing a reputation as one of the most innovative directors in Irish theatre. He directed all the productions at The Pike as part of a tiny, tightly-knit creative team.

The artistic manifesto of the new theatre they set up together read:

> Our policy is to present plays of all countries on all subjects, written from whatever viewpoint, provided they seem to us to be of interest and to be dramatically satisfying. As our theatre is a small, intimate one, we intend to avail of the opportunities afforded to stage productions which, for various reasons, would not be seen on either the larger or smaller commercial stages, and we hope to give theatre-goers an opportunity to see more of the struggle going on at present to introduce new techniques and new subjects in play writing.[1]

In just under two years, The Pike did more than fulfil the promise of its manifesto – it exceeded it. By producing the world premier of *The Quare*

Fellow, it paved the way for Behan to go international. By staging the first Irish production of Beckett's *Waiting for Godot* on 28 October 1954, it brought a world masterpiece of progressive drama to the home city of its author. Among the similarities the two plays shared is that, in both of them, we never see the character of the title on stage.[2]

Brendan had first met Alan Simpson and Carolyn Swift at the sculptor Desmond MacNamara's studio, where Simpson and Swift were regulars. To be asked there was considered a sign of acceptance by Dublin's literary aspirants and Brendan became a regular from 1947. This fortuitous introduction had taken place in March, just a few months after Brendan's release from the Curragh.

On first sight, Brendan found Alan Simpson, the man who was to make his career by producing his first serious play, somewhat intimidating – he struck Brendan as someone with whom he would be more likely to have a fist fight than a theatrical collaboration. Simpson, usually a mild mannered man, arrived at the MacNamaras in a rage and started flinging chairs at the walls and generally letting off steam. The reason for this behaviour was that his motorcycle had just been stolen from outside the nearby stage door of The Gaiety Theatre. Behan later confessed to Carolyn Swift, after she had married Alan Simpson, that witnessing that tantrum made him treat Simpson 'with the greatest respect and a certain amount of caution ever after.'[3]

The gestation of *The Quare Fellow* was a complex affair. Behan based the play on his experiences in Mountjoy Jail when the murderer Bernard Kirwan was hanged. In its first incarnation, he called it *Casadh Sugáin Eile (The Twisting of Another Rope)*. The title was a homage to Douglas Hyde, the Irish language scholar, cultural activist and the first President of Ireland. Brendan mistakenly believed that Hyde's play, *Casadh an tSugáin (The Twisting of the Rope)* had been the first Irish language drama presented on a Dublin stage.[4] Hyde's play, based on a scenario by W.B. Yeats, stirred actor and critic Frank Fay to write in *The United Irishman* that 'hope is strong within us again'. Behan admired Hyde, and believed any Irish play bearing a title similar to that of Hyde's would stand a chance of winning favour with Ernest Blythe, Director of the Abbey Theatre. The Abbey Theatre grew out of the literary revival that took place in the 1890s and played a major role in the forging of Ireland's resurgent national cultural identity. It was founded by, amongst others, Yeats, Lady Gregory and the playwright Edward Martin, all towering figures of the Irish literary renaissance. As a result, The Abbey Theatre and drama in general became something of a sacred cow in the nation's cultural life.

The first written reference by Behan to the earliest version of the drama appeared in a letter he wrote to Blythe on 18 May 1946. Having explained to Blythe his decision to fuse two works he was working on to form the play he called *The Landlady*,[5] he went on to say:

> ... I have written one Act of another play. *The Twisting of Another Rope* I call it, because everything is shown in the black cell in some prison. Two men are condemned to death and waiting for the Rope – I would send it with this but better not scare the Department of Justice before we have anything done. There is nothing political in it, of course. I'll send it to you if you like.[6]

Blythe did not take up the play. After his appointment in 1941, Ernest Blythe presided over one of The Abbey's most stagnant periods, producing dreary Irish kitchen-cottage dirge and rejecting most new writing if it did not conform to his aspiration of new Irish State drama. Behan believed that aspiration consisted mostly of The Abbey company of actors eating endless pans of fried rashers and sausages during a play, thus making them, in his opinion, the best fed actors on earth. A rejection by Blythe became a shared experience for many aspiring Irish dramatists. Hugh Leonard captures the authoritarian attitude of the man in his prose memoir, *Out After Dark*: 'I realised ... where his strength lay: he did not give a damn for the opinion of any man on earth.' Blythe did not give a damn for Brendan's innovative one-acter.

Continually rebuffed by the Abbey, Behan later began to hawk the play elsewhere. Micheál Ó hAodha of Radio Éireann remembers Brendan bringing him 'six pages of closely typed stuff, all swiddled up as if it had been in every pub ... merely a sketch with some sort of a synopsis'.[7] He advised him to rework it and bring it back. Behan got the same advice from Francis MacManus at RTÉ. He too had seen a rough fragment which he thought unsuitable unless it was given major attention. He turned one more time to The Abbey and Blythe advised him to extend the play.

There is some dispute over whether Blythe ever saw the final version of the three-act play Brendan later gave to Alan Simpson and Carolyn Swift. Carolyn Swift says Blythe insisted to her that Brendan never submitted the three-act version to The Abbey.[8] Behan's cousin, Seamus de Burca, disagrees. De Burca says Blythe not only saw it, but suggested to Brendan that The Abbey producer, Ria Mooney, should work with him on making the play fit The Abbey's requirements. He also claims Brendan rejected out of hand the very question of anyone interfering with his text – which seems strange considering his future assent to changes made by The Pike producers and to the more radical ones made by Joan Littlewood in her London productions. According to de Burca, Brendan sent the manuscript back to Blythe unchanged. Blythe was furious that Brendan had made no changes and that he had so lightly discarded the assistance of a person of Ria Mooney's standing to help make those changes. In his anger, Blythe physically threw the unaltered script back at the playwright. That episode ended Behan's relationship with the Abbey for some years to come.[9]

Brendan now began the search for an alternative producer for his play. He sent it to Hilton Edwards at The Gate. The play had no obvious leading role for his partner Micheal MacLiammóir and this may well have been the unspoken reason why The Gate rejected it and other plays. After The Gate's rejection, Brendan sent *The Twisting of Another Rope* to Cyril Cusack, one of Ireland's most famous actors of the period. He also turned it down, but later admitted that it was one of the great regrets of his life.[10] Carolyn Swift recalled that people gave various reasons for rejecting the work, 'but the truth was probably that, although the play provides a wealth of marvellous characterisations, it has no obvious lead in which the three actor-managers could star, there being some half-dozen equally dominating roles.'[11]

While the script of the play was lying around the house which Hilton Edwards shared with Micheal MacLiammóir in Harcourt Terrace, MacLiammóir's niece, the actress Sally Travers, happened to read it. She thought sufficiently highly of it to mention it to Alan Simpson and Carolyn Swift. They knew of Behan's writing from the *Irish Press* and from *Envoy*, and were interested to see how he might tackle the task of writing a play. When they read *The Twisting of Another Rope* they were 'slightly daunted, for the pages of the script were all of different sizes and qualities and the typing was the product of a number of different machines, all well past their prime. Moreover, the speeches were thick wedges of dialogue, nearly all with a minimum of four sentences, and full of subordinate clauses.'[12]

Nevertheless, they were convinced of the intrinsic quality of the work and wanted their company to produce it. They made Behan an offer of £25 for the rights and a four-week run at The Pike. They made the offer over the telephone to London where Behan was staying with his friends Joe and Kathleen McGill. He himself recalled being offered the slightly larger sum of £30, but The Pike file records the figure of £25.[13] Later there was a dispute and exchange of solicitors' letters over the rights, after Behan shamelessly re-sold them to Joan Littlewood behind the Simpsons' back.

With the play heading for production in Dublin, Behan left London for the South of France, passing through Paris. He found Paris little changed since his previous visit. The Metro had gone up 30 (old) francs and the government was coming in for less abuse than previous administrations during his visits. Many of his former friends had left and, since he was only over-nighting, he headed straight for an old haunt, the Pergola, where he found an affectionate welcome. He headed South the following day to stay with his friend Ralph Cusack. He met Sugar Ray Robinson in The Hollywood nightclub in Juan-les-Pins and then, after a few more days with the Cusacks, he returned to Paris. He made his way to the Gare Saint Lazare where he discovered that he had lost the luggage ticket needed to redeem his most valued possession, his typewriter, from Left Luggage. Behan's natural luck came to his aid again:

> I was arguing as best as I could to get it back before the train left, when a young clerk came up and asked me where I was from. I said Ireland and his face lit up as he bustled about.
> 'Syracusecque,' he muttered. 'Syracusecque,' and came back with the luggage and ten minutes to spare.
> 'Syracusecque,' he said in triumph, and shook my hand.
> 'The same to you,' said I, and was on the train and half way to Rouen, when I figured out that this incantation referred to Cyril Cusack, latest hero of the theatre-going population of the city behind me.[14]

Now that his play was in rehearsal in Dublin, Brendan wanted to be on hand. He returned home in early November to investigate the progress at The Pike. After just one reading Carolyn Swift realised a superb piece of drama was waiting to be unlocked from an excess of undisciplined writing.[15] Here began a trend which would attend Behan's relationship with the theatre for the rest of his writing career. Having refused to let the Abbey alter a word of his play, he now agreed with Swift and Simpson that they could make certain changes. The task fell to Carolyn Swift.

She thought he had an impressive grasp of drama, and knew how to construct a dramatic scene. This skill, she believed, came partly from years of attending his uncle's melodramas at The Queen's Theatre when he was a child. She also found a wealth of Dublin wit that his young ear had picked up and stored away as if one day he knew it would serve a higher purpose. All of this combined successfully with the fact that he was writing out of his experiences in prison. The play was an indictment of the barbarity of capital punishment, but nowhere did she find the message of the play impinging on plot and characterisation.[16] His treatment of plot was unconventional. There is little action but much dialogue and the building up of suspense through scenes of brusque realism.

Once Behan understood that her request for changes was not patronising but flowed from a genuine desire to improve it, Carolyn Swift found him quite amenable to her suggestions. There remained one final problem and that was the title. Alan Simpson felt *The Twisting of Another Rope* was cumbersome. He suggested it should emphasise the central focus on the condemned man, even though he never appears on stage. With Brendan's enthusiastic approval, the play was renamed *The Quare Fellow* and The Pike announced that it would open on Friday 19 November, 1954.

Brendan's association with the Press Group of newspapers did the advance publicity for the play no harm whatsoever. '... it has qualities which place it in the front ranks of modern international plays', 'Brendan Behan could well begin where Sean O'Casey left off', the *Evening Press* predicted two days later. *The Irish Times'* more restrained comment noted that the play had gone into rehearsal and that its subject matter 'is unusual in its discussion of the unpleasant subject of capital punishment and the reaction on the inmates of a prison'.

When rehearsals began, Brendan took to dropping into the theatre to watch. Simpson had no objection to his being there, but he soon found progress interrupted when Brendan and whatever drinking buddy he had brought with him began shouting encouragement at the actors. Carolyn Swift remembered him 'chortling at his own gags, after which he would nudge his bewildered companion and say, with a touchingly naïve mixture of pride and amazement: 'I wrote that!'

This was all very well at rehearsals, but the producers feared a drunken Brendan on opening night might prove too much for the cast in such a small theatre. They also knew Dublin theatregoers would not tolerate two performances – one on stage and one in the auditorium – the way London and New York audiences did in later years. To avert disaster, Steve Willoughby and her husband Tom, who were an important part of The Pike's support team, were detailed to keep Brendan in a reasonable state of sobriety. They managed to do this with considerable success and when the cry of 'Author, Author!' went up Brendan was in a fit condition to walk on stage, casually smoking a cigarette, hitch up his trousers and respond to the loud applause by singing *Red Roses for Me*. Behan's choice of a song by Sean O'Casey for a Dublin audience showed something of the often inspired but sometimes tedious showmanship that was to be his hallmark at first nights around the world.[17]

On Saturday, 20 November 1954 Brendan Behan woke up to find himself a celebrity in his home town. The reviews were the stuff of authors' dreams. 'When he finds himself technically the Irish theatre will have found another and, I think, greater O'Casey' predicted the *Evening Press*. 'Undoubtedly the finest [play] by a new dramatist seen in Dublin for years' acclaimed the *Irish Independent*. 'The most exciting dramatic experience which Dublin has had for many years', commented *The Times Literary Supplement*. *The Irish Times* critic said, 'One of the positive qualities – and there are many – of Mr Brendan Behan's play is its power of provoking thought. Like a modern novel, it rounds off neither character nor situation but passes the buck, as it were, to the customer'. One of the few negative voices raised against the play was that of Abbey director and playwright, Lennox Robinson. Ironically he had been asked to review it by Behan's own paper the *Irish Press*. The editor believed Robinson's weighty reputation would give his columnist's play an additional push. What he did not know was that Robinson had been involved in the play's rejection by the Abbey. Dr Robinson did praise the acting, and said that for that alone 'it must be seen again and again'.

It was inevitable that reviewers in Ireland would make a comparison with Wilde's *The Ballad of Reading Gaol*. In the *Evening Press* Gabriel Fallon found it 'more profoundly moving and deeply religious' than Wilde's great prison poem. Lennox Robinson, doggedly persisting with his negative views, believed it trivial by comparison. An important positive assessment of the production came from A.J. Leventhal, the critic and scholar. Dr Leventhal had succeeded Samuel Beckett as lecturer in French at Trinity and had added his influential voice to the campaign against the censorship laws in Ireland. He too saw the parallel with Wilde's poem. He wrote that Behan's sincerity in 'stressing the inhumanity of capital punishment can be as little doubted as Wilde's when he wrote his *Ballad of Reading Gaol*. This distinguished man of letters, whose review of *Ulysses* was censored in 1922, believed Behan's play to be a powerful piece of anti-hanging propaganda. The last judicial hanging in Ireland had taken place on 20 April 1954, at Mountjoy Jail, which added greatly to the play's powerful public impact. Military Intelligence took sufficient interest in it to keep an impressive collection of press cuttings relating to the production in Behan's G2 file. More ominously, the file also listed the names of everyone connected with the production. The notes failed, however, to unravel one successful ploy by the man playing the homosexual, Other Fellow. Mindful of the climate of the times, he concealed his identity under the pseudonym Patrick Clarke and this went undetected by the spooks at G2.

The bar-flies and literary begrudgers wondered what all the fuss was about. They asked one another what the slum boy with the assertive personality and talent for notoriety had done to achieve such status in the theatre – which in Dublin was a sacred forum. Those honest enough to admit it realised that in *The Quare Fellow*, Behan had looked beyond the well-defined frontiers of the Irish dramatic movement and opened up new possibilities for Irish theatre. He had also managed to break away from the straight jacket of Republican ideology. 'The effect of prison on most [literary] republicans ... was to redouble their political fervour: the effect on Behan, however, was to leave him with an abiding distrust of all commitments,' writes Declan Kiberd in his *Inventing Ireland:The Literature of the Modern Nation.*

> His plays are O'Caseyesque in their sharp critique of idealism, so sharp that they come perilously close to nihilism. Ultimately, they owe more to the absurdist theatre of Ionesco, Genet and Beckett than to their forerunners in the Irish dramatic movement.[18]

This debt to a foreign trend in drama rather than a native one was reason enough for it to be considered suspect by many in 1950s Dublin.

Beckett himself was supportive. He had been sent Gabriel Fallon's review and, on 7 February 1955, when writing to the Pike about their planned production of Godot, asked them to 'Remember me to the new O'Casey'.

The criticism most frequently levelled at *The Quare Fellow* is that it lacks climax because, in the last moments of the play, the hanging of the condemned prisoner takes place off stage. To take this view is to miss Behan's important point that capital punishment at the time was something that was shrouded in bureaucratic secrecy and not done in public view. If there is an anti-climax, it is deliberate, just as the prisoners' apparent cynicism and gallows humour about death are deliberate. Their reaction is understandable because of the horrific immediacy the man's fate had for his fellow inmates. It is counterbalanced by the compassionate humanity of Warder Regan who is the embodiment of Christian compassion and understanding. The consistency of theme and character of the play as *comédie noire* is sustained by the successful fusion of these two elements.

The play had an initial run of four weeks and played to full houses. Unfortunately, the production was not a financial success for The Pike. There was a large cast of over twenty players to pay, and the tiny seating capacity of the auditorium meant a four-week run was not an economically viable proposition. The loss was small, averaging around ten shillings per week, but even such small losses had a big impact on the delicately balanced finances of The Pike.

Alan Simpson and Carolyn Swift, however, had great faith in the play's worth. They began to negotiate to produce it in a larger theatre. Carolyn Swift made further revisions to the script, but this time she did meet some minor resistance from Brendan. The Olympia Theatre on Dame Street was the venue they favoured and they suggested to its managers, Leo McCabe and Stanley Illsley that they put on the play. Carolyn Swift recalled being met with a 'categorical refusal' from the two men. When she pushed the matter further, she was told it was because Brendan's brother, Seán Furlong, had been sacked from the theatre for selling the *Daily Worker* to patrons up in 'the gods' where he operated the follow-spot. Young Furlong's left-wing politics were so well-known in Dublin that when Brendan offered to introduce him to the Irish Ambassador in London, Dr F.H. Boland, the diplomat told him, 'I would love to meet him but I can't afford the luxury.'[19]

Since Dublin was throwing up its characteristic obstacles to a new production of *The Quare Fellow*, Simpson and Swift began to explore the possibility of a London production with Donald Albery of the Criterion Theatre in Piccadilly. Little did they know that Brendan was on the job himself. Before Christmas 1955, he contacted Swift and asked if he might have a copy of the re-written script so that he could enter it in a literary competition. In fact, the author was considering making his own arrangements for a London production of the work she and her husband had salvaged when nobody else was willing to produce it. It was ingratitude on a scale which few involved in the Pike production of *The Quare Fellow* could believe. Brendan, though never a pragmatic businessman, had his own agenda, and set his sights much further afield than Dublin. However, after his years in the wilderness, few, not even Alan Simpson and Carolyn Swift whom he had just unashamedly swindled, could find the heart to deny him the larger stage.

Beatrice

Brendan Behan married Beatrice ffrench-Salkeld in her local parish church, the Church of the Sacred Heart, Donnybrook, on 16 February 1955.[1] Brendan's family, friends and acquaintances were surprised that he got married. That he married a ffrench-Salkeld astounded them. Her family and friends had reservations of their own.

Brendan first met Beatrice in 1947, when he was twenty-four and she was twenty-one. Their social backgrounds and temperaments could hardly have been more different. Beatrice came from a family that straddled the upper middle-class and landed gentry. The Salkelds were an old English Catholic family from Cumbria. They could claim descent from Sir Richard de Salkeld, lord warden of Carlisle in the reign of King Edward III.

Cecil ffrench-Salkeld, Beatrice's father, was born in India in 1904, the son of Henry Lyde Salkeld, a colonial civil servant, born in Cumbria. His mother, Florence ffrench-Mullen came from an old County Galway family of gentry. When his father died of typhoid fever in 1908, she brought the boy to Dublin and set up house in Fitzwilliam Square. She was just twenty-eight years old. Under the Irish version of her name, Blanaid, she threw herself into the vortex of the Irish literary renaissance, writing plays and poetry. She also acted with the Abbey Theatre, and enjoyed some critical success in George Fitzmaurice's *The Country Dressmaker* when it played at the Court Theatre in London.[2]

Her son, Cecil, maintained a somewhat patrician reserve, but mixed in bohemian artistic company. Despite his colonial infancy, Cecil sympathised with the Irish Republican cause. He told Dublin friends that his first language was Irish, learned from his County Galway nanny in India; his second language, Hindi; and his third, English. As a young boy, he knew many of the central figures in the Independence movement, including Patrick Pearse and Eamon de Valera. To prevent him becoming too dangerously involved with the troubled politics of the emerging Irish State, Blanaid sent Cecil to Germany when he was seventeen. He attended the art academy in Kassel, where he studied under Ewald Duelberg and became part of the Neue

Sachlichkeit (New Objectivity) movement, set up in opposition to the vogue for expressionism. There he met his future wife, Irma Taesler. She was born in Silesia of a German father and a Polish mother. They returned to Dublin, where Cecil set himself up as a professional artist. They had two children: Beatrice, born on 31 December 1925 and named after Dante's heroïne, and her younger sister, Celia, who became a distinguished stage and radio actress.[3]

As an artist, Cecil enjoyed early recognition – at one time he exhibited with Picasso. But his natural indolence did not serve the advancement of his career. The family was not well-off when Beatrice was a child. To earn extra money, her mother worked as a governess to the O'Gorman family at 19 Leeson Street. Beatrice was educated at the prestigious Loreto Convent in St. Stephen's Green, Dublin. Afterwards, she enrolled in the nearby College of Art in Kildare Street. She was able to remain a full-time student there for just six months before the family's straitened circumstances forced her to take a job as a clerk in the Board of Works. During the day, Beatrice endured the tedium of her Civil Service clerkship while continuing to attend night classes at the College of Art. In 1950, she became a botanical assistant at the Museum of Natural History where, over the next five years, she combined her interest in botany with her considerable drawing skill.

She was an extremely beautiful young woman, her fine features and delicate pale skin set off by her thick dark hair. As a young girl, she took her Roman Catholic faith quite seriously, attending Mass and Communion daily. Her close friend from those years, Pauline Parker, remembered hearing her praying late into the night during their holiday stays at youth hostels in the countryside.[4] She was twenty-one before she took her first drink, and twenty-four before she had her first serious relationship with a man. Though naturally shy, she never lacked for male suitors. There were four lovers in her life before Brendan, two of whom she might well have married. One was an artist friend whom she had been in love with before she met Brendan. Their relationship ended after a year. She also had a romance with Ian Stuart, son of the novelist Francis Stuart, who later married Iseult, daughter of Kathleen Behan's former employer, Maud Gonne MacBride. The Salkelds had known the Stuarts since their days as neighbours in Glencree, County Wicklow, where the Salkelds lived before moving to Dublin.[5] Ian Stuart wrote to her proposing marriage but, on his sister's advice, he tore up the letter. His relationship with Beatrice ended quite soon afterwards, although they remained very good friends.

Beatrice's first meeting with Brendan was in her father's large Victorian house on Morehampton Road. Cecil was wont to bring home strays whom he met in Dublin's drinking haunts, and he brought Brendan home after a spree. Cecil was impressed by a remark of Brendan's – 'a job is death without dignity'

– which he overheard him deliver in a pub. Cecil had a lifelong gentlemanly
aversion to work. He did not lack for commissions, but hadn't the tenacity to
carry out many of them.

As the family listened to Shaw's *Widowers' Houses* on the radio, Beatrice
served Brendan tea and scones but otherwise paid him very little attention.
She thought of him then as just another waif from Cecil's world of literary café
society – the young aspirants to literary fame who happily listened to Cecil's
mandarin rhetoric. She remembered him as 'a slim, dark-haired boy in house
painter's overalls and an open shirt that defied a tie'.[6] She also remembered his
gaucheness.[7] Brendan later told her that he mistook her natural shyness for
snobbery.

Beatrice was not easily impressed by young men with literary aspirations.
Beatrice ffrench-Salkeld's immediate world was suffused with literary
achievement. She had known some of the giants of Irish literature – writers of
the stature of Liam O'Flaherty, whom she knew since she was five. The poet
Joseph Campbell and the novelist Francis Stuart were all friends of her
father's, as indeed was the young Samuel Beckett. A character based on Cecil
himself appears in Flann O'Brien's modernist comic novel, *At-Swim-Two-
Birds*. Beatrice's grandmother was a published writer whose poetry had
achieved considerable critical success.

Although they had met a few times since their first introduction, the first
meaningful meeting between Brendan and Beatrice was at a performance of
The Quare Fellow, near the end of its four-week run at the Pike Theatre in late
1954. Beatrice went to the play with her then boyfriend, and her father. After
the play, Brendan asked Cecil and Beatrice, without the boyfriend, to have a
drink with him in The Eagle Bar on the North Quays. It was a pub frequented
by dockers and Brendan and Cecil got a thrill from being served after official
closing hours. That evening, Brendan asked Beatrice to go racing with him at
Leopardstown on St Stephen's Day, 26 December. Beatrice remembers a
pleasant day, comfortable in each others' company, wandering between track
and bar, 'in air as chilled and bracing as a bottle of Bordeaux'. They spent
much of the day with Liam O'Flaherty. Later that evening, Beatrice returned
home to find her boyfriend waiting. After he started a blazing row about her
being out with Brendan Behan, whom he saw as an unsavoury character, she
decided their relationship was at an end. She began to think of marrying
Brendan. She had been thinking about marriage seriously since the late 1940s.
Pauline Parker, one of her closest friends from those years, remembers sitting
with her in St Stephen's Green. Beatrice suddenly turned to ask, 'How much
money, Pauline, do you think one needs in order to get married?'[8]

The couple's courtship was unconventional and brief. There would be few one-to-one meetings. Brendan had no truck with dining and dancing. He saw that side of Dublin life as belonging to a class whose habits were alien to him. What little money he had, he preferred to spend in the informal setting of Dublin public houses where he could best exercise his talent to amuse. It was in these places that he mostly wooed Beatrice. Here he could cover his natural shyness through alcohol and cocoon himself in the sycophantic society of his audience of cronies. It was a zone of unreality that excluded the risks of intimacy. Beatrice recalled that he objected to couples holding hands in public and he disliked public displays of affection, especially when sober. When drunk he could be sloppy and sentimental as well as gratingly argumentative.

Beatrice longed for moments alone with her lover. In private, his behaviour was entirely different. It was the memory of these rare times that sustained her when Brendan the showman was at his most outrageous. It was not the extrovert that she fell in love with and she never found that side of his personality especially attractive. She fell in love with the private man, the shy, self-conscious Brendan, with a nervous stutter, a man who wanted above all else to be loved and to succeed as a writer. Beatrice believed from the beginning that her unreserved love would help him fulfil that ambition. She resolved to accept Brendan, flaws and all, and disregarded her family and friends' doubts about her suitor. 'What could they know of the understanding Brendan and I had reached? I may have been a shy woman in my late 20s, but I was determined to make my own decisions.'9

She retained intense cameo memories of their courtship, like cinematic flashes. The most vivid, and the most joyful, were scenes from their pre-marriage stay in the Aran Islands: Brendan unusually silent in a dark bar on Inisheer, listening to the poems and songs of the islanders; Brendan sprawled on a fishing trawler, a bottle of whiskey in hand; Brendan swimming naked in Kilmurvey harbour, turning somersaults and referring to his bare bottom as 'one of the Sights of Aran'; Brendan dancing with her to céilí music and speaking to her in Irish.

Some of her memories of the courtship are less idyllic. There were incidents that presaged the turbulence of later years: Brendan, in fighting form, ejected from the flat of her art college friends in Anglesea Street in Dublin; Brendan gate-crashing a party at Clontarf Castle and dismissing her friends as 'bloody bourgeois swine'. Beatrice cried and Brendan failed to apologise. The pattern of their later married years was emerging even at this early stage of their relationship. But it was not until after they were married that Beatrice understood just how difficult the man she had decided to take on as a husband could truly be.

In January 1955, in a sudden gush of enthusiasm in a Baggot Street pub, Brendan suggested that he and Beatrice live together in a 'trial marriage'. With sledge hammer subtlety, he proposed that they 'shag off together to the South of France and give it a try'.[10] Beatrice would have none of it. It was marriage or nothing. 'We'll be married soon, Brendan,' she said, 'or we won't be going anywhere'.[11] Beatrice assumed that Brendan was afraid of losing his freedom to married life. She was acutely aware of the risks of moving in to live with Brendan as his mistress in the staid moral climate of mid-1950s Dublin:

> I loved Brendan, but I didn't believe my love would extend to a life together without marriage.
> Perhaps I was conventional, but I was not a puritan or I would never have wanted to marry him in the first place. He must have sensed my determination, for he asked me casually to fix a date in February, the month of his birthday, for our wedding.[12]

Beatrice has left a clear impression of her reasons for marrying Brendan and her feelings for her fiancé. Brendan's motivation is less documented. Beatrice was, of course, an attractive woman. There was certainly no pecuniary advantage in marrying a ffrench-Salkeld, but she was something of a social catch and this seems to have mattered more to Brendan than he ever admitted.[13] As already discussed, his sexuality was at least ambivalent, and, given his drinking, heterosexual desire may not have been his prime consideration. There is no doubt, however, that in his own rather inadequate way, he did love Beatrice. He surely looked forward to the domesticity, stability, emotional security and source of uncritical love that marriage to her offered.

They both agreed that the ceremony would take place in a Catholic Church. Beatrice insisted on Brendan attending Confession before the ceremony and taking Communion on the day. There remained only the business of a chat with the priest who was to perform the marriage ceremony. Beatrice and Brendan met Father Paddy Crean in Donnybrook a few days before the ceremony. The curate and Brendan clashed. According to Beatrice, Fr Crean asked her future husband if he was still a member of the Communist Party; reminded him that as an IRA member he had been excommunicated and said the Behan family had a history of causing industrial strikes. Brendan cut the conversation short by saying that a registry office would not raise such objections. That one remark persuaded Fr Crean to perform the ceremony without further argument. Brendan decided not to inform his family about the wedding until after the event. His story was that, firstly, he wished to avoid any publicity. Secondly, he excused his secrecy because of the endlessness of the Behan family's blood connections – if he invited one family member he would be obliged to invite the extended circle of relatives or suffer the consequences of leaving them out. There were those in the family who felt snubbed and disappointed.[14]

Beatrice believed that this element of conspiracy and concealment helped to seal the intimacy between herself and her intended husband. She decided to tell just her family and a few friends. She felt that her father should be the first to know. Cecil ffrench-Salkeld was something of an Oblomov – he liked to stay in bed. She approached him in his bed chamber, where he lay propped up against his pillows, reading. She broke the news casually and his reaction was equally casual. He merely cautioned her that if she entertained any notions of changing Brendan's lifestyle, she would do well to abandon them. In particular, he warned her about Brendan's drinking. In doing so, Cecil felt he was doing no more than his fatherly duty. But, behind any doubts Cecil may have expressed about Brendan's suitability as a husband, lay his persuaded belief that his future son-in-law had the talent to make a considerable contribution to Irish letters.[15] In return, Brendan enjoyed Cecil's fatherly attitude, and referred to him affectionately as the 'Dalai Lama'.

Beatrice's mother, Irma, was more concerned than her husband that her daughter had chosen to marry a hard-drinker. Beatrice's younger sister, Celia ffrench-Salkeld, found the idea of marrying Brendan Behan appalling. She knew of his reputation from her artist and actor friends and thought her sister would be unable to cope with a man like Brendan. Her attitude softened a little when Beatrice asked her to be her bridesmaid, and she later came to a generous acceptance of her brother-in-law's short comings. The only member of the family not to express surprise or even the slightest indignation was Beatrice's grandmother, Blanaid. She loved Brendan's company and adored his stories of Dublin life and of his involvement with the Republican movement.

Beatrice also told a handful of close friends. She told Pauline Parker and Nuala Maher. They were both amazed that she would even entertain the idea of marrying Brendan. All her friends agreed – they begged Beatrice to think over her decision. Despite all the well-intentioned advice, she had made her mind up quickly and resolutely and determined to carry out her decision:

> I heard myself saying that the world didn't know, or didn't want to know, the Brendan I knew. All right, he was a hard drinker and a rebel and an ex-jailbird, but when we were alone together, or when I drank in a pub with him, I was captivated by his voice and personality. I was

surprised, as his friends were, that he had survived his years in prison with such a zest for living. He would speak of matters which moved him deeply and experiences which distressed him. Where others saw a rebel I saw an idealist; where others saw a hard drinker I saw a man of humour and compassion. His was not the conventional romanticism of other young men I had dated; he needed me more than any other man I had known.[16]

The cloak-and-dagger atmosphere surrounding the arrangements for the wedding had a suitably dramatic quality for a man who was about to become a world famous playwright. Beatrice's greatest fear was that he would fail to turn up at the church because of some drunken mishap with the police. After all, he served seven days' imprisonment in Mountjoy Jail for drunk and disorderly behaviour less than a year before. She feared he might make some impulsive bid to maintain his freedom just before the ceremony. With that in mind, Beatrice made him promise that he would drive past her home on the morning of the wedding, before she left the house for the Church.

To avoid publicity, the ceremony was scheduled for 7 a.m. In the pre-dawn darkness of the wedding morning, Beatrice and her sister Celia peered through the curtains of her grandmother's bedroom at Morehampton Road, waiting for the signal that indicated that Brendan was on his way to Church. Her mother and father waited downstairs with Celia's boyfriend, the painter and set designer, Reginald Gray, who was to be Brendan's best man.

Beatrice had the same fears that any bride might have on her wedding day, and she had the added worry of Brendan's unpredictability.

> In the days and hours before her marriage a woman seeks to shut out her fears, dismissing doubts that she does not truly know the man she is about to marry. I had accepted my man without question. It didn't matter what others thought now.[17]

Just after 6.30 a.m., Beatrice heard a car horn sound outside her door. She knew then that Brendan was on his way to Donnybrook Church. Beatrice arrived at the Church a few minutes before the 7 a.m. bell sounded. The wedding party consisted of less than a dozen people. Were it not for a handful of early morning worshipers, the Church would have been all but empty. Brendan waited near the altar rails. Long after his death she still recalled his appearance that morning: 'He was wearing a navy blue suit with a white shirt and a dark green tie. His hair was neatly brushed and his face, freshly shaved, shone like a schoolboy's.'[18] Near him stood his best man and opposite stood

Beatrice's bridesmaid, her sister, Celia. Cecil walked his daughter to the altar. By 7.30 a.m., when they signed the Marriage Register, Beatrice ffrench-Salkeld had become Mrs Brendan Behan. The bride was twenty-nine and the groom was thirty-two.

During the signing of the Marriage Register, Irish Catholic Church hypocrisy raised its intrusive head. The priest refused to allow Reg Gray to sign as witness because he was not a Catholic. Joe Doyle, the Church sacristan, signed the register instead. When asked how his profession should be recorded, Brendan replied, 'I'm a writer, but for the purposes of the Dublin District Court, I'm an unemployed house painter'.[19] Brendan was furious about that final unnecessary act of Church interference and announced to the guests in a loud voice 'Thanks be to Jaysus that's over, let's go and have a few jars'.

Brendan, Beatrice, Cecil, Irma, Celia, Reg Gray, Beatrices's friends, Maura Scannell, Pauline Parker, Nuala Maher and two family friends Alice Hughes and a Mrs McCarthy comprised the entire wedding party. At the nearby Morehampton Hotel,[20] they ordered breakfast which Brendan suggested Beatrice's mother pay for. He announced to all that he would pick up the bill for the drinks. He offered the first drink to eighty-year-old Mrs McCarthy who through deafness ignored him. He shouted into her ear trumpet, 'Have a fucking jar, Mrs McCarthy', but it was to no avail, so he simply bought a round.

The wedding breakfast was simple. There were no formalities, or speeches. No telegrams were read, no wedding cake cut. The odd assortment of guests left after breakfast, and Cecil collected his car from his house which was near the hotel. He drove Brendan, Beatrice, Celia and Reg Gray to Crumlin to introduce Beatrice to her mother-in-law.

His mother, Kathleen, was not at home when the newly-weds called. Beatrice's first sight of her was as she walked along near Kildare Road: 'a wiry, grey-haired woman carrying a shopping bag'.[21] Brendan called out to her and the party left for Kennedy's pub in Harold's Cross. When Brendan introduced Beatrice as his wife, his mother, thinking he was joking, laughed. She simply did not believe him. She sang for the party, her large expressive hands keeping time to the singing. But when the party left Kennedy's at 2.30 p.m., Kathleen was still unaware that she had met her daughter-in-law, something they would later laugh about together.

Brendan and Beatrice moved on in a taxi to Morehampton Road to see Beatrice's grandmother, Blanaid. Having fulfilled familial requirements, Brendan took his new wife to Roberts' Café in Westmoreland Street where they ate onion soup and Beatrice contemplated her happiness and their forthcoming honeymoon in Paris:

> Even though the café was noisy, we were alone together for the first time since our wedding. I was too shy to tell Brendan of my feelings, although I hoped he was aware of my happiness as we talked about the morning's events. He remarked that the onion soup in Paris would be better.[22]

But before tasting the Parisian version, Brendan insisted they make a round of social calls which involved visiting friends' houses and several Dublin pubs. The main purpose of the visits was to borrow money for the honeymoon. Contributions came from Brendan's cousin, Jimmy Bourke and from *Comhar* editor, Riobárd MacGoráin. Beatrice had fourteen pounds of her own and together with the money Brendan borrowed, they had enough to pay their way to Paris. On their way to Westland Row Station, Brendan insisted on having a drink at the Lincoln Inn outside which a street musician played the Irish air 'The Coolin' on a fiddle. When he struck up the music, Brendan began to accompany him in his fine tenor voice. Heads appeared at the windows of nearby offices and shops and, when he finished, his listeners applauded.

As he was leaving to board the steamer at the North Wall, Brendan discovered he had forgotten his passport. This meant a journey to his parents' house in Crumlin, where Beatrice waited outside while he collected his passport and two clean shirts. He was now impatient to leave for Paris, but made one final call at the Liverpool Bar where the assembled dockers cheered the couple, thinking Brendan was off on a journey with his girlfriend and not his wife. At eight o'clock they boarded the ship to make the night crossing of the Irish Sea.

During that voyage, Beatrice had a first taste of the married life that lay ahead of her. Brendan spent most of the journey in the bar singing rebel songs with the men of the 1950s' diaspora who were returning to their jobs in England. She did not hear him enter their cabin in the early hours of the morning.

When the boat docked, they went on by train to Paris, arriving at the Gare du Nord during a light snowfall. They spent their first night in the down-at-heel Hotel de Milan and the next day Brendan took Beatrice on a tour of Behan's Paris. Beatrice was interested to see the hotel where Oscar Wilde fought his last battle with the unacceptable wallpaper and the house where, in Brendan's often-used phrase, 'that grand old woman of French Letters',

Colette, had lived. She was, however, dismayed at the amount of drinking the tour entailed. For the first time she realised the magnitude of the problem she had on her hands. They were in Paris without enough money to survive and what little there was Brendan was spending on drink.

> For what reason I did not know. I only knew it was the first time I had seen him on a prolonged bash.
> He could drink a lot of liquor without anybody noticing, and this surprised and disappointed me.
> It could not have been that he was unhappy. I was beginning to realise that beneath his extrovert surface he was a shy and nervous man. 'I'm afraid I'm not the great lover,' he said, 'despite what people think.'[23]

During the honeymoon, Beatrice saw the true depths of her husband's vulnerability. One evening, she found him sobbing in their hotel bedroom, berating himself for destroying their honeymoon and promising her 'diamonds, mink and a house' when their fortunes changed for the better. Beatrice cared only that her husband had wept for her. She dismissed their poverty as a temporary obstacle. In time, the material goods did come, but so did much pain and humiliation, which she endured with unfailing dignity.

The generosity of friends like *The Irish Times* Paris correspondent, Desmond Ryan, and the writer Ralph Cusack, who sent money from the South of France, made it possible for the Behans to spend a few further days in Paris. Brendan had also pitched up at the office of *Points*. Finding the editor out to lunch, he 'borrowed' his typewriter and pawned it to pay for their journey home.

As they left Paris, the biting cold snows that greeted them had begun to disappear, the Seine was calm, and they were absolutely penniless as they faced the prospect of finding a home in their native city.

Beatrice's parents provided a temporary solution to that problem when they offered the couple a room in their house. Brendan's in-laws were generally tolerant of his undisciplined behaviour but Irma Salkeld was only truly happy with him when she heard the sound of his typewriter clacking away. Her prohibition on alcohol in the house did not suit Brendan. He soon developed a routine of writing for a couple of hours in the morning. He sat unshaven in an ungirded Chinese silk dressing-gown given him by Cecil. In the afternoon he and Cecil would make a beeline for the nearest pub where they chatted away, often picking up the threads of a conversation started the evening before.

While this arrangement was all very convivial for Brendan and Cecil, and convenient for the newly-weds, Beatrice felt that living with her parents prevented her from getting to know her husband properly. She wanted to find a place of their own soon. Her mother precipitated the move by answering an advertisement for a one-bedroom flat in neighbouring Waterloo Road. Number 18, a typical example of Dublin's domestic Georgian architecture, became their first home. It was a flat at garden level with a large bright drawing room and a comfortable bedroom and kitchenette. They augmented the sparse furnishing with wedding presents, which included an armchair and a pressure cooker. Brendan soon added the mayhem of unshelved books and papers.

Between journalistic assignments, he continued to work on *Borstal Boy*. Beatrice has left this account of his approach to work:

> ... His methods were haphazard. He would type for a while and then get up from the table and walk around the flat, preoccupied, perhaps taking up a book to read. Then he would go back to the typewriter and type a further page or two. Occasionally he would leave the flat and go out for a walk. When he returned he would sit down at once and resume typing as though, during his walk, he had marshalled his thoughts. Before lunch he usually went to one of the local pubs and returned after closing time around three in the afternoon.[24]

Marriage introduced a new stability to his writing life. 'Chastity and soda-water, according to Proust's receipt, is what a writer needs when he's working', Brendan used to say in the early days of his married life. He was usually good about his journalistic deadlines, though in later years he was appalling about deadlines agreed with his publishers. His *Irish Press* series of articles, which began as a regular feature in April 1954 and continued until 1956, became the couple's main source of income. It was inadequate. To supplement it, Beatrice took a freelance job as an illustrator with *The Irish Times*. Though he had sworn on several occasions not to take up painting work again, Brendan did a few painting jobs in the first year of their marriage. When the rent of thirty shillings and the food and electricity bills were paid, there was little drinking money left for Brendan. Yet somehow he managed to always have enough to get drunk on and this alarmed Beatrice. When he had the money he loved to drink brandy which he quaffed like lemonade. She made a concerted effort to keep him away from hard spirits. In the early years of their marriage, he was not insensitive to the pain his drinking caused Beatrice. She soon realised, however, that there was little she could do about it.

Any dreams I had of a changed Brendan Behan were vanishing in the smoke of Dublin pubs in which I was thrown into the company of his drinking friends. Not that I objected to the company; but until now my drinking had been a couple of glasses of stout, and hangovers were hearsay to me. A man of extremes like Brendan turned convention upside down.[25]

Very little correspondence from Brendan to Beatrice exists, but in a verse letter he wrote her seven months after their wedding, he shows his concern for her anxiety over his drinking and the damage it was doing to his health. It is touchingly sensuous, but in the end, perhaps more cosy than sexual:

> To Beatrice
>
> When the timid eye looks at you
> fearful and full of guilt,
> In hope its woeful look will catch you
> smile across the quilt.
>
> Oh what hopes of reformation
> promises to stick to stout
> Beating breasts and condemnation
> of late stopping out.
>
> Curling up and dreamy fondling
> Going as far as it can yet
> Paws are moving, surer, loving
> Further than they should be let.
>
> Till the process is completed
> Grace and absolution said
> Purring, moves in, snuggles closer,
> Stretches happily in the bed.
>
> Why does any woman double
> give herself the nuisance that
> husbands are when with less trouble
> She could buy and train a cat?[26]

In bed at night she sometimes read him passages from Flaubert, Colette or Proust. When he was seriously hungover he liked to read her *Alice in Wonderland.* Once he turned to her suddenly and asked if she had ever had a lesbian relationship.

'Did you ever fancy another woman?' he asked casually.

'No,' I told him. 'I'm sorry to disappoint you, Brendan.'

I laughed at him among the pillows.

'I'm curious from a writer's point of view.'

I told him I had shared a bed with other girls in my hostelling days, but you could not by any stretch of the imagination call that lesbianism.

'Was there no feeling?'

'Not in any sense of the word.'

I took it for granted he was no different from other men who enjoy sex. I returned his love and forgot in those moments his other imperfections. His love was my reassurance. There was harmony in our giving each other our bodies, a fulfilment that made me whisper to myself, 'Brendan is mine.'[27]

Beatrice had only a brief opportunity to enjoy any form of conventional married life with Brendan. He was standing on the threshold of international fame and she sensed its imminent arrival. For this reason she cherished the ordinary things they did together in the months following their wedding: swimming at Seapoint, race meetings, visits to the dog track and walks in the Dublin mountains.

They spent their first Christmas together as house guests of the Guinness heiress, Oonagh Lady Oranmore and Browne, at her Irish estate, Luggala, near Roundwood, County Wicklow. Lady Oranmore and Browne hosted some of the most glamorous house parties in Ireland. An invitation was a mark of social standing. Lucian Freud had introduced Brendan to her just before the Dublin success of *The Quare Fellow*. They became good friends on that first meeting and remained so until Brendan's death. It has sometimes been claimed that he was invited to Luggala as some sort of prize exhibit of stage Irishness to entertain smart house guests from London and elsewhere. This was not the case. Over the years he became a cherished family friend and his hostess chronicled his every success in large leather-bound albums alongside the movements in society of members of her family. He was extremely proud of, and regularly boasted in the press about, his friendship with the family, invariable insisting on calling them 'the Guinnesses', which was not strictly correct. Oonagh was the daughter and a co-heiress of the Honourable Ernest Guinness and granddaughter of the Earl of Iveagh, chairman of the famous brewery that bears the family name. 'The Guinnesses have been good to the people of Dublin but then the people of Dublin have been good to the Guinnesses', Brendan would add as if to put a slight sting in the tail of his complementary remark about his grand friends. For all his flaunting of his working-class origins, Brendan sometimes displayed a more than latent snobbery.

It was Beatrice's favourite country house in Ireland and she felt at ease the moment her hostess's Rolls Royce brought them over the Sally Gap. Beatrice's social background enabled her to move in a relaxed way among the titled and distinguished house guests at Luggala. Brendan's behaviour often lacked elegance, to say the least, but he never fell from grace there, no matter how outrageously he comported himself while a guest. According to Brendan, the golden rule in the house was that 'you may say whatever you like so long you don't take too long about it and it's said wittily'.

The house has one of the most spectacular settings in Ireland. Having negotiated a precipitous drive the Behans passed Lough Tay with its white sandy beach protected by a sheer rise of mountain called 'The Fancy'. At the end of the drive stands the white-washed Gothic house. The Behans spent nearly all the Christmases of their married life here.

That first Christmas, the guests included Lucian Freud and his wife, the writer Lady Caroline Hamilton-Temple-Blackwood; another writer, Francis Wyndham (Brendan particularly like Wyndham's left-wing views); and the novelist Derek Lindsay (who wrote under the pseudonym A.A. Ellis but was known to his friends as Deacon because of his priestly manner). Oonagh's children, Garech and Tara Browne and Tara's school friend, Charles Murdock were also present.

Over the years Brendan became very fond of the informality at Luggala and he added his own rules to those of the house. The butler, Cummins, he addressed as Paddy, the chef's wife danced *The Blackbird* for him, and when asked to sing after dinner, he saw no reason to keep the lyrics on the right side of *risqué*. He sang *Lady Chatterley's Lover* to the air of *Land of Hope and Glory*.

> I went third-class with Lolita
> In a great grim ship.
> What on earth could be sweeter
> Than taking off her gymslip?

Or in later years, after the success of *The Hostage*, he would bellow out in the public school accent of some of the guests:

> In our dreams we see old Harrow,
> And we hear the crow's loud caw,
> At the flower show our big marrow
> Takes the prize from Evelyn Waugh.
> Cups of tea or some dry sherry,

Vintage cars, these simple things,
So, let's drink up and be merry
Oh, the Captains and the Kings.
So, let's drink up and be merry
Oh, the Captains and the Kings.

One Christmas, when wandering around the house in the early hours of the morning singing *Adeste Fideles*, he took a drunken stumble down the narrow back stairs and remained helplessly wedged there until his shouts were heard by a female servant, Sis Leonard. He commemorated the fall in a bread and butter thank-you lyric to his hostess.[28]

Lady Oonagh, Garech, Tara,
Three bright heads be twice as fair
This time twelve months (and
as hard a curse of mine lies on that stair).
The girl that danced *The Blackbird* lightly,
Michael Wilding, Harold Lloyd,
Tara's bow to shine as brightly,
Bless Caroline and Lucian Freud.[29]

It was at Luggala that Brendan got into a second social pickle over his self-advertised but possibly mythical 'Herod complex', or sexual interest in underage boys. While he was staying at the house over Christmas 1961, Miguel Ferreras[30] Lady Oranmore and Browne's partner accused Brendan of sexually interfering with Oonagh's son, Tara. Señor Ferreras, the Spanish dress designer who had a physique closer to that of a prize fighter, invited a very drunk Brendan outside and knocked him down. Brendan had no idea whom he was dealing with, nor indeed had Lady Oranmore and Browne. She later found evidence that Ferreras had been born José Maria Ozores Laredo in Madrid on 12 March 1922, and allegedly had served with the Blue divison on the Fascist side of the Spanish civil war and later with the German S.S. According to members of the Browne family, there appears to be strong evidence that he had taken the identity of Miguel Ferreras from the dead brother of a Cuban-born comrade. Tara's elder brother Garech was present at Luggala when Ferreras made his unsavoury allegations against Brendan. He recalled that the allegation was totally without foundation and no-one present in the house at the time believed it. Lady Oranmore and Browne wrapped Brendan in a Foxford blanket and took him inside. Brendan remained a close and much-loved friend of the family and of Tara Browne's. Señor Ferreras, on the other hand, was not to enjoy his position in that famous Irish household for very long after the incident. As a formality, Lady

Oranmore and Browne divorced Ferraras in 1964, but her position was and the position of the Browne family remains that Ferraras/ Ozores Laredo was never Lady Oranmore's husband because their marriage was never valid, and at the time of the ceremony, Lady Oranmore and Browne was, in effect, marrying a man who was legally dead.[31]

Returning from Luggala after that first Christmas, Brendan set about re-selling the rights to *The Quare Fellow*. Beatrice's early post-marital bliss, such as it was, ended after the play's success in London in May 1956. Memories of their early excursions, and memories of Brendan's routine of rising early, writing and bringing her breakfast in bed sustained her when the full horror of his debilitating alcoholism became the reality.

Within two years of marrying Brendan, the conventional life Beatrice had led was turned upside down. She was hurled into his chaotic rise to international fame. However, not surprisingly, along the way, her deep reserve of patience and their relationship came under severe strain.

PART THREE

1956-1964

Under Littlewood

Unbeknownst to itself, the socialist newspaper, *The Daily Worker*, was both the obstacle that prevented a further Dublin production of *The Quare Fellow* in 1955, and the communication channel that led to its spectacular success in London the following year. The Olympia Theatre had refused to put on the play because Brendan's brother, Seán, had been discovered selling the paper clandestinely up in the gods where he worked as a spot-light operator. Then, in that organ, Brendan saw a notice inviting playwrights to submit scripts to Joan Littlewood's Theatre Workshop in London. Beatrice packaged up what she remembered as 'a very tattered manuscript' of *The Quare Fellow* and sent it off.

The director Joan Littlewood was a socialist and a cultural iconoclast. She had set up a travelling theatre company in 1944, which aimed to reach a working-class, non-London audience with a new, realistic approach to drama. The company produced both classics and plays by twentieth century writers like Sean O'Casey and Brecht. With her partner Gerry Raffles, she found a London home for her work at the Theatre Royal, Stratford, in the depths of the working-class East End, where she set up her Theatre Workshop group. Like the Pike Theatre, the Theatre Workshop was committed to modernising the dramatic arts. Littlewood saw her job as 'creating a contemporary expression for a British popular audience'.[1] Interaction between actors and audience on a level mostly alien to British theatre was one of the principal motivations guiding her style of direction. Though her innovative work was gaining recognition among her peers in the theatre, Littlewood's company lacked the funding to carry her ideas to the wider popular audience which she wished to target.

Although, writers like Beckett and Ionesco on the continent, were turning time honoured notions of dramatic representation upside-down, most British theatre remained conservative. Then John Osborne's *Look Back in Anger* opened at the Royal Court on 8 May 1956. The production broke the barriers of the classic drawing-room dirge that dominated the West End at the time.

The huge impact of this production did much to encourage progressive companies like Theatre Workshop. English drama, now forced to compete with the immediacy of television, was about to be engulfed by a New Wave. Playwrights such as Osborne, Harold Pinter, and later, Joe Orton, redefined the nature of theatre, plot and character. Outmoded notions of 'good taste' no longer applied. It is not too large a claim to make for Littlewood's production of *The Quare Fellow* to say that it was an integral part of that revolution.

She and Gerry Raffles had heard of Brendan and his family's republican history through the Scottish poet, Hamish Henderson, but nothing had prepared them for the man they were about to do business with. According to an admirer of her work, John Russell Taylor, she did not look for a tidy, well-written, finished play but something with a spark of life that might be developed.[2] This pretty much fits her description of the manuscript she received from Behan. Joan Littlewood maintains that what she got in 1956 'was a bundle of notes, all covered with beer stains, none of which Brendan had ever read again since he wrote them'.[3] Things couldn't have been quite as bad as this – what she actually received was the typed script for the Pike production, which Behan had read several times as it went through rehearsal in Dublin. Whatever the physical condition of the play, on a first reading it struck Littlewood and Raffles as the work of 'a great entertainer'.[4] At the time, Littlewood was particularly keen for a successful production to enable her to extend the short-term lease she held on the old theatre beyond its looming expiry date. She thought *The Quare Fellow*, which fitted her ideological bill as well as her notions of popular drama, might be it.

It became a priority to get the playwright to London for negotiations. Twice, they sent him the fare, and twice he drank it. Brendan finally made it on a third attempt and he and Beatrice arrived in London to stay in the Bayswater flat of their artist friends, Joe and Kathleen McGill. Joe McGill had first met Brendan in Dublin when he opened the door of his father's house to a young boy waving a petition to General Franco seeking the release of Arthur Koestler.

Littlewood and Raffles met in the bar of the Theatre Royal at Stratford East. Joe McGill and Beatrice went along to support him because he was still incredibly shy when sober. It proved to be one of the key meetings of his career. The first meeting proved an unqualified success. Littlewood and Behan liked each other immediately. They both came from working-class backgrounds, they shared similar ideas about the future of theatre and they were both on the verge of making a lasting contribution to it. They also both firmly believed that the theatre should entertain its patrons. Beatrice Behan believed that Littlewood's eagerness to convey her feeling about the importance of involving the audience to Brendan was the element that cemented their working relationship from the very beginning:

> I can hear Joan saying to him, 'We must make them sit up Brendan. We must entertain them, jolt them out of their slumbers. We don't want them scratching their heads in bewilderment. Once you hear a cough or a sneeze, watch out. We must make them part of what's going on.'[5]

Beatrice had hoped that Brendan's decision to give his play to Theatre Workshop was the lucky break that would bring his work to a wider audience. Littlewood and Raffles found lodgings for the Behans in a shabby East End boarding house so primitive that it had no electricity. Their very basic room with its single bed and general air of decay did not strike Beatrice as a portent of imminent success. Her attitude towards the project softened considerably, however, when she attended the first rehearsal. Beatrice had no doubt that Littlewood's direction did much to improve the form and structure of the play.

Since that first collaborative effort between Littlewood and Behan a debate has raged about just how many of the textual changes made to *The Quare Fellow* and later to *The Hostage* were done without Brendan's total consent. The creative partnership between Behan and Littlewood – and that is definitely what it was – caused the artist Tom Nisbet to make the now often-quoted remark that 'Dylan Thomas wrote *Under Milkwood* and Brendan Behan wrote "under Littlewood" '. Like all such *bons mots* it is not without its grain of truth. Carolyn Swift believes that Littlewood's handling of *The Quare Fellow* was 'an emasculation' of the work; carried out in the misguided belief that an overseas audience would not be able to appreciate it undiluted. Joan Littlewood maintains that her textual changes met with no objection from the author.[6]

Nevertheless, those changes have provided fertile ground for textual scholars, particularly in view of Brendan's cavalier attitude towards his manuscripts. The change which most effects the core of Behan's original concept is the reduction of the role of the play's most articulate communicator, Warder Regan, whom Behan used as the central vehicle for his analysis of judicial hanging.

Ulick O'Connor assesses Littlewood's alterations as negative, in particular the diminution of the significance of Warder Regan's role. He believes that this central 'Christian humanist' character was regrettably sacrificed to keep a London audience entertained, to the detriment of the moral basis of the play. He holds that this presaged Brendan's future willingness 'to allow his plays to be worked over at Stratford East in order to accommodate popular taste' to the detriment of his development as a writer.[7] In Littlewood's defence, it must be stressed that before she began working with Brendan she showed him, in a specially arranged rehearsal, exactly how she proposed to direct his play and the type of changes required.

In later years, although she felt the textual changes made in rehearsal may have done some damage to the essence of the play, Beatrice Behan resented the view often heard in Ireland that Littlewood rewrote the play without Brendan's consent or sometimes even his knowledge.[8] She objected to her husband being represented as so weak that he would allow his work to be manipulated against his wishes. She saw his willingness to accept advice as a progressive step: Carolyn Swift's reasoned and unpatronising approach on the touchy subject of textual changes helped her husband to advance from his original stubborn rejection of Ernest Blythe's demands. Brendan now saw that an element of collaboration made for a better dramatic production. Having seen the favourable critical reaction in Dublin to this new approach, it was not unreasonable to expect that he would allow further changes at the hands of someone as experienced as Joan Littlewood.

Brendan began his working relationship with this first London production in a concentrated and serious manner. Sadly, he lacked the dedication to carry that through on a regular basis. He began to slip across the road to the pub at lunch time. Littlewood often insisted he return to discuss the changes she wanted to make to the text. At times, he was a very reluctant participant. A very serious work ethic pervaded the rehearsals. Joan Littlewood took her actors through gruelling rehearsal routines that taxed the resources of even the most patient members of the cast. She used the bleak grey open roof space to simulate a prison exercise yard. It was fun for the actors in the beginning, but she took it to such professional extremes that they eventually began to feel as if they were physically and spiritually part of a prison routine. Beatrice noted Littlewood's determination to ensure the final quality of the production and acknowledged that Littlewood's primary motivation was not money, even though her personal finances were in a perilous state. And indeed, Littlewood made very little money from any of her theatrical productions:

> As the first night approached I realised what an asset she was to Brendan. She was his kind of director, just as he was her kind of playwright. For both of them the success of the play was crucial. Brendan was unknown outside Ireland; Joan was striving to save her theatre. I was conscious of their intense ambitions for *The Quare Fellow*.[9]

The Pike management in Dublin was shocked to hear of Joan Littlewood's announcement of a London production. The rights were quite clearly and legally theirs. Alan Simpson and Carolyn Swift immediately attempted to have an injunction put in place, but they failed to secure one. The solicitor for the other side later told Simpson that while he had a clear cut case for an injunction, 'being in the right is not always sufficient in law'.

The week before the play opened, Littlewood and Raffles took Behan and Beatrice on a sentimental journey to Hollesley Bay. They set up a picnic within sight of the Borstal where he had been so happy and where he had learned to understand a people he had been brought up to hate. Later they visited the local pub 'The Shep', where friendly warders had once taken him for a drink. When they came outside, they saw, in the distance, a group of Borstal lads returning from a work detail. The memory stayed with Beatrice for the rest of her life.

> Brendan stood and stared after them. The sight had suddenly telescoped past and present. I could almost see him as one of those dark-haired boys. I wanted to retain the scene as much as Brendan wanted to retain it in his mind's eye, for he had come to Hollesley Bay this day to review again, after seventeen years, the scenes of his youth ...[10]

The Stratford East production of the play had its first night on 24 May 1956. Brendan invited several of his IRA colleagues. When he arrived in the auditorium, he looked around and said to Beatrice. 'I'd say there was two hundred years of penal servitude in those seats'. Many of the IRA men were still under Expulsion Orders and had slipped quietly into London to share their old colleague's moment of glory. When, as part of the performance, the Irish national anthem was played, the IRA men jumped to their feet. When *God Save the Queen* was played at the end of the performance, they remained firmly seated. Other Dublin friends came over specially for the performance, including John Ryan and Gainor Crist. Governor Joyce – 'the old Man' as he still called him – and his wife were also there to see their reformed Borstal boy's success. Brendan invited the retired hangman, Albert Pierrepoint, but he did not turn up. In an audience that included so many ex-lags it was, perhaps, just as well. The play's opening neatly coincided with a House of Commons debate on capital punishment. Some of the most influential theatre critics in London trekked out to the wilds of the East End to catch the opening of this unknown Irishman's first play. Also in the audience was the Labour MP, Sidney Silverman, one of the leading campaigners for abolition.

The production, with its all-male cast and two sparse sets by designer John Bury, powerfully captured the stultifying nature of prison confinement. The grim preparations for the execution – convicts digging the condemned man's grave, prison warders setting their watches in anticipation of his last minute eagerness to know the time – starkly contrasted with the jocular gallows humour of the inmates. In his review in *The Observer*, which appeared the Sunday after the first night, the key critic of the New Wave, Kenneth Tynan, reproduced the gathering tension: 'Meanwhile, almost imperceptibly, the horror approaches ... Dawn breaks, accompanied by the ghastly, anguished clatter of tin cup and plates against iron bars that is the tribute traditionally paid by the thousand convicts who will see tomorrow to the one who will not. The empty exercise yard now falls silent. The hush is broken by a unique *coup de théâtre*, Mr Behan's supreme dramatic achievement. An unseen humorist, bawling from some lofty window, embarks on an imaginary description, phrased as racily as a Grand National commentary, of the hundred yard dash from condemned cell to scaffold. They're coming to the straight now; the chaplain's leading by a short head ... A sad, bawdy ballad filters through from the punishment block.'[11] As the voice sang a verse from of *The Old Triangle* – 'In a female prison/There are seventy women/ I wish it was with them that I did dwell' – the jerk of the rope was heard off-stage and the curtain fell.

In London, as in Dublin, Brendan told anyone who praised his work on the first night, 'I didn't write this play. The lags wrote it'.[12] The audience reaction was astoundingly positive and, in his curtain speech, Behan gave full credit to Joan Littlewood's direction. At the first night party, Kenneth Tynan asked Brendan what he was doing in Mountjoy when the quare fellow was being topped. The writer told the celebrated young *Observer* drama critic that he was 'having a wank over a copy of *Picturegoer*'.

He and Beatrice spent a restless night in their room in the dingy lodging house. At first light, Brendan got up and went out to buy every daily newspaper he could find. The reviews could hardly have been more favourable. *The Times, The Daily Telegraph, The Daily Mail* all carried positive notices on that Friday morning. Kenneth Tynan's review sealed the play's fate. *The Quare Fellow*, Tynan wrote 'will belong not only in such transient records as this, but in theatrical history'.

> The English hoard words like misers; the Irish spend them like sailors; and in Brendan Behan's tremendous new play language is out on a spree, ribald, dauntless and spoiling for a fight. In itself, of course, this is scarcely amazing. It is Ireland's sacred duty to send over, every few years, a playwright to save the English theatre from inarticulate glumness.[13]

Tynan said Littlewood's production was a model of restraint, integrity and disciplined naturalism. This East End-Dublin collaboration had made the reputations of its author and its producer. It also helped make the reputation of a then unknown young Irish actor named Richard Harris. His portrayal of one of the convicts brought him to the attention of Arthur Miller who dropped in to see the play during its Stratford run.

Maurice Richardson, writing in *The New Statesman*, suggested it should transfer to the West End. 'Aunt Edna and the matinée-goers might stay away, but the Irish and the underworld would flock to it, to say nothing of us progressives'.[14] Richardson caught the mood of the times correctly. When it did transfer to the Comedy Theatre on 24 July, it was received as rapturously as it had been in the East End. *The Sunday Times* critic, Harold Hobson, said Behan deserved to take his place in the 'long line of Irishmen, from Goldsmith to Beckett, who have added honour to the drama of a nation which they have often hated ... *The Quare Fellow*, like Garcia Lorca's lament – *Llanto por Ignación Sanchez Mejias* – is a ritual elegy written in a prison yard. There is nothing else like it in London'.

The afternoon after his Stratford East triumph, Brendan met Anthony Cronin quite by accident in The French House pub in Soho. Cronin had moved to London and was working for *Time and Tide*. Brendan strolled into the pub with a few companions and a conspicuous bundle of newspapers under his arm. Cronin was unaware that his old friend of Catacombs days had just enjoyed a critical triumph. Brendan threw a copy of the *Daily Express* down on the table in front of him open at John Barber's feature article on himself. A classic Behan diatribe then followed. Cronin was at the same time a bogman and a bourgeois swine. He had chosen to advance the literary careers of his university contemporaries over that of the poor slum boy. To finish off he threw in a parting salvo about the Kavanagh libel trial. Cronin's friends enjoyed the performance and asked his name. 'His name is Brendan Behan,' he told them. 'Ah', came the reply, 'the famous Brendan Behan.' Cronin realised that Behan's years of fame had begun.

It was his drunken appearance on the BBC's prestigious *Panorama* programme in a live interview with the well-known and intellectually-inclined broadcaster, Malcolm Muggeridge on 18 June that made him a popular hero in Britain. It was the first episode in the long-running serial drama of the televised drunkenness for which he became notorious. It captured the imagination of the ordinary man in the street who revelled in seeing a working-class boy made good embarrass a venerable institution like the BBC.

Duncan Melvin, the press agent for Theatre Workshop, arranged the interview. Brendan and Beatrice had returned to Dublin but, at Littlewood's request, came back to London specially for the show.[15] Muggeridge arranged to meet Brendan at The Garrick Club. The Garrick, though not the stodgiest of London's gentlemen's clubs and with a strong theatrical tradition, was an odd choice of place to entertain a well-known firebrand. Behan arrived wearing a floral noose given to him at the airport by cast members from *The Quare Fellow*. The club bar did not serve draught beer, so Brendan settled into drinking Scotch in large quantities. He had not eaten since breakfast and Beatrice pleaded with him to eat something. He refused. Muggeridge ran through the format of the interview with him and left for the BBC studios at Lime Grove. Brendan continued drinking at The Garrick. When he arrived at Lime Grove he was well-oiled but not comatose. The rehearsal with Muggeridge went well, and programme producers believed they had a potentially brilliant interview on their hands. Then disaster struck. Brendan asked if he could go out to a pub for a quick beer. Instead he was reluctantly steered to the hospitality room where he began demolishing a bottle of whisky. There he met others who were due to conduct interviews or appear on the programme. He was introduced to Richard Dimbleby, archetype of the reverential BBC broadcaster. Brendan began to improvise a Dimbleby-style commentary on a royal visit. Based on previous Behan performances, one imagines it might have run thus:

> Her Majesty is now presenting the great silver trophy to the captain of the winning cricket team... 'Good God!' she says 'but you native types look fetching all in white.' Now in an extraordinarily spontaneous gesture, Her Majesty has taken a bat to the Royal consort ...

Woodrow Wyatt, whom he was to see again at Luggala that Christmas, was there to interview two War Office brass hats about Civil Defence. The other guests were a gaggle of impeccably turned out young ladies from a finishing school who were part of a feature on ladies' finishing academies. Brendan's remarks about what he would like to do with them forced them to flee the hospitality room to take refuge in the corridors.

By the time the red light came on, he was incredibly drunk. The BBC executives were in a panic and wanted to keep him off air. Muggeridge argued trenchantly for letting him on, so on he went, shoeless and with his shirt open at the neck by several buttons. Muggeridge received mumbled replies to his questions and, in the time-honoured tradition of all great TV interviewers, he provided his own subtitles by repeating the answers.

Muggeridge asked if he had met any interesting characters during his time in jail. He said he had met the murderer Neville Heath who objected to his use of bad language. Muggeridge finished by asking Brendan to sing and he obliged with an off-key rendition of *The Old Triangle*. Even while the interview was on air, the BBC switchboard was jammed with complaints. Behan had made television history by being the first man to appear drunk on a live chat show.

Around London the next day, he was a hero. Bus and taxi-drivers, newspaper sellers, publicans and citizens on the street stopped to congratulate him. Within a few days, more than two dozen magazine and newspaper articles covered the famous incident. It was as if in some God-given moment of self-realisation he had suddenly seen the publicity benefits of his own outrageous behaviour: One drunken television appearance appeared to have turned a struggling playwright into an overnight household name. Nearly forty years later, Joan Littlewood still wondered which was more important in Behan's success – her production or his public drinking: 'Whether it was *The Quare Fellow* or the drink that put Brendan on the map, I'll never know...'[16] The hacks in quest of the colour story were now in the palm of his hand and he knew it. He also knew they had an insatiable appetite for a story like his, and he provided every embellishment needed to maintain their hunger. His interviews with the print media following the broadcast showed his ability to manipulate journalists. Depending on the tone of the questions and the nature of the publication he was, variously, 'sorry or not sorry about his behaviour'; 'drunk or not so drunk on the programme'; 'ill or in the best of health'. The thing he most feared about his drunken TV performance, he told the *Daily Mail*, was that he might, in some way, have disappointed his old Borstal Governor.

> 'I'm sorry', he said, 'if I've let the governor of my old Borstal down and sorry if I annoyed Malcolm Muggeridge – a real English gentleman ... I love the Londoners. London is the greatest city in the world.'[17]

From that day on, few writers would make more skillful use of the media in furthering their literary careers than the lad with the nervous stammer from Dublin's Russell Street.

At the end of June he was back in Dublin, but now on his terms as a famous playwright. He must have savoured the vindication. Flann O'Brien, writing in *The Irish Times* the following month, produced a vivid vignette of his popular reception by the Dublin working-class with whom he so strongly identified. The voice is that of a Dublin plumber:

> 'Tell you wan thing about Mr Been. He wrut a play.'
> 'Right?'

'Right.'

'It was turned down be that crowd in the Mechanics Theatre, th'
'Abbey, and had to be put on in the heel of the hunt in some sort of
somewhere. Now it's in the middle of Lunnon. And they tell me it's
going across to America.'

'What's wrong with that?'

'Nothing at all.'

'Know what I mean? There's another crowd in this country that gets
out a wee book now an' again and has a whole crowd over the head of
it drinking small sherries in the High Berinian. Your man just clatters
a play off the typewriter and takes the whole world into his lap. What's
wrong with that?'

'Not a thing ...'[18]

Before 1956 had ended, the 'crowd in the Mechanics Theatre' had put on
a production of *The Quare Fellow*. The first Abbey production opened on
8 October and received the now predictable critical acclaim. The following
month, the play opened in Belfast and, in December, it was broadcast on Irish
radio.

Behan's presence at a public meeting was guaranteed to spark controversy.
While his play was running at the Abbey, the authorities at University College
Dublin banned him from chairing a student debate where he was to speak to
the motion: 'That this country needs a revolution'. Later the same week a
meeting he addressed at the Queen's University Belfast broke up in a near riot.
He was just warming to his theme, 'Her Majesty's Prisons Today', when a
number of squibs exploded and the meeting had to be abandoned.[19]

One can imagine Patrick Kavanagh having serious indigestion when he
opened his *Irish Times* on 13 October to find an unsigned profile of his former
adversary in the disastrous libel case. In this case, the piece praised the
achievements of its subject, but, perceptively, drew attention to the dangers
ahead:

> ... it is a canon of criticism that, after his first big success, there must be
> a sitting in judgement on a young writer to determine whether he will
> ever really add up to anything.
>
> The evidence is not all in ... There are obvious dangers. Brendan Behan
> is very much a 'character' – TV and the popular illustrated magazines
> have done their best to make him so. The 'character,' whose talk
> everyone enjoys, but whose writings no-one ever sees, is a familiar
> feature of the Dublin scene ... One hopes his native wit and good sense
> will see him through the treacherous shoals, and that the thin, reflective

man imprisoned in his lurid and showy frame will be allowed to have his say.[20]

The comment about no one ever seeing his writing had a sting to it: the author of the piece was saying Brendan's reputation had been made, not by his published work, but on a single commercial success with a London theatrical production. Behan was, of course, also working on *Borstal Boy*, which he began to publish serially in the Irish edition of *The Sunday Dispatch* from September that year. In November, *The Quare Fellow* was published in London by Methuen. Sometime that month, he wrote to Beatrice's friend, Nuala Harris, who was then living in Montreal. He was touchingly anxious that their friends living abroad should know of his success:

> The play is in its fifth week at the Abbey and we continue to get a hell of a lot of money out of it.
> I am in the American edition of 'Harper's Bazaar' in a month or two – I don't know when – I only know they paid me $150 for it – or for the right to reprint it from the English 'Vogue'- which I gave to Beatrice for a non-birthday gift, so look out for it – the 'Harper's Bazaar' I mean.[21]

Now his status was confirmed, Brendan felt free to unleash himself on the letters editors of newspapers and journals at home and in England. He wrote to *The Irish Times* berating Paddy Kavanagh's provincial ideas and lecturing on the values of traditional Republicanism. On 8 December, he wrote to the *New Statesman* having read Marlowe Hone's review of Stephen Rynne's book, *All Ireland*:

> We read (and write) the N.S. & N. for no chauvinistic reason of centuries right or wrong, but I think, as a Dublin man of working-class, Connolly and Larkin Socialistic origin, [I] would be a better Irish guide to your readers than Mr Rynne – a Downside Catholic Englishman who cannot even spell an Irish place name – or Mr Hone, who for all his splendid first name I do not know a damn thing about – nor even if he is one of the Hones, Nathaniel, Joseph, David, or Pogema Hone.[22]

This communication, with its irreverence and arrogant obscurity, is a good example of the Brendan Behan Letter to The Newspaper, a genre of which he remained extremely fond throughout his years of success.

Beatrice and Brendan now had more financial security than they had ever thought possible. Beatrice realised, however, that Brendan's drinking habits and his generosity to every freeloader or 'toucher' as they are called in Dublin, would always put strains on their finances. Just before Christmas, they decided to look for another more spacious flat. They found what they were looking for in a Georgian house at 15 Herbert Street. The poet, John Montague, was a neighbour. His wife Madeline was from Paris and Brendan enjoyed dropping into the Montague's flat to talk French with her. Montague remembers the Herbert Street period as one of the happiest and most productive in Brendan's life.

Just before Christmas 1956 Lady Oranmore and Browne's chauffeur drove Brendan and Beatrice down to Luggala. That year their hostess, conscious of the hectic time they had just put behind them, and anxious for them to have some privacy, accommodated them in 'trapper's cottage'. It was in an idyllic mountain setting some short distance from the main house. At Luggala, Brendan could reflect on what had been the most successful year of his life and, in his mountain retreat, he discussed with Beatrice what his next move should be.

God-Branded

It was Valentine Iremonger, the poet and diplomat, who, in late 1956, brought the existence of the partly finished *Borstal Boy* manuscript to the attention of Iain Hamilton, editorial director of Hutchinson. Iremonger recognised its originality and exhorted the London publisher to sign Behan up. As we have seen, *Borstal Boy* had had a long and torturous history. Behan had been working on an account of his Borstal days since soon after his release from Hollesley Bay.[1] It went through several incarnations. In May 1951 he had written to Sinbad Vail in Paris mentioning his work in progress which he then called *Borstal Boy*.[2] He sent an extract which Vail published in *Points* under the title 'Bridewell Revisited'. The extracted piece differed little from the opening section of the work which Hutchinson brought out under the title *Borstal Boy* in 1958.

In January 1957, Hamilton came to Dublin to see for himself. He booked into The Shelbourne Hotel on St Stephen's Green and then went on a hunt for Behan around the city but failed to find him. News of Mr Hamilton's arrival to Dublin had been announced in *The Irish Times* and the paper suggested he was scouting in Ireland for unpublished literary talent. His room at The Shelbourne Hotel was inundated with unsolicited manuscripts, from veterans of the War of Independence, the Civil War and a host of more personal conflicts.

Two days into his stay, Hamilton was sitting in the lobby of The Shelbourne at around 4 p.m. when Brendan and Beatrice rambled in. Brendan was carrying a tattered leather briefcase which contained the thirty-odd pages of the manuscript Hamilton wished to see. The now half-legendary figure of Behan was scruffy, unshaven, and a touch musty. He sized up Hamilton, the dapper Scots Presbyterian whom in different circumstances he might have despised.

Hamilton was conscious of the image he may have presented: 'A bloody Presbyterian Scots chancer on the make, too neatly dressed, with a moustache a little too British-military for comfort, a phoney out to tie him up and render

him down, if possible into publisher's profit?' Hamilton's assessment of
Brendan at that first meeting is strikingly original and seems to carry a
premonition that this was a man marked out for early destruction and even,
perhaps, a kind of beatification. He noticed not his wit, nor his drunkeness
but a holy aura:

> Whatever else he was, Behan was God-branded. I don't know how else
> to put it. Among other odours, that of sanctity was predominant. It
> might have been Coleridge's mariner who was talking to me.[3]

By the time Hamilton had finished a six-hour drinking session with Brendan,
he had secured the rights to *Borstal Boy* for Hutchinson. Later that night in
his bed in The Shelbourne, Hamilton read the thirty-page opening and saw
that he had 'the beginning of something extraordinary', Brendan received an
initial advance from Hutchinson of £350, which he soon dissipated in his
Dublin drinking haunts. Hamilton would have a long hard battle on his hands
to extract the finished product from Behan in time for its London launch in
October 1958.

The new Behan residence at Herbert Street was just a short amble from
Brendan's favourite circuit of public houses around Grafton Street. This did
not prove too much of a problem during their first months in the flat. Behan
had taken up a routine of getting up at seven in the morning and writing until
midday. These months were one of the happiest periods in Beatrice's married
life. Brendan began to appreciate that domesticity had its merits. They were
given a cat by the Salkelds and Brendan christened it Beamish (after the stout
made in Cork). He taught Beamish to do tricks, like standing on its hind paws
and saluting like a well trained squaddie or revolutionary – as Brendan
preferred to think. 'Give the IRA salute, Beamish' he would say to the cat
while dangling a piece of fish in front of it and the animal always obliged. He
was so proud of the cat that he entered it in a cat show held in Dublin's
Mansion House. He did not have a cat basket so he exhibited it in a meat safe.
This sentimental affection for cats was a side to his personality rarely on
display in the pubs.

This sudden onset of the work ethic and appreciation of the delights of
home were the result of a shocking discovery about his own state of health.
Beatrice had been alarmed the summer before by a sharp change in his
condition. One of the warning signs had been a dreadful hangover which
would not go away. It followed an all-night party with the stage hands after
the West End opening of *The Quare Fellow*. When he returned to Dublin
from London in 1956, she noticed he had an almost insatiable thirst for

liquids other than his usual intake of alcohol. He drank large quantities of lemonade, tea and even water. Beatrice also noticed that his face was swollen and his eating habits had become extremely erratic. After their second Christmas at Luggala, Beatrice became seriously worried about his health. She was eager to seek medical help for her husband and he was determined not to have it.

No amount of pleading with him to attend a doctor had any effect until she forced him to see Dr Roderick W. (Rory) Childers, who was based in Baggot Street Hospital which was conveniently situated near their flat. Ralph Cusack had introduced Brendan to Rory Childers around 1950. Brendan greatly admired Childer's late grandfather, Erskine Childers, author of the classic tale of espionage and sailing, *Riddle of the Sands*, who had been executed after taking the Republican side during the civil war. From parties at Luggala, Brendan also knew his father, Erskine Hamilton Childers, a minister in Mr de Valera's cabinet and a future President of Ireland.

He agreed to meet Dr Childers in a pub near the hospital. 'I wake up in the middle of the night', he told him, 'with a burning thirst which I am happy to quench with water, which is very unusual for me'. Childers surmised at once that Brendan was suffering from diabetes but he said nothing other than to advise him to admit himself to Baggot Street Hospital for tests. To his surprise, Brendan agreed. He was hospitalised on 27 July 1956. It was the first of a series of hospitalisations resulting from his diabetes.

It made headlines in the London papers. 'Fourteen-pint Behan Switches to Milk', *The Daily Mail* told its readers. 'I don't regret one minute of the past ten years', he told the reporter, 'but I must admit I don't remember much of them'. He claimed to have drunk fourteen pints of stout or two bottles of whiskey or the equivalent each day of those ten years. To prove to his interviewer that he was still working, he dragged his typewriter from the bedside locker and also pointed to twelve volumes of Proust's *Remembrance of Things Past* standing sentinel by his bedside.[4] It was classic Behan showmanship. The hospital staff enjoyed his unconventional antics. Being a Catholic hospital it served fish on Fridays. Brendan sent for Professor Victor Millington Synge to complain:

> Sir, there appears to be in this hospital a sort of weekly solstice, an occasion where you are not allowed to partake of flesh. Now, where I come from, which is the slums, there are only two times when you don't eat flesh. One is when you're too damn broke to buy it. The other is when you're too damn sick to eat it.[5]

On another occasion he rushed into the doctors' dining room screaming for Dr Childers. 'Rory, Rory, please rescue me from the Druids'. Apparently to his annoyance, a priest had offered his immortal soul some spiritual comfort. Shades of Fr Lane at Walton perhaps?

The more serious side to his hospital stay surfaced after the results of the tests were made known to him. He was diagnosed as having a mild form of diabetes. A small daily dose of insulin was prescribed and Professor Millington Synge advised him to carry a couple of sugar lumps at all times. 'Why doctor?,' he asked, 'is that in case I meet a horse?'

Three weeks after he had been admitted to hospital, he was released. With Beatrice, he walked the short distance to their flat. As they walked, he cursed his bad luck and asked over and over again why this malediction had to befall him, a man who prided himself on his physical powers and his ability to recover quickly from hangovers. Things would never be the same again. According to Dr Childers 'Thirst, as a symptom of diabetes, was to confound his life thereafter, creating an endless series of vicious cycles'.[6]

Brendan insisted on keeping the illness a secret from his family and again, just like their private conspiracy over the details of their wedding, Beatrice felt this new secret brought them closer together. He had been dependent on her from the moment they married, now the dependence increased. His ailment required a special diet which she did her best to keep him to. They often talked about his illness but he never mentioned the word 'diabetic'. As was usual with Brendan's major problems, he found the best way to deal with them was to ignore them and hope they would go away. This one would not and there was the constant nagging reminder of the medication he carried in his pocket lest he should drift into coma.

To put the trauma of the diagnosis behind him, Brendan threw himself into working on *Borstal Boy* and several other projects. He accepted two other commissions in early 1957. The first, from the BBC, was to write a short radio play for the Home Service. *The Big House* was broadcast in the Spring. It is an Anglo-Irish romp set against the background of Ireland's Civil War. The owners of the big house in question are forced to flee and the place is plundered by a Dubliner and a cockney. Much of the material he used is scavenged from his *Irish Press* articles. In its use of songs and jokes it is a forerunner to the raucous, music-hall style of his later play, *The Hostage*. Two of the play's most Behanesque creations are Granny Grunt and Granny Growl. In the best traditions of Behan's comic 'shawlies', or Dublin barrow women, they are fond of a drop. They reminisce about their fine men who made their careers in the British Army:

GRANNY GROWL [sobs a bit] Me tired husband, poor ould Paddins,
he was shot in the Dardanelles.
GRANNY GRUNT [sympathetically] And a most painful part of the
body to be shot.
GRANNY GROWL. And me first husband was et be the Asantees.
All they found of him was a button and a bone.
GRANNY GRUNT. God's curse to the hungry bastards.[7]

The piece was strongly tongue-in-cheek, and Behan wrote it as a deliberate
money spinner. He saw it as a distraction from his main work which was
completing *Borstal Boy*. Hutchinson were beginning to press for hard copy.

Brendan liked to give the impression that he had nothing but disdain for
the contractual nature of the relationship between publisher and writer. He
may well have held such views, but he showed himself to be quite canny in
guarding his own best interests when it came to such matters. He had double
sold the rights which belonged to the Irish producers of *The Quare Fellow*, but
they had not been able to secure a legal settlement against him. His conscience
troubled him about that act of disloyalty to Alan Simpson and Carolyn Swift.
He did something to salve it in the Summer of 1957 when their production
of Tennessee Williams *The Rose Tatoo* was deemed an 'indecent and profane'
performance and Alan Simpson as the producer was prosecuted. Brendan
turned up at the theatre one day after the London success of *The Quare Fellow*
and gave Simpson £100 towards the legal defence fund.[8] Hutchinson were
concerned that a similar contractual conflict might arise over *Borstal Boy*.
They thought it possible that Gerry Raffles of Theatre Workshop might
already have some rights to the work.

In early 1957, Brendan corresponded with the London publishing firm to
allay their fears. He sent Hutchinson a detailed account of all his contractual
relations with Raffles. In a letter to Iain Hamilton dated 12 March he wrote:

> Gerry Raffles rang up, and acted very hurt, and all to that effect, but the
> principle thing is that he wrote me a letter of which I shall send on a
> copy renouncing any right to have anything to do with the book. I am
> sending you a copy of this letter.[9]

Brendan and Beatrice went to London for the first broadcast of *The Big House*
in the Spring of 1957, and at the same time to deliver the almost complete
manuscript of *Borstal Boy* to Hutchinson. It was in their London offices that
he first met Rae Jeffs, who was publicity manager at Hutchinson at the time.
This well-mannered, exquisitely dressed, reserved English lady had never met

anyone quite like him in her life. Nothing in her English education prepared her for this meeting with Brendan Behan. He eschewed all formal introduction and instead swept her into his arms and began dancing with her to his own accompaniment of *Land of Hope and Glory* set to his own words of *I Should Have Been Born a Tulip*[10] A Behan convert from that moment on, Jeffs was to play a vital role in shaping his last years as a writer.

At this stage, the manuscript of *Borstal Boy* consisted of about 300 pages of typed foolscap. Brendan was reluctant to hand over the unfinished manuscript to his publishers as promised, and had left it with his luggage at the BBC. Hamilton and Jeffs handled the absurd cat and mouse game that ensued with stoic patience. A member of Hutchinson staff was sent with Brendan to the BBC only to be ejected from the taxi by the writer. Finally, after a drunken evening in a London pub Brendan agreed that Beatrice should go with Rae Jeffs to the BBC and retrieve the manuscript. Miss Jeffs had the manuscript firmly in her possession, but the drama wasn't over yet. She, along with Beatrice, returned to the pub where Brendan was drinking and was drawn into the escalating camaraderie of his ever increasing circle. She finally extricated herself and took a train from Great Portland Street tube station. When she alighted at South Kensington, she discovered she had left the manuscript, which had been so difficult to prise from its author, in the train. She rushed by taxi to St James's Park station and arrived just ahead of the train she had left at South Kensington. The manuscript, to her intense relief, was just where she had left it. It was the classic story: the only copy in existence of Behan's masterly tale of Borstal life was rescued for posterity by the most arbitrary good fortune.

If the battle to get the unfinished manuscript proved difficult, it turned out to be a mere skirmish compared with the efforts the London publishers were forced to expend to secure delivery of the remaining unwritten section. Hutchinson continued to advance money for the unfinished book until Iain Hamilton finally refused to advance any more until he had received the finished work. A lengthy correspondence between author and publisher shows just how difficult that task proved to be.

In early June, to escape Dublin, heavy drinking and idleness Brendan rented a two-storey stone cottage at Caorán Mór, near Carraroe in Connemara for himself and Beatrice. The writer Brendan is most often compared to, Dylan Thomas, spent time here in his boyhood. Brendan rejected the comparison saying all they had in common was that they got drunk and disgraced themselves in public.

After the mayhem of London and the ongoing worry about Brendan's drinking, Beatrice was relieved by the peace of Connemara and her husband's attempts to cut out alcohol:

> After the sticky heat of London, I find Caorán Mór paradise. Life moves slowly in Connemara. There is time for talk, and time itself is counted not in minutes but by the seasons. Brendan has come to write the final chapters of *Borstal Boy*. No alcohol for him now; just soda-water with a dash of lime.[11]

Adhering to his own interpretation of Proustian abstinence, he worked steadily on *Borstal Boy* while staying in Connemara. However before the book was finished he became restless for Dublin and for his old drinking haunts and returned there in early July. The letters to Iain Hamilton asking for money continued as did his promises to finish the book. 'Here's the finished copy to date, and I am truly sorry I have not sent you more' he wrote to Iain Hamilton on 8 July.[12] On 12 August he wrote from Herbert Street:

> I really am very sorry that I have not sent you the last of the book mss before this, but matters sometimes get very complicated. What is the good of telling you now, but I have some very fucked up snafoos in my affairs and am only now getting out of them. They were all financial, but I did not like to call on you again, so soon.
>
> However, in one fortnight from now, as God is my witness, you shall have the last word of *Borstal Boy*.[13]

The last word did not come until 18 September, when he sent the final section of the book to Hamilton. He found the necessary push to finish the book when Hamilton, on 13 September, told him there would be no more cash until the manuscript was delivered. When that was done, he told him, he could expect a great deal of money to come in the future. Within five days, Iain Hamilton had the final section of the manuscript on his desk.

Knowing Brendan's drinking habits and spending largesse, Iain Hamilton did not think it sensible to give him a huge injection of cash upfront. He felt an arrangement to pay a monthly sum would better serve Beatrice's interests. He came to an agreement with Brendan, whereby Hutchinson paid a monthly sum of £40 to a bank account in Upper Baggot Street, Dublin.

Submitting *Borstal Boy* brought with it both a sense of relief and of loss. He not only dated the letter accompanying the manuscript but also put the time of 11 p.m. on it. By the end of September he was writing to Hamilton saying, 'I miss my poor old book! Though long and lovingly I cursed it. However, there's more where that came from, as the mother of twenty said.'

Despite the continuing rapid advancement of his career and reputation in 1957, it was in that year that Brendan Behan commenced his descent into serious, and ultimately fatal, alcoholic decline.

The 'happy little bull ... crackling with affection for the world' as his Herbert Street neighbour, John Montague describes him, was by the end of that year beginning his transformation into a less than blithe, socially impossible, physically disintergrating, drunkard.

Few of his true friends doubted that the most enjoyable time to be around Brendan was when he was sober. But, as he became successful, he was increasingly rarely sober. He did not become more entertaining as the evening wore on. In fact, his friends noticed that he frequently lapsed into a tedious monologue that made conversation something of a one-way street. Once he had crossed a certain threshold of inebriation, Oliver St John Gogarty's dictum 'We may repeat our drinks but not ourselves' no longer applied to Brendan. He larded his speeches with well-worn Behanisms: 'If you are in good health, and have the price of a drink, death and love can be mourned in comfort'; 'If it's a thing I go in for in human beings, it's weakness. I'm a devil for it'; 'Dates are only for the police'; 'Every tinker has his own way of dancing and every cripple his way of walking'; 'Fighting is better than loneliness'; 'The only people I ever met who really believed in capital punishment were murderers.'

These disposable gems were scattered around the pubs in Dublin, London and later in New York. On first hearing these aphorisms were engaging. But, their sparkle faded after a second, third, fourth or further airing.

His drinking continued to lead him into brawls with the police. Fame did not help him here. On one occasion in April 1957, after a visit with Beatrice to his in-laws in Donnybrook, he had been taunted by police who recognised his now notorious figure. Beatrice and he were walking home together when a police car pulled in, and two officers decided to give the 'hardman' a difficult time. He refused to give his name, and they took him to Donnybrook police station. He was quickly released, but was so infuriated by the incident that he wrote to his father's old friend, Seán T. O'Kelly, then President of Ireland:

> ... the Guards who drove us home, remarked that it was 'only a bit of sport.'
> I do not regard it as a bit of sport, and if all else fails, and I cannot live in Ireland, without the dangers of this experience being repeated, well I shall make very certain, at the International Drama Festival in a fortnight's time, that publicists outside this country know the way I was treated.[14]

The letter demonstrates how well Behan understood the power of his new literary status and the political clout it gave him in Ireland. But, with the exception of this threatening letter to the President, he forbore to use it.

In the last months of 1957, two projects, one a commission and the other an idea of his own occupied his thoughts. The first was a play in Irish, commissioned by Riobárd MacGoráin, editor of *Comhar* and a driving force behind *Gael-Linn* (an organisation founded in 1953 to promote Irish language, literature and culture). In 1956, the organisation established an Irish language theatre in the Damer Hall, in the premises of the Unitarian Church, St Stephen's Green. MacGoráin had asked Brendan several times to consider writing a play for them. He hesitated at first but, soon after his return from Connemara in summer 1957, they met in McDaid's and Brendan outlined the plot of *An Giall*.

His decision to return to writing in Irish may seem curious. He was now a highly successful writer in English – what did he have to gain by writing in an obscure language for a tiny theatre in Dublin? The truth is he had never really resolved for himself his reasons for his earlier abandonment of Irish as the vehicle for his writing. Starting out as a writer he had 'imagined himself as the dramatist of a new Gaelic revival', and wished, through his Irish poetry, to bolster Ireland's sense that it was a 'spiritually independent' nation. His desire to in some way serve Ireland was not diminished but rather strengthened by his success.[15] There was also the question of his gratitude to Gael-Linn for its early support in publishing his poetry in *Comhar*. Sometimes, if he had a lot to drink and was in the company of Irish speakers, he would seek their assurance that he wrote Irish well. It still mattered to him. It also helped his reputation among his old IRA colleagues when some of them were beginning to question the rightness of his use of his knowledge of the movement to advance his own literary career.

Joan Littlewood later asked him to translate *An Giall* for her Theatre Workshop, and in its new form, *The Hostage*, it confirmed his international success. Some in Dublin saw this as a betrayal. That transposition from Irish to English, and the subsequent changes made while the play was in rehearsal, are the most controversial points in the virulent later argument over how much, and with what degree of authorial consent, Littlewood tampered with Behan's original work. Littlewood's version was certainly different – there were more characters, and it included song, and topical references. The changes have caused some Irish critics to condemn the English language version as trivial and destructive of the integrity of the original work. Be that as it may, according to MacGoráin it was always Brendan's intention to translate the play into English and he retained the right to do so. He also claims he intended from the beginning to have it performed abroad.

The plot of *An Giall* was uncomplicated. A young British soldier is kidnapped from Armagh barracks and held hostage against the release of an IRA Volunteer who has been sentenced to death for shooting two policeman in Belfast. There is some suggestion that the IRA may have been bluffing. Brendan claimed he based the play on a real life incident which took place in Northern Ireland : The IRA found themselves with a hostage they did not want to kill and so released him. In *An Giall*, however, the soldier ultimately dies during a police raid, accidentally smothered in the closet in which he was hidden. Colbert Kearney supports Seamus de Burca's view that the play was really based on an incident which occurred during the Suez crisis in 1956. On 10 December, a British officer, a young Lieutenant of the West Yorkshires named Moorehouse, was captured by the Egyptians in an alley way in Port Saïd, and later found smothered in a closet. He had been bound and gagged and locked in the cupboard of a house. The kidnappers had to abandon the house when it was raided as part of the British attempt to recover him. When his abductors returned to the house they found him suffocated, as was *The Hostage* in *An Giall*. The later Littlewood production goes further: he ends up shot.

Brendan did not meet Gael-Linn's deadline for the premier of the play and his work drifted in to them in dribs and drabs. It was not produced until 16 June, 1958. He had other things on his mind, including a novel which he was thinking about calling *the catacombs*. Iain Hamilton had been promised that he would get a first look at it for Hutchinson.

By November 1957, he was exhausted from the year's efforts, especially the task of finishing *Borstal Boy*. The insidious damp weather brought on a new health problem: he began to suffer from rheumatism. He found this particularly galling because he believed it to be an old person's disease. Beatrice sent him to a clinic to have it checked out. The affliction was probably partially caused by the harsh conditions he suffered in jails in England and in Ireland, but he was not happy at the prospect of further medical attention. Beatrice suggested that his condition might improve if they used his advance on *An Giall*, along with fees he was receiving for a series of articles from *The People* newspaper, to spend the winter in a warmer climate. It would also give him an opportunity to work on the play and the novel.

Beatrice answered an advertisement in *The New Statesman* which offered a villa for rent on the island of Ibiza. It was to cost five pounds a month, payable in advance. Just before Christmas, Beatrice secured the villa by sending on a month's rent. They decided to travel to Spain after spending Christmas at Luggala.

Early on the morning of Christmas Eve, they packed for Luggala. That year the other house guests included Cyril Connolly, Alex Cockburn, the psychiatrist Carl Lambert and his wife, Lady Veronica Woolfe (Caroline Blackwood's aunt), Derek Lindsay and their hostess, Oonagh Lady Oranmore and Browne and her sons Garech and Tara Browne.

In terms of his work, 1957 had been a tremendously good year for Brendan. As he and Beatrice left for Spain after New Year celebrations in Dublin, he resolved to finish *An Giall* and make significant progress with his novel *the catacombs*.

15

Trouble In Spain

Brendan Behan had not thought of going to Spain since he was fourteen. In 1937, his ambitious plans to join the International Brigade in the struggle against fascism had been foiled by a combination of his age and his mother's endeavours to prevent him. He so identified with the losing side in the Spanish Civil War that, in the personal profile he gave of himself after his first arrest in England, he invented a brother who was killed in that conflict. He continued to despise Franco, and, as he prepared to set out for Ibiza in January 1958 he told friends that, 'The sight I most want to see in Spain is Franco's funeral.' He remembered the small red-covered pamphlet that was sold in Dublin in the late 1930s to raise funds for medical aid for Spain. Brendan particularly remembered Austin Clark's review of it in *The Dublin Magazine.*[1] This little pamphlet contained W.H. Auden's *Spain 1937*. He quoted from it for friends before he and Beatrice left Dublin:

> What's your proposal? To build the Just City? I will.
> I agree. Or is it the suicide pact, the romantic
> > Death? Very well, I accept, for
> I am your choice, your decision: yes, I am Spain.[2]

They journeyed to Ibiza through London, Paris and Madrid. Brendan arrived with a thundering hangover in the village of San Jorge some five miles from the town of Ibiza. A taxi brought them to a hilltop villa; Brendan was dismayed by its remoteness. Beatrice, however, thought it the perfect location because it was sufficiently far away from the village taverns to keep Brendan off the drink. 'Good luck now', he said to the taxi driver, 'and fuck Franco'.

While he collapsed into bed, Beatrice explored the house. It was not luxurious. There was no electricity or running water, and only a primitive charcoal stove. The beauty of the villa's setting made up for its lack of domestic sophistication. A broad terrace gave an uninterrupted view of the surrounding hills and the Mediterranean in the distance. In the evening, the couple introduced themselves to Francisco, the owner of the local cantina. It was the type of rural bar and shop combination that they knew from Connemara. In its removal from twentieth century civilisation, the area in general reminded the couple of the West of Ireland. The weather, however, was infinitely better, even in January.

Neither Brendan nor Beatrice had even a rudimentary knowledge of Spanish. Undaunted, Brendan declared that 'Money speaks all languages and the language of thirst is universal'. He took out a wad of pesetas and pointed to the local brandy. It cost three pence a glass, and he pronounced it excellent. He declared Francisco's little establishment 'a gargler's paradise'.

Brendan made rapid inroads into their cash reserves. It didn't matter, he told Beatrice, because he had 'great expectations' – a number of cheques which were due to him for articles he had written for *The People*. Four weeks passed, and nothing arrived. He began writing to Iain Hamilton, asking him to send emergency funds to his Dublin bank for transferral to Ibiza. In a series of postcards, he told Hamilton that the work on *the catacombs* was 'begun anyway' and progressing apace.[3]

During his stay on Ibiza, he decided that the cover of *Borstal Boy* should carry a photograph of him from his teenage years. Unfortunately, he did not possess one. He hired a photographer, and persuaded a local island boy, who resembled him at that age, to pose with a large name tag around his neck which read 'BRENDAN BEHAN 47383501' in imitation of his Borstal mug shot. The photograph cost £10 of Brendan's own money, further depleting funds. It was money wasted. Iain Hamilton rejected the fraudulent photograph.

Brendan and Beatrice were now at the mercy of Francisco, who was willing to give them credit for food and drink at his establishment. It was not a bad arrangement, because the old Spaniard had taken a great liking to them both. It did mean a rather limited diet of local sausage, dried beans, fruit and a particularly bitter local wine which Brendan disliked.

Beatrice was happy with the simple routine caused by their temporary cash shortage. She got up at 6 a.m. each morning to stoke up the charcoal-fired terracotta cooking pots in the kitchen. They had breakfast together on the terrace and, at 8.30 a.m., Brendan began writing on his portable Remington. He worked on the second act of *An Giall* and, if he had writer's block or simply got bored, he changed over to working on his novel. By lunchtime he abandoned work for Francisco's bar.

Beatrice joined him in the evenings, and they became friends with several local people, including two brothers who had fought on opposite sides of the

Spanish Civil War. Brendan could never distinguish between the Falangist and the Republican brother, but managed to effect a reconciliation between the two while they were both carrying him home from the cantina one evening. They had not spoken to one another since 1937.

Brendan's views on Spanish politics got him into serious trouble following an incident in a bar in the town of Ibiza. He had learned that a local doctor, an *habitué* of a bar Brendan called 'Dirty Domingo's', had served in Stalingrad with Franco's Blue Division. The bar was also the local of a retired British Army Brigadier, who disliked Brendan on sight. During a visit to 'Dirty Domingo's', Brendan challenged the doctor about his military past. The doctor ignored him, but the Brigadier challenged Brendan's right to insult the man. A fight followed. During the course of it, the Brigadier's wife tried to intervene to save her husband and Brendan spat at her. He was thrown out of the bar and believed that would be an end to the affair.

A few days later, the local police took Brendan into custody and warned him that the authorities did not like his attitude. He was fined the equivalent of £3 and a deportation order was served on him.

Before this incident, the Behans had met another Irish couple staying on the island. Desmond Mackey, a handsome and charming Dublin man, and his beautiful chestnut-haired wife Ayllie who became their very good friends. It was Mackey's ingenuity that saved Brendan from the deportation order. He called on the Mayor of Ibiza and, in casual conversation, told him that he and Brendan had fought for Franco with General Eoin O'Duffy's Irish recruits during the Spanish Civil War. The Mayor was so impressed he tore up the deportation order on the spot. Predictably, Brendan was abusively furious when he learnt of the manner in which the affair had been managed, but the friendship survived intact.

Brendan asked Mackey, who was a competent photographer, to take photographs to accompany his articles for *The People*. The collaboration worked out advantageously. When the cheques arrived, the Mackeys and the Behans bought a thirty-gallon barrel of Alicante wine and gave free-flowing parties that endeared them to the citizens of San Jorge. So popular were these gatherings that the Mackeys' villa became know as Hangover Hill.

The isolation of their villa retreat had not proved the restraint to Brendan's drinking that Beatrice had hoped. On several nights he failed to make it back to their villa and slept on the roadside. Beatrice began to question why he would choose to do that instead of coming home to her:

> Sometimes I felt cheated and hurt, wondering why he had deserted our bed for the lonely road. He should have been beside me, his arms

around me, whispering tender words; for Brendan could be tender like any other man and this was to be our second honeymoon.

But I lay in a room of silence. There were times when I couldn't sleep until long after I had left him on the hillside and gone to bed. Did he expect me to lie down beside him, the two of us like tramps, under the night sky? It was absurd. 'Tomorrow I'll speak to him', I used to tell myself, 'but will he listen?'[4]

He didn't listen. He carried on just as before. The result was that he did not finish either of the works he had come to Spain to complete. *the catacombs* remained an unfinished fragment of 12,000 words. Spanish-Irish relations dominate the short piece. Brendan appears under his own name as a working-class writer, compiling his memoirs of his jail sentence served in England for political offences. He describes his boyhood involvement in Dublin with the fight against Fascism in Spain. Some of the verse pieces he uses in the work refer to the conflict:

> Sure with money lent by Vickers,
> We can buy blue shirts and knickers,
> Let the Barcelona Bolshies, take a warning,
> Though his feet are full of bunions,
> Still he knows his Spanish onions,
> And we're off to Salamanca in the morning.[5]

He later transposed the material essence of *the catacombs* into another unfinished work, the play *Richard's Cork Leg*.

Beatrice decided it was time to abandon what was no longer an Iberian idyll. The incident with the police had left a deep impression on Brendan. He became obsessed with his hatred for Franco, especially when he was drunk. His hail and farewell became alternately 'Hello and fuck Franco' or 'Goodbye and fuck Franco'. The last straw came for Beatrice when she saw two boatmen beating him with their oars after he had swum out to their craft to give them the benefit of his anti-Franco abuse.

The Mackeys gave a farewell luncheon and saw them to the steamer that would carry them to Barcelona where they journeyed onwards to Paris. Even Brendan's departure was not without its confusion and drama. He had somehow forgotten the manuscript of *An Giall* and his typewriter. It took all of Desmond Mackey's powers of persuasion to convince him that he would send them on after him. Beatrice and a very glum Brendan stayed on the deck of the steamer until the island disappeared. When they arrived in Barcelona, Brendan set off on a drinking spree in the bars of the Ramblas area of the city centre. Beatrice believed he was drinking because he was worried about the loss of his manuscript and typewriter. Desmond Mackey sent the typewriter on by the next steamer, but Brendan continued his binge. What had begun as a spree motivated by worry now continued as one punctuated by relief at the recovery of the typewriter, and further worry that Mackey had not sent the manuscript of the play. Beatrice was now desperate to get him back to Dublin and to whatever form of normality existed in their life there. At least the terrain was familiar, and there were family and friends to rely on if she needed them. What she feared most was that Brendan would have a breakdown and that, alone in a foreign country, she would not be able to cope.

Brendan insisted that they stop off in Paris before returning home. An American woman called Jacqueline Sundstrom, whom he had met on Ibiza, had invited him to discuss a Paris production of *The Quare Fellow*. Brendan and Beatrice left Barcelona by train and went to stay in Sundstrom's elegant house in St-Germain-en-Laye. According to their hostess, Mozart had stayed in the house as a boy. Over dinner, they agreed a deal for the Paris production. She gave Brendan a cheque the following morning for £100. Once the cheque was in his pocket, he wanted to leave for Dublin. They were driven to Orly Airport and boarded a flight for Dublin.

After lunch was served, an ashen-faced steward announced that the plane was returning to Paris because of a technical fault. Beatrice, who loathed air travel, panicked. Brendan tried to calm her. Two versions exist of what happened next. In one, Brendan is alleged to have run up to the cockpit door, attempted to gain entry and had to be restrained. The airport police arrested him when the aircraft landed. Beatrice maintained that this was untrue and that he merely ran to the exit door to be first off (one might think this story makes her husband appear in an even worse light than the other version). According to Beatrice, he was arrested after a row with Air France management over a ticket refund. Whatever the reason, the reality was that Brendan Behan had yet again landed himself in a police cell in a foreign country.

He spent the night in custody in Choisy-le-Roi. He was released next day after Jacqueline Sundstrom intervened. The experience had not been pleasant. One of the station officers had called him a tramp. He was locked up with two Algerians – which he said was the best part of the whole episode. He taught them to sing *Colonel Bogey*, which they did all night to annoy the police.

When he got out the following day, Sundstrom took him and Beatrice to dinner at Le Village, a restaurant off the Boulevard St-Germain. After dinner, the Behans boarded the night train to London from the Gare St-Lazare. When they reached Dieppe, a large contingent of pressmen were waiting.

Brendan told them that, while he loved France, he had no particular interest in dying for its national airline.

When they arrived back at their cold Herbert Street flat, they found a parcel from Desmond Mackey containing the lost manuscript of the unfinished *An Giall*. It was mid-April. The play was due to be staged in Dublin in June and Brendan was now under severe pressure to finish it.

There's No Place on Earth like the World

The year 1958 was a marvellous one for Brendan Behan. It seemed as if nothing could halt the onward march of his success, and the horrible cost that that success would exact was not yet apparent. In the eight months following his return from Ibiza, he achieved, at home and abroad, some of the greatest public triumphs of his career. *An Giall* opened to major critical acclaim in Dublin in June; its mutation, *The Hostage*, was received enthusiastically in London in October. *Borstal Boy* was hailed as a modern masterpiece soon after its publication in London the same month. New York critics acclaimed *The Quare Fellow* when it opened off Broadway in November.

After arriving back in Dublin in April 1958, Brendan worked towards finishing *An Giall*. It was due to open on Bloomsday, 16 June. The play's director, Frank Dermody, who had made his reputation at the Abbey, remonstrated with Brendan over the piecemeal fashion in which he delivered the script. Brendan later claimed to have finished the work 'in about twelve days or so', but that is incorrect. Under pressure from Dermody, he wrote the last section of the script in about that time. Further changes were made during rehearsals. Brendan attended those rehearsals, but not in his usual heavy-handed manner. Dermody was too experienced to allow him get in the way. Brendan quietly agreed to the changes suggested by the director, although he later complained about Dermody's 'Abbey Theatre naturalism'.[1]

According to Brendan, he based the play's setting on a house that existed in Nelson Street on Dublin's Northside. In Behan's time, the street housed an eclectic mix of poets, playwrights, ordinary folk and the odd scoundrel. His friend, Cathal Goulding, believes the *An Giall* house to have been a lodging house kept by a Madame Rodgers. 'Madame' was the title applied to keepers of bawdy houses, as well as a compulsory appellation for Dublin's revolutionary women. Madame Rodgers fitted the latter category. She gave succour to all manner of Republicans, including Claude Chavasse, upon whom Behan based his character Monsewer. Behan's creation was a cruel caricature of the Gaelic-speaking Englishman. The kilted, bagpipe playing gentleman was well-known enough to have been described by Frank O'Connor in his autobiography, *An Only Child*, in 1961. He was educated in the English public school and Oxbridge tradition, but when he discovered his Irish ancestry became an avowed Republican devotee. Behan used him to send up fanatical Irish Republicanism.

An Giall was received enthusiastically by the capacity first night audience. Supporters of Irish literature and drama were delighted that someone was producing 'modern' theatre in the language. According to Dr Aidan Doyle, who translated the play for the Behan estate, there was a paucity of new works coming out in Irish in the 1950s. Compared to the unstimulating diet of Irish theatre offered by The Abbey, this production was refreshing. It dealt with a contemporary theme and took place in an urban setting. Garech Browne, who was in the audience that evening, remembers people saying they felt they had been present at an important moment in the development of Irish theatre. He also recalls several members of the audience, both male and female, being moved to tears.[2] Brendan was not there to witness the tears or accept the adulation. A dose of first night nerves prevented him from attending.

The play received very favourable notices in the Dublin press. 'Cleverly written ... leaving ... an overall picture of excellence' *The Irish Times* critic wrote. 'Probably the best thing he has done so far', the *Evening Press* ventured. The *Evening Herald* considered it to be 'one of the most stimulating plays seen in Irish for many a day'.[3] When he read the notices he was overjoyed and suggested he make a speech on the second night but the producers refused his request. 'You were too bloody cowardly Brendan', Frank Dermody told him.[4]

Blanaid Salkeld (Beatrice's grandmother), a perceptive octogenarian, saw the play during the second week of its Dublin run. She rightly wondered what Brendan's IRA friends would think of it. His comic portrayal of Monsewer, the upper-class Englishman turned fanatical republican convert was particularly likely to irritate. Some IRA supporters were outraged by its less than heroic portrayal of the organisation, and felt betrayed by their old colleague. Others, who, like Brendan himself, were growing weary of the fanatics, saw the point of what he was doing, but were not willing to articulate it just then. Littlewood's English language version, *The Hostage*, caused intensified resentment. Dark mumblings in Dublin pubs suggested that Brendan sacrificed his Republican principles on the altar of the London stage. 'Success had gone to his head', some McDaidians claimed; others thought he was 'getting above himself.'

A week after *An Giall* opened, Brendan wrote to Iain Hamilton at Hutchinson to tell him of the play's success and to apologise for the delay in forwarding requested changes to *Borstal Boy*.

I enclose a piece from *The Irish Times* about my new play, partly an exculpation of my dotty dilatoriness in the matter of 'B.B.' I am attacked by some citizens who maintain that my poor old play is Pro-British! Jesus, I've heard it all now.

However, it is a tremendous success, and is being retained. Being Scots or Irish is a great thing in the days of our youth, when we look good in a kilt, and associate it with giving us a good excuse for tramping the mountains, but sometimes I wish I was born something else. Not French (Algeria) nor English (Cyprus and Kenya) nor Russian – my affection for them is in their role of spectres haunting Maynooth College – but Swedish or Mexican ... Gneu, gou, gu.

the catacombs goes like a bomb. I have thirty pages of it done, and will send them to you whenever you like.[5]

The Irish Times review which Brendan sent to Hamilton closed with the reviewer saying he 'hoped that Mr Behan translates his play into a language which more people can understand and more theatregoers enjoy'. The author had retained the translation rights when he sold the rights to *An Giall*. Joan Littlewood offered to stage his translation in Stratford East. The critical success of *The Quare Fellow* had not been enough to secure the financial structure of Littlewood's Theatre Workshop. She also had difficulty securing Arts Council funding in 1958, and needed a new play to keep her operation in Stratford East afloat. Before it would agree to giving a grant for a play's production, the Arts Council required to see the script two months in advance. In late June, Littlewood and her partner Gerry Raffles came to an agreement with Brendan for the London production of the translation of *An Giall*. They agreed on the title *The Hostage*. They explained their predicament and asked that he deliver the script as soon as he possibly could. Brendan agreed, and then set about doing the remaining tidying up of the *Borstal Boy* proofs.

William Koshland of Alfred A. Knopf, the American publishers of *Borstal Boy* assessing the manuscript, in a letter to Iain Hamilton, indicates how Behan's work was perceived at this crucial point in his career. Koshland wrote ardently about what he had just read.

As for me, I am quite overwhelmed by the writing itself, and the general excitement of the prose, its moving quality, and, as one of your first blurb writers put it so clearly, the case of an Irishman coming along, and proving just where the source of vitality in the writing of the English language lies. I have no doubt in my mind that you are right in hailing this as literature with a capital 'L'.[6]

Commercial and critical success did not, however, prevent Brendan from entertaining doubts about his abilities. He was addicted to flattery, but also hungered for the genuine praise of those whose opinion he respected. Voices that mattered to him had lauded his work from his earliest days as a writer. Seán O'Faoláin had visited him in prison and encouraged him to write. John Ryan believed implicitly in his talent and had published his early work. The editors of *The Irish Times* and *Irish Press* had expressed their confidence in him. His peers in the IRA quoted his juvenilia with reverence. After *The Quare Fellow* opened in London, his work had been compared to Sean O'Casey's. But in his own mind, the doubts still remained. Underneath the bluff exterior, and in particular when he was sober, Behan was riddled with self-doubt and crippled by shyness. Nowhere was that self-doubt more evident than in his perception of his worth as a writer. He wrote to Iain Hamilton about Koshland's assessment of *Borstal Boy*:

> Apart from your job in the venal side of the business, as a writer you know we have no proper view of our own work – we think we're James Joyces one minute and plain gobshites the next. I resolved long ago not to take it seriously, only when I read remarks like Koshland's.[7]

In early August, the Behans left Ireland to stay with their friends, Dr Olof Lagerlöf and his wife Dagny on the Swedish Baltic coast, where Brendan would be able to work on the proofs of his autobiographical novel and break the back of *The Hostage* translation in peace. The Behans had met the Lagerlöfs during a brief holiday they spent in Dunquin, on the tip of Dingle Bay in County Kerry. Dr Lagerlöf was an ophthalmic surgeon. He came from a distinguished Swedish family and had a passionate interest in Irish language and culture. He and his wife had stayed in the same guesthouse as the Behans in Dunquin. It belonged to an irrepressible local character called Krüger Kavanagh, a man much loved by generations of visitors to the area. The Lagerlöfs had a car and they took Brendan and Beatrice on motoring trips to places of local interest. Brendan taught the doctor Irish songs and history and, by the end of the holiday, Lagerlöf invited the Behans to come and stay in his summer house in Sweden. They now took up the opportunity.

They travelled to Copenhagen, where they took a ferry to Malmö. There they got confused by the train system and nearly ended up in Gothenburg. After two days of boat and train travel, they arrived in Stockholm at midnight to find their hosts away. Persistent ringing of the doorbell failed to rouse the sleeping housekeeper, so they had to spend the night in a hotel near the Lagerlöfs' home in Karlavägen. The following day, Dr Lagerlöf collected his guests and took them to lunch in one of Stockholm's historical literary restaurants, Den Gylden Freden. A beautiful flaxen-haired boy, celebrating his Confirmation day, delighted the company with his singing, but Brendan's rendition of maudlin Republican ballads resulted in the manager asking him and his party to leave.

Brendan came to the sudden realisation that Stockholm was not the sort of city where he could get drunk and find his usual boisterous public act acceptable. The following day he and Beatrice went with their host by ferry to Ljusterö and onward to the Lagerlöfs' summer-house at Linanäs. The Behans spent some relaxing weeks there. They were happy in the company of their host and his family and Brendan worked steadily on correcting the proofs of *Borstal Boy*. He got on particularly well with Patrick, the Lagerlöfs' young son. Many people who knew Behan well have commented on his extraordinary ability to communicate with children, and in this case, even the fact that the child spoke no English and Brendan no Swedish did not impede their rapport. One day, after the Behans left, Olof Lagerlöf found his son packing his toys into a bag. 'Where are you going?' his father enquired. 'I'm going to Dublin to see Brendan,' the boy replied. Dr Lagerlöf told him that Brendan would not have time to play with him, but the boy countered firmly with, 'I'm not going to play with Brendan, I'm going to live with him.' As the boy's father put it, the unlimited confidence Brendan inspired in a small Swedish boy 'illustrat[ed] beautifully the personal charm of the inner man'.[8] That trip was one of Brendan's least tempestuous forays abroad. The very respectable Lagerlöfs got off lightly.

The Behans left Sweden for London at the end of August. They spent most of September staying with Joan Littlewood and Gerry Raffles in their house in Blackheath, a suburb of Southern London. Littlewood had offered Brendan the use of her home to finish *The Hostage*. However, both Beatrice and Littlewood claim Brendan arrived in London with very little of the translation work done on the play. Olof Lagerlöf, on the other hand, insists he had completed the First Act by the time he left Sweden. Littlewood's production was due to open in Stratford East in October. There was considerable tension in the house at Blackheath when Brendan refused to knuckle down to work on the play. In mid-September, Littlewood and Raffles left for France. When they returned Brendan had made no substantial progress in producing the finished text of *The Hostage*. He spent most of his time in The Dragon pub in Blackheath. He had an uncanny knack for finding like-minded boozers wherever he was in the world. In The Dragon, he met Gladys, a former chorus girl who arrived with her shopping. The Commander, a dapper ex-British Navy man, was also a regular and rather fond of rum. So was a doctor who arrived with his black bag into which he put several miniature bottles of whisky before going off on his rounds.

Beatrice tried the carrot and the stick tactic to get him out of the pub and persuade him to work on the translation of the play. All she got in return was abuse. When drunk and obviously ashamed of his lack of progress with the play he could be horribly rude to her. She remembered him calling her 'a limey Tibetan whore' on one occasion. When sober, he apologised and called her 'Pet Behan'.[9]

There were also unpleasant scenes with Gerry Raffles, who felt Brendan was letting Theatre Workshop down. Beatrice, Joan Littlewood and Rae Jeffs have all referred to Raffles threatening Brendan with a gun. The dramatic gesture, straight out of Behan's own work, was not meant seriously, nor did Brendan take it so. But it had an effect.

Time was now seriously against him. On 24 September, with everybody involved in the production now under the metaphorical gun, the following announcement appeared in the British press:

> After several months of uncertainty, following the withdrawal of most of their grants, Theatre Workshop announced last night that the Theatre Royal, Stratford, would reopen on Oct.14th. The production will be the first of a new play *The Hostage*, by Brendan Behan, author of *The Quare Fellow*.

The Saturday before the play opened, Act Three was still missing. No text was sacred in the hands of Joan Littlewood. Her Theatre Workshop was a genuine artistic community in which no voice, even one as loud as Brendan's, was allowed to dominate. The traditional naturalism of the Irish version of the play was in quite a different style from Littlewood's. She felt it was important to hold on to the theme and sustain the tension behind the jokes and laughter as the threatened execution of the hostage drew near. Brendan was happy to comply with the changes she felt were necessary to mould the production to her methods. She applied similar objectives to her production of *The Hostage* as those she had applied to *The Quare Fellow*, but necessity forced her to be less loyal to the text. What Behan provided in the end was a workshop version tailored to Littlewood's specific needs. Those needs included producing exciting theatrical entertainment that filled theatre seats. To provide that, *An Giall*, as a traditional text, had to be sacrificed. The Irish play which had caused a stir in Dublin was a naturalistic tragedy; *The Hostage* was a tragi-comic musical extravaganza meant to entertain British audiences. Certain shock elements were therefore introduced which today would seem rather tame. Two homosexual characters, Rio Rita and 'her' black boyfriend, Princess Grace, appeared out of the ether somewhere between Dublin and London. Many of the references dated rather quickly and sometimes changed with the play's venue. Sister Rowe, Uffa Fox, Jayne Mansfield and even Evelyn Waugh don't quite have the same relevance for a modern audience that they had in 1958. These additions became necessary because Brendan's tardiness in providing a translation of his work left him with no option but to proceed with the workshop formula. Depending on his mood and to whom he was speaking, he alternated between cursing and rhapsodising about what Joan Littlewood had done to his play. After the critical success of *The Hostage*, he claimed her ideas suited his purposes admirably.

> Joan Littlewood, I found, suited my requirements exactly. She had the same views on the theatre that I have, which is that the music hall is the thing to aim at for to amuse people and any time they get bored, divert them with a song or a dance. I've always thought T.S. Eliot wasn't far wrong when he said that the main problem of the dramatist today was to keep his audience amused; and that while they were laughing their heads off, you could be up to any bloody thing behind their backs; and it was what you were doing behind their bloody backs that made your play great.[10]

Littlewood's theatrical direction may indeed have suited his requirements but her programme notes were somewhat off-key. Patrons, particularly Irish ones, looking at their first night programme were confronted with this picture of the playwright's political views:

> Brendan Behan needs no introduction to the patrons of this theatre. This playwright of the Irish and British peoples made an unforgettable impression with *The Quare Fellow* in May 1956. He has hatred for the political forces which divide and subject Ireland: but for the people – even if those people are the subject of antagonistic political forces – he has only love and understanding. If a stranger attacks Britain, no one will support this country more than Brendan Behan, but when he talks of Ireland – of a country where, outside of the cities, there are almost no young and active men left, where villages are now but rows of empty houses, where Irish butter and meat are dearer than they are in England, and where partition gives such a sense of continuing betrayal and defeat that the brilliant and useful ones leave for abroad to escape the internecine quibbling and denigration – he grows angry with the anger of a man who loves his native place as passionately as Shakespeare loved his.[11]

Brendan had many reservations about de Valera's Ireland. However it beggars belief that, in the hope of presenting him to an English audience as pro-British and, for all his IRA past, not really a bad sort of chap, he could have allowed that odd portrait of his country to appear on the programme for his play. The programme notes appear to be pure Littlewood at her romantic left-wing best.

On the opening night, Beatrice looked elegant and beautiful in a black cocktail dress. Brendan wore a dinner-jacket. The McDaid's contingent came from Dublin. Some but not all of his family attended. Rae Jeffs came with the journalist Brian Inglis, Lady Oranmore and Browne came with her sons Garech and Tara. Alun Owen, the Welsh playwright, and author of the script for The Beatles' *A Hard Day's Night* was also present. Beatrice's sister Celia Salkeld was in the cast, playing Teresa, the role he had written for her.

Once again, Kenneth Tynan powerfully evoked the impact of the play on its first night audience in his *Observer* review.

> Its theme is Ireland, seen through the bloodshot eyes of Mr Behan's talent. The action, which is noisy and incessant, takes place in a Dublin lodging house owned by a Blimpish veteran of the troubles. ... His caretaker is Pat ... a morose braggart who feels that all the gaiety departed from the cause of Irish liberty when the IRA became temperate, dedicated and holy. Already, perhaps, this sounds like a normal play ... Yet there are, in this production, more than twenty songs, many of them blasphemous or lecherously gay, some of them sung by the hostage himself.

Resurrected from death before the final curtain, the captive British squaddie slowly got up and began to sing. The words of his song became as famous a Behan ditty as his version of *The Old Triangle*:

> The bells of hell
> Go ting-a-ling-a-ling,
> For you but not for me,
> Oh death, where is thy sting-a-ling-a-ling?
> Or grave thy victory?

In his review, Tynan described the unconventionality of the play's dramatic parameters: 'As with Brecht, actors step in and out of character so readily that phrases like "dramatic unity" are ruled out of court: we are simply watching a group of human beings who have come together to tell a lively story in speech and song.'[12]

In his speech, Brendan thanked Joan Littlewood, the players and the audience and joined the cast in a chorus of one of the play's songs, *There's No Place on Earth like the World*. He told the house his play was a comment on Anglo-Irish relations but, if they wanted to know what it was about, they would have to find out from the critics in the morning.

The following morning, Tuesday 15 October, Brendan and Beatrice bought the daily newspapers and took the train from Blackheath to central London. During that half-hour journey, Behan had the reality of his fame as a writer confirmed for him in newsprint.

The reviews confirmed that, in allowing Joan Littlewood to shape his play, he had made exactly the right decision to secure its success. 'I do not know whether *The Hostage* is a masterpiece or not. It made on me the impression of a masterpiece ...' Harold Hobson wrote in *The Sunday Times*.

Brendan cured his first-night hangover in the George pub in Great Portland Street – his unofficial London headquarters. There he accepted the adulation of the camp followers – the 'ardents' as Dylan Thomas named them –and the media circus which now attended his every public move. In the midst of the confusion, he turned to Rae Jeffs and asked: 'All this will help my book, won't it?'.

That question demonstrated his lack of confidence in himself as a writer. With the success of *The Hostage* guaranteed, he was now anxious about how *Borstal Boy*, the work he cared for most, would be received. He need not have worried because all the indicators pointed towards a success. His publishers organised a pre-launch party in London on 18 October, at which he remained sober and in sparkling form. Rae Jeffs diplomatically steered him away from possible flash points. As he sang *The Bold Fenian Men* with Hugh Delargey, M.P. two teenage boys entered the room. Without pausing for breath he took two strong drinks from a passing waiter and handed them to both boys, Garech and Tara Browne. They accepted them without the slightest hesitation. Several respectable British middle-class ladies could not conceal their horror.

The party adjourned to Bertorelli's, a nearby Italian restaurant. Brendan got drunk and had a flaming row with Patrick Campbell, the son of Lord Glenavy. He accused Campbell of having policemen in his pedigree – the most heinous blot on any family's escutcheon, in Brendan's view. The scene became so nasty that the management asked the entire party to leave.

Birmingham was his next stop. He was booked for a live television interview with Kenneth Allsop. As before, he went into a Behan-style spin at the prospect. Beatrice and Rae Jeffs feared a repeat of his performance on *Panorama*. But, although he did get drunk, he performed brilliantly and got a standing ovation in the hospitality suite after the show. The following day he left Birmingham by train with Beatrice and Rae Jeffs. He found it necessary to get spifflicated drunk to unwind from the tension of his ordeal. As the train pulled into Euston, he locked himself in a lavatory and refused to leave. When he finally emerged onto the train's step, Rae Jeffs saw him standing there with his trousers down around his ankles and his shirt unbuttoned to reveal a bare chest. Looking at the world-famous playwright in that degrading condition, she saw him as desperately isolated; a man whose success had made no difference to his internal insecurity. Beatrice, looking at the man she had married, was reminded not just of those insecurities, but of the fact that she was now rarely alone with him. She also noticed how her own moderate drinking habits had changed.

> ... all these weeks seemed like a train journey on which I met strange or unfamiliar faces in the corridors for brief moments, unable to converse for long, swept along by the man at my side. I shared his success and was happy to do so, but there were few moments when we could be alone, except late at night or early in the morning when, tired, he wanted to lie in bed. The telephone would ring with calls from journalists and television executives. Brendan was more energetic than I; he expected me to keep pace with him, and I had no option but to do so, even though I now needed a couple of drinks where once I could have done without them. It was a choice between losing my husband to the world or drinking with him.[13]

Rae Jeffs was constantly in his company while the publicity drive for *Borstal Boy* steamed ahead. At that stage of their friendship, she still had sufficient distance to be an objective judge of what she witnessed. She noted how quickly he moved from sweetness to savagery. 'This was Brendan himself', she observed, 'even at war, his seesaw emotions pitching him up and down on a base of uncertainty that he could never shift'.[14] She also recognised that the temporary 'truce' brought on by alcohol only served to intensify the battle and 'weaken his ability to combat it.' Rae Jeffs was becoming one of those strong women on whom he so depended, in a direct line of succession from Granny English, through Sister Monica and Kathleen to Beatrice.

Borstal Boy came out on 20 October. Rae Jeffs counted 52 reviews in Ireland and England alone. The consensus opinion was that he had created a modern literary classic. The superlatives have been appearing on dust jackets since 1958 and are of a theme. Christopher Logue, writing in *The New Statesman and Nation*, was most effusive of all: 'The most important book of its kind to be published this century', he concluded. Lost among the deluge of acclamation was a piece in *The Irish Times* by Martin Sheridan, one of the most perceptive critiques of the book: '... a steaming *olla podrida* of a book into which the author seems to have cast practically everything that came to his hand'. Sheridan pointed out that what made the book different is what distinguishes any piece of original writing – 'An individual style and a fresh approach'.[15]

The first printing of 15,000 copies sold out almost immediately. The publicity staff at Hutchinson were inundated with requests for interviews. Foreign publishers sought the rights for France, Germany, Italy, Spain, Sweden, Norway, Denmark and Holland. Alfred Knopf published the book in the United States on 23 February 1959. All the American newspapers and periodicals reviewed it with the same enthusiasm it had received in England and Ireland. The novelist Brian Moore, writing in *The New York Times*, struck a discordant but incisive note when he wrote: 'A desire to be loved robs the memoir of power'. The warm reception for the book quickly established Behan's reputation in the United States. It was a country that naturally embraced the larger-than-life Behan image. Within a very short time, he would look to the US, and to New York in particular, as a place that offered a spiritual exile from Irish constraints. Meanwhile, there were visa problems to overcome before he was allowed enter the US. A diplomat friend in Dublin told him that the US immigration authorities had reservations about letting him in because of his prison record. He was already in love with the notion of America and deeply hurt by the suggestion that he was unwelcome. He reacted angrily to the rejection: 'It is only Americans who think America is important; no one else does'. He was particularly upset, because *The Quare Fellow* was due to open in New York on 27 November 1958. The production was directed by José Quintero in the Circle-in-the-Square Theatre, off Broadway. Brendan had not intended to be in New York for the opening, but he wanted to be in a position to go if he so desired. It turned out to be just as well he was not there to read the reviews. 'A loose sprawling loquacious play', *The New York Times* called it. Most of the other mainstream papers were also lukewarm about the play. However, Behan the 'character' had already captured the attention of the New York media. *Time* magazine ran a feature on him, describing him as a 'Falstaffian figure of a man ... the descendant of a distinguished line of eccentrics, rebels and house painters'. Behan's thunderous and immediate popularity as an American media celebrity was on the scale of another bedevilled Celt, the late Welsh poet, Dylan Thomas'.[16]

After the round of celebrations in London for *Borstal Boy*, Beatrice had brought him back to Ireland in October. Their Herbert Street flat depressed them both, especially when they discovered it was riddled with dry rot. Beatrice decided it was time for a move and began looking for a new flat to rent. When letting agents discovered the identity of her husband, they tended to refuse to let anything on their books to the couple. In November, a cousin of Beatrice's mentioned a house that was for sale at 5 Anglesea Road in the fashionable Dublin suburb of Ballsbridge. The Behans went to see it on a grey Saturday afternoon and instantly fell in love with it. It was a rebricked, Victorian terrace house with seven rooms and a long narrow garden running down to a river. Money was no longer a problem. Brendan told Beatrice there and then: 'It's my present to you'. The house needed serious refurbishment, and they were not able to move in until early in the New Year. Brendan painted a little sign for the gate – it read 'Cúig' – the Irish for five. That is the name by which the house became known. It was Brendan's last home in Dublin. He wrote to Iain Hamilton about the financial arrangements for the house at the end of November:

> We have bought a house after much searching, on Anglesea Road, rather a snob area, opposite the RDS. It costs 1,470 pounds, and we have 400 already, so if you could send the 750 pounds it means we could complete the purchase.[17]

In early December, *Borstal Boy* was banned in Ireland. He had expected this – books with far less racy language had suffered the same fate. When he learnt of the actual decision, however, he was overwhelmed by anger. His publishers had sent a consignment to Dublin for the Christmas market. It was stopped at the port and confiscated. Benedict Kiely, who already had three novels banned by 1958, remembers Brendan coming in to see him in the *Irish Press* to declare his utter indignation that a group of 'country yobs, so-called Civil Servants, sitting in a room in Merrion Square' had the right to forbid the circulation of his work.[18] When Australia and New Zealand followed suit, he decided the best form of attack was satire. He went around Dublin singing his own composition, to the tune of *McNamara's Band.*

> My name is Brendan Behan, I'm latest of the banned
> Although we're small in numbers we're the best banned in the land,
> We're read at wakes and weddin's and in every parish hall,
> And under library counters sure you'll have no trouble at all.

The annual invitation to spend Christmas at Luggala arrived. But the Behans had to decline. Christmas 1958 was a sad one for Beatrice, because her grandmother, Blanaid Salkeld, had died in mid-December. Brendan was also very distressed by her death, because she too was one of those strong women who loved him without reservation. They decided to spend a quiet Christmas with Beatrice's family in Morehampton Road. On Christmas Day, Brendan went to see his parents at Kildare Road. His relationship with his mother remained unchanged since childhood. As the years passed, nothing intervened to alter that. Sometimes Brendan arrived at her house with large wads of cash and swooped her into a waiting taxi. She loved the Wicklow mountains and that was where he especially enjoyed taking her. Brendan's relationship with his father never regained the closeness that they had enjoyed before their argument on the eve of his departure to bomb the Liverpool docks. It was Brendan's first Christmas in Dublin as 'international man of letters' and he revelled in the position. He was asked to be Master of Ceremonies at the switching on of Christmas lights in Dublin's Parnell Street. A huge crowd turned out to see him and he entertained them for half an hour in the biting December cold. No matter how busy he was, he always found time for children. In later December he wrote to a young schoolgirl, Mary Kiely, (daughter of his friend Benedict Kiely) at her convent school:

> Dear Mary,
> I should like to know what you mean by writing letters to Petro Flan[19] and not to me Breno Bee-han.
> And you may furthermore tell Sister Brigid if it was not a sin to hit a holy nun with a hammer – as all females should be hit regularly – Petro, Sister Brigid & you – I would take it very ill of her not to use me for geography lessons for the sixth and seventh.
> Regards to the Maureen & Ben [20] & the other kids & for sister Brigid (only a few because she's a nun).[21]

After Christmas, there was good news. The West End production of *The Hostage* was announced for June 1959. The play was chosen to represent Britain in the Théâtre des Nations Festival in Paris in April. Brendan was ecstatic. 'I can see the headlines', he boasted to friends in Dublin 'Ex-IRA jail bird represents the Empire in Paris'. To round off his unstoppable rise, it was confirmed that *The Quare Fellow* was to have a German language production in Berlin in March. Things had never looked better for Brendan Behan.

17

'Success is Damn Near Killing Me'

In early February 1959, the builders and decorators finished work on 5 Anglesea Road, and the Behans moved into their new home. Anglesea Road Ballsbridge is one of the most prestigious bourgeois addresses in suburban Dublin. Living there was a mark of Brendan's success and the Behans' social arrival. That February, it looked as if nothing could halt Brendan's upward trajectory. But, while Beatrice was happy with this change in their lives, property ownership did not hold sufficient attraction for Brendan to keep him at home. Instead of his city watering holes, he began using a circuit of pubs. Beatrice tried to keep him to the special diet prescribed by Dr Childers, but when he was drinking he refused to eat at all. If she thought he was liable to go on a day-long binge, she prepared a raw egg with milk and a small dash of sweet sherry to make it palatable. This was often his only food intake all day. He ignored his wife's concerns about his health. 'One just can't be angry with him for long' she told a reporter in early 1959. Beatrice's inability to sustain her anger fitted her into the deep-woven pattern of female forgiveness that had shaped Brendan's life. 'Poor dear Bren', Granny's boy had to have it no other way than his own.

The Hostage was due to open in Paris in April and Beatrice knew he would not get much work done once he arrived. She persuaded him to take a room in the La Touche Hotel in the seaside village of Greystones, less than twenty miles from Dublin's city centre. Beatrice thought the move might help to progress work on *the catacombs*. Brendan also said he wanted to do some work on a film script. Little progress was made. He arrived in Greystones on the evening of 3 March and later, at 1 a.m. in the morning, disaster struck. While he was sitting at the bar of the La Touche Hotel on the evening of his arrival, a man asked if he might join him for a drink. All went smoothly until Brendan discovered his companion was an ex-policeman. He unleashed a torrent of abuse and left the hotel in a very bad temper. The manager of the La Touche Hotel believed Brendan was sober when he left the bar.[1] But sometime after midnight, he appears to have had some sort of seizure at Church Road,

Greystones. A doctor examined him at the scene but ironically he concluded that it was a matter for the police. The doctor may have assumed that he had merely passed out from excessive drinking. His report to the police indicates that this was the case.

Brendan was arrested and taken to Greystones police station. Again he was charged with drunk and disorderly behaviour. He appeared before the District Court in Bray, County Wicklow on 6 March. He insisted on his Constitutional right to have the case heard in Irish, knowing that this would cause considerable difficulty for the policemen giving evidence and make good copy for the newspapers. His insistence on the use of Irish did indeed cause the intended disruption; at times the proceedings descended into farce. *The Irish Times* carried this report the following day, 7 March 1959:

> Mr Brendan Behan, playwright and author, aged thirty-six, Anglesea Road, Dublin, was yesterday fined forty shillings at Bray District Court by District Justice Manus Noonan, for being drunk and disorderly at 1 a.m. at Greystones, Co. Wicklow, on the morning of 4 March last.
> Mr Behan insisted that the case should be heard in Irish. He admitted that he was drunk and apologised for his language. Witnesses said that he called policemen murderers, scruffhounds and dirtbirds.[2]

After the trial, Brendan went to a pub near the courthouse and told reporters 'I gave them their forty shillings' worth. It was worth every penny'. Reports of the trial appeared in the British and American press, and journalists were frantically seeking interviews with him. Beatrice convinced him the publicity would do nothing to enhance the forthcoming productions in Berlin and Paris, and would only diminish his stature as a writer. She was angry because the judge at the trial had suggested she was losing control of her husband. He agreed to keep his head down, while Beatrice made arrangements for their visit to Berlin.[3] They were due in Berlin a week after the trial.

The management of the Schiller Theatre, where the production of *The Quare Fellow* was to be staged, sent airline tickets, but Beatrice returned them and arranged rail and boat tickets instead. It was a bad move because it gave Brendan more drinking time on a journey that took them nearly 80 hours to complete. At Hamburg, a group of German sailors boarded the train and Brendan spent the evening drinking with them. He arrived in Berlin in very poor shape and immediately took to the schnapps bottle like a long lost friend. The couple stayed in a suite in The Stein Platz Hotel where, within hours of arriving, Brendan gave a press conference. He then headed for East Berlin, where he had a row with the staff of a newspaper because they refused to let his driver come in with him. 'So much for Communist equality,' he declared and stormed out. He attended rehearsals at the Schiller Theatre the next day. While he was there, Beatrice received a telephone call at their hotel from Alan Baker of the British Institute in Berlin. The management of the theatre had asked Baker to intervene, because Brendan had been making what they described as 'inflammatory speeches' during rehearsals. He came to the hotel and explained to Beatrice that a foreign author of Brendan's international standing could easily inflame political passions in the city. Would she have a word with her husband? Baker also thought it sensible to try to prevent Brendan from attending the opening night. He invited the Behans to his house in the suburb of Charlottenburg for dinner on the evening of the première. Alan Baker tried his best to make him late for the opening but Brendan was too wily to fall for the ruse and insisted on going to the theatre.

Baker tried one final stratagem to delay the party which consisted of Baker, his wife Hannah, their daughter Alannah, Beatrice and Brendan. He drove further out into the suburbs instead of heading for the city. When they had passed one particular block of flats three times, Brendan unleashed a string of expletives and Baker relented and drove to the Schiller Theatre. The performance had already started. At the end of it, Brendan took his curtain call, thanked the players and expressed the hope that East and West Berlin would one day be united again. He then sang *The Old Triangle*. He was dishevelled, tieless and patently the worst for drink. He made his speech with his hands in his pockets – a capital offence against the German ethics code. There were shouts of 'Disgraceful' from the audience. The German audience and German critics proved immune to Behan's usually potent charms. The day after the performance, St Patrick's Day, 17 March 1959 the critic of *Die Welt*, Friedrich Luft, panned him utterly:

> This is a notice of a disaster, an account of a total artistic failure. Rarely has it been so difficult to maintain one's seat in Berlin's Schillertheater as during the German première of Brendan Behan's *Der Mann von Morgen Früh*.
> In England, this author has a reputation for a certain brand of notoriety. He is an Irishman. He was born in the slums of Dublin. His youth was spent in the back room of a bordello ... At a young age he became associated with the bombers among the enraged Irish ...
> In this, his prison drama, he makes a plea against capital punishment. The boredom produced by the result is, however, deadly. The Schillertheater stalls reacted with various kinds of theatrical slumber – amongst them snoring from many sides.

What makes this play so ineffective? It is weak dramatic form ...
The author, motivated by a smattering of applause stumbled onto the
stage in a state of total drunkenness and just managed to gather himself
sufficiently to address an audience which had just woken up. We were
told of his opposition to the conflict between East and West.
Mercifully the rest of his speech was cut short by the lowering of the
curtain. And then – at last – came the first, liberating whistles.[4]

Beatrice held that the production was at fault and not the play. She felt the
whole thing was over ponderous and the actors' lengthy pauses weighed down
the dialogue. Her prediction that antics of the sort Brendan had recently been
fined for in County Wicklow would not be well received in Germany, turned
out to be correct. She knew the German mind. Her mother was German. Her
father had lived and studied there. She herself had been there as a young girl
and relatives of hers still lived in Berlin. Brendan was devastated by the notices,
but tried to hide his feelings by shouting louder and more outrageously. 'Nazi
swine!' 'Nazi murderers!' he roared around the lobby of his hotel. Nobody
listened, nobody cared. The Berlin visit could hardly have been a greater
disaster if Brendan had planned to make it so. He and Beatrice spent a few
more days in Berlin before leaving for Paris. One night before his departure,
he had supper with a group of prostitutes in the restaurant of the Zoobahnhof.
One complained with loud indignation when she saw his flies were
accidentally unbuttoned when he came back from the lavatory. 'That is the
German mentality for you, even the shaggin' whores have an ethics code', he
later enjoyed telling friends. As he left for Paris, he resolved not to repeat the
same mistakes he had made in Berlin. Paris still meant a great deal to him and
acceptance there was more important than acceptance in Berlin or elsewhere.

Jacqueline Sundstrom, who was preparing her production of *The Quare
Fellow* with the translator Boris Vian, met them when they arrived in Paris.
She took them to their hotel room in the Hotel Royal and later, over lunch on
the Faubourg St Honoré, they discussed details of the production. George
Wilson, an Irishman living in Paris, was also involved in the production. He
had been eager to meet Behan, having worked for some months on his play. He
was unprepared for the appearance of the person he met:

I had not in the least expected his physical appearance. He was a man
who appeared unhinged; during my two months of work on his play, I
had constructed for myself a quite different image of him, but that was
a matter of no importance.
We went out together. He seemed to me rather sad, and very reticent.
He saw a rehearsal of his piece and said to me, 'It's very good, better
than what I wrote' – but that was a sally.

I saw later that he only ever talked in riddles. It was a defence.
Over-sensitivity? I do not know.[5]

On the evening of 3 April, Theatre Workshop's production of *The Hostage*
opened at The Sarah Bernhardt Theatre. The audience of 1,250 included
several ambassadors, and leading Paris social figures like Jean-Louis Barrault,
Lady Diana Cooper and Brendan's old friend, Desmond Ryan of *The Irish
Times*. Beatrice, dressed in a blue and silver iridescent brocade dress and
silver slippers, was ecstatically happy with her husband's behaviour that
night. Brendan was sober and in total control. He had refused any alcohol
offered him on the day of the première. Beatrice later wrote in her
autobiography, *My Life With Brendan*, that of all the moments she had
shared with him in theatres around the world, this was the most pleasant:

> When we arrived at the Sarah Bernhardt Theatre, the foyer was
> crowded with guests in evening dress.
> I recognised an occasional familiar face, and waved. The red carpets
> were down, the chandeliers sparkled, and a guard of honour lined the
> staircase, magnificent in their black and white uniforms with gold
> epaulettes.

There were ten curtain calls at the end of the performance. When the cry of
'Author, Author!' went up, a sober Brendan appeared at the edge of his box to
acknowledge the applause. Speaking in French, he said how happy he was to
be among 'the most civilised people in the world'. A post-opening dinner was
given in his honour at La Mediterranée. The following morning's newspapers
brought extremely favourable reviews from the critics. Martini, the drinks
company, gave a cocktail party in his honour. New friends were made and
entertained during the Paris visit. Brendan took a group of students on a tour
of his old drinking haunts, the Mabillon, the Pergola, the Reine Blanche, the
Royale. In bawdy lyrics, he lambasted the literary veterans of '20s and '30s
Paris as the group progressed from one café to the next:

> I absolutely must decline
> To dance in the streets
> for Gertrude Stein,
> And as for Alice B. Toklas,
> I'd rather eat a box of Fucking chocolates.[6]

Of the other new friendships made on that visit, the one that caused the
greatest occasion for comment was that with his fellow playwright Shelagh

Delaney. Delaney was a working-class girl from the North of England. Young, tall, and attractive, she was making a name in the theatre with her play *A Taste of Honey*. She had come to Paris with Joan Littlewood's entourage. She was smitten by Brendan or, perhaps, by his success. One morning at an outside table at the Pre-aux-Clercs, she naïvely told Beatrice she was in love with Brendan. Beatrice was annoyed but not unduly distressed:

> Shelagh was a teenager ... I knew she admired his achievements in the theatre and he was possibly flattered by her admiration. Women had not pursued him until now, but he had become a celebrity and, whilst I admired Shelagh's frankness, I was convinced I knew Brendan better than any other woman. I had no illusions. There would always be women infatuated with Brendan, I told myself.[7]

Nothing came of Shelagh Delaney's youthful infatuation. He had still not abandoned his 'Herod Complex' and that too surfaced in conversation, but less frequently than in the days of The Catacombs. Beatrice correctly believed she had little to worry about when it came to the issue of her husband's fidelity.

He remained sober throughout the Paris celebrations until his resolve slipped at a dinner hosted by Jean-Louis Barrault. From that point on he returned to his old ways with a vengeance. However, Cognac did not suit his temperament and drinking it to excess got him into several ugly fist fights. He drank so much that, when he arrived in London a week after the Paris opening, Rae Jeffs of Hutchinson found him 'dishevelled, dejected and utterly exhausted'. She also began to feel the difficulties of communicating with him 'as he hid, alternately spiky and moronically morose, under a shell'.

The BBC wanted another interview, this time the interviewer was Derek Hart. When pressed about his success, Brendan reacted angrily, 'I go to better beds, if you like,' he shouted at Hart, 'but I sleep less well'.

Brendan returned to Dublin. He grew restless after only four days and took a flight to London. Dublin soon tired of his stories of triumphs abroad – such triumphs had no immediacy in a city still dominated by parochial opinion. A success at the Abbey had more meaning than a success in the West End. In London, however, he felt he had many admiring, tolerant and loyal friends.

This time Brendan boarded a plane for London without informing any of his London friends of his intentions. Beatrice telephoned Rae Jeffs to announce Brendan's imminent arrival in the city. Within hours he arrived at Hutchinson. Jeffs was concerned about the progress of their commissioned title *Brendan Behan's Island*, which was to be his personalised account of his native land, illustrated by the English artist Paul Hogarth.

Amongst the people whose houses he frequented was Irish hostess, Naureen Smythe. In her house, 'Brantwood' in Putney, he used to meet George Hodnett, a friend from the days of the Pike Theatre. Hodnett, an affable eccentric, slept in a sleeping bag under loose floorboards in Mrs Smythe's drawing room. Behan and himself often returned to the house late at night and gained entry through a downstairs window which their hostess always left off the latch for them.

Jeff's worst fears were realised when Brendan took off on an unbridled drunken binge around London. She was horrified to see a talent she so firmly believed in, dissipate itself in such an abandoned fashion. Loyally she accompanied him from pub to pub pouring him into taxis and holding him up when he was no longer able to stand. The experience pained her deeply. What he needed was hospital treatment, but she knew that the mere suggestion of it would send him scuttling off to the nearest pub. Before he went back to Dublin, he turned to her one day and said:

> Success is damn near killing me. If I had my way, I should prescribe that success should go to every man for a month; then he should be given a pension and forgotten.

Brendan returned to Dublin at the end of May. Beatrice was appalled when she saw him. He had lost a great deal of weight and had difficulty walking. In despair, she wrote to Rae Jeffs:

> I'm worried to death, but no one can control a man like Brendan. It is too much for anyone. He drinks too much and won't eat at all. He has been told to stop drinking completely. But what can I do with him?[8]

Beatrice pleaded with Brendan not to go to London for the opening of the West End production of *The Hostage*. It was to open on 11 July at Wyndham's Theatre and she dreaded the consequences of another West End success.

Feeling exhausted and very ill, he agreed to go with her to Carraroe in Connemara. They took the cottage they usually rented. This time it proved no respite from drink. There was little else to do, except listen to drunken old bores in village pubs retell their stories and sing their songs.

The press were hounding him for interviews in Carraroe. The main focus of media interest was his alleged affair with Shelagh Delaney. In the end it became such a bother for Shelagh Delaney that she issued a statement denying that there was any truth in the rumour.

Joan Littlewood also realised that Brendan was now very ill. She remarked on the poor shape he had been in on the Continental tour and expressed her fears for his longterm health prospects. She was right to be concerned. About a week before leaving for the West, Brendan had had a seizure in the seaside suburb of Dun Laoghaire. It was diagnosed as epileptiform, a spasmodic condition or fit associated with his diabetes and alcohol problem. In Carraroe, he had another fit on the beach and ended up in Galway hospital. A young doctor took Beatrice aside and told her that unless her husband stopped drinking, he would be dead within eighteen months. During his week in Galway hospital, Brendan had six further seizures. On his release Beatrice took him directly back to Dublin by taxi.

> I tried not to give way to despair on the journey, but that was my mood when Brendan ordered the driver to stop at pubs along the way so that he could drink stout and whiskey. I didn't want to loose him, but watching him drink, I told myself he needed me now more than ever before.[9]

Back in Dublin, Beatrice made him see his GP, Dr Terence Chapman, who had begun to take a special interest in Brendan. Chapman was a cultured man with an interest in the theatre. He gave Brendan the same warning he had got in Galway. 'Stop drinking or prepare to die soon'. Brendan replied, 'Alcoholics die of alcohol, don't they, doctor?'

Dr Chapman arranged for him to enter Baggot Street hospital where his diabetes had first been diagnosed. Two days later he discharged himself. 'I can't sleep in that fucking place' he told Beatrice. He turned up on their doorstep early in the morning, wearing his coat on top of his pyjamas and carrying his clothes over his arm. Brendan ordered Beatrice, whose father was in hospital and whose mother was also very ill, to pack their bags for London. When she refused, Brendan snapped at her and announced he would go on his own. His primary motivation for going to London was to bask in the glory of *The Hostage's* West End production. Absent on its first night, he had sent a telegram that was read on stage by one the actors: 'Tell the audience I was asking for them'.

The Manchester Guardian commented that:

> For once it was an occasion which would have been heightened if the author could have taken his deserved call. But he is still in a 'foreign

land' and will be welcome in London whenever he can come to see his
own play so well done!

The ink was barely dry on that article, before Brendan was on a plane for
London.

Officials at London airport were startled to see his unshaven, tousled-
haired form, dressed in a dinner jacket, making its way to the bar. When
sufficiently fortified, he left for Celia Salkeld's flat in Paddington and rested
there briefly before making his way to the Salisbury pub near Wyndham's
Theatre. On his way in to the performance he joined a street busker, sang with
him and passed the hat around, greatly augmenting the man's takings. After
that performance, he was geared up for the next act of his personal drama. No
sooner had the curtain gone up on *The Hostage* than he began his additional,
impromptu contribution to the play. He laughed loudly at his own jokes,
joined in the singing of the play's songs, engaged in banter with the actors,
abused the audience, and finally scrambled up onto the stage to do the
ultimate stage Irish act, dancing what passed for a jig. The management
brought the curtain down on him and the theatre cleared quickly. He had
disgraced himself again and enjoyed every moment of it. The theatre's owner,
Sir Bronson Albery, banned him from the premises, and left specific
instruction to his staff only to allow him in if he was carrying written
permission. He didn't care about Sir Bronson's ban because there was hardly
a newspaper in England that had not carried a report of his antics.

To most outsiders he appeared to take unashamed delight in his
outrageous disruption of the production of his plays. At the time, only
Beatrice and a handful of very close friends knew that his extraordinary
behaviour was that of a very sick man, who had become the pathetic victim of
his own self-created image. Coupled with his physical illness, were the
psychological problems of his natural shyness and his long standing 'Granny's
boy complex'. It was from this morass of an emotional and physical history
that the insufferable show-off emerged. His past, his success and his own
inadequacies were creating a monster. It took great fortitude and courage to
stand by him. From 1959 onwards only a handful of people did so.

The doorman at Wyndham's, acting on orders, refused him access to the
theatre when he tried to join the audience for another spontaneous authorial
contribution. 'Nobody's giving orders to Brendan Behan,' he shouted, but the
impassive doorman barred his entry. He went back to Desmond
MacNamara's house in Hampstead and collapsed into bed. When he awoke
early the following morning, he took himself to Number 4 Market Mews,
Shepherd's Market, the London home of Lady Oranmore and Browne. Only

her son Tara was at home. He did his best to entertain Brendan and tried to get him to have some breakfast. After about an hour, he passed out and Tara, in a state of great distress, telephoned Beatrice in Dublin. Beatrice then got in touch with Rae Jeffs who arranged for her doctor to come to Market Mews. Brendan had rallied by the time the doctor arrived and was in good enough spirits to insult both he and Rae Jeffs before leaving Market Mews without making his destination known. Within an hour, he was arrested and taken to Saville Row police station. Desmond MacNamara and Theatre Workshop's publicity agent, Duncan Melvin, bailed him out. Though it is impossible to be certain, as he was not examined by a doctor that day, it seems likely that he was not drunk but had fallen into another diabetic coma on a Mayfair Street.

At Bow Street Police Court the next day, he was charged with being drunk in a public street. A titter went around the Court when the Magistrate asked the routine question: 'Anything known'. He was fined five shillings. Outside the Court, a large group of reporters waited for him recalled that some prostitutes who had just concluded their business before the 'Beak' called out: 'Good old Brendan, come back soon luv'.

Donal Foley, with whom Brendan had worked when Foley was London Editor of the *Irish Press*, remembered thirty car loads of reporters in a cavalcade following Brendan when he left the Court for the airport. There was a stop along the way. Brendan got his own back on the hacks by commenting only in Irish. To Brendan's satisfaction, Foley, who knew the language, made a large sum on translation. At the airport, Brendan sang *The Red Flag* and boarded his plane for Dublin.

A similar media frenzy awaited him at Dublin Airport. He ignored reporters eager for a Dublin angle, and went straight home where Beatrice put him to bed. He was puffy in the face and vomiting constantly. The following day, he was admitted again to Baggot Street Hospital. This time he stayed for two weeks. While there he wrote a piece for *The People* newspaper. It was a defiant admission of his alcoholism and a pledge to reform:

> I'm not proud of being an alcoholic, but neither am I going to apologise to anybody for being one.
> I might also mention the people who abuse me for giving a 'wrong' impression of the Irish abroad.
> Frankly, I don't care two hoots what impression I give. Nobody ever paid me anything for being Irish. I know I can cure myself from drink and that's what I am doing here in hospital. Remember that during that skite last week my average consumption was between two and three bottles of whiskey a day, washed down with, maybe, a dozen or two of

stout or beer.

Since I came into hospital on Wednesday I cut that down to a dribble and I took nothing yesterday or today. And – with the possible exception of the little bottle hidden in the water jug – I will take nothing until I come out a new man ... I'll go back to work then and take an occasional drink just like I used to before all this rumpus started a few months ago. I'll go out for walks with Beatrice then and we'll go to the sea and we'll talk just like we used to. I know people are always gossiping about how we get on, why we got married, and 'I don't know how his poor wife puts up with it all, and her such a sweet, quiet creature, too!'

Well. I'll tell you. It happens that Beatrice and I like each other very much and when I'm on the wagon we go out and talk and laugh like so many other couples. Beatrice is a wonderful girl.[10]

The confessional tone of the piece was highly unusual for Brendan. He was not a natural public dirty-linen washer. Now he told his readers why he drank so much: '... I'm a lonely so-and-so and I must have people around me to talk with'.

Beatrice was extremely pleased with his progress. When she collected him from the hospital, she felt that there had been a genuine improvement in his health. After the stern warnings he had received in Baggot Street Hospital, his resolve to stay off alcohol now appeared to be firmer than perhaps it had ever been in his drinking life.

He resumed work on *the catacombs*, but did not seriously advance it. He described its contents for a number of people, including Rae Jeffs. He even read her the opening paragraph down the telephone to London:

There was a party to celebrate Deirdre's return from her abortion in Bristol. Ciaran, her brother, welcomed me, literally with open arms, when I entered the Catalonian Cabinet Room where the guests were assembled. Even her mother, the screwy old bitch, came over with a glass of whiskey in her hand, 'You're welcome, Brendan Behan.' Bloodywell, I knew why I was welcome. It was I squared the matter for Deirdre to go over to England and have her baby out under the National Health Service, so to speak.

In newspaper interviews, he began to speak of his next play. It struck Rae Jeffs that what he had described to her as the theme of *the catacombs* seemed to be identical to the theme of the play. When she asked him about it, he merely winked at her. *The Hostage* continued its successful run in London. Princess

Margaret attended one evening and the press reported that she laughed heartily at the jokes, especially those about her family. When Brendan was asked about her reaction he said: 'And why wouldn't she enjoy it. Don't I know her husband well'. (The princess's husband, Anthony Armstrong-Jones had photographed Brendan in Dublin). Brendan went back to London to see his play before it finished its run and managed to attend a performance without disrupting it.

By the end of 1959, the media in the United States had started to intensify its coverage of Brendan. In November, he was invited to do a link-up telecast from Dublin for Ed Morrow's show, *Small World*. The half-hour programme had as its theme 'The Art of Conversation'. Brendan was on a panel with comedian Jackie Gleason and literary critic John Mason Brown in New York and Morrow chaired the programme from London. *The Hostage* was due to open in New York in September 1960 and Brendan thought his appearance would prepare the way for his storming of that city. It was an unmitigated disaster. Brendan was drunk and incoherent. If his intention had been to repeat his performance on Malcolm Muggeridge's show to capture the headlines in the US, he had made a serious miscalculation. The newspaper reports did not refer to his drunkenness, and the programme producers cut out most of his performance in the edit. He was furious when he saw the programme. What little of him that remained in the programme gave the impression of an inchoate idiot. Jackie Gleason said he came across 100 per cent proof – not by an act of God but by an act of Guinness.

In the period before Christmas he started to do the rounds of his old Grafton Street drinking haunts in Dublin. He dispensed largesse to a coterie of drunks and camp followers but, by Christmas Eve he had had enough, and travelled with Beatrice to Luggala for Christmas. The house guests that Christmas included the actor Peter O'Toole, Lord Kilbracken, the poet John Montague and his wife Madeline and David J. Lichtig. Garech Browne recalls that Brendan's drinking that Christmas was on a more moderate scale than in former years and that he drank no spirits.

His restraint continued in the immediate post-Christmas period. The English media kept up its discussion of his work, and Rae Jeffs informed him of what was said. He wrote to *The Sunday Times* about recent comments on the religious value of his work:

10 January, 1960

Sir,
Though I am very pleased to read Mr Harold Hobson's notices of my work, and indeed enjoy any mention of anything I write by anyone, I seldom write or talk about it myself.

I was glad that Canon McKay considers that *The Hostage* among the four plays that he mentions has 'a religious value for any thinking Christian.'

The Catholic Herald and *The Tablet* recognise my work as that of a Catholic. Which I am, though a bad one. I could not write as I do if I were not some kind of one.

In my own country I have been accused of blasphemy. So, of course, has that great Christian, Seán O'Casey. Mr Evelyn Waugh was recently quoted as saying: 'I can see nothing objectionable in the total destruction of the earth, provided it is done, as seems likely, inadvertently.'

Now, to me, that is blasphemy.

So are the speeches on Apartheid by those other religious men, the South African Government, and the son of the manse, Montgomery.

Brendan Behan.[11]

Paul Hogarth had already completed his illustrations for *Brendan Behan's Island* and was worried that there would be no text to accompany them. It was Hogarth's agent who suggested to Iain Hamilton that Brendan might use a tape recorder. When Brendan raised no objection to the method, Miss Jeffs went to Dublin in January 1960. Over a three-week period, she recorded the 40,000 words that constituted the text of the book. Behan excused himself for abandoning his Remington in favour of this new method by saying,

> If the Mycenaean Greek poets could do it, then so can I ... I do not set myself up as an authority on these matters, but if Homer is to be believed, the Greeks wrote their books by improvising them in talk. Now I'm getting in on their act.

Brendan's ability to excuse his failings was considerable, but on that particular front he was bringing self-deception to a new level. Rae Jeffs went back to London satisfied that, while the tape recording could never be a substitute for Brendan's writing, at least it gave him hope that he could continue to produce books of some worth. This was the first of three books he would dictate for later editing by Rae Jeffs. His decision to work in this way was probably the beginning of the end of his career as a writer. Though he did not yet know it, he had by this time written his last complete work in his own hand. Only unfinished fragments remained to haunt him.

As usual, fate conspired to shatter Brendan's determination to moderate his drinking. His brother Dominic's play *Posterity Be Damned* had had a controversial run at The Gaiety Theatre in Dublin. Brendan had attended the first night. Some members of the audience considered it to be blasphemous. Others were annoyed at Dominic's portrayal of the IRA as misled idealists. Behan did not really approve of there being more than one famous writer in the family. Members of the audience hurled abuse at the author from the floor and Dominic was never really convinced that Brendan had not joined in. However, when Alan Simpson and John Ryan announced the London opening of *Posterity Be Damned* at the Metropolitan Theatre on Edgware Road, Brendan told Beatrice that it was his duty to be there for this family occasion. 'After all', he declared, 'it's not every day two brothers have plays running simultaneously in London'.

Rae Jeffs took charge of him and tried to ensure he was in a fit state to meet his parents when they arrived at Euston. He was not. He looked so unkempt that she took him to a gentleman's outfitter off the Euston Road. While she was talking to the assistant, Brendan took all his clothes off and dumped them in the middle of the shop. When she turned around he was standing stark naked, awaiting his new kit. A fresh bout of drinking had left him in a near comatose state but he insisted on attending a rehearsal of Dominic's play with Kathleen and Stephen. He fell asleep in the theatre but unfortunately woke up in time for his comments to be noted by the press attending the rehearsal. 'Rubbish' he shouted 'there were no murderers in the IRA'. In the following day's newspapers, those comments translated into simply 'Rubbish'. Relations between the two brothers had been strained for many years and Brendan did not find it easy to deal with his feelings about the prospect of his younger brother becoming a rival literary success. Dominic, however, though given to exaggeration and licence, was generous in his assessment of Brendan after his death, and willing to forgive a great deal because he believed that much of the unpleasantness between them was a result of his brother's ill-health.

After the incident at the rehearsal of Dominic's play, Brendan went on a three-day binge. At the end of it Rae Jeff's finally got him to see a doctor. Using her influence with Brendan, which was now quite considerable, Rae Jeffs managed to convince him that he was truly sick and needed hospitalisation. The diagnosis was predictable. Diabetes and advanced cirrhosis of the liver. The doctor advised that he should be taken to hospital in Dublin. Unfortunately, no airline would agree to take him without an accompanying doctor. The situation was so serious that he was given a bed in a public ward at Middlesex Hospital. He was still asking for whisky as a nurse sedated him.

He found himself under the care of a Dr Nabarro, who suggested that he might benefit from psychiatric treatment at the hospital. The doctor wasn't convinced that Brendan's problems were entirely due to his drinking. However, the very idea of any form of psychiatric treatment horrified Brendan. 'I'll have nothing to do with the headshrinkers', he used to say. In the meantime, the editor of *The Observer*, David Astor, had taken a personal interest in Brendan's case. Beatrice came to London and discussed with him the best way forward. On 2 April, Brendan even signed a note giving David Astor *carte blanche* to suggest the best way to deal with his problem.

> I agree that David Astor should supervise medical treatment for me and I authorise him to prepare such measures as he sees fit.

> (Sgd. Brendan Behan)

Astor suggested a clinic for alcoholics run by a Dr McKeefe at Warlingham Park in Surrey. The doctor had heard about Brendan's case and was prepared to take him on. In the end, Brendan rejected the idea. When he had regained sufficient strength to leave hospital he did so. He believed he could kick his alcoholic addiction using only his own will-power. 'I want to try and work this out in my own way, and I'll write and swim and go for walks again as I used to do. If I fail, perhaps I can come back ...', he told Rae Jeffs. And indeed, for the next nine months, with only one unfortunate slip in America, not a drop of alcohol passed his lips.

America My New-Found Land

Brendan's outrageous behaviour, both in public and in private, put his relationship with Beatrice under the sort of strain that would sunder most marriages. John Montague recalls that the inner reserves she demonstrated in the Herbert Street days had survived the batterings of the last, tumultuous year. It allowed her to handle the truly awful position in which Brendan commonly placed her, in a way that few women could have managed. Beatrice was acquainted with the ways of the heavy-drinking man before she met Brendan. Her father was one, but Cecil's drunkenness was very different to Brendan's. For the most part it led into indolence rather than self-destruction. Beatrice's background had given her no preparation for the bellicose and abusive nightmare that was Brendan Behan when drunk. Now that he was sober, Brendan had a chance to confront at least some of his inner demons and he seemed confident that he was capable of doing so. His wife hoped that with Brendan off the drink, some of the old wounds caused by his behaviour would heal.

The couple revisited the North West of Ireland, travelling around half-a-dozen or so of its small towns and villages, staying sometimes with friends but most often in guest houses. It was a sort of second honeymoon in their favourite part of the country. By 1960, five years after he married Beatrice, he became somewhat obsessed with the need to produce children. Beatrice also wanted children, but first she wanted to help Brendan to regain and maintain his health, so that any child they might have would stand a reasonable chance of having a father there to look after it.

Back in Dublin, he began a regime of walking, swimming and running and in a very short time he looked remarkably well for a man who had abused his body so exhaustively. The most difficult part of this self-cure was being in a city like Dublin, where alcohol was a prop for every social occasion. Initially, he avoided going to public houses because the temptation was just too great. Later on, he drifted back because he missed the company. On a previous attempt to give up alcohol he drank orange juice but 'friends' and journalists looking to bait the bear, sometimes spiked it with vodka. Now he drank soda water because it was clear in colour, tasteless and could not be adulterated without his knowledge. As part of his psychological approach to his self-cure, he began to speak of his 'problem' in the past tense. 'I *had* a drink problem', he used to say at the time, 'I couldn't get enough of it'. He scattered his gems of self-analysis about rather freely: 'One's own ill-health and death are unspeakable calamities and that is all I can say about them. I am not a priest but a sinner. I am not a psychiatrist but a neurotic. My neuroses are the nails and saucepans by which I get my living. If I were cured, I would have to go back to house-painting.'

The Bailey pub and restaurant in Dublin's Duke Street played an important part in the last four years of his life, both when he was on and when he was off the drink. He went there principally because it was owned by his friend, John Ryan, but also because the staff were kind to him. Austin Byrne joined The Bailey staff in 1960 and, like many others who had an opportunity to observe Brendan from behind a bar counter, believes his physical tolerance for alcohol was quite low. He confirms the view generally held by those who served him drink that he was unmanageable when drunk but boisterous and usually well-behaved when sober.[1] Now that he was sober again, he began to enjoy lunching at the upstairs restaurant in The Bailey. Dublin's *erste Gesellschaft*, such as it was, dined here. The regulars included Lady Murphy, the wife of Sir George, a governor of the Bank of Ireland, Mrs McCartan-Mooney who was related to Winston Churchill, Erskine Childers, father of Brendan's doctor friend, Rory, the Hon. Patrick Campbell, Siobhán McKenna, and members of the Guinness family. Even the Aga Khan dropped in during Horse Show week. Brendan engaged them all in conversation at one time or another and revelled in their company because, fundamentally, he was a terrible snob and a shameless name-dropper. By 1960, apart from the odd excursion into sentimentality, he had little interest in the realities of working-class life. His slum background still made very colourful newspaper copy, however, and he served it up in large helpings whenever it advanced his career.

He attended several Dublin social events in the summer of 1960 without drinking. They included a twenty-first birthday dinner for Garech Browne in Jammet's restaurant, held on 25 June and hosted by his father, Lord Oranmore and Browne. Being sober allowed him to sit back and observe people in a way he might not have done when drunk. During dinner he noticed Lady Cusack-Smith, that great doyenne of the Irish hunting field, blowing her nose in her napkin. The scene lodged in his mind and it helped him form his standard definition of a lady. 'A real lady is a woman who can blow her nose in her napkin and not worry about it.'[2]

Once he had rediscovered the relative advantages of sobriety, he began to think seriously about getting down to writing again. The new play he talked about was very much on his mind, as was his unfinished novel. To some, including, perhaps, himself, it was a confusing business to distinguish between these two works. It remained so. However, despite having succumbed to the temptations of the tape recorder, he was determined to return to writing, and to prove that he could be appreciated for his literary talent, as well as for his talent to amuse.

The journalist, Alan Bestic, visited him at Anglesea Road at the end of the Summer and was surprised by his abstinent industry:

> In a large, comfortable house in Ballsbridge, one of Dublin's most fashionable suburbs, Beatrice Behan is brewing tea by the gallon these days. Her Husband Brendan, the boisterous, bewildering 'Quare Fella' [sic] is pushing it down by the potfull as he pounds at a typewriter with stubby fingers. For perhaps the first time in his life, he is writing a play without the aid of porter, whiskey, brandy, Chateauneuf-du-Pape, or any similar lubricant.[3]

He had, of course, done most of his serious writing without the inspiration of alcohol, but that was not the popular perception. By now it was nearly impossible for a journalist to write about even the sober Brendan without making some reference to the man as a legendary boozer. As he prepared to leave for the opening of *The Hostage* in New York, he was especially conscious that his reputation as a drunk had preceded him. When Leonard Field, one of the producers of *The Hostage*, tried to book Brendan and Beatrice into the Algonquin Hotel, the establishment refused to have them. Andrew Anspach, the hotel's managing director, told Field that the Algonquin's dignity might be damaged by Brendan's behaviour. He suggested he put his guest up at The Chelsea, because it was 'more Bohemian'. Anspach finally relented when he heard Brendan was on the wagon and that his wife would accompany him. Just before leaving for New York, Brendan learned that Corgi had bought the paper-back rights of *Borstal Boy* for £5,000.[4] When his plane touched down at Idlewild on 2 September, he was sober and in splendid form.

It was inevitable that Brendan would embrace New York and it would in turn take him to its heart. It was his kind of city. At anytime of the day or night he could find companionship in its insomniac soul:

In New York, at three o'clock in the morning, you can walk about, see crowds, read the papers, and have a drink – orange juice, coffee, whiskey or anything. It is the greatest show on earth, for everyone.[5]

'I think New York is a fabulous place,' he said soon after arriving. 'I think it ought to be investigated by a committee – the whole town, the twenty million people in it – for being jolly.' He was so pleased with the city that he wrote to his father-in-law, Cecil ffrench-Salkeld: 'This is a great town. We should all have come here years ago'.[6]

He had a well-formed idea of what he wanted to see in America:

I would like to see in New York the Rockefeller who said that he would like to see me in Ireland.
I would like to see and pay my respects to Big Daddy Burl Ives, Lee Tracy, Studs Lonigan, Billy Graham, Tom Lehrer, the Empire State Building, the Saint Patrick's Day Parade on Fifth Avenue, Costello's saloon on Third Avenue, Robert Frost, Marilyn Monroe, back and front, the most unforgettable character you know, the Mafia, the Mizrachi, the Daughters of the American Revolution, the Ivy League, Niagara Falls, Nick the Greek, the Governor's pitch in Albany, William Faulkner, the Yankee Stadium, a love nest, a hot dog stand, a jam session, the Golden Gloves, and the candidates for the presidential election.[7]

When Brendan arrived, the presidential electoral battle between Kennedy and Nixon was in full swing. He made it quite clear to reporters and to his hosts at the many parties he was invited to that he was backing his 'fellow-countryman'. 'I'm for Kennedy,' he told *The New York Times*, 'because he's of the Roosevelt party and Roosevelt was a great man.' John F. Kennedy's ancestors, Brendan claimed with overstatement tailored to suit at least some of his American audience, came from a part of Ireland where 'the apples grew alongside the road and the people were so honest they never touched them.' When Kennedy won, he did not forget to acknowledge Behan's support. An invitation to his inauguration arrived at 5 Anglesea Road, addressed simply to *Mr & Mrs Brendan Behan, Dublin, Ireland.*

Brendan the showman was what interested the New York media, just as it had interested their counterparts in London. But there were perceptive commentators among them who saw his serious side. Arthur Gleb of *The New York Times* was one:

The playwrighting Behan (as opposed to the performing Behan) has depths of seriousness, sensitivity, tenderness and erudition. These depths are not easy to dredge up from the self-created legend. For Mr

Behan finds it difficult to avoid the temptation of saying what he knows
will make good copy. (Having once been a reporter himself, he has
affection, but little reverence, for the breed.)[8]

On this, his virgin visit to America, the country he called his new-found land,
the press was relatively moderate. It was however, all too easy for less
thoughtful American journalists to label him 'the Irish Dylan Thomas' or 'the
Irish Jean Genet'. The comparative tags seemed so appropriate – he was a
convivial drinker and an ex-jailbird. Later, as Brendan slid inevitably towards
his destruction, it was this type of journalism which elbowed out more serious
analysis in the battle for the thousands of US newspaper and magazine
column inches that chronicled his fall.

If it was predictable that Brendan and New York would fall in love with
one another, it was also predictable that he would fall off the wagon there.
Within a few weeks of his arrival, he had established his social pitch much as
he had done in Dublin, Paris and London. The only difference was that in
New York, the variety of bars, restaurants and night clubs, provided a greater
mix of humankind for Brendan to entertain and be entertained by. His
adamant resolution to remain sober did not prevent him from going to places
where drink flowed in great quantity. Third Avenue was a favourite part of his
beat because it contained a whole group of bars with strong Irish associations.
In McSorley's, Costello's, 'Ma O'Brien's', P.J. Clarke's, Kearney's and Mike
Sheehan's, he was instantly recognised and lionised. In those places, he found
something of the camaraderie he loved about Dublin pubs. The Chelsea and
the Bristol Hotels, Jim Downey's and Sullivan's on 8th Avenue, the Oasis Bar
on 23rd Street, the 'White Horse' which had been much frequented by Dylan
Thomas, all played their part in the drama of Behan's New York life. So too
did a host of other establishments. Many of their owners, managers and staff
became his friends, in days of good behaviour and of bad. But in the not-too-
distant future, in days of very sad behaviour, some of them would deny him
with an alacrity which would make Judas a worthy candidate for canonisation.
In the end it didn't really matter; Brendan took from these establishments and
from their patrons, barmen and owners, whatever he needed to suit the
demands of the moment. Just as in Dublin, they were his audience, his
bankers, and his research centres. In some he was understood, in others he was
misunderstood. The passage of time has transformed the reality of the role
these establishments played in his life into a legend. They provided the
backdrop for the posthumous myth.

Brendan's principal business in New York was to attend the first night of
The Hostage. Caroline Swann, the co-producer of the Broadway production of

the play, wanted to present it just as she had seen it produced in London, complete with the same cast and director. That created a number of tricky problems. She later remembered the prolonged battle with Actors' Equity and the Immigration Department to get them to allow Joan Littlewood and her troupe to come to America. In the end, most of the original cast did get to New York, many of them for the first time. The time spent on these negotiations meant that there was little rehearsal time and certainly no time for an out-of-town try-out. Much of the play needed translation into American English if it was to be understood by a New York audience. Joan Littlewood and the cast rose to the challenge. That particular need was hardly going to pose a problem for Littlewood, whose methods thrived on improvisation.

> Miss Littlewood incited the production into existence by stirring a talented cast into performances that had the spontaneity of *commedia dell'arte*. 'She never allowed interpolations to become stale', commented Caroline Swann on the changes made for the production.[9]

Littlewood scanned the newspapers for topical subjects and they went into the ever-changing presentation of the play. Sober, Brendan was also a useful participant in the process of 'inciting' *The Hostage* into existence.

It opened at the Cort Theatre on 20 September. The reception was enthusiastic and there were several curtain calls. Brendan made a tamer-than-usual speech and he and his party went off for a brief first stop at Sardi's where he was toasted with champagne. From there, they moved on to Jim Downey's Steak House for the main celebration. He got a standing ovation as he entered the restaurant. By coincidence, F.H. Boland, the Irish diplomat who had petitioned the British Home Secretary for the lifting of the Order prohibiting Brendan from entering Britain, was dining in Downey's that evening. He was celebrating his election as President of the General Assembly of the United Nations. It was a great night to be Irish in New York.

In the tradition of New York first nights, the party swung on merrily in anticipation of that tense moment when the copies of the main morning newspapers arrived. Despite the pressure of a Broadway opening, Brendan stuck to soda-water. The reviews were mixed. The New York critics seemed unwilling or unable to amend the language of standard criticism to accommodate the level of theatrical innovation involved in the Behan-Littlewood collaboration. There was nothing of Kenneth Tynan's readiness to abandon the old pigeonholes of conventional terminology. 'To the critic', Tynan told his readers in London in 1958, '... the correct assignment of compartments is as vital as it is to the employees of Wagon-Lits.'[10] All of this still seemed so terribly relevant in New York in 1960. In those days, there were six New York reviewers – the Butchers of Broadway as they were traditionally called. Of the six, it was Howard Taubman of *The New York Times* whose opinion carried most weight. He hedged his bets sufficiently to allow his readers the privilege of making up their own minds:

> ... a grab-bag of wonderful dreadful prizes. Organised chaos is the handiest description of it ... Even in Mr Behan's undisciplined invention he reveals a flair for drama. There are ... some splendid hits in the course of this fusillade, but they are balanced by embarrassing misses.

Of Littlewood's production, Taubman said it had 'an abundance of fresh ideas, some excellent and some in poor taste. Like Mr Behan's writing, her staging would not be harmed by discipline.'

His punch line guaranteed that the punters rolled in: 'Mr Behan is an original, and so is *The Hostage*. If you are willing to shuttle madly between delight and distaste, you might try dancing to Mr Behan's Irish jig.' The *New York Post* and *The Herald Tribune's* critics also had their reservations but, like their colleague in *The New York Times*, they said nothing that was likely to prevent theatregoers making their way to the Cort Theatre.

In *Brendan Behan's New York*,[11] Behan left this typically humorous comment on the power of the New York critics:

> Now if you get six out of six good reviews, you can ask the President of the United States to sell you the White House, though I don't think this has ever happened. If you get five good reviews, you are doing fairly well and you have to start worrying about 480 Lexington Avenue, which is the home of the income tax.
>
> It is not a bad kind of worry though in its own way, if you have got to have worries, and I suppose everyone has to have them. If you have four, you can afford to give a party, or at least you can afford to attend the party which is usually given for you. If you get three good reviews, it's time like to go home to bed, but if you only get two, you stay there the whole of the following day and don't go out until after dark. If you get one good review, you just make an air reservation very quickly, to get back to where you came from, but if you get six bad reviews, you take a sleeping pill. You might even take an overdose![12]

He also offered a more serious condemnation of theatrical criticism: 'Critics are like eunuchs in a Harem. They're there every night, they see it done every night, they see how it should be done every night, but they can't do it themselves.'

Behan had no need to entertain fears about the critics and their power. *The Hostage* was a box-office success. It took $24,000 during the first week of its run at the Cort and it ran there for three months before transferring to the Eugene O'Neill Theatre.

On the afternoon of 20 September, Brendan sat quietly in his suite in the Algonquin receiving congratulatory telephone calls. In the midst of the maelstrom of idolisation, he found some time to do a decent act for an old friend in Dublin. He sent a postcard to fellow-writer, James McKenna. It speaks for the generous side of Behan's personality. Brendan rarely hesitated in using his new-found celebrity to push the work of other writers who had been kind to him in the past. In a letter dated 6 January 1957, he wrote to the *Spectator* to comment favourably on a poem it had published by Valentine Iremonger, the man who had brought *Borstal Boy* to the attention of Iain Hamilton.[13]

On this occasion, McKenna had written a musical play, *The Scatterin'*, produced by Alan Simpson and John Ryan in Dublin to great critical acclaim. Ryan described it as possibly 'the world's first Rock musical'. McKenna would later help write the film script of *The Quare Fellow*. Behan had been accused, especially in Dublin, of being extremely jealous of the rise of other Irish writers of his generation (leaving sibling rivalry aside). Yet, at one of the greatest moments of his career, he offered to use his New York contacts to promote McKenna's work:

> The play is much talked about here – if you send me an mss to the above address [the Algonquin] I know people that are interested.[14]

Brendan's own growing reputation and the demands it placed on him were beginning to swamp him. He had not yet managed to edit the transcripts of his recordings for *Brendan Behan's Island*, despite a visit to New York by Iain Hamilton. US publishers and agents were bombarding him with requests to get involved in various projects. He accepted advances for quite a few, including $12,000 from publisher Bernard Geis for a sequel to *Borstal Boy*. Geis became a loyal friend who hauled him out of several embarrassing predicaments during future visits to America. Eventually, he became Executor of Brendan's Will. There were others who just wished to make a quick buck – a concept to which Brendan himself was not adverse.

It was, without doubt, the success of his plays that turned Behan into a sought-after New York personality. What made him a national figure in the United States, however, was the reputation for outrageous behaviour that the media so readily propagated for him. Television played the biggest part in publicising his bad boy image.

His recorded appearance on *Small World* the previous year was still talked about in New York. Before he left New York in December, he had appeared three times on the most popular talk show in the United States, *The Jack Paar Show*. In a media-conscious society, a mere appearance on this programme conferred celebrity status. To do so three times within three months, as Brendan did, and to perform brilliantly, as he also did, made him a media icon. Despite his ability to project himself via the medium; television appearances terrified him. Without the fortification of alcohol, they were nightmare experiences for him. Yet when he was in top form, conversation came easily to him. During one of his appearances with Paar, he opined on American women: 'It's the land of permanent waves and unpermanent wives. The sort of man most American women want to marry is the fellow with a will of his own – preferably made out in her favour.'

Between his appearances with Jack Paar on his show and with David Suskind on *Open End*, Brendan had been a panellist with some of the biggest celebrities in America. They included Tennessee Williams, Jack Lemmon, Anthony Quinn, Peter Ustinov and Hermione Gingold. He had always possessed a sense of himself as a 'character' in the Dublin sense of the word. It was his defence mechanism against his fundamental shyness. But it took success in the United States to absolutely convince him that he was a celebrity in his own right. For that moment of revelation, he remained eternally grateful and loyal to America.

Because he was not drinking, Brendan had an opportunity to get to know the geography of New York. He went for long walks during the day and, on this first visit, he established contacts in distant and diverse quarters of the city. Greenwich Village was a favourite daytime haunt. Sobriety made little difference to his constant quest for nocturnal diversions. At night he moved to the bars of Third Avenue. It was usually the early hours of the morning before he returned to Beatrice at the Algonquin.

Brendan fell spectacularly off the wagon on 26 October. That morning, he had a minor argument with Beatrice about a cashmere coat that he had bought at Brooks Brothers for a very substantial sum. He went to the Cort Theatre in the late morning. At around 3 p.m., he made his way to the Monte Rosa restaurant at 128 West 48th Street for a late lunch with Beatrice and two companions. It seems the morning's domestic tiff had soured his mood for the day. When they were seated for lunch, Brendan ordered a bottle of champagne. Beatrice asked him to reconsider and think of the consequences. He ignored her and loudly told the waiter to bring the champagne. When further pleas to think again had no effect, Beatrice got down on her knees beside his chair and begged him not to drink, again in vain. By the time he left the restaurant for that evening's performance of his play at the Cort, he had consumed seven bottles of champagne. Such was the ferocity with which he recommenced his drinking that he refused a champagne glass and drank from a large water tumbler. The curtain went up on *The Hostage* at 7.30 p.m. and Brendan arrived just after 8 p.m. When the front of house staff saw his condition they tried to keep him out of the auditorium. Determined, Brendan made his way in through the stage door. The best efforts of the stage managers could not keep him off the stage. He made an inaudible speech, cavorted with the cast, sang, danced and exhorted the audience to tell their friends to come along. As ever, his personal performances on stage were somehow linked with his box office whenever it waned.

The episode had a nasty sequel. Perry Bruskin, the show's stage manager, was arrested for punching photographer Frank Castrol, and smashing his camera when he tried to take a picture of Brendan's off-stage antics.

While Bruskin was appearing in the Night Court before Magistrate Morton R. Tollers, Beatrice was hauling Brendan back to The Algonquin. He threw back a few large whiskeys in the lobby and returned with gusto to his old singing, dancing, hollering form. He woke at midday on 27 October, with a monumental hangover and nasty sense of contrition.[15] He renewed his vow to abstain and had only one further drinking session before returning to Dublin.

While he was away from Ireland, an interview he had recorded with Eamonn Andrews had been broadcast on 29 November. Unlike previous TV performances, this one showed him at his most humorous. The purpose of the interview, Andrews told his audience, was to try to discover what makes Brendan Behan tick. When asked to describe himself he gave this revealing reply:

> Whistler, the English painter, remarked that the world is divided into two classes: invalids and nurses. I'm a nurse ... I'm a nurse in the sense that in my plays and in my books I try to show the world to a certain extent what's the matter with it, why everybody is not happy. The fact, of course, that in my private life I'm rather a gloomy person has nothing at all to do with my public ministry – if I may so describe it. But what makes me tick? I don't know. Sometimes I wonder how long effectively I'm going to tick. I'm a person put into a position that in some ways suits me, but in other ways doesn't. I'm a very ordinary person. A great number of people say that with their tongue in their cheek, but I say it with my tongue in my gums. I've a great deal of fame, a certain amount

of glory, a certain amount of infamy. I can only repeat, with John Keats, saying, 'God help the poor little famous'.

He and Beatrice arrived in Montreal on 8 December. Two engagements brought him to Canada; an appearance at the *Comédie Canadienne* and a lecture at McGill University. He had some days to spare before both engagements and time to formulate an opinion about the city. If he had a love affair with America, his relationship with Canada turned out to be quite the reverse. Montreal was under heavy snow, and temperatures were -15°C which did little to improve Brendan's mood. He found that he was not at all as well-known there as he was in New York. The cold and snow kept him caged in his hotel room for much of the time. The novelist and broadcaster, Tony Aspler, drove him to the top of Mount Royal so that he might see the snow-covered city lying below. His reaction was to make the sign of the cross and urinate in the snow.

'This is a city of hatreds,' he declared, 'I can smell it'. He spent as much time as he possibly could in the French quarter. In cafés, restaurants and bars, he sang the Marseillaise and again hit the bottle in dramatic style. When two journalists came to interview him, he snatched the microphone of their tape recorder and proceeded to 'vilify Canada and Canadians with a stream of invective remarkable for its sustained invention and elegance of phrase. He ended on the note that all he wanted to do was get back to the Big Apple, to civilisation...'[16]

McGill University was a most unsuitable venue for a drunken Behan performance. Brendan assumed it was French-speaking, which it was not. Tony Aspler remembered him speaking in French for seventeen minutes on the theme of De Gaulle and the Algerian crisis. He followed that with a verse of 'The praties they are small over here', sang the French national anthem, danced the inevitable jig, and left the hall to a mixture of cheers and indignation.

Brendan was put to bed in his hotel. A doctor came and gave him an injection of Vitamin B Complex and told Beatrice what she already knew about her husband's health. His second engagement in the city was cancelled and he left Montreal hating it but, not surprisingly, having left his mark on it.

The Behans returned to Ireland to spend Christmas at Luggala. It was the first and only Christmas Brendan spent there without touching a drop of alcohol. His New York triumph had been sullied by his failure to remain abstemious but, with the New Year came a new resolution.

19

The Bells Of Hell

In February 1961, Joan Littlewood flew to Dublin to encourage Brendan to finish the play he told her he was working on. She wanted to put it on in London as soon as she could wrest the script from him. But he had been unable to write for nearly a year. Furthermore, he was now committed to the raft of projects he had signed up for in New York but did not have the will to commence, let alone complete.

In the sitting-room of his house in Ballsbridge, he sat Joan Littlewood down and enthusiastically outlined the plot of the play that he named *Richard's Cork Leg*.[1] He acted out the parts as he read. Its central characters are two prostitutes, Maria Concepta and Rose of Lima. These ladies are making an annual pilgrimage to a cemetery near Dublin to visit the grave of Crystal Clear, a prostitute who had been brutally murdered twenty years previously in the Dublin mountains. (This much of the rather loose plot is based on a fact). The play is populated with familiar Behan characters – prostitutes, puritanical Protestants, revolutionaries, two supposedly blind men (the Hero Hogan and the Leper Cronin), Fascists and a black mortician inspired by a trip to California's Forest Lawn, a commercial cemetery notorious for its grimly euphemistic, 'modern' approach to the business of death. The lack of plot is made up for by rhetoric, wit and song. However, since it remains an unfinished draft it seems unfair, if not impossible to judge it. It was edited with additional material by Alan Simpson for its first performance at the Abbey Theatre eight years after Behan's death. His cousin, Colbert Kearney, says that if Brendan had approached the play in happier times, he would gradually have discovered his theme and structure. Joan Littlewood thought the same, but decided she was not going to gamble with it this time. There was too little of substance for her to work on, and too little time in which to do it. Beatrice remembered Littlewood's reaction:

> Joan judged a play on its merits and not in relation to its author's reputation ... She didn't reject the play out of hand, but she withheld

her final judgement. She believed that Brendan's reputation was such
that his work should be of a standard equal to his talent.

In this case the standard certainly was not, and Littlewood knew it. Brendan
must have been aware of the play's failings too, but that did not prevent him
being angered by her rejection. In an absolute rage at Littlewood's decision,
he went to his old sponsors Gael-Linn who had produced the Irish version of
what became *The Hostage*. He offered them a draft in Irish of a one-act play,
A Fine Day in the Graveyard. It had all the defects and few of the virtues of
Richard's Cork Leg. This act of desperation signaled that Brendan had become
the victim of his own reputation – he expected Gael-Linn to take the work on
the strength of his name alone.

On the morning of 8 February, he received a telephone call from Gael-
Linn informing him that they required serious changes to his play before they
could accept it. Although they politely suggested that he might resubmit it in
a longer reworked version, Brendan interpreted the call as a rejection. Brendan
had never learned to cope with rejection of any kind. That an Irish language
organisation in Dublin should dare reject the work of a world-famous
playwright, was a massive blow to his increasingly battered ego. His very rapid
descent into irrevocable decline dates from this rejection. Something inside
him snapped. He left the house in a hurry and went on a morning bender
around several pubs. At about 5 p.m. he went to 'Smyth's of the Green' – the
Dublin equivalent of Fortnum and Mason – and enquired about the price of
four bottles of champagne. The following day was his thirty-ninth birthday
and he wished to bring them home for a little celebration to mark the day.
When an assistant, Thomas Byrne, told him it would be thirty-five shillings a
bottle, Brendan erupted and called him 'a thief, a robber and an "ejit".'
Brendan was then offered a cheaper brand of champagne, but that incensed
him further. He slapped another assistant on the head and unleashed a torrent
of foul language about the shop. The more nervous customers fled, while
those with a sense of theatre stood around awaiting developments. They were
disappointed. One of Symth's directors, Kenneth Fox-Mills, bundled
Brendan into one of the back offices. There was a further scuffle, this time
involving Fox-Mills. Joan Littlewood was with him, and tried but failed to get
him to leave in a taxi. The police were called, and Brendan was arrested and
taken to College Street police station where he assaulted the Station Sergeant,
Patrick McCarthy, and two other police officers.

On 17 February, he appeared before District Justice O'Hagan, at District
Court Number 2. This time, according to the court report, the list of charges
were impressive. He was charged with assaulting Kenneth Fox-Mills and

having used threatening, abusive, insulting words; and behaviour which might have occasioned a breach of the peace. He was also charged with malicious damage to property; assaulting the policemen and violent behaviour at the police station.

The newspapers reported that, at the hearing, one of the biggest crowds ever seen at the District Court had jammed the galleries. A broad spectrum of Brendan's friends turned up to support him. They ranged from the stallholders of Moore Street and university students to his friends Garech Browne, Lord Gormanston and the English painter 'Boots' Bantock. Some of his friends wore freesias in their lapels, giving the whole thing an almost festive air. However, many of his friends worried that Brendan was again heading for a custodial sentence in Mountjoy Jail. Joan Littlewood was there as a witness. Brendan arrived wearing dark glasses and a three-piece navy blue suit. It was all a little bit of Hollywood by the Liffey.

The hearing lasted over three hours. Brendan was defended by Con Lehane, Solicitor and prosecuted by the assistant State Solicitor, Thomas McDonagh. The medical evidence was crucial, not just to a successful outcome to the case, but as an indicator of Brendan's overall problem with alcohol. The defence made much use in evidence of the emotional upset Brendan suffered on the morning of the incident because of the rejection of his play by Gael-Linn.

Dr Rory Childers told the court that Brendan had been a patient of his for four years. He said the defendant was a diabetic and his system had an intolerance for alcohol. He added that Brendan was much less able to assimilate alcohol than an ordinary person, and had been advised that it would be in his own best interests not to drink. Dr John Dunne from Saint Brendan's psychiatric hospital, Grangegorman, Dublin, said Brendan's low metabolic tolerance made him more easily unbalanced by the consumption of alcohol than the average person. Dr Dunne offered the opinion that Brendan must have consumed sufficient alcohol to make him suffer from a temporary aberration of his reason. An emotional upset to an artist suffering from these kinds of health problems could be catastrophic, Dr Dunne concluded.

The medical evidence helped enormously in securing a non-custodial sentence, as did some of the police evidence. Sergeant McCarthy told the Judge he remembered Brendan making a generous donation to the police benevolent fund because of some kindness the police had done for his family.

Brendan accepted responsibility for creating a disturbance at Smyth's while in an emotionally-perturbed condition. Justice O'Hagan found each charge proved and fined him £30 on the main charges, along with nineteen pounds five shillings compensation. In conclusion, the justice told Brendan to take the advice of Sergeant McCarthy who had said in court: 'I would respect him as a citizen if he would conduct himself. He is a man who should never drink'.[2]

Beatrice, though she never gave any public indication of it at the time, knew she had lost the hard-fought battle to keep her ailing husband sober. Being intensely shy and private, she found it difficult to confide her thoughts on the matter even to her close friends. The ffrench-Salkeld reserve did not allow her wear her heart on her sleeve:

> What was I to think? I tolerated the fact that he was drinking again, although I was disappointed that he had broken out after his long months of sobriety in New York. He returned to his old haunts, and when I tried to advise him his sharp-tongued remarks stung me.[3]

During the early months of 1961, his drinking returned to its old level. Dublin was and remains a city that places a low premium on celebrity. Brendan found that his drunken behaviour in pubs did not meet the tolerance he had expected as an international celebrity. He was living on borrowed fame as well as on borrowed time. In Dublin, the fame and notoriety drawn from the success of two plays and an autobiographical book was beginning to wear thin. He talked so much about *Richard's Cork Leg* in his last years, that it became something of a Dublin legend for its non-appearance. The indulgence he had found in the Dublin of the '40s and '50s was beginning to vanish with the changing times. The interiors of Victorian and Edwardian pubs were being unceremoniously ripped out and replaced with bland formica substitutes. Women began going to pubs in greater numbers. The upbeat forward-looking Ireland of Seán Lemass was overtaking the austerity of his predecessor, de Valera's dreary Eden. In the 1960s, the slobbering pub bore began to find a less tolerant drinking environment in the changing capital than heretofore.

Brendan found himself barred from several public houses, including some in his own immediate neighbourhood. For Beatrice this was mortifying, but she chose to suffer in silence. She attributed his behaviour to his inability to return to his writing and the fact that he was now reduced to speaking his books into a tape-recorder.

> I shared the indignity when he was thrown out of local pubs and told he wasn't wanted as a customer. I knew he could not live on the reputation of *The Hostage* and *Borstal Boy* forever. I wanted him to write more plays and novels, but I knew the real Brendan would not emerge from a tape-recorder ... Brendan was a spontaneous and witty talker, and even in his most painful moments he struggled to express himself

on tape, but no matter how hard Rae [Jeffs] worked, and she was a persistent woman, her method seemed to me to be divorced from true feelings and thoughts ... Sometimes he would stop talking and walk out of the room, telling her, 'I can't go on.' I sympathised with him. I knew he was trying to repeat with a tape-machine what he had achieved so effectively with his pen, and to no avail.[4]

Even though he was now drinking as heavily as ever, Beatrice was pleased that at least she had him at home in Dublin. She felt safer knowing that if he came to any harm, Dublin was a small city and she would be near at hand if he got into trouble. Once he had fallen back into his old ways, it was certain that he would get into trouble.

Three days after the February trial, Brendan wrote to a New York impresario, Alexander H. Cohen, who had invited him to compère a jazz revue that he planned to bring on tour across the United States. Beatrice asked him to reject the quite substantial offer (reported to be $3,000 a week) to act as the show's host. Brendan was so seriously ill that Beatrice thought a return to the United States while he was still drinking, could be enough to kill him. At first, he took her advice and returned the $500 advance Cohen had sent him:

Dear Mr Cohen,

After a great deal of discussion and consideration, I have decided that I cannot appear on your show, 'Impulse' [this] March. Owing to commitments to my publishers, both in America and England, as well as pressure from my London producer who expects my new play to open at the end of March, I find myself in this position. I am sorry for any inconvenience which may arise out of this, and I hope at some future date to avail of your offer in New York.[5]

Within a month of writing that letter, he changed his mind. Cohen sent him a renewed offer that he found impossible to reject. Reluctantly, Beatrice packed their bags and they arrived in New York just in time for Brendan to be refused permission to march in the St. Patrick's Day parade. The invitation to do so had come from the Gaelic Society of Fordham University. He was rejected by the parade committee chairman, Henry Hynes, who, together with fellow committee man, Judge James J. Comerford, declared Brendan, 'a common drunk' and a 'disorderly person'. He was stung by the rebuff, but passed it off as the bigotry of the 'lace curtain Irish'. These were the conservative, successful, mostly second generation middle-class Irish

Americans, who resented Behan's displays of 'paddywhackery' because they felt they had struggled so hard to leave all that behind. Now here he was, the most talked about Irishman in America, being invited to Kennedy's inauguration and fêted on coast-to-coast television, throwing his 'Oirishness' and his 'broth of a boy' routine in their faces. Their representatives resolved that he would not hijack March 17, the most sacred day in the Irish calendar in New York by turning it into a Behan spectacle. There was a bitter anti-Behan editorial in the *Daily News* on 16 March. It ran:

> For our part, we're glad Justice Comerford thumbed Behan to the sidelines. Tomorrow's parade should be much the better for the absence of a show-off whose antics, frankly are threatening to become as boring as Lady Loverley's chatter or any six imitators of Edgar Browne, Charlie McCarthy and Mortimer Snerd. Jersey City, you can have him.

Behan got some kind of revenge when the same newspaper carried his reaction to the banning: 'There are three things I don't like about New York; the water, the buses and the professional Irishman. A professional Irishman is one who is terribly anxious to pass as a middle-class Englishman.' He delivered a further salvo in the pages of *Newsweek*: 'The way to win friends and influence people in the US is to have a judge say nasty things about you. ... I now have a new theory on what happened to the snakes when Saint Patrick drove them out of Ireland. They all came to New York and became judges.'[6]

Brendan's habit of firing off broadsides to the newspapers, at home and abroad gathered pace in the early 1960s. As in his professional writing, he now often preferred to dictate his words rather than record them on paper. He telephoned his letters, late at night to various news desks. Dermot Mullane remembers receiving one such telephoned blast in the newsroom of *The Irish Times*. Behan decided his letter was to appear in Irish. Mullane, who had been educated at an English public school, explained that his knowledge of the language was not up to the task. Undaunted, Behan insisted he take the letter down and went on to spell it out phonetically. Sadly this late night collaborative effort has been lost to posterity.

The day after St Patrick's day, *The New York Times* reported that Brendan and Beatrice had spent the day in Jersey City at the invitation of Mayor Charles S. Witkowski, who entertained them to lunch and presented Brendan with the key to the city. Brendan's cousin, Paul Bourke, who lived in New Jersey, drove them across for the ceremony. At its conclusion, Brendan, waving his Golden Key, declared: 'At the end of the Holland Tunnel lies freedom. And I choose freedom'.

He and Beatrice left New York by train for Toronto to arrive in time for the opening of Alexander Cohen's jazz extravaganza, *Impulse*, which was to have its out-of-town try out at the O'Keefe Centre on 21 March. They stayed at the Royal York Hotel, where Brendan gave a press conference upon arrival. He had been drinking heavily on the train. One reporter noted that a male companion who had travelled with him was so under the weather that when he reached forward to light a cigarette, he fell flat on his face. The media reports the next day portrayed Brendan Behan 'cursing, guffawing and snorting,' and in the condition now generally expected of him. He was asked what he knew about jazz, and his reply can hardly have been encouraging to Alexander Cohen: 'I can't read a note of music but I can certainly read a cheque'.[7]

Soon after they settled into their hotel room, Brendan began receiving abusive telephone calls. He was told to go back to Ireland where he belonged. Beatrice believed the calls came from the Anti-Republican Orange lobby in Toronto, who despised his Republican past. Brendan gave as good as he got, and many of the callers probably regretted bothering to register their dislike.

Nina Simone and about forty other leading jazz artists were billed in Cohen's show. Brendan arrived drunk and unrehearsed. He swaggered onto the stage to introduce the show, but only managed to mumble incoherently. The audience became restless. Had it been a more intimate space, he might have managed to establish a rapport, but it was a vast and soulless modern auditorium and he looked a tiny pathetic figure on stage. He was making an embarrassing spectacle of himself yet again, and Beatrice knew it. 'My husband the writer, was making a fool of himself for a couple of thousand dollars. It was a cruel dissipation of his talent'. After that disaster, Cohen announced that the show would not be opening in New York. Brendan was not the show's only problem; the jazz content was also sorely lacking, but had he made an effort he might have managed to rescue the show.

After a late dinner, the Behans returned to their hotel. Brendan demanded a drink from the night porter. The porter told him he could not have one. When he became abusive, a house detective was called. He advised Brendan in curt tones to go to his room, and Brendan landed a punch straight in his face. A second detective arrived and they bundled Brendan into his room. Within minutes, he was out again and engaged in a fist fight with both detectives. From their room, Beatrice could hear the detectives punching Brendan and through her tears she thought 'Am I losing control of him?'[8] The sad answer to that question was yes. She had lost control of him and, from this point on she was reduced to being a tolerant but powerless witness to his inexorable rush towards self-destruction.

The inevitable court appearance followed the next day. There were two charges of assault and one of causing a disturbance. He was released on bail of $1,500, put up by an Irish friend, Eamonn Martin, who was living in Toronto. The court released him into Beatrice's care and he went on a two-day drinking skite in Toronto.

Their Dublin friend, Petronella O'Flanagan had a sister in Toronto who was a doctor. In desperation, Beatrice asked for her help. Brendan turned up in a bar and after much effort, was persuaded that he needed hospitalisation. When he saw how determined Beatrice was, he left for Sunnyside Hospital where he collapsed into a diabetic coma. He was put under the care of a Dr. Pratt, who told Beatrice what she had heard so many times before. However Dr Pratt startled her by asking if Brendan had ever had a serious head injury. She told him about his tendency to get into fights and about his prison experiences. Pratt suggested that neurological tests might reveal an important link to Brendan's drinking disorder. Brendan objected in the most violent manner to the suggestion that, as he put it 'there is anything wrong with my fucking brain'. He had become increasingly concerned from 1950 onwards that he was going to be locked up in some type of mental institution. The threat of neurological tests made up his mind to leave the hospital at the earliest opportunity.

When he failed to make an appearance on the day assigned, the court issued a warrant for his arrest and a detective was placed outside the door of his hospital room. When he did appear, he was fined $200 and released.

As soon as he felt able to manage the journey, he and Beatrice left for New York before going on to San Francisco where *The Hostage* was due to open on 2 May. Beatrice, who detested flying, decided to go by train to the West Coast. Brendan flew on ahead of her, promising to be at the station to greet her when she arrived. She found him collapsed in a hotel room, surrounded by empty champagne bottles and unopened mail. He had fallen into another diabetic coma. Good fortune attended him again. Jim McGuinness, who had published Brendan in the *Irish Press* when he was a struggling writer in Dublin, was now working in San Francisco. Using his influence with a local doctor, McGuinness managed to secure a bed for Brendan in St Mary's Hospital, where many of the nursing staff were Irish. The familiar old routine was in place again. Beatrice arrived to visit one day and found him entertaining the other patients and in great spirits 'as if he were just in hospital for the removal of an in-grown toenail'.[9]

After getting out of St Mary's, he didn't take a drink for a few days but he was soon back on stage interrupting performances of *The Hostage* and making the headlines in the local papers. During his stay in San Francisco, he made a visit, accompanied by a posse of reporters, to The No Name Bar in Sansalito. There he met a man called Charles Gould. Gould, then a twenty-five-year-old barman, but now a rare books dealer in Oregon, had seen Behan on television. His interest in this powerful and unconventional personality was aroused, and he went to see the San Francisco production, which he especially recalls for the topicality of its references to American events. Behan was drinking champagne from a tumbler and singing what Gould called 'dirty songs'. He approached Behan to congratulate him. All Behan wanted to know was if Gould thought he looked 'soused' when he made his speech from the stage, to which he replied 'just about as soused as you are now'. When the bar's patrons and the attendant reporters began to draw away from the swaggering, staggering drunk, Gould was struck by the pathos of the moment.[10]

Most people involved in the San Francisco production were pleased when Behan announced his intention to go to Los Angeles when the show closed. The stage manager of *The Hostage*, Bernie Pollock, and his bride-to-be, Beulah Garrick, who played Miss Gilchrist in the touring production, were leaving for L.A. and Beatrice and Brendan went with them. Garrick insisted that if Brendan came on the trip, he would have to remain sober. Up to a point, he did. As usual any emotional upset sent him back to the bottle. This time it was over accommodation. They had been staying at the Montecito Hotel in Hollywood with Bernie and Beulah but, when their friends proposed moving, on their own, to an apartment, Brendan was angry. He disappeared for over twenty-four hours and was eventually found drinking in a bar in Hollywood that was patronised mainly by homosexuals. He was surrounded by several of the patrons who were feeding him drink and were highly amused by his talk. A promise of champagne if he agreed to leave succeeded in extracting him from the company.

In the midst of all the chaos and disorganised living, Brendan found time to write long letters home. His brother Rory received detailed accounts of the places he visited and the people he met:

> I am having a holiday – from what? – you may well ask – here. It's a screwy kind of place. Full of good kindly famous people. In Frank Sinatra's nite club they played Irish airs for me when I went in last night and Groucho just rang up to say he's calling for us in the morning. He and Harpo are friends of ours from New York. Harpo and I (and Harry Truman) share a new publisher.[11]

In between name-dropping to the people at home, Brendan liked to engage in more physical exercise. While staying at the Montecito he began using the local YMCA because it had an Olympic-size swimming pool. There, in late May, he met a very good-looking young Irishman called Peter Arthurs. His life story had many of the classic elements of a 'wannabe' – youthful poverty, struggle, stow-away romance and the desire for success in the New World. Arthurs' background had a natural appeal for Brendan. Peter Arthurs also claims that Brendan found him sexually attractive, and he has made a very frank admission claiming that Behan engaged in homosexual sex with him. He is the only man to have done so in print.

Arthurs was twenty-eight when he met Brendan. He came from Dundalk, County Louth, where he was born on 1 November 1933 into a working-class family. His father was an alcoholic, whom, Arthurs claims, beat him if he failed to come home without drinking money for him. His methods of getting this money varied. According to his account, it included allowing tourists and sometimes soldiers from a nearby barracks to fellate him in a public lavatory for a small amount of money. By the age of 15, his life was already crowded with incident. He had worked as a butcher's boy, a plumber's mate, a milkman's assistant and a circus-hand. He eventually became a mess boy on a Norwegian tanker that took him to Aruba, where he switched ships for New York. There he took the first step toward fulfilling his ambition to become an actor. A 'bit part' in the movie, *The World's Greatest Sinner*, further fuelled his star-struck ambitions. Hopes of advancing his acting career through an introduction to the television writer, David Gregory, brought him to Hollywood when Behan was living there. The encounter at the YMCA swimming pool, with the now famous Irish writer, must have seemed a good omen to a young man eager to advance his acting career. He recognised Behan from newspaper photographs and television appearances. Behan also recognised something appealing about Arthurs apart from his Irish accent because they remained close companions for three years after this first meeting. If, as he had often claimed to friends from The Catacombs period onward, Brendan sexually fancied the 'working-class youth of firm limb', Arthurs was a very fine example of it. He had been a boxer since the age of twelve and an able-bodied seaman since his late teenage years. In *With Brendan Behan*,[12] his memoir of his three-year friendship with Brendan, Peter Arthurs has left a hard-hitting assessment of Brendan's personality and of what he believes to have been his true sexual nature. Norman Mailer, who knew Behan in New York, said in an endorsement that the memoir revealed sides of Behan never presented before. He still accepts Arthurs' account of his friendship with Behan as fundamentally true.

Arthurs gives explicit details of Behan's sexual advances to him. They consisted mostly of Brendan fellating him in drunken *mêlées* and repeatedly asking for further sexual favours. Arthurs also recalled that Brendan relished the actor-sailor's stock of stories of on-ship buggery. Arthurs displayed none of the prudishness or prejudice about homosexuality one might have expected from a lad brought up in a provincial Irish town. Of his experience of homosexuality on board the ships he worked on as a teenager, Arthurs wrote:

> The practise of homosexuality was looked upon as an essential emotional outlet. Mutual masturbation and sodomy amongst the teenagers were the two most common acts.[13]

One of the things he most disliked about Brendan was his hypocritical pretence when he met homosexuals who were 'out of the closet'. He became uneasy and feigned shock, especially if the meeting occurred at an up-market Hollywood party. If this view of him is correct, then somewhere between the ages of nineteen and thirty-nine, Behan abandoned his very tolerant belief that a man's sexuality was his own business. Fame has its pressures and Brendan was no less susceptible to them than the next person.

What emerges from Peter Arthurs' account of their friendship is a catalogue of paradoxical Behan identities, which give it the ring of authenticity that acquaintances like Norman Mailer accept as accurate. Inevitably, some of Behan's friends thought Arthurs was on the make. Brendan allowed Arthurs to believe that he would use his influence for him with the Hollywood moguls who were beating a path to his door with offers for screen plays. Brendan spoke of a part for the handsome young man in the film version of *The Quare Fellow*.

Brendan had introduced Arthurs to Beatrice the day he met him at the YMCA. She thought him a likeable fellow. Arthurs disapproved of the rough way Brendan treated Beatrice when he was drunk. He tackled Brendan about his physical abuse of Beatrice. Of their friends, old and new, Arthurs was the only one to write about the beatings Behan inflicted on Beatrice. They usually occurred when he was very drunk and were accompanied by horrendous verbal abuse. When Arthurs reproved him for his unmanly behaviour, Beatrice usually came to her husband's defence. Since Brendan's death and his elevation to the status of literary icon, the question of any physical abuse of Beatrice has tended to be ignored. The reality, however – and this is a view shared by many who knew them after 1960 – is that she was regularly at the receiving end of his violent rage. Again, she bore it because she knew she was dealing with an extremely sick man.

Peter Arthurs proved useful when Beatrice needed someone to help her get Brendan out of his bar room brawls. On 31 May, quite soon after meeting Arthurs for the first time, Beatrice telephoned him when Brendan was arrested following yet another drunken episode, this time in a Hollywood bar, Magoo's. He had abused the barman when he refused to serve him a drink. At his court appearance, Judge Delbert E. Wong fined him $250.

After the trial and the usual publicity that came with it, Brendan decided he wanted to get out of Hollywood. Peter Arthurs drove Beatrice and Brendan to Mexico. On 12 July, from Tijuana, he sent John Ryan a postcard in which he remembered the old McDaid's brigade, including, Paddy Kavanagh:

Dear Hemingway Ryan,

A strange thing – I was thinking of [Patrick] Swift and [Anthony] Cronin and all when I saw this – I shed a tear of tequila into my vaso.

F. Scot Behan

I'd better say Kavanagh would love this place – I'm quite sure he wouldn't – I hope he's well.[14]

The Mexican holiday was distinguished by nothing much other than the shedding of tears into numerous *vasos* in a round of bar crawling. There was a visit to a bull-fight where Beatrice and Arthurs were on tenterhooks lest Brendan, in his drunken state, carry out his threat to join the matadors in the ring. He changed his mind when he saw blood drawn. The Mexicans, no doubt baffled by his toothless drunken mutterings, ignored Brendan for the most part. The trip was not a success. He picked rows with Arthurs over the most trivial matters, all childishly aimed at winning some sort of domination over him. Arthurs described Brendan's mental age as swinging on a wide arc that sometimes stopped at around that of an eight-year-old.

After the Mexican trip, the trio returned to Hollywood where Brendan eased up only very slightly on his drinking. In mid-July, the Behans arrived in New York to find that The Algonquin would not accept them as guests. The newspaper reports of Brendan's behaviour in Hollywood frightened the management into rejecting their reservation. As always, any form of rejection cut Brendan to the quick. Being turned away by The Algonquin was tantamount to being rebuffed by the city itself. He reacted in the predictable fashion. The pubs of the dockland area of Hoboken were favoured with his custom on this visit. Their main attraction was that they opened at 5 a.m. Beatrice had booked their passage home to Ireland for 28 July. He was eventually found wandering around in Hoboken early on the morning of 29 July through the kindness of a policeman, Dan Kiely. He had seen him wandering, shoeless, and in a dazed state in the docks area. He locked him in a cell. When Beatrice came to take him home, Kiely suggested that she allow him to take Brendan to New Jersey State Hospital, where he was admitted to the psychiatric wing.

Soon after Brendan's release from hospital, he and Beatrice sailed for Ireland. Beatrice knew the return home would not prevent him drinking, but she always felt she could manage his drinking better on home territory. On the journey, he vowed once again to stop and apologised for the way he had behaved to her.

When at large in Dublin, as he now was, it had always been Brendan's habit to drop in unannounced at the Dublin homes of his friends. In two such houses he was able to indulge his passion for traditional Irish music and song. The composer Seán Ó Riada, whose brilliant arrangement for the score of the film *Mise Éire* had been hugely popular in Ireland, gathered an impressive group of skilled Irish musicians around him in his house in Galloping Green. Brendan, drunk or sober, was welcome here and his inexhaustible stock of ballads and Irish airs were a valued contribution to an evening's entertainment. His other port of call on the traditional music circuit was a mews house at 41 Quinn's Lane, near Leeson Street, where Garech Browne with Paddy Maloney was about to found The Chieftains. Indeed so much a part of that circle was Brendan that the name The Quare Fellows had been mooted as an alternative for them.

These social diversions in private houses were not enough to keep Brendan occupied and out of the public houses. By late September, Beatrice wrote to Rae Jeffs for help:

> These days, concern about Brendan and myself is a rare thing – I mean genuine and constructive. At the time I received your letter I had just got Brendan into a nursing home by ambulance in a state of complete collapse. He stayed two days – and then did his usual trick of running out behind the doctor's back. Ten days later, BB is off again on the beer. He is today still bashing away regardless, money flying in all directions.[15]

Rae Jeffs acted immediately on Beatrice's request that she ask David Astor, editor of *The Observer*, to suggest a cure in London. The loyal Jeffs now believed that 'the bad in Brendan was slowly swallowing up the good'. She showed David Astor, Beatrice's letter and he wrote to Brendan to try to get him to come to London.

After consultation with *The Observer's* medical correspondent, Dr Abraham Marcus, they booked Brendan into a private clinic run by a Dr Glatt in the East End of London. Glatt had known of Brendan's problem through the newspapers and Rae Jeffs did her best to fill in the case history.

In October, Beatrice brought him to London. Rae Jeffs met them at Euston and she took them to the French House in Soho. It was to be a pre-cure luncheon. During that gloomy meal, Brendan told Beatrice he would not enter the clinic unless she stayed with him day and night. Of course, he thought this to be an impossible request, but Rae Jeffs slipped out and telephoned the matron who gave permission for Beatrice to stay in the hospital each day until it was time for Brendan to sleep. This did not satisfy him, and he announced that he would cure himself. When Beatrice asked him to consider her position and her health and well-being, he replied that he was happy to agree to a fifty-fifty split of their assets if she found that agreeable.

In silence, they went to the Holborn Hotel where they stayed for another week. They attended the film version of *The Quare Fellow*, which opened at the Rialto Cinema, Leicester Square. Brendan railed against Arthur Dreifus's interpretation of his play. A great deal of the action took place outside of Mountjoy Jail and the Quare Fellow's wife was introduced mainly so that she could have an affair with Warder Crimmin. However, the scene which Brendan had specifically insisted be included for Peter Arthurs to act in was cut.

Before leaving London, he had a meeting with Iain Hamilton at Hutchinson. Hamilton, who was leaving to become editor of *The Spectator*, was anxious that the editing of *Brendan Behan's Island* be completed before he left. The meeting was not successful. There was a suggestion that someone else, possibly even a member of his family, might do the job. That annoyed him and he later announced that he would do it himself. Before he left London, he told Rae Jeffs that he believed all the world was against him and his writing was being mutilated without his consent. Again he insisted that he would edit his own work from now on.

On 11 December, he was re-admitted to Baggot Street Hospital in Dublin but discharged himself two days later. It was the presence of Dr Victor Millington Synge that drew Behan repeatedly back to this hospital.[16] He was the leading Irish specialist in the treatment of diabetes, but this was not Behan's reason for seeing him. He had the most profound respect for Synge's intellect. He spoke Russian, Italian, French, German, Spanish and once wrote a reference for a Chinese student in perfect Mandarin. He was also a nephew of the playwright, John Millington Synge. Few medical men had the controlling effect on Behan which Synge could command. He never discharged himself if Synge was on duty, and the doctor had infinite patience with Behan's gregarious and disruptive behaviour.[17]

At Christmas, Brendan and Beatrice again went to Luggala. Other house guests that year included the sculptor Eddie Delaney and his wife Nancy, the painter Edward Maguire, the poet John Montague, Lord Kilbracken and Lord Gormanston. It was here, on Christmas Eve after dinner, that Brendan fell victim for a second time to his self-declared 'Herod complex' and suffered a brutal beating at the hands of Miguel Ferreras.[18]

Disintegration

After Christmas, Brendan received a telegram from Perry Bruskin informing him that his off-Broadway production of *The Hostage* was opening in Greenwich Village on 5 February. An invitation to New York was not something Brendan was likely to pass up lightly. On 2 February, he took a taxi from Dublin to Shannon Airport and an onward flight to New York in time for the opening. He travelled alone. Still banned from The Algonquin, he took up residence at The Bristol where Peter Arthurs found him in poor shape, eating Chinese take-away food from a newspaper on the floor of his room. The new production of *The Hostage* received extremely good reviews and Brendan was back in high demand by the media. He was a little wary of their attention on this occasion. A rumour was circulating in New York bars that he was about to become the father of a child by a woman with whom he was having an affair.

The woman in question was an Irish girl called Valerie Danby-Smith, Ernest Hemingway's former assistant. In 1959, at the age of 18, Danby-Smith left Dublin and went to live in Madrid with little more than a promise of freelance work from *The Irish Times*. In May of that year, she went to interview Hemingway in his hotel in Madrid. The meeting was so successful that, soon afterwards, she became his assistant and began travelling with him, mostly in Cuba and Spain. On a visit to Cuba, they dined with Castro. There were rumours of an affair with Hemingway. He did propose to her but she turned him down. Later she married his son, Gregory Hemingway.

Brendan revered Hemingway. His suicide in July 1961 had had a profound effect on Behan. In Hemingway's hard-drinking image, Behan saw his own reflection and his suicide forced him to confront his mortality. Brendan met Danby-Smith in New York and, though she had ceased to work for Hemingway, her name was still associated with his. Peter Arthurs remembers visiting her with Behan at a New York apartment where Hemingway had lived. Valerie Danby-Smith is one of the few women with whom Behan had an extra-marital affair. Nothing in these last years of turmoil hurt Beatrice more than the gossip in Dublin, London and New York about her husband's affair with another Irish woman.[1]

At the time of the affair, it was claimed that Brendan was the father of a male child born to Valerie Danby-Smith in New York on 12 February 1962.[2] Behan's friend, the impresario, Chesley Milliken, recalls being in Brendan's hotel room in the Bristol Hotel when a telephone call came through to say his son had been born. According to Milliken, Behan was thrilled by the news. Peter Arthurs wrote of receiving a transatlantic telephone call from Beatrice telling him to advise Brendan to deny that he was the father.[3] It was widely accepted in New York that he was the father of the child. Norman Mailer, who recalls Valerie being very much in love with Behan at the time, is quite certain Brendan Behan is the father of the child. Mailer, who saw the boy in his first years, says one look at the child left him in no doubt that he was Brendan Behan's son.[4] The story of Brendan's parentage of the child became one of the main topics of conversation in the Third Avenue bars. Brendan's brother Rory in Dublin received a photograph of the boy from America.[5]

There was no other particular purpose to Brendan's being in New York, except to escape being in Dublin. He spent most of his time in his favourite bars with Peter Arthurs as nursemaid in attendance. He did some work on *Richard's Cork Leg* in his room in the Bristol and received an offer to write a screenplay for *Borstal Boy*. In mid-March he returned to Dublin.

His physical decline had reached a point where he was frequently unable to dress or shave himself and the task fell to Beatrice. He was admitted to hospital again but discharged himself as usual. Beatrice took him back to Connemara in the first week of June and they stayed there for most of the Summer. When the lease on their cottage expired, he seemed not to want to leave. While they were there, he received the news that the French Theatre Critics' Association had selected *The Hostage* as the best play of the season in Paris. News also reached him that the Book Society had selected *Brendan Behan's Island* as its October choice. *The Observer* bought the rights to two extracts. After the second of the two appeared on 2 September, a Dublin solicitor wrote to the paper claiming a client of his had been libelled in it. Brendan agreed to go to London to discuss the problem with lawyers representing Hutchinson and *The Observer*. After a thoroughly unsatisfactory meeting in the offices of Rubenstein, Nash & Co. with Brendan rambling and incoherent, the matter remained unresolved. He was distressed at the idea of having to give in to the charge of libel and disgusted at the notion of settling by printing an apology in *The Observer*. He interpreted the umbrage taken by those libelled as an act of betrayal directed against himself. It was another excuse to have a drink. The usual pattern ensued – binge-drinking, followed by admission to hospital. During a brief period of health, he managed to make a coherent speech at a literary luncheon hosted by the *Yorkshire Post* at Harrogate. He joined a distinguished panel of writers and speakers chaired by Lord Boothby. The Countess of Harewood represented her husband, who was patron of the event. When she admired the tie Brendan was wearing – he had bought it on his Mexican holiday – he, like any good Republican Socialist on receipt of a compliment from the nobility, 'spun around the room like a top showing it off to all the guests.'[6]

He spent the week after *The Yorkshire Post* luncheon in the bars of Fleet Street and the markets. He drank around the clock. Sometimes, when no other source was available to him, he cured his hangover with tonic wine sold in chemists. His outward appearance began to change. His body became bloated, his skin blotchy and his walk changed from its usual swagger to a shuffle. He was admitted on two separate occasions to the Westminster Hospital and on both he discharged himself before his treatment was finished.

He refused all entreaties by David Astor and his medical correspondent, Abraham Marcus, to enter a hospital and stay there. Dr Marcus predicted that unless Brendan stopped drinking he would be dead within a year. Eventually, he ended up in a clinic for alcoholics by accident. On Sunday 30 September, Brendan was wandering around Victoria looking for an Irish friend who ran a guesthouse in the area. By complete chance, he knocked on the door of a private drying-out clinic. The doctor in charge, seeing his condition, ordered him to be sedated and put to bed. Beatrice and Rae Jeffs came to the clinic. They agreed to put Brendan on a course of 'aversion' therapy. The concept was considered advanced in those days and involved putting the patient on drugs that, if mixed with alcohol, would induce convulsive vomiting. That Brendan did not discharge himself immediately after this suggestion indicated how very unwell he was at the time. Beatrice's parents, Irma and Cecil were still both ill in Dublin, so Beatrice asked Rae Jeffs to supervise Brendan's progress. While the treatment was progressing, the legal action over the alleged libel in *Brendan Behan's Island* proceeded. The High Court in Dublin gave leave for summonses to be served on Hutchinson and *The Observer*, and granted an application to temporarily halt the circulation of the disputed material.

News of the legal action sent journalists to scour London for Brendan's whereabouts. His supporters thought it wise to move him, and he revelled in the subterfuge involved. He especially enjoyed being registered under the name 'John Browne'. He was moved first to Chelsea and then to South Kensington. Christopher Gore-Grimes, a Dublin solicitor, took instructions in London for the progression of the libel action and Brendan displayed singular lucidity when giving his opinion of how he thought the case should be handled.

It looked as if the aversion therapy might be working. Then, suddenly there was a setback. Brendan began to get double vision and his doctors in London, like the doctor in Canada felt that pressure on the brain might be relieved by an operation. Beatrice was now back in London. She discussed the possibility of the operation with him. He was adamant that under no circumstances would he submit to any form of brain surgery. He still feared the stigma of mental illness. Beatrice came to the clinic every day. She saw him wasting away daily, but thought he had finally accepted that he was a very ill man. Samuel Beckett came to visit him and was saddened to see his decline from the lively, if tediously drunk, character who had turned up unannounced at his Paris flat just ten years previously.

Brendan was allowed out of the clinic in the company of a male nurse. On these occasions he visited his old London drinking places, but took only tea and soft drinks. Rae Jeffs encouraged him to come to her office at Great Portland Street and look over copies of his *Irish Press* articles with a view to publishing them as a collection with illustrations by Beatrice. Hutchinson, at Rae Jeffs suggestion, also agreed to publish the novel, *The Scarperer*, which had appeared under a pseudonym in *The Irish Times*.

With an advance of £450 in his pocket, Brendan headed for the South of France. It was to be a rest cure in Speracèdes, in the hills above Nice where his old friends Ralph and Nancy Cusack had a perfume farm. Beatrice went on ahead. Brendan travelled to Paris with a male nurse, Joe McGarrity, who had looked after him in London. Initially, the doctors at the clinic were against the trip but felt slightly more at ease when he agreed to take his nurse with him.

Beatrice hoped the atmosphere in Speracèdes would have a calming effect on Brendan. Unfortunately he overstayed his time in Paris and arrived in Nice station in agitated form. He had lost his Brooks Brothers cashmere overcoat on the train and that was enough to start him drinking again.

They spent only a few days at the Cusacks' house before moving to a small, local hotel. Brendan was now knocking back large quantities of red wine and brandy, and suffered another collapse. During his stay in the hotel, he got into a fight with a local man and smashed the man's head through a glass door. He spent the night cooling off in the local police cell.

Beatrice bluntly put it to him that he should take either the pills or alcohol. To her total dismay he told her in no uncertain terms, he would stick with alcohol. They parted in Nice; Beatrice left for Dublin and Brendan went back to London.

In October, Eamonn Andrews contacted Brendan's cousin, Seamus de Burca. He wanted to feature Brendan's father, Stephen Behan, in the British television programme *This is Your Life*. The show's format was the surprise reunion where subjects were lured to the studio unawares, to be serially greeted by as many of the family, friends and acquaintances as could be brought to the studio. The show was filmed in Dublin and Brendan was invited to participate. He returned to Dublin in an alcoholic stupor. The old animosity between himself and his brother, Dominic, surfaced during the recording of the programme – fortunately it was off-camera. Brendan never really accepted that there was more than one writer or performer in the Behan family. That bitter jealousy which had led him, as a boy, to push his brother Seamus down the stairs at Russell Street screaming, 'She's my granny, not yours', remained unresolved in his relationship with Dominic, all those years later. His relationship with his father also remained uncertain. Family and friends are quite certain that he loved his mother much more than he did his father. Brendan's memory, in spite of being clouded over by alcohol for much of his life, was long and sharp. He had not forgotten the quarrel on the eve of his departure for Liverpool when he was sixteen. He had buried the axe, but he had marked the spot with care. When he began earning very large sums of money from his writing, he made a point of giving his mother money but rarely showed much generosity towards his father.

Curiously, on his return to Dublin for the recording of the show, it was to his family home at Kildare Road that he looked for comfort. Increasingly, he began to stay there and not at his own house in Anglesea Road. Relations between himself and Beatrice had become bitterly strained by the end of 1962. She was no longer able to cope, not just with his drinking, but also with his restlessness. There was also the question of his affair with Valerie Danby-Smith in New York. He had often stayed away from home in the past but, after his return from London, he stayed away so frequently that Beatrice found the strain almost unbearable. A further indication of how bad things were coming up to Christmas was their decision not to accept their annual invitation to Luggala. They had spent so many happy Christmas holidays there that Beatrice refused to have those memories shattered by turning up with Brendan when relations between them were at such a low ebb. On Christmas morning, he telephoned Rae Jeffs and chatted clearly and coherently, especially about the satisfactory resolution of his pending libel case. They also discussed the publication of his collection of *Irish Press* articles and chose the title *Hold Your Hour And Have Another*, which was a favourite pub expression of his.

In January 1963, he began talking about going to New York to undergo treatment with Dr Alter Weiss whom he had met through Perry Bruskin. In fact, the doctor had died since Brendan last saw him. What he really wanted was to escape Dublin, a city that daily grew less and less tolerant of his behaviour. Being there was also a daily reminder that as a writer he was now finished. He told Beatrice he needed to go to New York to deal with his obligation to Bernard Geis to complete the sequel to *Borstal Boy*, for which he had been paid handsomely. It was another feeble excuse to escape reality and further underlined to Beatrice that he was a very sick man.

On 26 January, he was again admitted to Baggot Street Hospital. When Dr Richard Brennan examined him, he found such severe infection in the genital area that he advised circumcision to prevent it recurring in future. The condition appears to have been a consequence of his neglected diabetes, which can produce a chronic version of something like female vaginal thrush in men. Brendan agreed to the operation. It was performed under local anaesthetic. When it was over, he offered to test its success on the nurse in attendance. He remained in hospital until 8 February.

One of his great pleasures in these days was to engage the services of a taxi driver for the day, or sometimes several days, and take long excursions into the countryside. A casual meeting with Nicholas Gormanston in the bar of The Shelbourne Hotel prompted one such expedition. Brendan's father was briefly interned during the Civil War at Gormanston Military Camp in County Meath. The camp was close to Gormanston's family seat, an impressive Gothic castle. After World War II, the Franciscan Order bought it to use as a school. The taxi journey also took them to the town of Drogheda where, in the local cathedral, Brendan enquired of a rather startled priest if they might see 'the head of Blessed Oliver Cromwell'. He meant the head of the martyred seventeenth century Archbishop, Blessed Oliver Plunkett, later to be a Saint, which was contained and venerated in a shrine there. When Gormanston remarked that the body of the martyr was at Downside, his old school, Behan quickly scribbled on a card containing a relic of the holy man: 'Give the head back its body'.[7]

In the last week of February, Beatrice's mother received an incoherent telephone call from Brendan, who was at London airport *en route* to New York. He had nothing with him other than the clothes on his back. With cash injections from Bernard Geis, Brendan was able to stay in the comfort of The Bristol Hotel until the management lost patience with his behaviour. He was found running naked around the lobby, vomiting on other guests, and throwing racist comments around without restraint. Thus he was ejected from yet another New York institution. Managers and owners of many of the bars he drank in also asked him to take his custom elsewhere. Peter Arthurs remembers him at this time as 'a perambulatory skeleton, a man who was in the cataclysmic spring of his dotage'. The journalist and writer, Pete Hamill, feels Behan was 'drinking to get rid of the world' and described him, when drunk, as having 'a snarl on his face which was generalised, not focused, and therefore directed not at the world but at himself'.[8] Norman Mailer believes Behan's drinking came from a belief that 'everything in life had conspired to put him in flames'. He also believes that it was firmly rooted in his Borstal and prison experiences. He says that, in prison, Behan formed allegiances which he perceived as necessary to protect his ego. Thereafter, he made all his allegiances on a win or lose basis, and, no matter what the outcome, he used drink as his armour in this deadly battle.[9]

Just when he was asked to leave The Bristol, he met the dancer and choreographer, Katherine Dunham, in Bernard Geis's office. Geis and Dunham arranged for Brendan to move to the Hotel Chelsea on West 23rd Street, where the dancer and her retinue took care of him. It was the perfect solution to Brendan's problems, and gave him an opportunity to enjoy being pampered and pitied. Dunham's rescue was not a philanthropic exercise. When Beatrice arrived to join him in The Chelsea, the accountant Dunham shared with Bernard Geis presented her with a bill for the enormous sum of $1,500. If Beatrice was taken aback at the bill which was supposed to represent her husband's expenses for a month, she was even more surprised when she was told by the managing director of the Chelsea, Stanley Bard, that he understood she was divorcing her husband. Bard seemed genuinely amazed when she asked to be taken to Brendan's room. Beatrice thought he must know something that she didn't. She found Brendan passed out in his room. She sat in a chair watching him until he opened his eyes. She made up her mind to confront him with the divorce claim. Although he had told a number of people in New York that he was going to divorce Beatrice, he said to her that the talk of their separation was also news to him. When pushed, he admitted having had an affair with Valerie Danby-Smith. It was the first and only such admission he made to Beatrice.

She already knew about Valerie Danby-Smith and the rumour that the baby she had just given birth to was Brendan's. Beatrice felt doubly betrayed because, before she left Dublin, her doctor had told her she was pregnant and would give birth in November. Suffused with anger she decided not to tell Brendan about her pregnancy just then. Beatrice was in an extremely difficult position. She had no money of her own, nor was she likely to inherit any from her family. After eight years of marriage to a man whose abuse of alcohol had turned him into a monster before her eyes, she was exhausted. The salvation or ruination of their relationship hung on this New York reunion. Relations between them were patched up sufficiently to allow at least a breathing space for reflection. During the first week of May, Beatrice told Brendan she was pregnant. She was convinced that the news did not register immediately and she repeated it again two days later. His reaction was swift and decisive. He went to the lawyers Greenbaum, Wolff and Ernstbat at 285 Madison Avenue and made his Will leaving his entire estate to Beatrice.[10] The sudden realisation that he was to have a child with Beatrice made him do the first responsible thing he had done in two or three years. His brother Brian believes that he might indeed have attempted to divorce Beatrice, had he not learnt that she was carrying his child.[11]

The presence of Rae Jeffs and her daughter Diana also helped restore some sense of calm to the Behans' frayed relationship. His editor had a soothing effect on Brendan, and was one of the few people who knew how to handle him in a tricky situation. Rae Jeffs came to New York to begin taping *Confessions of an Irish Rebel*, the work that was to be the second instalment of Behan's autobiography. She felt he was fit for the project, because of the somewhat possessive (not to say expensive) care Katherine Dunham and her team had taken of him.

Two weeks after the first taping sessions began, Behan had produced about 50,000 words of the book. The usual distractions, as ever, applied. There were constant diversions in The Chelsea itself. The most colourful was the composer George Kleinsinger. He kept an extraordinary menagerie of exotic birds and reptiles in his penthouse apartment in the hotel. Kleinsinger became Brendan's father confessor. One evening, he declared to him that he thought himself a phoney and a fraud. Having absolved him of that sin, the genial composer then had to deal with Brendan's fears about death and the afterlife. He had always been obsessed with death, but now it became a daily preoccupation although, in braver moments, he would mock the reaper: 'I'm only staying alive to save funeral expenses,' he told anyone who enquired too closely about his health.

Another neighbour in The Chelsea was Arthur Miller. Brendan took to using Miller's telephone for his more expensive transatlantic calls. Miller was not impressed by this, nor was he convinced by Brendan's talent as a writer. Miller did not have George Kleinsinger's patience for Behan's late-night drunken gibberish. Norman Mailer's patience with him was also wearing out, and he too felt he had to rebuff him in the end.

In the midst of all the mayhem, Rae Jeffs made a brief trip back to London, but returned to loyally battle on with her tape recordings. In June, he suffered a serious relapse. Beatrice and Rae Jeffs found him in a state of semiconsciousness in his room in The Chelsea. Dr Max Tasler succeeded in getting him a bed in the University Hospital where, during the night, he fell into one of his now frequent comas. In the morning, he emerged to wander about the hospital, wearing only the top-half of his pyjamas, screaming for drink and his clothes. He was so disorientated by this last attack that he believed himself to be in a mental hospital in Dublin.

The money Brendan secured from his various advances had now dwindled to almost nothing. An approach to his bank for the money to go home produced only a blank communiction from the manager: 'Mr Behan's account is not in funds'. Luckily, Beatrice remembered an uncashed cheque for royalties for *The Hostage* that she had secreted in her handbag for an eventuality such as this. Rae Jeffs and the Behans secured tickets for the *Queen Elizabeth* to Southampton and, on 3 July, they sailed for England. Brendan stayed sober for his last few days in New York. He confessed to Beatrice that he believed he would never return there again. During the sailing, Brendan had to be removed from the dining-room after he became obnoxiously insulting to his fellow diners. Beatrice abandoned her post, and sat finishing her pudding, leaving Rae Jeffs to get him to his cabin. There, an officer, ironically confusing him with another famous Irishman, the late First Lord of the Admiralty and wartime Minister for Information in Churchill's cabinet, addressed him as 'Mr Brendan Bracken.' On arrival at Southampton, the Behans went on to London where Brendan undid all the good which his last few sober days in New York had achieved. He signed a contract with Hutchinson for a companion volume to *Brendan Behan's Island*. It was to be his panegyric on New York, illustrated by Paul Hogarth and called *Brendan Behan's New York*. It would be the last of his tape-recorded books.

By late July, he was back in Dublin. John Ryan saw a great deal of him on his return. Indeed, Ryan's bar and restaurant, The Bailey, on Duke Street, was one of the few places where he knew he was welcome. Ryan recalled those last days in The Bailey:

> One would have to rifle the annals of Bacchus to find a more determined nuisance in drink. If he wasn't falling on you and spilling drinks over you, he was mauling your wife or girlfriend to the accompaniment of an unbroken dirge of truly 'foul' language. He would punch and claw you if he felt you weren't giving him one hundred per cent attention – not the easiest thing to mime when you were hearing some story you had heard a million times before.

Ryan's tolerance was impressive. One day, feeling that the clientele of The Bailey was ignoring him, Brendan stood on a stool and exposed his genitals.

Even the publication of *Hold Your Hour And Have Another* in September did not seem to give him any joy. He did not seem to care about the many good notices it received. His contribution to the book had been very little – it was Rae Jeffs who made the selection of articles and bashed it into a publishable text. Brendan rarely spoke about these taped books in Dublin. He knew that behind his back the literary gossips had dismissed him as a washed-up writer. John Ryan remembered him being thoroughly ashamed of resorting to speaking his books into a tape-recorder. 'They require their pound of flesh,' he told Ryan, 'and I suppose I owe it to them'.

Friends now fled when they saw him entering a pub. Even the 'touchers' – the bums who hung about with him just on the off-chance of getting a free drink – began to grow weary of him. Of the few genuine friends who did stand by him, one of the most loyal was Bill Finnegan, a former barber turned taxi-driver. Finnegan collected him in the morning from Anglesea Road and drove him wherever he wished to go. What is more important, he delivered him back home at night and helped Beatrice put him to bed.

But, in these last months, he relied most of all on the friendship of his old IRA colleagues. The literary society he had worked so hard to become a part of had rejected him, but these few IRA men still found time for him. He had never completely abandoned them during his years of fame. To them he remained much as they had always seen him – a brother-in-arms who had served the cause, if perhaps, a little naïvely. These men included Mattie O'Neill, Cathal Goulding, Paddy Whelan, Paddy Kelly, Liam Brady, Charlie Gorman, Mick Kelly and Paddy Collins. They were prepared to ignore his boasting about his glory days in London and New York, and the vast sums of money he had earned there. His name-dropping e.g. 'As Norman Mailer, Arthur Miller, Groucho Marx said to me' cut very little ice with these men.

At the end of August 1963, Rae Jeffs came to Dublin to begin taping the New York book. Within two months, they had recorded the substance of it. As had become the established practice, his faithful editor was left to make sense out of a mass of often incoherent rambling. Thanks to Jeffs' persistence the book came out but, like *Confessions of an Irish Rebel*, it was not published until after his death.

Between November and Christmas, it became clear to Beatrice that if Brendan was to live, even just a few more years, something quite drastic had to be done. Treatment for alcoholic disorders was still in its infancy in Ireland and it was rare for people with drink problems to commit themselves to institutions for treatment. A horrible disgrace was attached to committal for the treatment of any form of addiction. However, friends advised Beatrice that she had no other option but to commit him. It required her signature and that of three doctors. Beatrice had already been forced by circumstances to sign papers committing her father, Cecil, to an institution for treatment for drug and alcohol abuse. She had no other option open to her, and she knew her father would benefit from the treatment. Brendan was a different matter. When he learnt of the possibility that she might commit him to an institution he told her: 'If you do that, and I come out alive, that day I will drink myself to death'. That comment made up her mind to the inescapable. All she could do with the aid of his then doctor, Terence Chapman, was to make him as comfortable as she possibly could until the inevitable happened.

From November to Christmas, Brendan had few intervals of sobriety. On 7 November he was back in hospital in Dublin. This time, he stayed for a week. A particularly low point came with the assassination of John F. Kennedy on 22 November. Brendan was in The Bailey with John Ryan and Anthony and Thérèse Cronin when they heard the news on the wireless. The instant the announcement was made, he ordered a taxi to the American Embassy. The next day, the morning papers reported that, amongst the first to sign the book of condolence, was the author Brendan Behan.

The following day, 24 November, Beatrice gave birth to a baby girl in the Rotunda Hospital. Brendan went to the hospital every day, sometimes smuggling in bottles of Guinness for Beatrice. She stayed in hospital until the first week of December and even then she asked if she could stay on a few more days. The baby was christened in St Andrew's Church, Westland Row, where both Brendan and Beatrice had themselves been christened. They named the little girl Blanaid, after her grandmother, Blanaid ffrench-Salkeld. Brendan arrived at the end of the ceremony. Rae Jeffs was god-mother. Brendan gave a celebratory luncheon party in the bourgeois environs of The Dolphin Hotel. He was still in a theatrically sombre mood after the death of Kennedy. There could hardly have been a person in Dublin who met him in the days following the shooting that he did not tell of how the great man had invited him to his official inauguration. The invitation card remained on the mantelpiece of 5 Anglesea Road, even though he had not attended the event.

If his behaviour towards the memory of the great was respectful, his behaviour towards his wife was despicable. He treated Beatrice in a way that no human being could reasonably be expected to tolerate. His nastiness manifested itself most openly when other people were in the house. Ian Stuart, who had wanted to marry Beatrice, called at 5 Anglesea Road one evening to visit her and to see the new baby. When Brendan discovered who was there he shouted to her from his bed: 'Come upstairs, and cut my fucking toe-nails.' That was one of his more moderate outbursts.[12]

Beatrice left the maternity ward a determined woman. She decided that her first concern must now be her baby. Brendan had to be prepared to take second place. Dr Terence Chapman came to the house every morning to give him an insulin injection. Some days Brendan was there, other days he was not. As Christmas approached, it became increasingly obvious to Beatrice that second place in the Behan household was not a position Brendan was willing to assume. He absented himself completely during Christmas week and spent his time distributing large sums of cash and drink to the many free-loaders to be readily found in Dublin pubs. On Christmas Eve, Beatrice received a message to say Brendan had been taken to Baggot Street Hospital in a comatose state. When she visited him on Christmas Day, he had just been given Extreme Unction – the last rites of the Roman Catholic Church.

21

The Final Curtain

On New Year's Eve 1963, Beatrice Behan celebrated her 38th birthday. Half-a-dozen of her friends called to her house to mark the occasion. At midnight she looked at her watch and said to her guests, 'Well, Brendan has missed it, but he'll be home soon.' Her power to put a brave face on a truly desperate situation astounded even her closest friends. Brendan was gravely ill and he had been missing for more than two days. He had discharged himself from hospital on 29 December, on the pretext that he was unable to sleep there. Three staff doctors went searching for him in the nearby pubs but were unable to find him. He had made his way to his parents' house in Crumlin where his mother put him to bed. During the night he stumbled out on to the roadside and some hours later a neighbour found him lying in a pool of blood. His head had a large open wound from which he had lost quite a lot of blood.

On New Year's morning 1964, Beatrice Behan was wakened by a loud knocking at her door. The police had come to inform her that Brendan had been taken to the Meath Hospital. At the hospital, he was unable to tell her, or the police, what had happened. Beatrice refused to believe that someone in Crumlin, where his family lived, could have beaten him up. He may have been mugged, because it was known that he carried large wads of cash on him; alternatively he may have fallen. The cause of his injury remains an unsolved mystery. On top of his other medical problems, he had developed pneumonia. In a groggy voice and heavily sedated he turned to Beatrice and said: 'We'll be happy again'. Just a short time before, he had told Rae Jeffs that he regretted causing Beatrice so much pain. He said he felt he had married a gentle soul who had become hardened by nine years of marriage to him. After all the suffering, Beatrice still felt great warmth and compassion for him as she recalled in her autobiography:

> I cried in bed at night, no longer comforted by the warm presence of
> Brendan beside me. If he did come into the house he would sleep

downstairs on the sofa or in the small return room off the landing. I clung desperately to the last vestiges of our marriage. When you have loved a man, and when you have experienced the joys of giving, it is hard to accept the cold, cruel detachment that is the enemy of love.

Contrary to all medical prediction, he rallied again and discharged himself from hospital. Dublin pub gossips daily expected the news of his death. He astounded the bar flies and others by walking, albeit shakily, into The Bailey.

Dr Chapman told Beatrice that even at this late juncture it was possible to save Brendan if he would agree to stop drinking and undergo treatment. When the doctor suggested further treatment, Brendan just shrugged his shoulders and said: 'Alcoholics die of alcohol'.

A tax bill for £8,000 was hanging over his head and causing him considerable anguish. 'They banned *Borstal Boy* and now they want money for it. They object to my work and now they want my morally tainted money', he would scream with incredulity. For most of February and March, Beatrice saw him only intermittently. In the middle of February she was walking near Baggot Street when she heard him calling her. She turned to find him in a taxi with Desmond Mackey, their friend from Ibiza days. 'Come to the mountains' he appealed to her, 'we're going on a skite'. She felt she could have been talking to a stranger and reminded him that they had a baby at home and then walked on.

He talked incessantly about returning to New York to finish his book on that city. Rae Jeffs had gone back to London. Without her there was no question of doing any work on anything, not even on a short article he was asked to write as a tribute to John F. Kennedy.

On the evening of 10 March, Beatrice was at home listening to the wireless. She answered a sharp knock at the door and when she opened it saw Brendan slouched in the back of a taxi. His friends Paddy Kelly and Charlie Joe Gorman brought him home as they had often done before. Beatrice took one look at him and ordered the taxi to take him straight to the nearest hospital. He was brought to the Meath. The hospital was aware of his record from the previous admission. They decided to put him on peritoneal dialysis immediately. This was before the days of kidney machine dialysis. Peritoneal dialysis involved introducing a saline solution into the abdominal cavity with the intention of reducing the urea content. It was not a comfortable procedure for the patient.

Beatrice believed he would revive, as he had done so many times, in so many hospitals. A young doctor who seemed shocked at the number of times Brendan had been admitted to hospital took Beatrice aside and told her he thought it unlikely that he would leave hospital this time because he was so seriously ill. She had heard it all before and refused to accept that his resilience would not see him through yet another crisis.

Between his admission on 10 March and his final critical moments on 20 March, he slipped in and out of coma several times. He became incontinent from 12 March and on 17 March, Dr H.I. Browne inserted a dialytic catheter to help with the problem. He became extremely agitated after the minor operation and was given Paraldehyde to calm him down.

It has been suggested that someone smuggled a bottle of brandy into the hospital for him and it was that which finally killed him. The blood tests done on him in his last days do not show the presence of alcohol but then no specific test for alcohol was made. Beatrice recalled a friend of Brendan's coming to her in tears and begging her forgiveness for having brought the brandy in. However, from Brendan's condition as indicated on the medical records, it would have been necessary to force feed him the brandy because he certainly was in no condition to sit up and drink it. It is quite likely that it was intercepted by staff at the hospital.

Just before lunchtime on 20 March, Beatrice received a telephone call from the hospital advising her to come as quickly as possible. A tracheotomy had been performed at 1.30 p.m. the previous day to ease his breathing. Even though he was unconscious and the doctors held out no hope for him, Beatrice persuaded herself that she had seen him in worse states and that it was only a matter of time before he rallied around again. His temperature began to rise from normal to nearly 103°F at 6 p.m. that evening. At 8.15 p.m. his condition began to deteriorate rapidly. At 8.35 p.m. he was pronounced dead. His Death Certificate records the cause of death as 'Hepatic Coma /Fatty Degeneration of the Liver'. In simple language, he died of alcohol abuse. He had lived a month into his forty-first year.

Beatrice was at his bedside at the end. His parents, who had kept up a near constant vigil at his bedside, had been there that afternoon with John Ryan. Kathleen told Ryan she believed her son would not last beyond that day. They went to The Bailey to rest and have a drink. The hospital called them to say that Brendan had died and they went immediately to Baggot Street. His last words, like most such recorded death bed utterances, may well be apocryphal but they have the ring of a true Behanism. When a kindly nun adjusted his pillows and wished him God's blessings, he is said to have opened one eye and whispered: 'Thank you, sister, and may you be the mother of a Bishop'.

In a city of Dublin's size, news travels fast. Within half an hour, a crowd had gathered outside the hospital. The artist James Power arrived to make a death mask. The morning newspapers conclusively proved his often-quoted dictum that the only bad publicity is one's own obituary. Every major newspaper in the world reported his death and the obituaries were of a theme. They generally began 'Wild boy of Irish letters is dead' and invariably, as these things usually do, hailed him as a thoroughly decent fellow.

His body was removed to the parish church at Donnybrook where he and Beatrice had been married. On Monday 23 March, the once-excommunicated IRA man was given the full dignity and ceremonial of a Roman Catholic burial. The funeral Mass was attended by the titled, the untitled, the famous and the unknown. Rae Jeffs, her daughter Diana and Joan Littlewood came from London. Jacqueline Sundstrom came from Paris. The City of Dublin was represented by the Lord Mayor, the President by his ADC, the Government by the Deputy Prime Minister. The distinctive white head dress of his favourite nuns, the Sisters of Charity, showed above the crowd. Christy Browne, the author of *My Left Foot*, was there in his wheelchair. Carolyn Swift, who was amongst the first to express her belief in his talent was also there. His friends Garech Browne and Lord Gormanston arrived a little late just as he would have expected.

As the Mass ended, a group of his IRA comrades slipped quietly up towards the tricolour covered coffin to act as honour guard and pall-bearers. Outside, the cold March sun shone brightly as the cortège moved off towards Glasnevin Cemetery. Respectful citizens lined the city streets, watching in silence as the hearse passed. So legendary was his generosity in his final years that one old Dublin lady said aloud as the hearse passed: 'Well, the poor of Dublin can go back to work now'.

At Glasnevin, the scene of his reckless shooting incident in 1942, his great friend, Mattie O'Neill, gave the oration:

> There was life throbbing in every vein of him. It is heartbreaking to see
> all that gaiety and all that bravery going under the soil at Glasnevin.
> His memory will be green as long as Dublin lies on the Liffey.

Then, the tiny figure of fourteen-year-old Peter McNulty, a member of Brendan's old Republican youth movement, Fianna Éireann, stepped forward at the head of the grave and sounded *The Last Post* and *Réveille*. The mourners filed away in silence leaving a distressed Beatrice to her thoughts. Later on, an IRA honour party stood at either side of the freshly covered grave and fired the traditional salute over it. The wheel had come full circle and the organisation to which he had dedicated his youth, claimed him back in death as one of their own.

By a curious coincidence, later that day, Carolyn Swift sold the old Pike Theatre, the scene of the triumph that had launched him on the world literary stage.

When John Ryan came back privately to look at his dead friend's grave, he reflected how time would take up Brendan Behan's theme, tone it down into history and, later, embroider it as legend. And so it was.

Bibliography

1.   THE PUBLISHED WRITINGS OF BRENDAN BEHAN

The dates are those of first publication.

The Quare Fellow (London: Methuen, 1956).
Borstal Boy (London: Hutchinson, 1958).
The Hostage (London: Methuen, 1958).
Brendan Behan's Island; An Irish Sketchbook (London: Hutchinson, 1962).
Hold Your Hour And Have Another ((London: Hutchinson, 1963).
The Scarperer (New York: Doubleday, 1964).
Brendan Behan's New York (London: Hutchinson, 1964).
Confessions of an Irish Rebel (London: Hutchinson, 1965).
Poems And Stories (Dublin: The Liffey Press, 1978).
The Complete Plays (London: Methuen, 1978).
After the Wake (Dublin: O'Brien Press, 1981).

2.   PRIMARY SOURCES

The present author was the first to have access to three important sources of primary material which relate to Brendan Behan's prison years. The most valuable has been the many unpublished letters written from Borstal and prisons in England and Ireland and contained in files in the British Home Office. Other important material includes medical reports, psychological assessments, reports by prison and Borstal officials and these have proved invaluable in writing the first complete account of Behan's years in jail based on such source material. The locations are as follows:

The Home Office

Queen Anne's Gate, London. The Home Office has three substantial files on Behan which cover the period 1939 to 1958. The author saw the material in the Home Office but there were plans to remove it to the Public Records Office at Kew. An important file, containing many unpublished letters from Borstal, was to have remained closed until the year 2007, but the Home Office kindly agreed to allow access to it. It was then decided that all restrictions on the file should be lifted.

Military Intelligence (G2)

Military Archives, Cathal Brugha Barracks, Rathmines, Dublin. The file on Behan was opened in 1939 and closed in 1968 (four years after his death). Again, like the Home Office files these contain many unpublished letters and documents which relate to Behan's incarceration in Mountjoy, Arbour Hill and the Curragh. These files were especially useful in compiling an account of Behan's IRA activities in Ireland.

Department of Justice

St Stephen's Green, Dublin. The department files are extremely important because they contain, *inter alia*, the correspondence between Behan and department officials relating to Behan's efforts to have his writings published while he was in prison in Ireland.

Other collections:

The following institutions have holdings of Behan manuscripts, letters, recordings or related material: The National Library of Ireland, The Abbey Theatre, The Library of Trinity College Dublin, The Library of University College Cork, The National Archives Dublin, The Morris Library, University of Southern Illinois at Carbondale, The Public Records Office London, Suffolk Record Office Ipswich, BBC Archives, RTÉ Archives.

3.   DISCOGRAPHY

The Quare Fellow, Spoken Word A-24.
The Hostage, Columbia DOL 329/DOP 729.
Brendan Behan: Irish Folk Songs and Ballads, Spoken Arts SA 760.

4.   SELECT BIBLIOGRAPHY OF SECONDARY SOURCES

For an extremely comprehensive annotated bibliography of criticism see EH Mikhail, *Brendan Behan: An Annotated Bibliography of Criticism* (London: Macmillan, 1980).

BOOKS

Arthurs, Peter, *With Brendan Behan* (New York: St. Martin's Press, 1981).
Bair, Deirdre, *Samuel Beckett: A Biography* (New York: Harcourt, 1978).
Behan, Beatrice, *My Life With Brendan* (London: Leslie Frewin, 1965).
Behan, Brian, *With Breast Expanded* (London: MacGibbon and Key, 1964).
Behan, Dominic, *My Brother Brendan* (London: Leslie Frewin, 1961).
Behan, Kathleen, with Brian Behan, *Mother of All the Behans* (London: Hutchinson 1984).
Bowyer Bell, J., *The Secret Army: The IRA 1916-1979* (Dublin: Poolbeg Press, 1989).
Boyle, Ted E., *Brendan Behan* (New York: Twayne Publishers, 1969).
Brown, Terence, *Ireland: A Social and Cultural History 1222-1985* (London: Fontana, 1981).
Carlson, Julia (Editor), *Banned In Ireland* (London: Routledge, 1990).
Cronin, Anthony, *Dead As Doornails* (Dublin: Dolmen Press, 1976).
Cronin, Anthony, *The Life of Riley* (London: Panther, 1964).
Cronin, Anthony, *Samuel Beckett: The Last Modernist* (London: Harper Collins, 1996).
de Burca, Seamus, *Brendan Behan: A Memoir* (Dublin: Proscenium Press, 1971).
Eachach, Vivian Uibh and O Faoláin Donal (Editors) *Felie Zozimus: Brendan Behan* (Volume 2), (Dublin: Gael-Linn, 1993).
Esslin, Martin, *An Anatomy of Drama* (London: Maurice Temple Smith, 1976).
Farson, Daniel, *Sacred Monsters* (London: Bloomsbury, 1988).
Fitz-Simon, Christopher, *The Boys: A Biography of Micheal MacLiammoir and Hilton Edwards* (London: Nick Hearn Books, 1994).
Foley, Conor, *Legion of the Rearguard: The IRA and the Modern Irish State* (London: Pluto Press, 1992).
Gerdes, Peter R, *The Major Works of Brendan Behan*. (Bern: Herbert Lang; Frankfurt: Peter Lang, 1973).
Harmon, Maurice, *Seán O'Faoláin: A Life* (London: Constable, 1994).
Hosey, Seamus (Editor), *Speaking Volumes* (Dublin: RTÉ/Blackwater Press, 1994).

Inglis, Brian, *Downstart: An Autobiography* (London: Chatto & Windus, 1990).

Jeffs, Rae, *Brendan Behan: Man and Showman* (London: Hutchinson, 1966).

Joyce, C.A., *By Courtesy of the Criminal* (London: Harap, 1955).

Kearney, Colbert, *The Writings of Brendan Behan* (Dublin: Gill & Macmillan, 1977).

Kearns, Kevin C. *Dublin Pub Life & Lore* (Dublin: Gill & Macmillan, 1996).

Keogh, Dermot, *Twentieth-Century Ireland: Nation and State* (Dublin: Gill & Macmillan, 1994).

Kiberd, Declan, *Inventing Ireland: The Literature of The Modern Nation* (London: Jonathan Cape, 1995).

Littlewood, Joan, *Joan's Book: Joan Littlewood's Peculiar History As She Tells It* (London: Methuen, 1994).

MacEoin, Uinseann, *The IRA in the Twilight Years, 1923-1948* (Dublin, 1997).

McCann, Sean, (Editor), *The Wit of Brendan Behan* (London: Leslie Frewin, 1969).

McCann, Sean, (Editor), *The World of Brendan Behan* (London: New English Library, 1965).

MacLiammóir, Micheal, *Theatre In Ireland* (Dublin: Cultural Relations Committee of Ireland, 1964).

Mikhail, E.H., *Brendan Behan: Interviews and Recollections* (2 Vols.) (London: Macmillan, 1982).

Mikhail, E.H., *The Letters of Brendan Behan* (London: Macmillan, 1992).

Norman, Diana, *Terrible Beauty: A Life of Constance Markievicz* (London: Hodder and Stoughton, 1987).

O'Connor, Ulick, *Brendan Behan* (London: Hamish Hamilton, 1970).

Porter, Raymond J., *Brendan Behan* (New York & London: Columbia Press, 1973).

Rose, A.G., *Five Hundred Borstal Boys* (Oxford: Blackwell, 1954).

Ryan, John, *Remembering How We Stood* (Dublin: The Lilliput Press, 1987).

Smith, M.L.R., *Fighting for Ireland: The Military Strategy of the IRA* (London: Routledge, 1995).

Simpson, Alan, *Beckett and Behan and a Theatre in Dublin* (London: Routledge, 1962).

Swift, Carolyn, *Stage by Stage* (Dublin: Poolbeg Press, 1985).

White, Edmund, *Genet* (London: Chatto & Windus, 1993).

NEWSPAPERS AND PERIODICALS

The Bell

Envoy

The Dublin Magazine

Points (Paris)

The Irish Times

Sunday Press

Irish Press

Sunday Independent

The Times (London)

Fianna (Magazine of Fianna Éireann)

The United Irishman

The Irish Democrat

The Daily Worker

The New York Times

The People

The Daily Mail

The Daily Express

New Statesman

The Spectator

Guardian

Irish Digest

L'Express (Paris)

Veckojurnalem (Stockholm)

Manchester Evening News

Globe and Mail (Toronto)

The Montrealer

Washington Post

Evening Press

Evening Herald

Commonweal (New York)

Globe Magazine (Toronto)

New York Herald Tribune

Theatre Arts (New York)

Pike Newsletter (Dublin)

Observer (London)

Newsweek

Time

Footnotes

Chapter 1 – Granny's Boy

* **NOTE**: The author's interviews cited herein took place, mainly, over the period 1992-1997. They have not been given specific dates because, in most cases, the initial contact was sustained until the time of publication, by further meetings, telephone calls and letters. Information was repeated, confirmed and supplemented as the author became better acquainted with his sources.

1. According to a marriage certificate held at the General Record Office, Kathleen and Stephen Behan were married on 28 July 1922.
2. Kathleen's brother was Peader Kearney, author of the Irish National Anthem, *The Soldiers Song*; Kathleen Behan, with Brian Behan, *Mother of all the Behans*, Poolbeg, (Dublin), 1994, p. 37.
3. Cathal Goulding, 'Kathleen Behan, An Appreciation', *The Irish Times*.
4. Kathleen Behan, with Brian Behan, *Mother of all the Behans*, pp. 37-43.
5. *Author's interview with Seán Furlong.
6. Painting now in the National Gallery of Ireland. See John O'Grady, *The Life and Work of Sarah Purser*, Fourcourts Press, (Dublin), 1997.
7. Bob Bradshaw, 'Early Behan: Republican Life in the Dublin of the '30s and '40s', *The Irish Times,* 9 July 1970, p. 12.
8. Kathleen Behan, with Brian Behan, *Mother of all the Behans, p. 51.*
9. Seamus de Burca, *Brendan Behan: A Memoir,* privately published, (Dublin), 1993, p.7.
10. *Author's interview with Seamus Behan.
11. He is said to have attended either the diocesan seminary at Knockbeg in County Carlow or the Jesuit seminary at Tullabeg in County Offaly but an extensive search of the records of both institutions has failed to establish a connection with either seminary. I am grateful to Rev Fr Stephen Redmond SJ, for his kind assistance.
12. Ulick O'Connor, *Brendan Behan,* Hamish Hamilton, (London), 1970, p.13.
13. All births, marriage and death dates for Brendan Behan's family used herein have been checked against relevant official documentation held at the General Record Office in Dublin.
14. Colbert Kearney, *The Writings of Brendan Behan,* Gill & Macmillan, (Dublin), 1977, p.4.
15. Ibid.
16. The family believed that Christina English did not establish her property empire until after her second husband's death. However, Patrick English's death certificate, which shows him dying at number 13 Russell Street suggests that the empire was already growing before his demise.
17. Kathleen Behan, with Brian Behan, *Mother of all the Behans*, p. 52.
18. Ibid., p.53

19. Ibid.
20. Brian Behan, *With Breast Expanded,* MacGibbon and Kee, (London), 1964, p. 12.
21. The street now contains a block of corporation flats called 'Brendan Behan House'.
22. Dominic Behan, *Teems of Times and Happy Returns,* Heineman, (London), 1961, p. 53.
23. Ibid., p.55.
24. Kathleen Behan, with Brian Behan, *Mother of all the Behans,* p. 60.
25. Brendan Behan, *The Confirmation Suit,* (first published), *The Standard,* Easter 1953, p. 5, reprinted in *Brendan Behan's Island, An Irish Sketchbook,* Hutchinson, (London), 1962, pp. 147-153.
26. Brendan Behan, *Brendan Behan's Island, An Irish Sketchbook,* p. 148.
27. Brian Behan, *Spectator,* CCXIII, 17 July 1964, pp. 77-79.
28. Colbert Kearney, *The Writings of Brendan Behan,* p. 11.
29. Seán McCann (Editor), *The World of Brendan Behan,* New English Library, (London), 1965, p. 56.
30. *Author's interview with Brian Behan.
31. Brendan Behan's Birth Certificate from Number 4 District of the Superintendent Registrar's District of Dublin, entry number 158 shows his father's place of address as 79 McCaffrey's Estate, the Mount Browne home of Kathleen's brother Peadar Kearney. This was most likely used as an address from which Stephen would not be traced when he left Kilmainham Jail. Brendan Behan's own more colourful account is given in *Brendan Behan's Island, An Irish Sketchbook,* p. 14.
32. Alan Simpson (Editor), *Behan: The Complete Plays,* Methuen, (London), 1995, p. 202.
33. Anthony Cronin, *Dead as Doornails,* Poolbeg, (Dublin), 1976, p. 7.

Chapter 2 – Northside Childhood

1.   Kathleen Behan, with Brian Behan, *Mother of all the Behans,* pp. 59-60
2.   Brendan Behan, *Confessions of an Irish Rebel,* Hutchinson, (London), 1985, p. 88.
3.   No official record for the child exists.
4.   *Author's interview with Seamus Behan.
5.   Kathleen Behan, with Brian Behan, *Mother of all the Behans,* p. 52
6.   This document is considered later in this chapter.
7.   Dominic Behan, *Teems of Times and Happy Returns,* p. 99.
8.   *Author's interview with Seamus Behan.
9.   Same interview.
10. Same interview; Also, see Brendan Behan, *Borstal Boy,* Hutchinson, (London), 1958, p. 27.
11. Brendan Behan, *Borstal Boy,* p. 27
12. Ibid.
13. Dublin slang for 'girlfriend'.
14. Brendan Behan, *Borstal Boy,* p. 27
15. Seamus de Burca, *Brendan Behan: A Memoir,* pp. 40-41.
16. Brendan Behan, *Hold Your Hour and Have Another,* Hutchinson, (London), 1963, pp. 85-86.
17. Ibid.
18. Ulick O'Connor, *Brendan Behan,* p. 25.
19. For a portrait of Stephen Behan, see Seamus de Burca, *Brendan Behan: A Memoir.*
20. *Author's interview with Seamus Behan.
21. List compiled from Cobert Kearney, *The Writings of Brendan Behan;* Seamus de

Burca, *Brendan Behan: A Memoir*; and *author's interview with Cathal Goulding.

22. Brendan Behan, *Borstal Boy*, p. 80.
23. *Author's interview with Cathal Goulding.
24. *Author's interview with Brian Behan.
25. Seamus de Burca, *Brendan Behan: A Memoir*, p. 10.
26. Patrick J Bourke (1883-1932), born in Dublin. Formed his own theatre company and acted in his own plays. Wrote and performed one of the first full-length feature films made in Ireland, *Ireland a Nation* (1913).
27. For a list of other productions which Behan may have seen at the Queen's, see Seamus de Burca, *Brendan Behan: A Memoir*, p. 12.
28. *Author's interview with Seamus Behan.
29. See Leon Ó Broin, *The Unfortunate Mr Robert Emmett*, 1958.
30. Bob Bradshaw, *Early Behan, The Irish Times*, 9 July 1970, p. 12.
31. Kathleen Behan, with Brian Behan, *Mother of all the Behans*, p. 64; Ulick O'Connor, *Brendan Behan*, p. 21.
32. *Author's interview with Brian Behan.
33. Recalled by Brian Behan.
34. Ulick O'Connor, *Brendan Behan*, p. 21.
35. Brian Behan, *With Breast Expanded*, p. 13.
36. Peter Fallon (editor), *Red Jam Roll, the Dancer, After the Wake*, O'Brien Press, (Dublin), 1981, p. 103.
37. Ibid., p. 104.
38. Date taken from the Register of St Vincent's school. I am grateful to Sr May Nyhan, Principal, and Ms Beverley Tormey, school secretary, for access to St Vincent's School records.
39. Brendan Behan, 'The School by the Canal', *Irish Press*, [n.d.].
40. Ibid.
41. Ibid.
42. *Author's interview with Sr Louise of the Sisters of Charity, Dublin.
43. *Author's interview with Michael Coogan.
44. Brendan Behan, 'The School by the Canal', *Irish Press*, [n.d.].
45. There are variants of this story. Kathleen, in her autobiography, says she was told she was 'rearing a genius' but the more moderate language used in Sr Louise's story seems more likely. See Kathleen Behan, with Brian Behan, *Mother of all the Behans*, p. 75; and Ulick O'Connor, *Brendan Behan*, p. 23.
46. St Vincent's school register.
47. Brendan Behan, *Hold Your Hour and Have Another*, pp. 191-192.
48. Brendan Behan, *Borstal Boy*, p. 340.
49. *The Irish Times*, 21 March 1964, p. 9.
50. Ibid.
51. An inner city area near Behan's home.
52. Brendan Behan, *Hold Your Hour And Have Another*, p. 95.
53. *The Irish Democrat* (Dublin) I, Number 32, 6 November 1937, p. 3; also see EH Mikhail, *Letters of Brendan Behan*, pp. 7-8.
54. Recollections of Ms Bred Costello and Brother O'Donnell, *The Irish Times*, 21 March 1964, p. 9.
55. Ulick O'Connor, *Brendan Behan*, p. 23.
56. *The Irish Times*, 21 March 1964, p. 9.
57. Cobert Kearney, *The Writings of Brendan Behan*, p. 14.
58. *The Irish Democrat* as cited in footnote 53.

59. Author's interview with Cathal Goulding.
60. Ulick O'Connor, *Brendan Behan,* p. 17.
61. EH Mikhail, *Letters of Brendan Behan*, Macmillan, (London), 1992, p. 5.
62. Beatrice Behan, *My Life with Brendan,* Leslie Frewin, (London), 1973, p. 72.
63. Born Constance Gore-Booth, 1868-1927, daughter of an Anglo-Irish family from County Sligo. She became the first woman in Europe to hold a ministerial portfolio.
64. J Boyer Bell, *The Secret Army: The IRA 1916-1979*, Poolbeg, (Dublin), 1990, p. 16.
65. *Fianna,* (Wolf Tone Commemoration Number), Volume 1, Number 1, June 1922; Ulick O'Connor, *Brendan Behan, p. 23.*
66. Seamus G O'Kelly, 'I knew the real Brendan Behan', *Irish Digest,* (Dublin), LXXVIII, Number 12, June 1964, pp 67-70, *The Irish Times,* 21 March 1964, p. 9.
67. Ibid., p. 67.
68. *Author's interview with Cathal Goulding.
69. Seamus G O'Kelly, 'I knew the real Brendan Behan', *Irish Digest,* (Dublin), LXXVIII, Number 12, June 1994.
70. *Fianna,* October 1935 – June 1936, p. 130.
71. Professor Colbert Kearney was the first to observe this; See *The Writings of Brendan Behan, p. 21.*
72. Brendan Behan, *Confessions of an Irish Rebel,* p. 209.
73. See Ulick O'Connor, *Brendan Behan,* p. 32; also Seamus G. O'Kelly, *Irish Digest,* (Dublin), LXXVIII, Number 12, June 1964, pp. 67-70.
74. Brian Behan, *With Breast Expanded,* p. 16.
75. Dominic Behan, *Teems of Times and Happy Returns,* p. 141.
76. Ibid.
77. Dominic Behan, *My Brother Brendan,* Leslie Frewin, (London), 1961, pp. 14-15.
78. Information from Brendan Behan's prison medical file.
79. Kulak is a nineteenth-century Russian village term meaning 'tight-fisted'.
80. Same interview.
81. Same interview.
82. Kathleen Behan, with Brian Behan, *Mother of all the Behans,* pp. 89-90.
83. Brian Behan, *With Breast Expanded*, p. 23.
84. Kathleen Behan, with Brian Behan, *Mother of all the Behans*, p. 90.
85. Ibid., p. 92.
86. Brian Behan, *With Breast Expanded*, p. 23.
87. Census of Population in 1936.
88. Reported by John Ryan, owner of The Bailey, founder of *Envoy* magazine, painter and writer.
89. Kathleen Behan, with Brian Behan, *Mother of all the Behans*, p. 97.
90. Ibid., p. 93.
91. Dominic Behan, *My Brother Brendan,* p. 31.
92. *Author's interview with Cathal Goulding.
93. Same interview.
94. *Wolfe Tone Weekly,* 4 September 1937, p. 7.
95. The date of publication is sometimes incorrectly given as *The United Irishman,* May 1938. *The United Irishman* had ceased publication at this time.
96. *Wolfe Tone Weekly,* 24 December 1938, p. 7. The other two stanzas of the poem are:

Proudly they step forward to face the traitors' guns,
O, Ireland, pain is thine tonight but pride in these thy sons,
Four volleys from the rifles held by the green-clad foe,

Speed unto God the souls of Rory, Liam, Dick and Joe.
Dear Mother, thou art weeping, but gaze not at the night,
See, where morning's crimson rays give hope to Freedom's fight.
And listen to the breezes sigh their message.

Chapter 3 – Boy and IRA Man

1.   *Author's interviews with Cathal Goulding, Seán Furlong, Seamus Behan and Paddy Whelan.
2.   *Daily Express,* 19 February 1940
3.   Ulick O'Connor, *Brendan Behan, p. 36*
4.   *Author's interview with Cathal Goulding.
5.   Brendan Behan, *Confessions of an Irish Rebel.*
6.   See examples of such letters in Chapter 4.
7.   *Author's interview with Seamus Behan.
8.   Same interview.
9.   Same interview.
10. Reprinted in *Wolfe Tone Weekly,* 23 August 1939, p. 1.
11. Ulick O'Connor, *Brendan Behan,* p. 41.
12. Home Office file P.Com 9/1907.
13. *Interview with Seamus Behan.
14. From list of personal belongings in Home Office file P.Com 9/1907.
15. A letter dated 23 January 1940 apologises to a friend for not being able to see him as arranged because he had to 'seize the opportunity while there was no watch on the North Wall'. It indicates that he had made a few trips back and forth to the port, to investigate the police presence there. Home Office file 45/25068.
16. I am extremely grateful to Mr Gerry Daly of Dublin Port and Docks Board for making this information available to me. There was no sailing to Liverpool from Dublin on 1 December and the next sailing of the Lairdscastle on 2 December would not accord with the details of Behan's arrest on 1 December.
17. Russell's travel permit number 37315 was issued on 28 November 1939. In a letter written soon after his arrest Brendan confirmed that he travelled under the name 'Peter Russell'. The police report on the missing document – a valuable wartime item – confirms that Russell was not known to be a member or have any involvement with the IRA and that the document was stolen from his coat. Extensive correspondence relating to the document in the Department of Justice files on Behan.
18. Brendan Behan, *Borstal Boy,* p. 9.
19. Ibid., p. 10.
20. Ibid., p. 9.
21. Information contained in a suppressed letter to an unidentified friend. Home Office file 45/25068.
22. Brendan Behan, *Borstal Boy,* p. 12.
23. Ibid., p. 13.
24. Ibid.
25. Home Office file P.Com 9/1907.
26. Brendan Behan, *Borstal Boy, p. 76.*
27. Home Office file P.Com 9/1907.
28. Brendan Behan, *Borstal Boy,* p. 76,
29. Medical report in Home Office file P.Com 9/1907.
30. Seán McCann (Editor), *The Wit of Brendan Behan,* Leslie Frewin, (London), 1969, p. 86.

31.　*Author's interview with Brian Behan.
32.　Ulick O'Connor, *Brendan Behan,* pp. 48-9.
33.　Brendan Behan, *Borstal Boy*, p. 61.
34.　Home Office file P.Com 9/1907.
35.　Stephen gave his employer as: C Goulding, 15 Cadogan Road, Dublin.
36.　Report of J Holt, Governor, HM Prison Walton dated 25 January 1940. Home Office file P. Com 9/1907.
37.　Memo from Principal Warder to Governor in Home Office file P.Com 9/1907.
38.　Suppressed letter dated 13 December, Home Office file P.Com 9/1907.
39.　Ibid.
40.　IRA's name for the Special Branch.
41.　Brendan Behan, *Borstal Boy*, p. 12.
42.　All quotes are from a letter to Mrs Fitzsimons of 21 Avonmore Terrace, Cabra, Dublin. The letter was suppressed by the authorities at HM Prison Walton and remains on Home Office file 45/25068 in the British Home Office.
43.　Copy of letter in Home Office file 45/25068. This letter was suppressed and never sent out.

Chapter 4 – Behan in Borstal

1.　Letter to Seán Furlong dated 23 January 1940. Home Office file 144/23212.
2.　Governor's memo of 6 February 1940. Home Office file P.Com 9/1907.
3.　I have been unable to find a record of the letter in the Home Office file but this fragment is quoted in Kathleen Behan, with Brian Behan, *Mother of all the Behans*, p. 103; and EH Mikhail, *Letters of Brendan Behan*, p. 9.
4.　Letter to Seán Furlong, 23 January 1940. Home Office file 144/23212.
5.　Ibid.
6.　Letter to Mick Whelan, 23 January 1940. Home Office file P.Com 9/1907.
7.　Letter to Seán Furlong, 23 January 1940. Home Office file 144/23212.
8.　Brendan Behan, *Borstal Boy*, p. 138.
9.　Ulick O'Connor has pointed out that an altogether different account of that evening, with Brendan instigating the shout of 'Up the Republic', was written by Brendan Behan in *The Bell* in June 1942. See Ulick O'Connor, *Brendan Behan, pp. 50-51.*
10.　*The Irish Times*, 8 February 1940, p. 6. See also *The Evening Mail* and *The Irish Times* of the same date.
11.　Brendan probably meant Sir Joseph Byrne. His mother would have known him when he was Inspector General of the Royal Irish Constabulary. Oriel House near Dublin's Amiens Street was the Head Quarters of the Criminal Investigation Department.
12.　David Nelligan was Michael Collins' chief informer in Dublin Castle during the War of Independence. He later became head of the Special Branch.
13.　Francis Behan.
14.　Irish for "laid low".
15.　Fifteen shillings – 75p.
16.　Suppressed letter to Kathleen Behan. Home Office file P.Com 9/1907.
17.　Brendan Behan, *Borstal Boy*, p. 159.
18.　This and preceding quotes are from the report of Dr A P Lewis, Medical Officer, Feltham Boys' Prison, dated 29 February 1940. Home Office file P.Com 9/1907.
19.　CA Joyce has left a very readable account of his theories on Borstal in his book *By Courtesy of the Criminal: The Human Approach to the Treatment of Crime*, George G Harrap & Co, (London), 1955.

20. Brendan Behan, *Borstal Boy*, p. 275.
21. CA Joyce, *By Courtesy of the Criminal: The Human Approach to the Treatment of Crime*, p. 13.
22. Ibid., p. 85
23. Brendan Behan, *Borstal Boy,* p. 212.
24. Ibid., p. 252.
25. Ibid., p. 262.
26. *Sunday Press,* (Dublin), 5 April 1964, p. 12.
27. 'Charlie Millwall' was the name Brendan used in *Borstal Boy* to disguise the identity of a friend who died when his ship, the *Southampton*, was sunk off the Straits of Gibraltar during World War II. It has not been possible to establish the identity of this boy despite extensive enquires at the British Ministry of Defence and the Home Office.
28. Brendan Behan, *Borstal Boy,* p. 242.
29. Ibid.
30. Report of FEJ Curtes, Hollesley Bay. Home Office file P.Com 9/1907.
31. Brendan Behan's medical records. Home Office file P.Com 9/1907.
32. Letter from Seán Furlong dated 10 March 1940 forwarded to Hollesley Bay from Feltham.
33. Mr Justice Singleton was the trial judge who sentenced Mrs Furlong and her daughters in Birmingham.
34. Irish for 'goodbye to you'.
35. Mrs Furlong's daughters Emily and Evelyn who were jailed with her.
36. Letter to Mary Ann Furlong dated 10 November 1940. The letter was suppressed by the authorities at Hollesley Bay and it was given back to Brendan for re-writing. Home Office file P.Com 9/1907.
37. *Sunday Press*, (Dublin), 5 April 1964, p. 12.
38. Both reports in Home Office file P.Com 9/1907.
39. *Sunday Press*, (Dublin), 5 April 1964, p. 12.
40. Called 'Anne Lafeen' in *Borstal Boy*.
41. Brendan Behan, *Borstal Boy,* p. 367.
42. Ibid., pp. 351-352.
43. Ibid., p. 359.
44. *The Courteous Borstal,* manuscript in Morris Library, Southern Illinois University. Professor Colbert Kearney has made an important contribution to our understanding of its significance. See Colbert Kearney, *The Writings of Brendan Behan*, pp. 84-85.
45. Home Office file P.Com 9/1907.
46. Letter to R Bradley from CA Joyce, Home Office file P.Com 9/1907.
47. Two separate memos in the Home Office files deal with this episode.
48. CA Joyce, *By Courtesy of the Crime: The Human Approach to the Treatment of Crime*, p. 15.
49. The declaration, in his own hand, is in Home Office file 45/25068.
50. Brendan Behan, *Borstal Boy,* p. 377.
51. Ibid., p. 378.

Chapter 5 – Six Months of Freedom

1. There has been some confusion with regard to the date of his release. He was released on 31 October 1941 and arrived back in Dublin on 1 November 1941. Some accounts have him arriving back in Ireland a month later but the terms of the Expulsion Order from Britain make this impossible. It specified that he leave within 48 hours.

2. Interview given by FH Boland in 1970 to Dr Dermot Keogh, quoted in *Twentieth-Century Ireland – Nation and State*, Gill and Macmillan, (Dublin), 1994, p. 111.

3. *Author's interview with Cathal Goulding.

4. Irish for the 'Irish police'.

5. Confirmed by his brother Seán Furlong, who was in the Communist Party of Ireland.

6. Brendan's nickname at Borstal.

7. Copies of both telegrams are in the Military Intelligence file G2/C/154 held in the Military Archives, Cathal Brugha Barracks, Dublin.

8. Military Intelligence file G2/C/154. The speech is reproduced almost completely. The only passage omitted here attacks members of de Valera's government and suspected IRA informers. It is reproduced here as per the typed copy in Behan's file. The file does not state so, but it is most likely, that the speech was taken down by police note takers, as was the practice at such Republican gatherings.

9. See Kathleen Behan with Brian Behan, *Mother of all the Behans*, p. 106.

10. Máirtín Ó Cadháin to Declan Kiberd, April 1969. Quoted in Declan Kiberd, *Inventing Ireland – The Literature of the Modern Nation*, Jonathan Cape, (London), 1995, p. 513.

11. The account of the shooting incident contained herein is drawn from the proceedings of the Special Criminal Court, Behan's Military Intelligence file G2/C/154, the Department of Justice files on Behan, contemporary newspaper reports, and *interviews with Cathal Goulding and Seamus Behan, combine to give an invaluable reconstruction of the events.

12. Brendan Behan, *Confessions of an Irish Rebel*, p. 35.

13. Ibid., p. 36.

14. The resemblance between the names Flaherty and 'Cafferty' – the pseudonym which Behan gives his accomplice in *Confessions of an Irish Rebel* – has given rise to the idea that Brendan was accompanied by Dick Flaherty, an IRA comrade. None of the sources interviewed for this book support this thesis. Seán Furlong, Brendan's brother, who also served in the IRA, believes it possible that Brendan had a companion during the first moments of his escape but claims that he was alone while he was on the run.

15. Brendan Behan, *Confessions of an Irish Rebel*, p 37.

16. Ibid., p 40.

17. Ibid., p 41.

18. Most likely number 15 Blessington Street, the home of his aunt Margaret Corr and her son George Bendal.

19. Brendan Behan, *Confessions of an Irish Rebel*, p 53. The last sentence of this quotation is an almost exact repetition of what he claims to have said when arrested in 1939 in Liverpool. See Brendan Behan, *Borstal Boy*, p. 9.

20. *Author's interview with Cathal Goulding.

21. In February 1945, O'Kelly became the second President of Ireland as successor to Douglas Hyde.

22. *Author's interview with Cathal Goulding.

23. Like so much else to do with Behan's life these dates are often given incorrectly. The dates as given here are taken from the Department of Justice files on Behan, Reference number B18/5468.

24. Brendan Behan, *Confessions of an Irish Rebel,* p 56.
25. Tony Gray, *Ireland This Century,* Little, Browne and Company, (London), 1994, p. 144; Brendan Behan, *Confessions of an Irish Rebel,* p 57.
26. Brendan Behan, *Confessions of an Irish Rebel,* p 57.
27. Ibid.
28. Ibid.

Chapter 6 – Mountjoy Jail

1. Details from Mountjoy Convict Register. By permission of the Governor of Mountjoy Jail.
2. Brendan Behan, *Confessions of an Irish Rebel,* p 60.
3. Term used by left-wing IRA men at the time.
4. As is often the case with Behan's description of his period in jail, this one is also highly inaccurate, as previous chapters show he did not spend all this time in Liverpool prison but it suited him to allow others to think that he did.
5. Seán McCann (Editor), *The World of Brendan Behan,* p. 67.
6. Seán Ó Briain, *The Irish Times,* 21 May 1964, p. 8.
7. Letter dated 14 March 1940 in the National Archives, Dublin.
8. Brendan Behan, *Confessions of an Irish Rebel,* p. 58.
9. 'Pearse, my dear friend'.
10. Mrs Peadar Kearney and her son Colbert.
11. Poem written after the death in Mountjoy Jail of hunger striker, Thomas Ashe.
12. The letter is quoted here almost in full. For the remainder of text see EH Mikhail, *Letters of Brendan Behan,* p. 16.
13. The departmental memo in Behan's file does not record why parole was refused or the Minister's opinion of Brendan.
14. Irish poets admired by Peadar Kearney.
15. A complete list of these visits is appended to Behan's Military Intelligence G2 file.
16. Borstal detention.
17. Penal servitude.
18. Military Intelligence G2 file.
19. I have been reliably informed by a number of Freddie May's friends that this was the case.
20. *Author's interview with Frederick May's friend, the late Humphrey Langan.
21. Original of this letter is in the Department of Justice file B18/5468. The letter was forwarded from Mounjoy to the Department of Justice on 17 October 1942.
22. Berry (who later came to national prominence during the 1970 Arms Crisis) said as much in a note attached to May's request. Now in Behan's Department of Justice file.
23. Department of Justice file B18/5468.
24. Brendan Behan, *Confessions of an Irish Rebel,* p 63.
25. Twelve unpublished manuscript pages of *The Courteous Borstal* are now in the Morris Library at the University of Southern Illinois. These, along with *I Became A Borstal Boy*, the autobiographical piece that appeared in *The Bell* in 1942 can be considered works in progress for *Borstal Boy* published in 1958. The absence of any mention of *I Became A Borstal Boy* in prison and Justice Department records suggest that its publication was not a matter for their jurisdiction since the piece had been written and submitted before Behan's arrest and conviction in April of that year.
26. Department of Justice file B18/5468. Letter published here for the first time.
27. See footnote 6.

28. Justice Department memos copied to Military Intelligence file G2/C/154.

29. Memo dated 7 October 1942 in Department of Justice file B18/5468.

30. See footnote 5.

31. This is the title given the story by Behan in a letter from prison. The description of the story on his Military Intelligence file G2/C/154 gives the title as 'The Green Invader'.

32. His half brother, Seán Furlong.

33. Michael Traynor and Dominic Adams, IRA colleagues.

34. Letter dated 4 December 1943, now in New York University Library. See EH Mikhail, *Letters of Brendan Behan*, pp. 27-28.

35. Military Intelligence file G2/C/154.

36. The manuscript is in the Library of University College Cork. The story was first published in *Brendan Behan, Poems and Stories*, Denis Cotter (Editor), Liffey Press, (Dublin), 1978, limited edition of 500 numbered copies.

37. Colbert Kearney, *The Writings of Brendan Behan*, p. 29.

38. Seán McCann (Editor), *World of Brendan Behan*, p. 67.

39. Seán O'Faoláin to Catherine Rynne. See Seán McCann (Editor), *The World of Brendan Behan*, p. 171.

40. Excepting the sign-off and signature this represents the compete letter – Department of Justice files B18/5468.

41. Department of Justice files B18/5468.

42. Ibid.

43. Ibid.

44. Ibid.

45. Unfortunately no mention is made of the content of the material sent to O'Faoláin.

46. Military Intelligence file G2, 24 March 1943.

47. Seamus de Burca, *Brendan Behan, A Memoir*, p. 19.

48. EH Mikhail, *Letters of Brendan Behan*, p. 27.

49. Recalled by Tom Doran, Brendan Behan's fellow prisoner at Arbour Hill.

50. Brendan Behan, *Confessions of an Irish Rebel*, p. 61.

51. Ibid., p. 62.

52. There has been some confusion with regard to the date of his move to and duration of his confinement in Arbour Hill. The official records show that he arrived at 14:55 on 15 July 1943 and was transferred to the Curragh Camp on 12 June 1944.

Chapter 7 – Arbour Hill and The Curragh

1. Brendan Behan, *Confessions of an Irish Rebel*, pp. 55-56

2. Colbert Kearney, *The Writings of Brendan Behan: A Memoir*, p. 48

3. Memo to Provost Marshal, 21 December 1943.

4. Letter to Bob Bradshaw, 4 December 1943 in E. H Mikhail, *Letters of Brendan Behan*, p. 28. Original in New York University Library.

5. Brendan Behan, *Confessions of an Irish Rebel*, p. 63.

6. Seán Ó Briain, *Irish Press*, (Dublin), 21 May 1964, p. 8.

7. Ibid.

8. Memo from Provost Marshal to Comdt Michael Lennon dated 23 February 1944 – Military Intelligence G2 file.

9. Letter dated 19 May 1944 in Military Intelligence G2 file.

10. Ibid.

11. Memo in Military Intelligence G2 file.

12. Seamus de Burca, *Brendan Behan: A Memoir*, p. 18.

13. Despite extensive searches these letters have not been found at the time of writing.
14. In a letter to Tom Wall, an internee at the Curragh, he referred to a play he had just finished. This was probably the Theobald Wolfe Tone commemorative work.
15. Brendan Behan, *Confessions of an Irish Rebel*, p. 78.
16. Ibid., p. 69.
17. I am grateful to Anne O'Neill for this document. This is its first publication.
18. Máirtín Ó Cadháin, *As an nGeibheann*, (Dublin), 1973, p. 201.
19. Cobert Kearney, *The Writings of Brendan Behan*, p. 46.
20. Harry L Craig was Assistant Editor at *The Bell*. He was renowned for his disordered life and it is quite possible that he mislaid the manuscripts Brendan refers to in this letter of 25 October 1945 – Military Intelligence G2 files.
21. Letter dated 7 January 1946 – Military Intelligence G2 file.
22. For the complete text of this letter see EH Mikhail, *Letters of Brendan Behan*, p. 31.
23. See Chapter 11.
24. Letter to the Governor of the Curragh in Military Intelligence G2 files.
25. Military Intelligence G2 memo.
26. Brendan Behan, *Confessions of an Irish Rebel*, p. 68.
27. Military Intelligence G2 file.
28. A Republican friend of his father's.
29. Letter dated 16 July 1946 in Military Intelligence G2 file.
30. Extract from letter written in Irish. The English translation quoted here is from the copy of the letter in the Military Intelligence G2 file.
31. Military Intelligence G2 file.
32. Brendan liked to give the impression that he was one of the last prisoners to leave the Glasshouse. The parole paper in the Military Intelligence G2 file shows that he was once again taking licence with the details of his prison days. The Government Minutes for 17 December 1946 show that the remainder of his sentence was remitted with effect from 18 December 1946. National Archives Dublin – file S.12813.

Chapter 8 – Adrift in Dublin Bohemia

1. Seán O'Faoláin, *An Irish Journey*, Longmans, Green & Co, (London), 1940, p. 272.
2. Anthony Cronin, *Dead as Doornails*, p. 3.
3. Quoted in the splendid and scholarly account of Dublin drinking establishments: *Dublin Pub Life and Lore* by Kevin C Kearns, Gill & Macmillan, (Dublin), 1996, p. 67.
4. Ibid.
5. Brendan Behan, *Confessions of an Irish Rebel*, p. 67.
6. Ibid., p. 88.
7. Ibid., p. 81.
8. Translated by Dr Aidan Doyle.
9. Translated by Dr Aidan Doyle.
10. Sometimes mistakenly called *Winson Green*.
11. A much fuller account of the meeting and the fall-out from it is contained in Ulick O'Connor, *Brendan Behan*, pp. 110-112.
12. Ibid., p. 113
13. Ibid., p. 135
14. Brendan Behan, *Confessions of an Irish Rebel*, pp. 112-113
15. Colbert Kearney, *The Writings of Brendan Behan*, p. 52
16. Translated by Dr Aidan Doyle. The poem was first published in Irish in *Comhar* in October 1947.

17. Several works of fact and fiction feature *the catacombs*. See Anthony Cronin, *The Life of Riley* and his memoir *Dead as Doornails;* JP Donleavy, *The Ginger Man;* and John Ryan, *Remembering How We Stood* and others.
18. Anthony Cronin, *Dead as Doornails*, p. 5.
19. Brendan Behan, *Confessions of an Irish Rebel*, pp. 136-37.
20. John Ryan, *Remembering How We Stood*, p. 18.
21. *Interview with Freddy May's friend, the late Humphrey Langan.
22. Same interview.
23. Anthony Cronin, *Dead as Doornails*, p. 10.
24. Ibid., p. 8.
25. Ibid., p. 10.
26. Ibid.
27. John Ryan, *Remembering How We Stood*, p. 69.
28. Ibid.
29. Brendan Behan, *Confessions of an Irish Rebel*, p. 139.
30. Ibid., p. 116.
31. Anthony Cronin, *Dead as Doornails*, pp, 9-10.
32. Ibid., pp. 16-17.
33. See chapter 12 below.
34. *Author's interview with Brian Behan.
35. *Author's interview with Allen Ginsberg.
36. *Author's interview with Brian Behan.
37. Anthony Cronin, *Dead as Doornails*, p. 11.
38. Anthony Cronin's observation of him at this time.
39. There has been some confusion with regard to this date. It has been claimed that he did not begin work with Chapman until 1950. Several sources, however, some of whom met him in Newry at this time, confirmed to the author that this earlier date is correct.
40. Seán A Browne, Brendan Behan Lived Here, *Brass Tacks*, January 1991, Number 50, for details of Chapman in the Newry days.
41. The trial was reported on the front page of the *Evening Herald* on 14 August 1948.
42. There is considerable confusion about the date of his move to Paris. It is usually given as August 1948 but the records at Mountjoy clearly show that he was not released until 13 September 1948.

Chapter 9 – Between Paris and Home

1. Home Office File 45/25068.
2. In *Confessions of an Irish Rebel*, Brendan gives the impression that his first trip to Paris took him through Newhaven. I am grateful to Desmond MacNamara for pointing out to me that the first trip was direct from Cork and not through England. This information accords with information of his movements in the Home Office files.
3. It has not been possible to establish the exact date of this first arrival in Paris but it was between the 20 and 25 of September 1948.
4. Brendan Behan, *Confessions of an Irish Rebel*, p. 144.
5. Ibid., p. 145.
6. Ulick O'Connor, *Brendan Behan*, p. 148.
7. Reprinted in James Campbell, *Paris Interzone*, Secker & Warburg, (London), 1994, p. 23.
8. First published in *Comhar*, August 1949. Translation by the poet Valentine Iremonger.
9. *Comhar*, August 1949. Translation by the poet Valentine Iremonger.

10. *Comhar*, March 1952. Translation by Colbert Kearney.

11. *Author's interview with Seamus Behan.

12. First published in *Points*, Number 15.

13. This police report appears in the Home Office files on Behan.

14. Behan's own translation.

15. An extensive search of the Paris magazines in which Behan claimed to have written pornography has not uncovered the story. The description of the proposed legal action was told in detail to the present author by a nephew of the two ladies involved. He remembers Mr Lehane coming to the family home and advising strongly against the action.

16. In 1970, Ulick O'Connor drew attention to the existence of the story and it was first published in *Brendan Behan Poems and Stories*, Denis Cotter (Editor), The Liffey Press, (Dublin), 1978. The edition was limited to 500 numbered copies.

17. Ibid., p. 27.

18. Ibid., p. 28

19. Ibid., p. 31

20. Brendan Behan, *Confessions of an Irish Rebel*, p. 207

21. A gold emblem worn in the jacket lapel and issued as an award for proficiency in the use of the Irish language.

22. Translated by Colbert Kearney.

23. Colbert Kearney, *The Writings of Brendan Behan*, p. 55.

24. Translation by Colbert Kearney.

25. For the complex history of that process of gestation see Colbert Kearney, *The Writings of Brendan Behan*, pp. 81-116.

Chapter 10 – Pursuing Honour In His Own Country

1. Quoted in Seán McCann (Editor), *The World of Brendan Behan*, p. 186.

2. The articles appeared in *Comhar* between October 1952 and April 1953.

3. Translation by Colbert Kearney.

4. Michael O hAodha, 'The Behan I Knew', *Feile Zozimus*, Volume 2, *Brendan Behan, The Man, The Myth and The Genius*, Gael-Linn, (Dublin), 1993, p. 21.

5. *The Irish Times,* 28 December, 1951.

6. *Irish Press,* 7 January 1952.

7. I am extremely grateful to Mr Brian Lynch at RTE for his patient searches of the station's archives for material relating to Behan's broadcasting career.

8. *The Irish Times,* 28 March 1952.

9. *The Irish Times,* 28 December 1952.

10. The play is sometimes mistakenly called *The Garden Party* but the script of the original production carries the title *A Garden Party*.

11. From the RTÉ production script. See also Brendan Behan, *The Complete Plays*, Methuen, (London), 1978, p. 330.

12. The farm at Rosybrook in County Louth is still owned by the Kearney family.

13. Produced by the Pike Theatre Club in 1958. The second part of the programme was *The Big House*, commissioned from Behan by the BBC.

14. The date is sometimes incorrectly given as June 1953, but the Home Office files which related to his arrest while he was on this assignment specify the date as 26 October 1952.

15. There are reports of the trial in *The Irish Times* on 5 November 1952 and in the *Evening Mail* of 4 November.

16.   16. Some accounts of the trial inaccurately suggest that he was remanded for a further three days by the magistrate. This was not the case. He left England the following day. Information in Home Office file 45/25068.

17.   Brendan Behan, *Confessions of an Irish Rebel*, p. 225.

18.   Home Office file 45/25068.

19.   Its broadcast title, according to RTÉ's archives, was *A Coat for Confirmation*.

20.   The story can be found in the collection *After the Wake*, edited by Peter Fallon, O'Brien Press, (Dublin), 1981. The collection is still in print in paperback.

21.   First published in novel form in 1964.

22.   Translation by Colbert Kearney.

23.   Chuter Ede, the then British Home Secretary.

24.   *The Evening Mail,* (Dublin), 22 November 1951, p. 4.

25.   Letter dated 3 January 1954. Home Office file 45/25068.

26.   Peter Kavanagh, *Sacred Keeper; A Biography of Patrick Kavanagh,* The Goldsmith Press, 1979, p. 263.

27.   *The Evening Herald* of 2 April 1954 has an account of the trial.

28.   The volume published by Hutchinson in 1963 contained line drawings by Beatrice Behan.

Chapter 11 – The Rise of The Quare Fellow

1.   Manifesto now in the papers relating to The Pike Theatre and history of the theatre, in the Library of Trinity College Dublin.

2.   For an elaboration of this point and an excellent discussion of the characteristics shared by the two plays see *Beckett and Behan; Waiting for Your Man* in *Contemporary Irish Drama: From Beckett to McGuinness*, Anthony Roche, Gill & Macmillan, (Dublin), 1995.

3.   Carolyn Swift, *Stage by Stage*, p. 41.

4.   That honour went to PT McGinley's *Eilís agus an Bhean Deirce*.

5.   E H Mikhail, *Letters of Brendan Behan*, pp. 30-32.

6.   Ibid., p. 31.

7.   Peter René Gerdes interview with Ó hAodha, January 1965.

8.   Carolyn Swift, *Stage by Stage*, p. 138.

9.   Seamus de Burca, *Brendan Behan: A Memoir*, p. 22.

10.   Ibid., p. 23.

11.   Carolyn Swift, *Stage by Stage*, p. 138

12.   Ibid., pp. 138-39.

13.   Pike Theatre files in Trinity College Dublin Manuscript Department and see also Brendan Behan, *Confessions of an Irish Rebel*, p. 242 for Behan's own recollections of the sale of the play to the Simpsons.

14.   Brendan Behan, *Confessions of an Irish Rebel*, p. 244.

15.   *Author's interview with Carolyn Swift.

16.   Same interview.

17.   I am indebted to Carolyn Swift and Steve Willoughby for this information about the first night of *The Quare Fellow* and for generously giving of their memories of this important phase in Behan's development as a writer.

18.   Declan Kiberd, *Inventing Ireland: the Literature of the Modern Nation*, Jonathan Cape, (London), 1995, p. 513.

19.   *Author's interview with Seán Furlong.

Chapter 12 – Beatrice

1.   The place of marriage is sometimes incorrectly given as Westland Row.
2.   *Author's interview with Jarlath ffrench-Mullen.
3.   For further information see Cyril McKeon's article on ffrench-Salkeld in *Martello*, Winter 1992, pp. 1-5.
4.   *Author's interview with Pauline Parker.
5.   *Author's interview with Ian Stuart.
6.   Beatrice Behan, *My Life with Brendan*, p. 43.
7.   Ibid., p. 43.
8.   *Author's interview with Pauline Parker.
9.   Beatrice Behan, *My Life with Brendan*, p. 44.
10. Ibid., p. 40
11. Ibid.
12. Ibid., p. 41.
13. *Author's interview with Seamus Behan.
14. Same interview.
15. *Nuala Maher remembers Cecil ffrench-Salkeld's view of Brendan's literary skills. Interview with the author.
16. Beatrice Behan, *My Life with Brendan*, p.44.
17. Ibid., p. 52.
18. Ibid., p. 56.
19. *Author's interview with Senator Joe Doyle.
20. Now Sachs' Hotel, Morehampton Road.
21. Beatrice Behan, *My Life with Brendan*, p.57.
22. Ibid., p. 58.
23. Ibid., p. 61.
24. Ibid., p. 67.
25. Ibid., p. 69.
26. Written on 23 September 1955 and entitled 'To Beatrice'.
27. Beatrice Behan, *My Life with Brendan*, pp. 65-6.
28. I am extremely grateful to the Honourable Garech Browne and to his mother, the late Lady Oranmore and Browne for access to photographs, guest books and other material relating to Behan's association with Luggala.
29. Poem in the collection of the late Lady Oranmore and Browne.
30. Born José Maria Ozores Laredo in Madrid on 12 March 1922.
31. *Interview with the Honourable Garech Browne. The alleged incident with Tara Browne is mentioned in *Silver Salver: The Story of the Guinness Family*, (London), Granada, 1981, p. 148. The book's author, Frederick Mullally, gives the impression that the story is true.

Chapter 13 – Under Littlewood

1.   Peter René Gerdes, *The Major Works of Brendan Behan*, Herbert Lang, (Bern), 1973, p. 225.
2.   John Russell Taylor, *Anger and After*, Harmondsworth, (London), 1963, p. 101.
3.   *The Sunday Times*, 22 March 1964.
4.   Joan Littlewood, *Joan's Book: Joan Littlewood's Peculiar History As She Tells It*, Methuen, (London), 1994, p. 468.
5.   Beatrice Behan, *My Life with Brendan*, p.83.

6.   Joan Littlewood, *Joan's Book: Joan Littlewood's Peculiar History As She Tells It,*
     p. 469.
7.   Ulick O' Connor, *Brendan Behan*, p. 199.
8.   *Author's interview with Beatrice Behan.
9.   Beatrice Behan, *My Life with Brendan*, p. 84.
10. Ibid., p. 79.
11. Kenneth Tynan, *The Observer*, 27 May 1956, p. 11.
12. Carolyn Swift, Beatrice Behan and John Ryan all heard him making that remark. He
     also made it to several reporters.
13. *The Observer* (London), 27 May 1956, p. 11
14. *New Statesman* (London), 2 June 1956, p. 626.
15. This is another date in Behan's life about which there is some confusion. Various
     accounts give it as the day after the opening night, one week after the opening night. It
     did not take place at Lime Grove until 18 June.
16. Joan Littlewood, *Joan's Book: Joan Littlewood's Peculiar History As She Tells It,* p.
     472.
17. *Daily Mail*, 20 June 1956, p. 1.
18. Flann O'Brien, [Brian O'Nolan], *The Irish Times*, 23 July, 1956, p. 6.
19. For an account of the University College Dublin meeting see *The Irish Times*, 24
     October 1956 and for the Belfast meeting see the *Irish Press*, 27 October 1956.
20. *The Irish Times*, 13 October, 1956.
21. EH Mikhail, *Letters of Brendan Behan*, p. 79.
22. The phrase in Irish 'póg mo thóin' means literally 'kiss my arse'.

Chapter 14 – God-Branded

1.   At this point he had been working on the manuscript for ten years.
2.   Ulick O'Connor brought the existence of this important correspondence to a wider
     audience. Behan's letters were first published in *Points*. See EH Mikhail, *Letters of
     Brendan Behan*, p. 43 for the complete correspondence as published.
3.   Iain Hamilton has left an engaging memoir of his meeting with Behan in *Encounter*,
     XXIII (October 1964), pp. 36-7.
4.   This account appears in *The Daily Mail*, 3 August 1956, p.3.
5.   Dr Rory Childers.
6.   Dr Rory Childers gave an account of their friendship in *Chicago Today*, III 1966, pp.
     50-54.
7.   Brendan Behan, *The Complete Plays*, p. 379.
8.   *Author's interview with Carolyn Swift.
9.   EH Mikhail, *Letters of Brendan Behan*, p. 97.
10. Rae Jeffs has left a very detailed and endearing account of her friendship with
     Brendan Behan in her memoir *Brendan Behan, Man and Showman,* Hutchinson,
     (London), 1966.
11. Beatrice Behan, *My Life with Brendan*, p. 92.
12. EH Mikhail, *Letters of Brendan Behan*, pp. 86ff.
13. Ibid., p. 124.
14. Ibid., p. 104.
15. This is the most convincing assessment of his return to the Irish language I have
     found. It is Colbert Kearney's, *The Writings of Brendan Behan*, p. 119.

Chapter 15 – Trouble In Spain

1.   Austin Clarke, *The Dublin Magazine*, XIII, April-June 1938 pp. 77-8.
2.   The poem was written by Auden in 1937 and the royalties from the edition published by Faber & Faber that year went to medical aid in Spain.
3.   Postcard to Iain Hamilton, [dated January only but possibly sent in mid January] see EH Mikhail, *Letters of Brendan Behan*, p. 142.
4.   Beatrice Behan, *My Life with Brendan*, p. 104.
5.   Used in *the catacombs*, for the first publication of the extant fragment of this unfinished novel see *After the Wake*, pp. 57-97.

Chapter 16 – There's No Place on Earth like the World

1.   Brendan's recollections of *An Giall* appeared in *Brendan Behan's Island*, p. 16-17.
2.   *Author's interview with the Honourable Garech Browne at Luggala, County Wicklow.
3.   All notices quoted here appeared on 17 June 1958.
4.   Ulick O' Connor, *Brendan Behan* p. 204.
5.   Letter from Herbert Street dated 22 June 1958 (Feast of St Joseph Stalin) as Behan puts it. See EH Mikhail, *Letters of Brendan Behan* p. 149.
6.   Letter to Behan from Hamilton 16 May 1958. See EH Mikhail, *Letters of Brendan Behan* p. 148.
7.   EH Mikhail, *Letters of Brendan Behan*, p. 147.
8.   EH Mikhail, *Recollections*, Volume 1, Macmillan, (London), 1982, p. 103.
9.   Beatrice Behan, *My Life with Brendan*, p. 126.
10. Brendan Behan, *Brendan Behan's Island,* p. 17.
11. Programme for *The Hostage*.
12. Kenneth Tynan, *The Observer*, 19 October 1958, p. 19.
13. Beatrice Behan, *My Life with Brendan*, p. 148.
14. Rae Jeffs, *Brendan Behan, Man and Showman*, p. 72.
15. Martin Sheridan, 'Within the Gates', *The Irish Times*, 25 October 1958, p. 6.
16. Blanking Success, *Time*, Volume 72, 8 December 1958, pp. 78-80.
17. Letter to Iain Hamilton dated 26 November 1958. See EH Mikhail, *Letters of Brendan Behan*, p. 162. The reader should note the shortfall of £320 is as per Behan's original letter.
18. *Author's interview with Benedict Kiely.
19. Petronella O'Flanagan, an Irish journalist, cat lover and friend of the Behans.
20. The recipients mother and father.
21. Letter to Mary Kiely. See EH Mikhail, *Letters of Brendan Behan*, p. 165.

Chapter 17 – 'Success is Damn Near Killing Me'

1.   Ulick O' Connor, *Brendan Behan*, p. 228.
2.   *The Irish Times*, 7 March 1959, p. 9.
3.   *The late Beatrice Behan to the author.
4.   Friedrich Luft, *Die Welt*, 17 March 1959.
5.   George Wilson, *Les Lettres Français*, Number 1022 (26 March 1964 – 1 April 1964), p. 8.
6.   Recollected by the writer David Nathan.
7.   Beatrice Behan, *My Life with Brendan*, pp. 163-4.
8.   Rae Jeffs, *Brendan Behan: Man and Showman*, p. 92.

9.   Beatrice Behan, *My Life with Brendan*, p. 169.
10. *The People*, 19 July 1959, p. 6.
11. *The Sunday Times*, 10 January 1960, p. 32.

Chapter 18 – America My New-Found Land

1.   *Author's interview with Austin Byrne.
2.   *Author's interview with the Honourable Garech Browne.
3.   *Irish Digest*, LXIX, number 4, October 1960, p. 13.
4.   This represents approximately £69,000 at 1997 values.
5.   Brendan Behan, *Brendan Behan's New York*, Hutchinson, (London), 1964, p. 12.
6.   EH Mikhail, *Letters of Brendan Behan*, p. 182.
7.   Letter to the *New Yorker*, Volume 36, 10 September 1960, p. 131.
8.   Arthur Gleb, *New York Times*, 18 September 1969, Section II, pp. 1-3.
9.   For Miss Swann's complete account see *Theatre Arts (NY)*, XLVI, November 1962, pp. 26-7.
10. Kenneth Tynan, *The Observer* (London), 19 October 1958, p. 19.
11. Another of the books he spoke into a tape-recorder. It was not published until after his death.
12. Brendan Behan, *Brendan Behan's New York*, p. 46.
13. *Letters of Brendan Behan*, p. 86, the letter, as Professor EH Mikhail points out, was never published.
14. Postcard in the possession of Carolyn Swift.
15. Arthur Noble, Howard Wantuch and Sidney Kline reconstructed the days' events in the *Daily News* next day. Beatrice Behan told the present author the additional facts.
16. Tony Aspler, 'Brendan Behan's Last Wake in Montreal', *The Montrealer*, XL September 1966.

Chapter 19 – The Bells of Hell

1.   See Brendan Behan, *Brendan Behan's New York*, p. 117 where he explains the title. When *Exiles*, Joyce's play, was rejected for lack of humour he said to Sylvia Beach, perhaps if he gave the character Richard a cork leg it might jolly it along a bit!
2.   I have relied on a number of sources to reconstruct the day in court. They include *The Irish Times* report of the case on 18 February 1961, and the recollections of the Honourable Garech Browne who was in the court room for the hearing.
3.   Beatrice Behan, *My Life with Brendan*, p. 180.
4.   Ibid.
5.   Letter dated 21 February 1961 in the Library of the Performing Arts, Lincoln Centre, New York.
6.   *Newsweek*, 27 March 1961, p. 28.
7.   *Globe and Mail* (Toronto), 18 March 1961, p. 13.
8.   Beatrice Behan, *My Life with Brendan*, p. 183.
9.   *Beatrice Behan to the author.
10. *Author's interview with Charles Gould.
11. EH Mikhail, *Letters of Brendan Behan*, p. 196.
12. Peter Arthurs, *With Brendan Behan*, St Martin's Press, (New York) 1981, and *author's interview with Peter Arthurs.
13. Peter Arthurs, *With Brendan Behan*, p. 24.
14. E.H. Mikhail, *Letters of Brendan Behan*, p. 202.

15. Extract from complete letter published in Rae Jeffs, *Brendan Behan, Man and Showman*, p. 149.
16. Between 27 July 1956 and 24 December 1963, Behan was admitted to the Royal City of Dublin Hospital, Baggot Street on eight separate occasions.
17. I am grateful to Dr WS Jagoe for this information.
18. For an account of the incident see chapter 12.

Chapter 20 – Disintegration

1. Mrs Valerie Hemingway (neé Danby-Smith) wrote to the author to say: 'I note your request for my memories of Brendan Behan for your forthcoming biography. A great deal of time has passed, and having given it some thought, I don't think that I have anything to contribute ...'
2. Birth registered in Manhattan. Certificate Number 5360.
3. *Author's interview with Peter Arthurs.
4. *Author's interview with Norman Mailer.
5. *Author's interview with Paula Furlong, second wife of Rory Furlong.
6. Rae Jeffs, *Brendan Behan, Man and Showman*, p. 174.
7. *Author's interview with Lord Gormanston.
8. *Author's interview with Pete Hamill.
9. *Author's interview with Norman Mailer.
10. Author has consulted registered copy after grant of probate.
11. *Author's interview with Brian Behan.
12. *Author's interview with Ian Stuart.

All works by Brendan Behan appear in bold type.